Penguin Masterstudies

Pure Mathematics

Ian Dawbarn was educated at York [illegible] at Oxford University where he receive[illegible] ics at Davies's College, London. He has [illegible] *ern Mathematics* in the Penguin Passnotes series, as well as *Applied Mathematics* in this series, and is an examiner for a major GCE Board.

Penguin Masterstudies
Advisory Editor: Stephen Coote

Pure Mathematics

Ian Dawbarn

Penguin Books

Penguin Books Ltd, Harmondsworth, Middlesex, England
Viking Penguin Inc., 40 West 23rd Street, New York, New York 10010, U.S.A.
Penguin Books Australia Ltd, Ringwood, Victoria, Australia
Penguin Books Canada Limited, 2801 John Street, Markham, Ontario, Canada L3R 1B4
Penguin Books (N.Z.) Ltd, 182–190 Wairau Road, Auckland 10, New Zealand

First published 1986

Made and printed in Great Britain by
Richard Clay (The Chaucer Press) Ltd, Bungay, Suffolk
Filmset in Monophoto Times by
Northumberland Press Ltd, Gateshead

The publishers are grateful to the following Examination Boards for permission to reproduce questions from examination papers:

Associated Examining Board, University of Cambridge Local Examinations Syndicate, University of London School Examinations Department, University of Oxford Delegacy of Local Examinations, Southern Universities' Joint Board.

Contents

Chapter 2 Sequences and Series

Chapter 3 Polynomial Functions and Equations

Chapter 4 Further Results for Quadratic Equations and Their Roots

Chapter 5 Gradients, Differentiation and Integration for Polynomial Functions

Chapter 6 Other Power Functions, Implicit Functions, Further Geometry, and Parametric Equations

Chapter 7 Rational, Exponential and Logarithmic Functions

Chapter 8 Trigonometric Functions and Equations

Chapter 9 Vectors

Contents Table

Introduction

This book contains all the material required by the Pure Mathematics Core adopted by all GCE Examining Boards. It can be used as a revision guide or as a companion to text books or course notes.

All of the techniques and methods are developed in the early chapters, applied to the simplest type of functions (polynomials). Later chapters extend the results to rational, exponential, logarithmic and trigonometric functions. There also chapters covering sequences, series and vectors.

The first chapter contains background material of O-level topics.

Theory is fully illustrated with examples and each chapter has a section of worked examples showing how results and methods may be used to answer examination type questions. There are also sections of examination questions as exercises for the reader. Numerical answers are given at the back of the book.

A comprehensive contents list will help you find particular topics, and page references throughout the text link topics together. There is also a contents table which cross references types of function with particular techniques (solution of equations, differentiation and so on).

A list of formulae for areas and volumes, and tables of derivatives and integrals are included, as is an index of terms and definitions used in the text.

Advice for examinations appears in a 'Do's and Don't's' section.

When using this book, remember that Mathematics can only be learnt by practising. Try the exercises and check the working of the examples, making sure that you understand each step.

Examination questions are identified by Board, but you need not restrict your answers to those of only one Board.

The companion volume, *Applied Mathematics*, completes the syllabus of a combined Pure and Applied Mathematics A-level.

Acknowledgements

I am grateful to all my students and colleagues, past and present, who have contributed to the ideas and development of this book. In particular I would like to thank Mr S. Kaveh for useful discussions and criticism.

1 Background Material

Readers who have followed an O-level course in Mathematics will have sufficient background for this book. (For concise summaries, see *Mathematics* or *Modern Mathematics* in the Penguin Passnotes series.) Some essential topics are presented in this chapter for easy reference.

Section 1 Arithmetic and Algebra

1.1 Rules for Indices (Powers)

The index (or power) notation is used to show repeated multiplication. Thus, $2 \times 2 \times 2 = 2^3$, $a \times a = a^2$, $x^1 = x$.

Rules for manipulating indices

Rule	*Examples*
(1) $a^m a^n = a^{m+n}$ for any number a and any powers m, n	$(2^2) \times (2^3) = (2 \times 2) \times (2 \times 2 \times 2)$ $= 2 \times 2 \times 2 \times 2 \times 2 = 2^5$
(2) $a^m \div a^n = a^{m-n}$ for any number a and any powers m, n	$\frac{2^5}{2^3} = \frac{2 \times 2 \times \not{2} \times \not{2} \times \not{2}}{\not{2} \times \not{2} \times \not{2}} = 2^2$
(3) $(a^m)^n = a^{mn}$ for any number a and any powers m, n	$(3^4)^2 = (3 \times 3 \times 3 \times 3) \times (3 \times 3 \times 3 \times 3) = 3^8$
(4) $a^n b^n = (ab)^n$ for numbers a, b and power n	$(2^2)(3^2) = 2 \times 2 \times 3 \times 3 = (2 \times 3) \times (2 \times 3) = (2 \times 3)^2$
(5) $a^0 = 1$ for any $a \neq 0$	$(2^0)(2^1) = 2^{0+1} = 2^1$ from (1) Dividing by 2 $\Rightarrow 2^0 = 1$
(6) $a^{-n} = \frac{1}{a^n}$ for any $a \neq 0$	$a^0 \div a^n = a^{0-n}$ from (2) $\Rightarrow 1 \div a^n = a^{-n}$ from (5)
(7) $a^{1/n} = \sqrt[n]{a}$ (nth root of a)	$(a^{1/n})^n = a^{n/n}$ from (3) $= a^1 = a$

Rule	*Examples*
(8) $a^{m/n} = \sqrt[n]{a^m} = (\sqrt[n]{a})^m$	$a^{m/n} = (a^m)^{1/n}$ from (3) $= \sqrt[n]{a^m}$ from (7) and $a^{m/n} = (a^{1/n})^m$ from (3) $= (\sqrt[n]{a})^m$ from (7)

These are the only manipulations permitted when using indices.

Warning: Although $(ab)^n = a^n b^n$, $(a+b)^n$ is *not* $a^n + b^n$ (see page 68). The example

$$(1+1)^2 = 2^2 = 4$$
$$1^2 + 1^2 = 1 + 1 = 2 \neq 4$$

is sufficient to show this.

A special case is with $n = \frac{1}{2}$, so that $\sqrt{a+b}$ CANNOT be 'simplified' as $\sqrt{a} + \sqrt{b}$ (a very common mistake in examination scripts at all levels!). If you are in any doubt about the validity of an operation, try it with some test numbers.

Roots and powers are **inverse** operations. Thus, $(\sqrt{a})^2 = a$ and $\sqrt{a^2} = a$.

1.2 Manipulating Fractions

A fractional number is of the form $\frac{a}{b}$, where a and b are whole numbers. b is the **denominator** and a is the **numerator**.

The value of a fraction is unchanged when *both* numerator and denominator are multiplied or divided by the same quantity.

Thus,

$$\frac{2}{3} = \frac{4}{6} = \frac{200}{300}$$

Also,

$$\frac{a}{b} = \frac{ax}{bx} = \frac{a^2}{ab}$$

But $\frac{a}{b}$ is *not* equal to $\frac{a^2}{b^2}$ unless $a = b$ (top multiplied by a, bottom by b). Fractions with *equal* denominators can be added (or subtracted) by adding or subtracting the numerators:

$$\frac{1}{2}+\frac{5}{2}=\frac{6}{2}=3, \qquad \frac{a}{b}-\frac{3x}{b}=\frac{a-3x}{b}$$

Notice the simplification $\frac{6}{2}=\frac{3}{1}=3$. By dividing out all factors common to top and bottom, the fraction is put in *lowest terms.* If the result of a calculation is a fraction, it should always be put in lowest terms. This applies equally well to *algebraic fractions*. Thus, $\frac{2ab}{4a^2x}$ should be simplified to become $\frac{b}{2ax}$ by dividing top *and* bottom by $2a$. Make sure that you divide *all* terms; for example $\frac{2+x}{4}=\frac{1+\frac{1}{2}x}{2}$, *not* $\frac{1+x}{2}$.

Two fractions with different denominators can be added (or subtracted) by first multiplying by suitable factors so that the denominators can be made equal.

Examples

1. $$\frac{2}{3}-\frac{5}{4}=\frac{8}{12}-\frac{15}{12}$$

(multiplying by 4 in the first fraction, 3 in the second)

$$=\frac{8-15}{12}=-\frac{7}{12}$$

12 is the **least common multiple** (LCM) of 3 and 4. It is the smallest number divisible by both 3 and 4.

2. $$\frac{a}{c}+\frac{b}{d}=\frac{ad}{cd}+\frac{bc}{cd}=\frac{ad+bc}{cd}$$

3. $$1+\frac{1}{a}=\frac{a}{a}+\frac{1}{a}=\frac{a+1}{a}$$

Two fractions can be multiplied by multiplying tops and bottoms directly.

Examples

1. $$\frac{2}{3}\times\frac{5}{7}=\frac{10}{21}$$

2. $$\frac{a}{b}\times\frac{c}{d}=\frac{ac}{bd}$$

When dividing by a fraction, turn it upside down and multiply.

Examples

1. $\frac{2}{3} \div \frac{5}{4} = \frac{2}{3} \times \frac{4}{5} = \frac{8}{15}$

2. $3 \div \frac{9}{a} = \frac{3}{1} \times \frac{a}{9} = \frac{a}{3}$ (dividing out common factor 3)

$\frac{a}{b}$ is called the **reciprocal** of $\frac{b}{a}$. Thus, 2 and $\frac{1}{2}$ are reciprocals.

A *proper* fraction has a numerator smaller than its denominator:

$\frac{2}{3}$ is proper, $\frac{11}{3}$ is **improper**

An improper fraction can be written as a **mixed number** by dividing out;

$$\frac{11}{3} = 3\frac{2}{3}\left(\equiv 3 + \frac{2}{3}\right)$$

When finding a root or power of a fraction, you may treat numerator and denominator separately.

Examples

1. $\left(\frac{a}{b}\right)^3 = \frac{a^3}{b^3}$

2. $\sqrt{\left(\frac{16}{25a^2}\right)} = \frac{\sqrt{16}}{\sqrt{25a^2}} = \frac{4}{5a}$

1.3 Use of Brackets

Brackets are used to avoid ambiguities in calculations. For example, $2 + 3 \times 5$ could be calculated as either 17 or 25. (*Note*: different calculators may well interpret in either of these ways.) Inserting brackets, $(2 + 3) \times 5$ can only mean 25. Brackets show the *order* in which steps of a calculation should be done.

Examples

1. $2(x+3)$ means add 3 to x and *then* multiply by 2.

2. $(x+1)^2$ means add 1 to x and *then* square.

3. $\frac{1}{2}(1+\frac{1}{2}(1+\frac{1}{2})) = \frac{1}{2}(1+\frac{1}{2}(\frac{3}{2})) = \frac{1}{2}(1+\frac{3}{4}) = \frac{1}{2}(\frac{7}{4}) = \frac{7}{8}$.

The dividing bar of a fraction has the same effect as a pair of brackets. Thus, $\frac{2+x}{3}$ could be written as $\frac{(2+x)}{3}$.

THE RULES OF SIGNS

When multiplying or dividing positive and negative numbers,

$+(+) = +$	$(+)\div(+) = +$	which may be remembered with the table	$\begin{array}{c\|cc} & + & - \\ \hline + & + & - \\ - & - & + \end{array}$
$+(-) = -$	$(+)\div(-) = -$		
$-(+) = -$	$(-)\div(+) = -$		
$-(-) = +$	$(-)\div(-) = +$		

Note how brackets imply multiplication.

Examples

1. $2\times(-3) = -6$

2. $(-2x)\div(-3y) = \dfrac{2x}{3y}$

3. $1-\dfrac{x-1}{2} \equiv \dfrac{2}{2}-\dfrac{(x-1)}{2} = \dfrac{2-(x-1)}{2}$

$$= \frac{2-x+1}{2} \quad [-(x) = -x, -(-1) = +1]$$

$$= \frac{3-x}{2}$$

Note carefully the sequence of steps in example 3. A common mistake is to write $\frac{2-x-1}{2}$ after removing the brackets. A – to the left of a pair of brackets changes the signs of *all* terms inside these brackets.

Always use brackets when combining fractional terms. Thus,

$$\frac{2+x}{3} - \frac{5-2x}{6+x}$$

should be written as

$$\frac{(2+x)}{3} - \frac{(5-2x)}{(6+x)}$$

for clarity.

On page ..., it was observed that $(a+b)^2$ is *not* a^2+b^2. The correct expression is found by multiplying out

$$(a+b)^2 = (a+b)(a+b) = a(a+b) + b(a+b) = a^2 + ab + ab + b^2$$

$$\boxed{\Rightarrow \quad (a+b)^2 = a^2 + 2ab + b^2}$$

Similarly,

$$\boxed{(a-b)^2 = a^2 - 2ab + b^2}$$

Another useful result is:

$$\boxed{a^2 - b^2 = (a-b)(a+b)}$$

These three results should be *understood* and *memorized*!

1.4 Calculations

When performing calculations or manipulating formulae, write down enough steps to show what you are doing. Errors are more easily traced and corrected and, in the case of an examination answer, method marks can be awarded. A methodical approach to *all* working is essential when studying mathematics.

Always check the result of *each* part of a calculation – a small error early in your calculation may result in pages of incorrect and unnecessary working!

When using an = sign, ensure that the expressions on either side are actually equal.

If a given degree of accuracy is required for a problem, make sure that you follow the instruction. Your working should be to at least one higher degree of accuracy and then rounded off to the required accuracy *at the end* (so the working to produce an answer to two decimal places should be done to at least three-decimal-place accuracy). It is not always necessary, or desirable, to express your answers as decimals. Fractions, root signs, etc. can be left in the answer *unless otherwise specified.*

When using a calculator, make sure that you understand how to operate it correctly – read the maker's manual! A calculator is only as accurate as its user.

Section 2 Numbers and Sets

2.1 Sets, Union and Intersection

A set is a collection of items called the **elements** or **members** of the set.

Sets are denoted by capital letters and can be defined by: (a) listing the elements between curly brackets, $A = \{1, 2, 3, 4\}$, for example; (b) providing a rule for determining membership, for instance $B = \{x: x \text{ is divisible by } 3\}$. In this example, x represents a general member of B.

Elements are denoted by small letters.

The symbol $\in$ is used to mean 'belongs to'. Thus $6 \in B$, $2 \in A$. However, 4 is not in B, so we write $4 \notin B$.

When listing the members of a set, each element appears once only. The order is not important. Two sets are equal if they have exactly the same elements; thus $\{1, 2, 3, 4, 10\} = \{10, 2, 3, 1, 4\}$.

For a finite set A, $n(A)$ is the number of elements in A (or **cardinality** of A). For example, if $A = \{a, b, c, d\}$, then $n(A) = 4$. The set $B = \{x : x \text{ is divisible by } 3\}$ is **infinite** and cannot be represented by a finite list of elements. However, we may write $B = \{3, 6, 9, \ldots\}$ and understand by $\ldots$ that the list continues. If all the elements of set A also belong to set B, A is called a **subset** of B and we write $A \subset B$ (which includes the possibility of $A = B$). $A = \{1, 2, 3\}$ and $B = \{0, 1, 2, 3, 4, 5\}$, then $A \subset B$.

UNION AND INTERSECTION

Another way to define a set is in terms of other sets. Two sets A and B may have some elements in common. These common elements form the **intersection** of A and B, written as $A \cap B$.

Example

$A = \{1, 2, 3, 4, a, b, c\}$, $B = \{2, 4, c, d, z\} \Rightarrow A \cap B = \{2, 4, c\}$

The elements of two sets can be combined to form a larger set, called the **union** of A and B, $A \cup B$.

Example

$$A = \{-1, 3, 7, 9\} \quad B = \{-2, -1, 0, 1, 2, 3\}$$
$$\Rightarrow A \cup B = \{-2, -1, 0, 1, 2, 3, 7, 9\}.$$

Notice the relation $n(A \cup B) = n(A) + n(B) - n(A \cap B)$.

The *empty set* $\varnothing$ contains no elements at all, $\varnothing = \{\ \}$.

The *universal set* $\mathscr{E}$ contains all possible elements. In practice, $\mathscr{E}$ is restricted to contain only the type of element involved in a particular problem. For any set A, $\varnothing \subset A \subset \mathscr{E}$.

The complement A' of set A contains all elements *not* in A.

Example

If $\mathscr{E} = \{0, 1, 2, 3, 4, 5\}$ and $A = \{1, 3, 5\}$, then $A' = \{0, 2, 4\}$.

Notice that A' depends on the choice of $\mathscr{E}$.

It follows from the definition of A' that $A \cup A' = \mathscr{E}$ and $A \cap A' = \varnothing$. Also, $\mathscr{E}' = \varnothing$, $\varnothing' = \mathscr{E}$.

If two sets A and B satisfy $A \cap B = \varnothing$, they are said to be **mutually exclusive**. They have no elements in common and do not **overlap**.

If sets A, B, C, ... satisfy $A \cup B \cup C \cup \ldots = \mathscr{E}$, they are said to be **exhaustive**.

2.2 Number Sets

These are the type of set we shall be mostly concerned with.

The **natural numbers** $\mathbb{N} = \{0, 1, 2, 3, \ldots\}$.

The **integers** $\mathbb{Z} = \{\ldots -3, -2, -1, 0, 1, 2, 3, 4, \ldots\}$.

The **rational numbers** (fractions) $\mathbb{Q} = \{\pm \frac{p}{q}: p \text{ and } q \in \mathbb{N}\}$.

Notice that $\mathbb{N} \subset \mathbb{Z} \subset \mathbb{Q}$, since a natural number is a positive integer and an integer is a fraction ($z = \frac{z}{1}$, for example). Not all numbers can be expressed as fractions.

IRRATIONAL NUMBERS

An **irrational** number is a number that cannot be written in the form $\frac{p}{q}$, where p and q are integers. One such number is $\sqrt{2}$.

The irrationality of $\sqrt{2}$ was known to the Ancient Greek mathematicians. $\sqrt{3}, 2 - \sqrt{5}, \ldots$ are also irrational.

The union of the sets of all rational and irrational numbers is called the set of **real numbers**, $\mathbb{R}$.

Real numbers can be represented by points on a number line

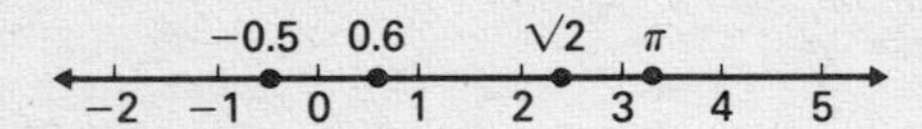

Notice that it is impossible to write an irrational number as a terminating decimal (1·414 is only an approximation to $\sqrt{2}$).

Other number sets of interest are

$$E = \{\text{even numbers}\} = \{0, \pm 2, \pm 4, \pm 6, \ldots\}$$

and

$$O = \{\text{odd numbers}\} = \{\pm 1, \pm 3, \pm 5, \ldots\}$$

(An acceptable alternative definition requires even and odd numbers to be strictly positive.)

The **prime numbers** $P = \{2, 3, 5, 7, 11, 13, \ldots\}$ have the property that they have no factors other than 1 and themselves.

2.3 Venn Diagrams

Relations between sets can be illustrated on diagrams. $\mathscr{E}$ is represented as a rectangle and other sets by simple shapes (circles, for example) inside this rectangle:

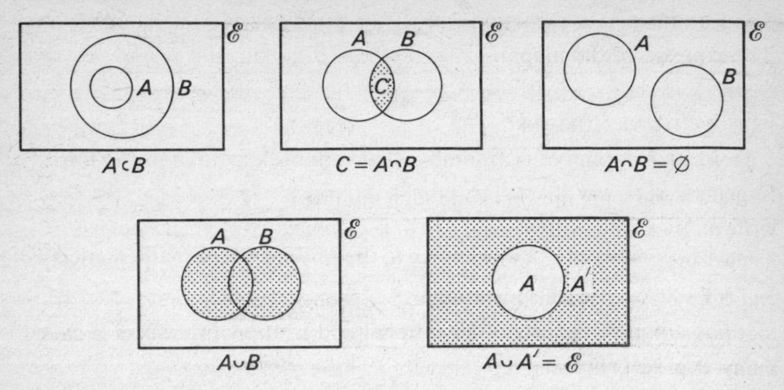

Section 3 Mappings and Functions

3.1 Mappings

A mapping, or *map*, associates the elements of one set with those of another.

Example

The ages of 5 students are shown in the table:

Name of student	Alan	Barbara	Claire	David	Eddy
Age (yrs, months)	17,6	18,1	17,3	17,9	18,1

The set {Alan, Barbara, Claire, David, Eddy} is *mapped* to the set {17,3, 17,6; 17,9; 18,1}. The mapping can also be shown by a diagram:

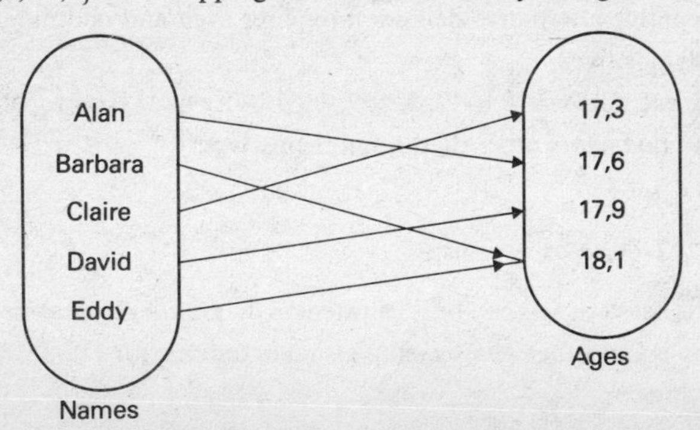

The set of names is the **domain** of the mapping, while the set of ages is the **range set** of the mapping. Each name in the domain is mapped to its **image** in the range. Denoting the mapping by the letter m

$$m(\text{Alan}) = 17{,}6, \text{ or } m\!:\text{Alan} \mapsto 17{,}6$$

In general, if A and B are the domain and range of mapping m, then we write $m\colon A \to B$. If, further, $m(a) = b$ (b is the image of a), then $m\colon a \mapsto b$.

Two mappings are equal if they have the same domains *and* ranges *and* rules of association. Notice that two names (Barbara and Eddy) are mapped to the same age (18 years 1 month). Such a map is called **many–one**. Several domain elements may have the same image.

A **one–one** map associates each domain element with a different image.

A **one–many** map associates several images with each domain element, but no two elements have the same image.

A **many–many** map associates several domain elements with not necessarily different images.

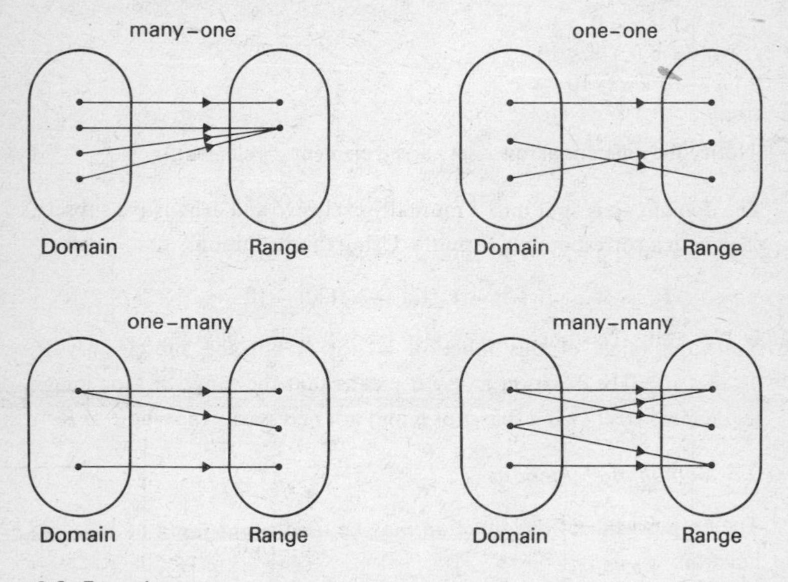

3.2 Functions

A **function** is either a one–one or many–one mapping. We shall usually stipulate that the domain and range are both number sets (this is the traditional characterization of a function; however, some texts may allow more general sets).

Note that a function *can only map a number to one image.* Thus, $m: x \mapsto$ square root of x, with domain the set of positive numbers, is a mapping but *not* a function. Every positive number has two square roots (4 has square roots $+2$ and -2).

If we use the symbol $\sqrt{\ }$ to mean the **positive root** only, then $f: x \mapsto \sqrt{x}$ is a function on the domain $\{x : x \in \mathbb{R},\ x \geqslant 0\}$. This is an example of a function defined by a **formula**. We can also write $f(x) = \sqrt{x}$. The **variable** x represents any element of the domain. For example, $f(9) = \sqrt{9} = 3$. **Any** letter may be used to represent a variable. The formulae $f: a \mapsto a^2$, $f: b \mapsto b^2$, $f: \alpha \mapsto \alpha^2$ all represent the same function *if* they have the same domain.

A function may need more than one formula in its definition.

Example

$f: \mathbb{R} \to \mathbb{R}$ is defined by

$$f: x \mapsto \begin{cases} 1 \text{ if } x < 0 \\ x \text{ if } 0 \leqq x \leqslant 10 \\ 10 \text{ if } x > 10 \end{cases}$$

(Notice the different arrows: set $\to$ set, element $\mapsto$ element.)

The domain, $\mathbb{R}$, is split into 3 mutually exclusive and exhaustive subsets, each with a corresponding formula. Using this definition,

$$f(-3) = 1, f(2) = 2, f(20) = 10$$

Note: the range of this function is not $\mathbb{R}$ but the subset $\{y : y \in \mathbb{R},\ 0 \leqslant y \leqslant 10\}$. The notation $f: A \to B$ means that the range of f, or image set denoted by $f(A)$, is a *subset* of B and not necessarily the whole of B.

3.3 Combining Functions

The output value of one function may be used as the input of a second function.

Example

Let $g: \mathbb{R} \to \mathbb{R}$, $g(x) = x^2$, $f: \mathbb{R} \to \mathbb{R}$, $f(x) = x + 1$. Then, $g(2) = 2^2 = 4$. Input to f, $f(4) = 4 + 1 = 5$. The combined functions map 2 to 5. This combination is also a function, called the **composition** of g *followed by* f. It is denoted by fg. Thus,

$$fg(2) = f(g(2)) = f(4) = 4 + 1 = 5$$

A formula for fg can be calculated in much the same way:

$$fg(x) = f(g(x)) = f(x^2) = x^2 + 1$$

(replacing x by x^2 in the f-formula).

We have to be a little careful about domains. Since $g(x) \in \mathbb{R}$, the domain of f, then $fg(x)$ is properly defined.

In general, if $f: A \to B$ and $g: C \to D$, then fg is defined if the range of g is a subset of the domain of f.

Diagrammatically,

x → [g] → g(x) → [f] → fg(x)

x ∈ domain of g   g(x) ∈ domain of f

Example

f has domain $\{x \in \mathbb{R}: 0 \leqslant x \leqslant 3\}$ and is defined by $f(x) = \frac{x+3}{2}$. g has domain $\{x \in \mathbb{R}: -1 \leqslant x \leqslant 2\}$ and is defined by $g(x) = 2x + 2$.

Find a formula for $gf(x)$, giving its domain of definition.

Answer

$$gf(x) = g\left(\frac{x+3}{2}\right) = 2\left(\frac{x+3}{2}\right) + 2$$

$$= x + 3 + 2$$

$$\Rightarrow gf(x) = x + 5$$

This is defined if

$$0 \leqslant x \leqslant 3 \quad \text{(domain of } f\text{)}$$

and

$$-1 \leqslant f(x) \leqslant 2 \quad \text{(domain of } g\text{)}$$

So we must satisfy

$$0 \leqslant x \leqslant 3 \qquad (1)$$

and

$$-1 \leqslant \frac{x+3}{2} \leqslant 2$$

simultaneously. The second inequality reduces to

$$-5 \leqslant x \leqslant 1 \qquad (2)$$

(See page 101.)

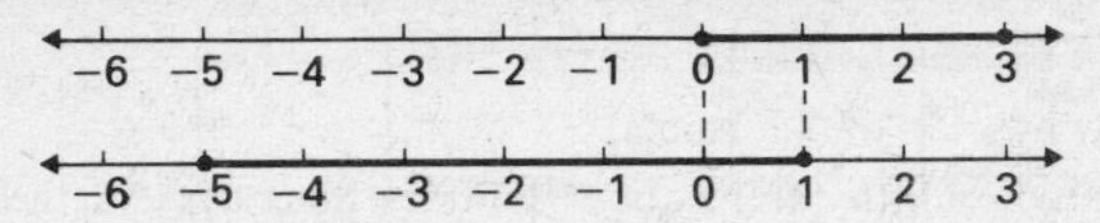

(Range of values of *x* indicated by a thickened line. The filled circles show that end points of intervals are included.)

The overlap (intersection) of these sets is $\{x : 0 \leqslant x \leqslant 1\}$ which is the domain for gf (i.e. gf is undefined for any values of x outside this interval).

It is important to note that the compositions fg and gf are different functions.

Exercise

For f and g of the example above, find a formula for $fg(x)$ and state its domain of definition.

Answer

$$\frac{2x+5}{2}, \text{ for } x = 2 \text{ only}$$

3.4 Identity and Inverse Functions

The **identity function** $I : \mathbb{R} \mapsto \mathbb{R}$ is defined by $I(x) = x$. Each element of the domain is left unchanged by I. If f is any function, $fI(x) = f(x)$ and $If(x) = I(f(x)) = f(x)$. Thus, $fI \equiv f \equiv If$.

Let

$$f : x \mapsto \frac{x+1}{2}, \; g : x \mapsto 2x - 1 \text{ (on domain } \mathbb{R})$$

Then,

$$fg(x) = f(2x-1) = \frac{(2x-1)+1}{2} = x$$

Similarly, $gf(x) = x$. Thus, $fg = gf = I$. f and g are **inverse functions**; they 'cancel' each other out. The inverse of f is denoted by f^{-1}, and satisfies $f^{-1}f = ff^{-1} = I$.

Warning: $f^{-1}(x)$ does NOT mean $\frac{1}{f(x)}$; -1 is *not* an index here!

The domain of f^{-1} is the range of f.

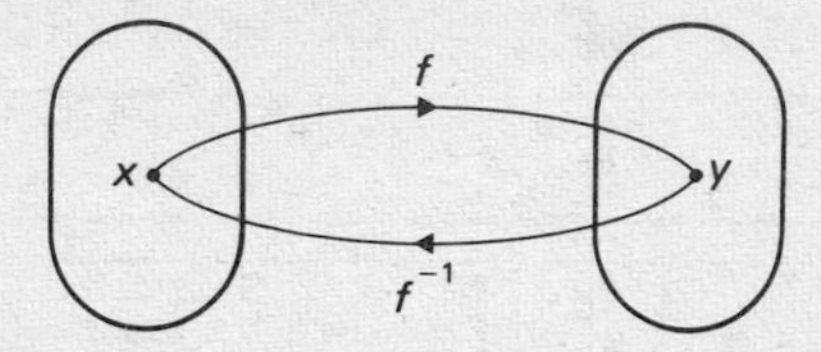

Note: Not all functions have inverses. In particular, a many–one mapping does not have an inverse function since any inverse would be one–many and hence not a function. For a function to have an inverse, it must be one–one.

f	f^{-1}
$x \mapsto x+2$	$x \mapsto x-2$
$x \mapsto 2-x$	$x \mapsto 2-x$ (self inverse)
$x \mapsto 2x$	$x \mapsto \frac{1}{2}x$
$x \mapsto \frac{2}{x}$	$x \mapsto \frac{2}{x}$ (self inverse)
$x \mapsto x^2$	no inverse (not one–one)

3.5 Graphs

If the image $f(x)$ is denoted by y, then the function f corresponds to the set of **ordered pairs** $\{(x, y): x \in \text{domain of } f,\ y = f(x)\}$.

An ordered pair (x, y) can be represented by a point in the plane, with **coordinates** x and y with respect to two fixed **axes**. The diagram overleaf shows the point P with x-coordinate 1 and y-coordinate 3. It represents the ordered pair (1, 3).

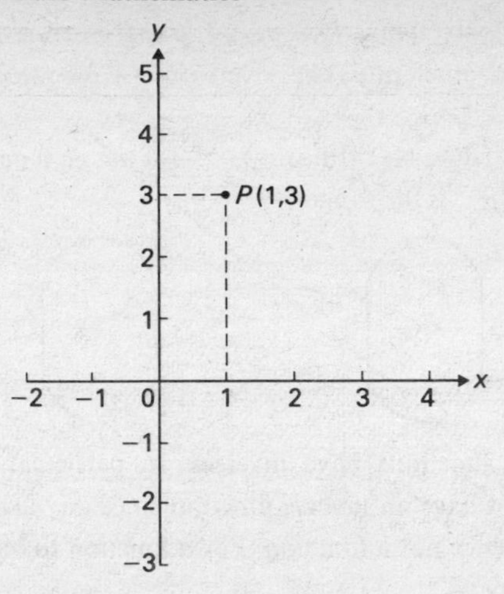

The **coordinate axes** are at right-angles and meet at the **origin** O with coordinates $(0, 0)$.

Numbers in the domain are represented along the left–right axis. Numbers in the range are represented along the up–down axis. The same scale need not be used for both axes.

The set of points corresponding to all the ordered pairs (x, y) is called the **graph** of the function f.

Examples

1. f has domain $\{0, 1, 2, 3\}$ and $f: x \mapsto 2x$. The graph is

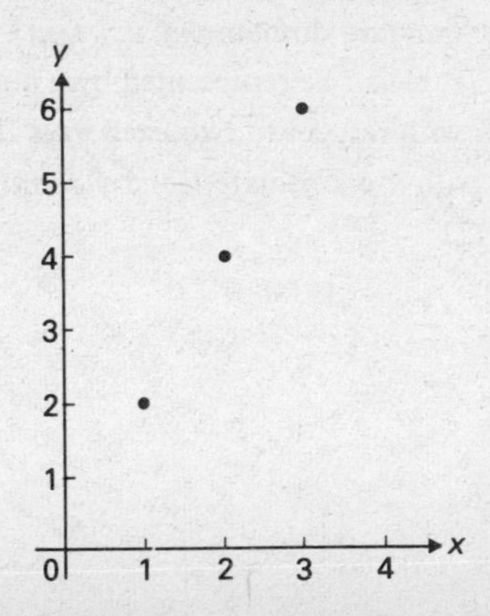

2. f has domain $\mathbb{R}$ and $f: x \mapsto x + 1$. The graph is

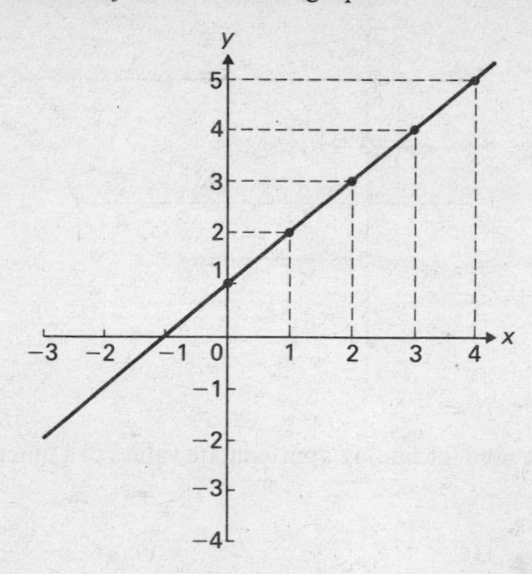

(The diagram shows points with x coordinates between -4 and $+4$; since $\mathbb{R}$ is infinite, it is impossible to show the whole graph.)

The first example shows a **discrete** graph composed of isolated points. *These points must not be joined* since f is undefined for $x < 0$, $0 < x < 1$, $1 < x < 2$, $2 < x < 3$, $x > 3$.

The second example shows a **continuous** graph.

In general, a graph may be composed of continuous segments and isolated points.

Example

The function f defined on domain $\{x: -2 \leqslant x \leqslant 3\}$ by

$$f: x \mapsto \begin{cases} 1 \text{ for } -2 \leqslant x < 0 \\ 0 \text{ for } x = 0 \\ -1 \text{ for } 0 < x \leqslant 3 \end{cases}$$

has graph

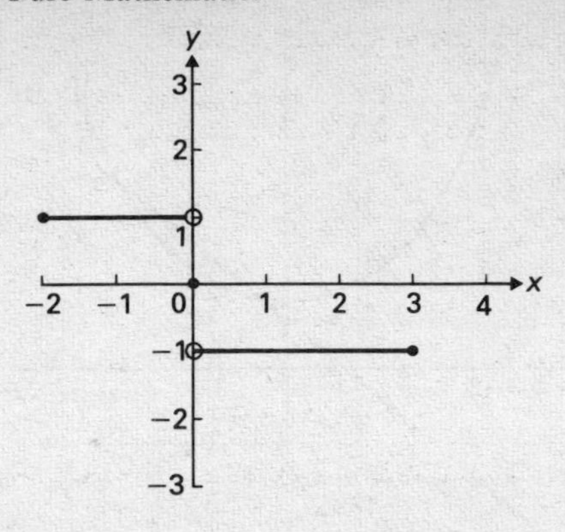

Graphs can be used for finding approximate values of a function.

Example

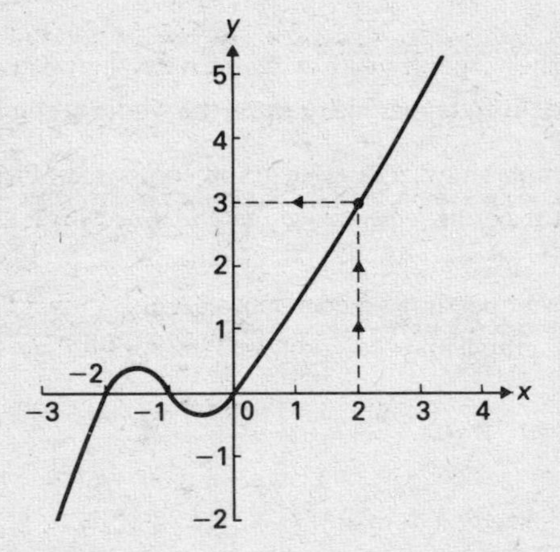

From the graph, $g(2) = 3$.

Conversely, a graph may be used to find domain values corresponding to a given image value

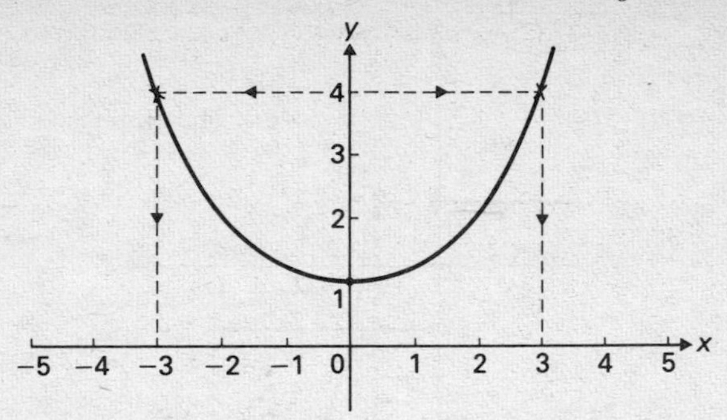

From the graph, $h(-3) = 4$; also, $h(3) = 4$ (so that h is many–one and has no inverse).

These methods are useful when *accurate* graphs are drawn. Later sections show how graphical and numerical methods can be combined for greater accuracy (page 164).

3.6 Odd and Even Functions

An **even** function satisfies the condition $f(-x) = f(x)$ for all x in the domain of f.

The graph of an even function is **symmetric** about the y-axis.

Example

$f(x) = x^2 + 1 \Rightarrow f(-x) = (-x)^2 + 1 = x^2 + 1 = f(x)$. The graph is

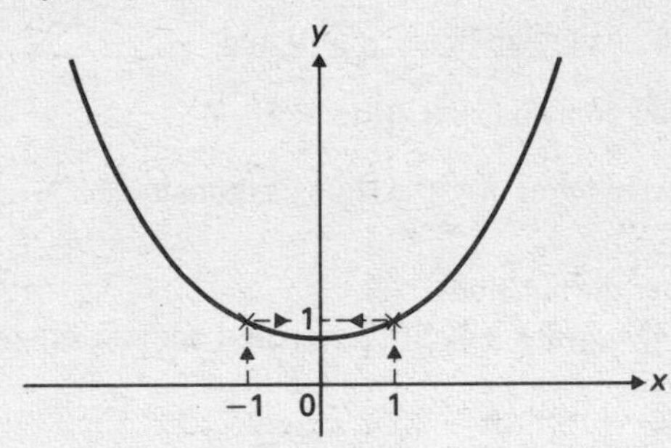

Symmetric

An **odd** function satisfies the condition $f(-x) = -f(x)$ for all x in the domain of f. The graph of an odd function is **antisymmetric** about the y-axis.

Example

$f(x) = \frac{1}{x^3} \Rightarrow f(-x) = \frac{1}{(-x)^3} = -\frac{1}{x^3} = -f(x)$. The graph is

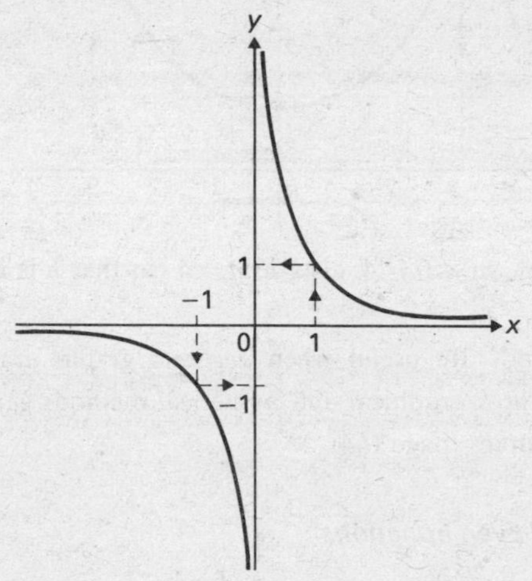

Antisymmetric

3.7 Exercises

1. $A = \{x: -3 \leqslant x < 5\}$, $B = \{x: 1 \leqslant x \leqslant 11\}$ are subsets of $\mathbb{R}$. Illustrate $A \cap B$ by thickening a part of the number line.

2. $f: x \mapsto 2x + 3$ on domain $\{x \in \mathbb{R}, x > 0\}$ and

   $g: x \mapsto \frac{1}{1+x}$ on domain $\{x \in \mathbb{R}, 0 < x < 5\}$.

   Express $fg(x)$ in terms of x and state its domain.

3. State whether the functions
   (*a*) $f: x \mapsto \frac{1-x}{x^2+2}$ (*b*) $g: x \mapsto \frac{x^4+1}{x^2-1}$ (*c*) $h: x \mapsto \frac{x}{x^2+1}$

   are even, odd or neither.

2 Sequences and Series

Section 4 Sequences

4.1 Sequences

In this section, we consider functions with domain $\mathbb{N}$. Let f be such a function. The images $f(0)$, $f(1)$, $f(2)$, ... form an **ordered sequence** of numbers. Unlike a list of set elements, these numbers must be written in the correct order.

Example

The functions $f: n \mapsto 3n^2$, $n \in N$ generates the sequence 0, 3, 12, 27, ...

NOTATION

Letting $a_0 = f(0)$, $a_1 = f(1)$, ..., $a_n = f(n)$, ..., the sequence is written as $a_0, a_1, a_2, \ldots, a_n, \ldots$, or $\{a_n\}$. The subscript determines the position of the number in the sequence. a_0 is the first term, a_1 the second; in general, a_n is the $(n+1)$th term of the sequence or **general term**.

Note: $a_n \equiv f(n)$ is usually defined by a formula; however, a sequence may be defined in terms of the properties of its terms, or in more general ways (see page 45 for example).

Warning: An alternative convention is to write the sequence as a_1, $a_2, \ldots, a_n, \ldots$, where a_n is now the nth term (corresponding to taking the domain of the function as $\{1, 2, \ldots\}$). You should make sure that you use the appropriate convention for a given problem.

A sequence may be finite $a_0, a_1, \ldots, a_n$ or infinite $a_0, a_1, \ldots$ We now look at the properties of two special types of sequence.

4.2 Arithmetic Progressions

(Progression is another word for sequence.)

Example

The terms of the sequence 2, 5, 8, 11, ... increase successively in steps of 3. Knowing this, we can calculate further terms. The next two terms are 14, 17. Such a sequence is said to be *arithmetic.*

Suppose that $a_0, a_1, a_2, \ldots, a_{n-1}, a_n, a_{n+1}, \ldots$ is an arithmetic progression. The difference between successive terms must be constant. $a_n - a_{n-1} = d$, say, where d is the **common difference** of the progression. Thus, $a_n = a_{n-1} + d$ for $n = 1, 2, 3, \ldots$ Given a value for the first term, a_0, further terms can be calculated with this **iterative formula** (see page 45). If the first term is a, then the second term is $a_1 = a + d$, the third term $a_2 = a_1 + d = a + 2d$, and so on. The progression can be written in terms of a and d as

$$a,\ a + d,\ a + 2d,\ a + 3d,\ a + 4d,\ \ldots$$

The nth term of the progression is $a + (n - 1)d$

The sequence is generated by the function $f: n \mapsto a + nd$, where $n = 0, 1, 2, \ldots$

Examples

1. $-1, 0, 1, 2, 3, \ldots$ $\quad a = -1, d = 0 - (-1) = 1$
2. $3, -1, -5, \ldots$ $\quad a = 3, d = -1 - 3 = -4$
3. $0{\cdot}5, 0{\cdot}55, 0{\cdot}6, 0{\cdot}65, \ldots$ $\quad a = 0{\cdot}5, d = 0{\cdot}55 - 0{\cdot}5 = 0{\cdot}05$

Notice how the common difference is found by subtracting any two consecutive terms.

4. The sequence 3, 11, ... is arithmetic. Calculate its 12th term.

Answer

$$a = 3,\ d = 11 - 3 = 8$$

$$12\text{th term} = a + (12 - 1)d$$

$$= 3 + 11 \times 8 = 91$$

Note: In this example, we needed the information that the sequence was arithmetic to calculate further terms. *Do not* assume that a sequence is arithmetic unless you are told so. For example, given the sequence 1, 2, 3, 4, 5, 6, 7, you *cannot* say that the next term is necessarily 8 – although it would be a reasonable guess.

4.3 Arithmetic Mean

The **arithmetic** mean of two numbers x and y is defined as $\frac{x+y}{2}$. If p, q, r are 3 consecutive terms of an arithmetic progression, then q is the arithmetic mean of p and r.

This property can be used to prove that a given sequence is arithmetic.

Example
A sequence is defined by $a_n = 3 - 2n$. Show that the sequence is arithmetic.

Answer 1

$$a_{n+1} = 3 - 2(n+1) = 3 - 2n - 2 = 1 - 2n$$

$$a_n \quad = 3 - 2n$$

$$a_{n-1} = 3 - 2(n-1) = 3 - 2n + 2 = 5 - 2n$$

so

$$\frac{a_{n+1} + a_{n-1}}{2} = \frac{5 - 2n + 1 - 2n}{2} = \frac{6 - 4n}{2} = 3 - 2n = a_n$$

Therefore, the sequence is arithmetic.

Answer 2
A quicker way is to show that consecutive terms have a constant difference.

$$a_{n+1} - a_n = 1 - 2n - (3 - 2n) = -2$$

which is constant and so the sequence is arithmetic.

4.4 Geometric Progressions

Example
The terms of the sequence 2, 4, 8, 16, ... are successively multiplied by the factor 2. The next two terms are 32, 64. Such a sequence is said to be **geometric**. Suppose that $a_0, a_1, a_2, \ldots, a_n, \ldots$ is geometric. The ratio of consecutive terms must be constant. $\frac{a_n}{a_{n-1}} = r$, say, where r is the **common ratio** of the progression.

Thus, $a_n = (a_{n-1})r$ for $n = 1, 2, 3, \ldots$ Given a value for the first term, a_0, further terms can be calculated with this iterative formula.

If the first term is a, then the progression in terms of a and r is $a, ar, ar^2, ar^3, \ldots$

The nth term of the progression is ar^{n-1}.

Examples

1. $-1, 1, -1, 1, -1, \ldots \qquad a = -1, r = -1$
2. $4, 2, 1, \frac{1}{2}, \ldots \qquad a = 4, r = \frac{1}{2}$
3. $3, 0{\cdot}6, 0{\cdot}12, \ldots \qquad a = 3, r = 0{\cdot}2$

The common ratio is found by dividing any two consecutive terms.

4. The sequence 1, 3, 9, ... is geometric. Calculate its 10th term.

Answer

$a = 1, r = \frac{3}{1} = 3$. 10th term $= (1)(3)^9 = 19683$.

4.5 Geometric Mean

The geometric mean of the positive numbers x and y is defined as $\sqrt{xy}$. If p, q, s are 3 consecutive terms of a geometric progression, then q is the geometric mean of p and s.

Proof

$q = pr$ and $s = qr = pr^2$, hence $\sqrt{ps} = \sqrt{p^2r^2} = pr = q$. Conversely, $q = \sqrt{ps} \Rightarrow \frac{q}{p} = \frac{s}{q}$. Consecutive terms have a constant ratio and so the sequence is geometric.

Example

Show that the sequence defined by $a_n = 2^{2n}$ is geometric.

Answer

$\frac{a_{n+1}}{a_n} = \frac{2^{2n+2}}{2^{2n}} = 2^2 = 4$, which is constant.

Warning: These are two special types of sequence. Most sequences are neither arithmetic nor geometric. Do not assume that a sequence is one of these types *unless* you are told so or can prove it!

4.6 Convergent Sequences and Limits

Consider the sequence $\frac{1}{2}, \frac{2}{3}, \frac{3}{4}, \frac{4}{5}, \ldots$

The general term is $a_n = \frac{n+1}{n+2}$ (for $n = 0, 1, 2, 3, \ldots$).

Since $\frac{n+1}{n+2} = \frac{n+2-1}{n+2} = \frac{n+2}{n+2} - \frac{1}{n+2} = 1 - \frac{1}{n+2}$ and $\frac{1}{n+2}$ steadily decreases as n increases, then a_n approaches more and more closely to 1 as n increases. We write this as

$$a_n \to 1 \text{ as } n \to \infty$$

('a_n tends to 1 as n tends to infinity') and say that the sequence is **convergent** with **limit** 1.

We can also write this as $\lim_{n\to\infty} (a_n) = 1$.

Examples

1. $1, \frac{1}{2}, \frac{1}{3}, \ldots, \frac{1}{n}, \ldots$ is convergent with limit 0.

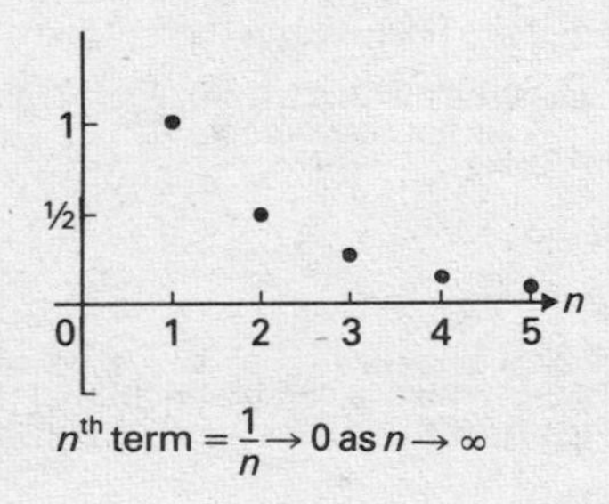

n^{th} term $= \frac{1}{n} \to 0$ as $n \to \infty$

2. $3, \frac{1}{3}, -\frac{1}{5}, \ldots, \frac{3-2n}{1+2n}, \ldots$ is convergent with limit -1.
(As an exercise, calculate the first 10 terms of this sequence and verify that they do approach the value -1.)

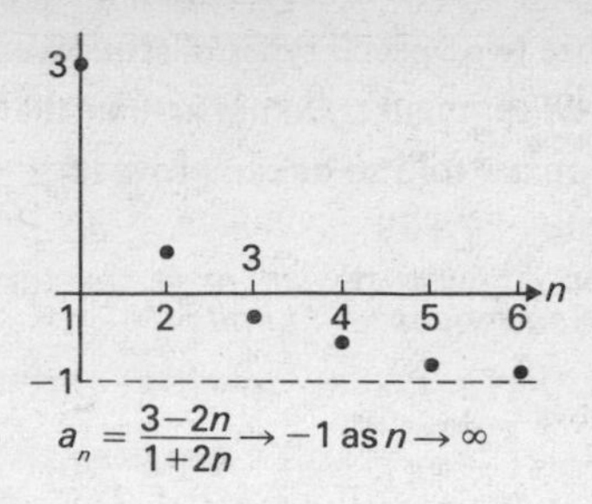

$a_n = \dfrac{3-2n}{1+2n} \to -1$ as $n \to \infty$

3. 1, 2, 3, 4, ... is not convergent. The terms increase without bound. A convergent sequence must have a *finite* limit. In fact, no arithmetic progression can be convergent, *unless the common difference is zero.*

4. $-1, 1, -1, 1, \ldots$ The sequence of alternating $+1$s and -1s is not convergent.

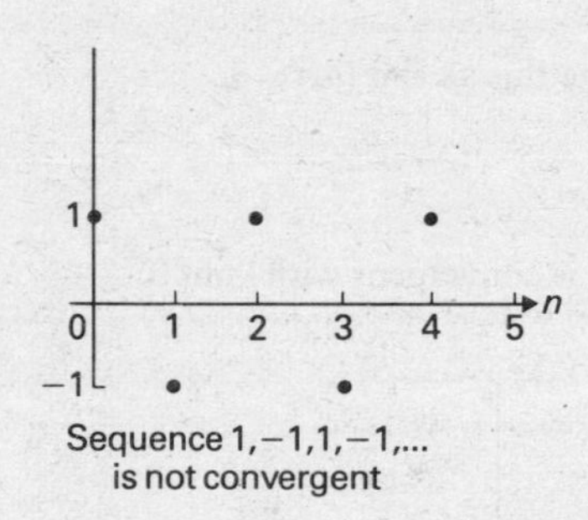

Sequence $1,-1,1,-1,\ldots$ is not convergent

4.7 Calculating Limits

The limit of a convergent sequence can be calculated from the formula for the general term.

Examples

1. $a_n = \frac{n-2}{n+1}$ is the general term of the sequence $-2, \frac{1}{2}, 0, \frac{1}{4}, \frac{2}{5}, \ldots$

Rewriting

$$a_n \equiv \frac{n+1-3}{n+1} = \frac{n+1}{n+1} - \frac{3}{n+1} = 1 - \frac{3}{n+1}$$

$$\lim_{n\to\infty}\left(\frac{3}{n+1}\right) = 0 \Rightarrow \lim_{n\to\infty}(a_n) = 1$$

2. $u_n = \frac{n^2+3}{2-n^3}$. A more general technique is to divide all terms of this fraction by the highest power of n, in this case, n^3. Thus, $u_n = \frac{\frac{1}{n}+\frac{3}{n^2}}{\frac{2}{n^3}-1}$. Since $\frac{1}{n}\to 0$, $\frac{1}{n^2}\to 0$ and $\frac{1}{n^3}\to 0$ as $n\to\infty$, then $u_n \to \frac{0}{1} = 0$. The sequence converges to 0.

Note: $\frac{0}{a} = 0$ for any $a \neq 0$. However, $\frac{a}{0}$ and $\frac{0}{0}$ are undefined quantities since division by 0 is not permitted. $\frac{a}{b}\to\infty$ as $b\to 0 (a > 0)$ is a shorthand for the statement that $\frac{a}{b}$ increases without bound as b decreases to zero.

3. $b_n = a + (n-1)d$ is the general term of an arithmetic progression. $b_n \to \infty$ as $n\to\infty$ and so the sequence does not converge.

4. $c_n = ar^{n-1}$ is the general term of a geometric progression. If $-1 < r < 1$, then $r^{n-1}\to 0$ as $n\to\infty$ and the sequence converges to zero. If $r > 1$ or $r < -1$, the terms increase (in magnitude) without bound, and so the sequence is divergent. If $r = 1$, $c_n = a$ for all n and so the sequence has constant value and converges (in a very trivial way). If $r = -1$, the sequence is $a, -a, a, -a, \ldots$ and does not converge.

To see that $r^{n-1}\to 0$ as $n\to\infty$ if $-1 < r < 1$ observe that (for $r > 0$) $r^n = rr^{n-1} < r$, and so the terms of the sequence get smaller and smaller as n increases. (For example, $r = \frac{1}{2}, r^2 = \frac{1}{4}, r^3 = \frac{1}{8}, \ldots$)

4.8 Iterative Sequences

Arithmetic and geometric progressions are examples of **iterative sequences**, in which terms can be generated successively.

$a_n = a_{n-1} + d$ for an arithmetic progression.

$a_n = ra_{n-1}$ for a geometric progression.

Other examples

1. Use the iterative formula $a_{n+1} = 2a_n - 3$, $n = 1, 2, 3, \ldots, a_1 = 2$ to generate the first 4 terms of the sequence.

Answer

$$a_2 = 2a_1 - 3 \qquad \text{(with } n = 1)$$
$$= 4 - 3$$
$$= 1$$

$$a_3 = 2a_2 - 3 \qquad \text{(with } n = 2)$$
$$= 2 - 3 = -1$$
$$a_4 = 2a_3 - 3 = -2 - 3 = -5$$

The first 4 terms are 2, 1, -1, -5 (which is neither geometric nor arithmetic).

2. The sequence

$$1, 1, 2, 3, 5, 8, 13, 21, \ldots$$

is generated by adding two consecutive terms to find the next one. The iterative formula is

$$a_{n+1} = a_n + a_{n-1} \qquad (n = 1, 2, 3)$$

and

$$a_0 = 1, a_1 = 1$$

In this case, the first two terms must be specified since the formula for a_{n+1} contains both a_n and a_{n-1}. This is known as the **Fibonacci sequence**. For a discussion of this sequence and how it arises in nature, see Martin Gardner, *More Mathematical Puzzles and Diversions* (Penguin).

In later sections (167), iterative sequences are used to find approximate solutions to equations.

Section 5 Series

5.1 Arithmetic and Geometric Series

A **series** is formed by adding successive terms of a sequence. For a finite sequence, a_0, a_1, $\ldots$, a_{n-1}, the corresponding finite series is $a_0 + a_1 + \ldots + a_{n-1}$.

(*Warning:* some authors use the terms sequence and series interchangeably. In this book, the now conventional usage series = sum of a sequence is followed. In other texts, the context should make the meaning clear.)

ARITHMETIC SERIES

The arithmetic progression $a, a + d, a + 2d, \ldots, a + (n - 1)d$, has first term a, common difference d and n terms. The sum of the first n terms of this progression

$$S_n = a + (a + d) + (a + 2d) + \ldots + (a + (n - 1)d)$$

can be expressed as a formula in terms of a, d and n

$$\boxed{S_n = \frac{n}{2}(2a + (n - 1)d)}$$

Proof

By definition

$$S_n = a + (a + d) + \ldots + (a + (n - 2)d) + (a + (n - 1)d)$$

Backwards:

$$S_n = (a + (n - 1)d) + (a + (n - 2)d) + \ldots + (a + d) + a$$

Adding term by term

$$2S_n = (2a + (n - 1)d) + (2a + (n - 1)d) + \ldots + (2a + (n - 1)d) + (2a + (n - 1)d)$$

Since all n of these terms are equal,

$$2S_n = n(2a + (n - 1)d)$$

$$\Rightarrow \quad S_n = \frac{n}{2}(2a + (n - 1)d)$$

Noticing that $S_n = \frac{n}{2}(a + (a + (n - 1)d))$, we can also write $S_n = \frac{n}{2}(a + l)$, where l = last (nth) term.

EXAMPLE

An arithmetic progression has first term 3 and third term 7. Find the sum of the first 12 terms.

ANSWER

Third term, $a + 2d = 7, a = 3 \Rightarrow 2d = 4 \Rightarrow d = 2$

$$S_{12} = \frac{12}{2}(6 + 11 \times 2) = 168.$$

GEOMETRIC SERIES

The geometric progression $a, ar, ar^2, \ldots, ar^{n-1}$ has first term a, common ratio r and n terms. The sum of the first n terms is denoted by $S_n = a + ar + \ldots + ar^{n-1}$. In terms of a, r and n

$$\boxed{S_n = a\left(\frac{1 - r^n}{1 - r}\right) \qquad \text{(if } r \neq 1)}$$

Proof

$$S_n = a + ar + ar^2 + \ldots + ar^{n-2} + ar^{n-1}$$

Multiply by r

$$rS_n = ar + ar^2 + ar^3 + \ldots + ar^{n-1} + ar^n$$

Subtract $(1 - r)S_n = a - ar^n = a(1 - r^n)$
(middle terms all cancel on the right)

$$\Rightarrow \quad S_n = a\left(\frac{1 - r^n}{1 - r}\right) \quad \text{if } r \neq 1$$

(For the case $r = 1$, the first n terms are all equal to a. Thus, $S_n = a + \ldots + a = na$.)

Example

The first 3 terms of a geometric progression are 2, 1, $\frac{1}{2}$. Find the sum of the first ten terms, correct to 4 decimal places.

Answer

$a = 2, r = \frac{\text{second term}}{\text{first term}} = \frac{1}{2}, n = 10.$

$$S_{10} = 2\left(\frac{1 - \left(\frac{1}{2}\right)^{10}}{1 - \frac{1}{2}}\right) = 2\frac{\left(1 - \frac{1}{2^{10}}\right)}{\frac{1}{2}} = 4 - \frac{4}{2^{10}} = 3{\cdot}9961$$

(to 4 decimal places)

5.2 Infinite Series

In some cases, it is possible to give a meaning to the sum of an **infinite** sequence $a_0, a_1, a_2, \ldots$ Denoting the sum of the first n terms of a series by S_n,

$$S_1 = a_0,\ S_2 = a_0 + a_1,\ S_3 = a_0 + a_1 + a_2, \ldots$$

The **partial sums** $S_1, S_2, S_3, \ldots$ form a sequence. For some series, this sequence of partial sums converges.

Example

Taking the geometric progression of the last example,

$$S_{10} \simeq 3{\cdot}9961,\ S_{20} \simeq 3{\cdot}9999961, \ldots$$

The partial sums appear to approach more and more closely to 4. In fact, the sequence $S_1, S_2, \ldots, S_{10}, \ldots, S_{20}, \ldots$ does converge with limit 4.

Proof

$$S_n = 2\left(\frac{1-0{\cdot}5^n}{1-0{\cdot}5}\right) = 2\left(\frac{1-0{\cdot}5^n}{0{\cdot}5}\right) = 4 - 4(0{\cdot}5)^n.$$

As $n \to \infty$, $(0{\cdot}5)^n \to 0$ and so $S_n \to 4$.

We *define* the sum of the infinite series $2 + 1 + \frac{1}{2} + \frac{1}{4} + \ldots$ to be this limit; thus, $2 + 1 + \frac{1}{2} + \frac{1}{4} + \ldots = 4$. Of course, we cannot physically add infinitely many terms. We interpret this **infinite sum** by saying that, as more and more terms are included, the total approaches as near to 4 as we want.

In general, for a sequence $a_0, a_1, \ldots, a_n, \ldots$, $S_n = a_0 + \ldots + a_{n-1}$ is the sum of the first n terms. If the sequence of partial sums $S_1, S_2, \ldots, S_n, \ldots$ converges with limit S, then we call S the sum of the infinite series $a_0 + a_1 + \ldots$ We say that the series **converges with sum S** and write symbolically $S = a_0 + a_1 + a_2 + \ldots$ We were able to calculate the infinite sum $2 + 1 + \frac{1}{2} + \ldots$ because $(0{\cdot}5)^n \to 0$ as $n \to \infty$.

In general, the infinite geometric series $a + ar + ar^2 + \ldots$ converges if $-1 < r < 1$. For this case, the sum of the infinite series is given by

$$\boxed{S = \frac{a}{1-r}}$$

Proof

The partial sum $S_n = a(\frac{1-r^n}{1-r}) = \frac{a}{1-r} - (\frac{a}{1-r})r^n$. If $-1 < r < 1$, then $r^n \to 0$ as $n \to \infty$ (try calculating $0{\cdot}7^{10}, 0{\cdot}7^{20}, \ldots$, for example). Thus,

$$\lim_{n\to\infty} S_n = \lim_{n\to\infty}\left(\frac{a}{1-r} - \left(\frac{a}{1-r}\right)r^n\right) = \frac{a}{1-r}$$

Note

If $r = 1$, $S_n = a + a + \ldots + a = na \to \infty$ as $n \to \infty$.

If $r = -1$, $S_n = a - a + a - a + \ldots$, so that $S_1 = a$, $S_2 = 0$, $S_3 = a, \ldots$ The sequence of partial sums is $a, 0, a, 0, a, 0, \ldots$ which **oscillates** between 0 and a and so does *not* converge. The strict inequalities $-1 < r < 1$ *are* necessary for convergence.

Example

Show that the geometric series $1 + 0{\cdot}1 + 0{\cdot}01 + \ldots$ converges and express the sum to infinity as a fraction.

Answer

$r = \frac{0\cdot1}{1} = 0{\cdot}1$ and so $-1 < r < 1$, which is required for convergence. $a = 1$, $r = 0{\cdot}1$, the formula for the sum to infinity

$$S = \frac{a}{1-r} = \frac{1}{1-0\cdot1} = \frac{1}{0\cdot9} = \frac{10}{9}$$

Note: This result shows that the **recurring decimal** $1{\cdot}11111\ldots \equiv 1{\cdot}\dot{1}$ is equivalent to the fraction $\frac{10}{9}$.

Summary

An arithmetic series has terms $S_n = a + (a + d) + \ldots + (a + (n-1)d)$.

The nth term of the series is $a + (n-1)d$.

The sum of the first n terms is $\frac{n}{2}(2a + (n-1)d)$.

A geometric series has terms $S_n = a + ar + ar^2 + ar^3 + \ldots + ar^{n-1}$.

The nth term of the series is ar^{n-1}.

The sum of the first n terms is $a\left(\frac{1-r^n}{1-r}\right)$.

If $-1 < r < 1$, then the infinite series $a + ar + ar^2 + \ldots$ converges with sum $\frac{a}{1-r}$.
An infinite arithmetic series *cannot* converge because its terms do not decrease in magnitude.

5.3 The Σ notation

The series $a_0 + a_1 + \ldots + a_n$ can be written more compactly as

$$\sum_{r=0}^{n} a_r$$

Σ (Greek capital S) stands for *sum*,
a_r is the general term of the sequence,
'$r = 0$' below the Σ tells you to start with term a_0,
'n' above the Σ tells you to stop with term a_n,
The subscripts increase from 0 to n in *steps of 1*.

Examples

1. $\sum_{r=1}^{10} r \equiv 1+2+3+4+5+6+7+8+9+10.$

This is an arithmetic series with first term 1, common difference 1, and 10 terms. Thus,

$$\sum_{r=1}^{10} r = \frac{10}{2}(2 + 9 \times 1) = 55.$$

2. $\sum_{r=0}^{3} 3^r = 3^0 + 3^1 + 3^2 + 3^3 = 1 + 3 + 9 + 27$
$= 40$ (geometric)

3. $\sum_{r=1}^{n} (2r-3) = -1 + 1 + 3 + \ldots + (2n-3)$

4. $\sum_{s=5}^{2n} c_s = c_5 + c_6 + \ldots + c_{2n}$

The following results are useful for simplifying Σ expressions:

1. $\Sigma(a_r + b_r) = \Sigma a_r + \Sigma b_r$

Proof

$$\sum_m^n (a_r + b_r) = (a_m + b_m) + (a_{m+1} + b_{m+1}) + \ldots + (a_n + b_n)$$

$$= (a_m + a_{m+1} + \ldots + a_n) + (b_m + b_{m+1} + \ldots + b_n)$$

$$= \sum_m^n a_r + \sum_m^n b_r$$

2. $\Sigma k a_r = k \Sigma a_{r'}$, where k is a constant (independent of r).

Proof

$$\sum_m^n k a_r = k a_m + k a_{m+1} + \ldots + k a_n = k(a_m + \ldots + a_n) = k \sum_m^n a_r$$

Notice that, where the subscript is obvious, the '$r =$' can be left off; for example, $\sum_1^4 b_r$ means $\sum_{r=1}^4 b_r$.

5.4 $\sum_1^n r$, $\sum_1^n r^2$ *and* $\sum_1^n r^3$

Formulae for the sums of these three important series can be calculated.

1. $\sum_1^n r \equiv 1 + 2 + \ldots + n$. This is arithmetic with first term 1, common, difference 1 and n terms. From the formula of page 47

$$\boxed{\sum_1^n r = \frac{n}{2}(2 + (n-1) \times 1) = \frac{1}{2}n(n+1)}$$

Example

Calculate $\sum_{10}^{20} r$.

We could regard this as an arithmetic series with first term 10, common difference 1, and 10 terms, and use the formula of page 47. However, we can use the result above directly.

$$\sum_{10}^{20} r = \sum_1^{20} r - \sum_1^9 r$$

$$= \frac{1}{2} \times 20 \times 21 - \frac{1}{2} \times 9 \times 10 = 210 - 45 = 165$$

2. $\sum_{r=1}^{n} r^2 \equiv 1^2 + 2^2 + \ldots + n^2$. This is neither arithmetic nor geometric.

To calculate this sum, we first consider the related series $\sum_{r=1}^{n} r(r+1)$.

First notice that $3r(r+1) = r(r+1)(r+2) - (r-1)r(r+1)$.

Letting $r(r+1)(r+2) = u_r$, we can write $3r(r+1) = u_r - u_{r-1}$.

Thus,

$$3\sum_{r=1}^{n} r(r+1) = \sum_{r=1}^{n} 3r(r+1) = \sum_{r=1}^{n} (u_r - u_{r-1})$$

$$= (u_1 - u_0) + (u_2 - u_1) + (u_3 - u_2) + \ldots + (u_n - u_{n-1})$$

$$= -u_0 + u_n$$

since all the middle terms cancel.

However,

$$u_0 = 0 \times 1 \times 2 = 0$$

$$\Rightarrow \quad 3\sum_{r=1}^{n} r(r+1) = u_n = n(n+1)(n+2)$$

$$\boxed{\Rightarrow \quad \sum_{r=1}^{n} r(r+1) = \frac{1}{3}n(n+1)(n+2)}$$

This uses the **method of differences**. The general term is expressed as the difference of consecutive terms of another sequence. When these are summed, all terms except the first and last cancel out.

Now, since

$$\sum_{1}^{n} r(r+1) = \sum_{1}^{n} (r^2 + r) = \sum_{1}^{n} r^2 + \sum_{1}^{n} r$$

then

$$\sum_{1}^{n} r^2 = \sum_{1}^{n} r(r+1) - \sum_{1}^{n} r$$

But both sums on the right are now known.

$$\Rightarrow \quad \sum_{1}^{n} r^2 = \frac{1}{3}n(n+1)(n+2) - \frac{1}{2}n(n+1)$$

$$= \frac{1}{6}n(n+1)(2(n+2)-3)$$

$$\boxed{\sum_1^n r^2 = \frac{1}{6}n(n+1)(2n+1)}$$

This final result can be quoted *without proof* in examination questions, unless instructions otherwise are given.

Example

Calculate the sum $10^2 + 11^2 + \ldots + 50^2$.

Answer

$$10^2 + 11^2 + \ldots + 50^2 = (1^2 + 2^2 + \ldots + 50^2) - (1^2 + 2^2 + \ldots + 9^2)$$

$$= \sum_1^{50} r^2 - \sum_1^{9} r^2$$

$$= \frac{1}{6}50 \times 51 \times 101 - \frac{1}{6} \times 9 \times 10 \times 19$$

$$= 42640$$

3. $\sum_{r=1}^{n} r^3 = 1^3 + 2^3 + \ldots + n^3$. Example 10 on page 62 gives a proof that

$$\boxed{\sum_1^n r^3 = \frac{1}{4}n^2(n+1)^2}$$

This result also may be used without proof.

5.5 Proof by Induction

Formulae and relations such as

$$\sum_{r=1}^{n} r^2 = \frac{1}{6}n(n+1)(2n+1), \quad n = 1, 2, \ldots$$

which involve the positive integral variable n, can be proved by the **method of induction.** The steps of such a proof are:

1. Show that the relation is true for $n = 1$ (or whatever is the least value of n).
2. *Assuming* that the relation holds for some value $n = m$, *show* that it then holds for $n = m + 1$.

These steps then allow us to deduce that the relation holds for all values of n.

Picture this as a ladder.
The rungs represent values of n for which the relation is true:
(1) asserts that the first rung can be reached;
(2) enables the next rung up to be reached from wherever you are.

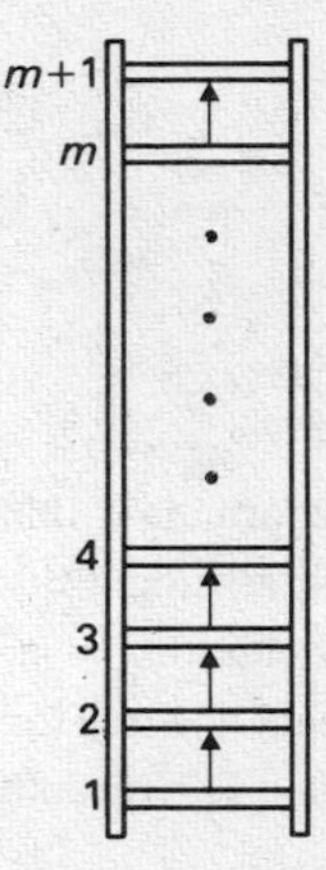

Thus, having reached rung 1, we can then reach rung 2, and then rung 3, and so on, to reach any rung.

Examples

1. Prove, by induction, that $\sum_{r=1}^{n} r^2 = \frac{1}{6}n(n+1)(2n+1)$

Proof

For $n = 1$, LHS $= \sum_{r=1}^{1} r^2 = 1^2 = 1$, RHS $= \frac{1}{6} \times 1 \times 2 \times 3 = 1$. Therefore, the relation holds for $n = 1$.
Now, assuming that it holds for $n = m$,

$$\Rightarrow \quad \sum_{r=1}^{m} r^2 = \frac{1}{6}m(m+1)(2m+1) \qquad \text{inductive hypothesis}$$

$$\Rightarrow \quad 1^2+2^2+\ldots+m^2 = \frac{1}{6}m(m+1)(2m+1)$$

$$\Rightarrow \quad (1^2+2^2+\ldots+m^2)+(m+1)^2 = \frac{1}{6}m(m+1)(2m+1)+(m+1)^2$$

(Add $(m+1)^2$ to both sides)

$$\Rightarrow \quad \sum_{r=1}^{m+1} r^2 = \frac{1}{6}m(m+1)(2m+1)+(m+1)^2$$

$$= \frac{1}{6}(m+1)(m(2m+1)+6(m+1))$$

(Factorize)

$$= \frac{1}{6}(m+1)(2m^2+7m+6)$$

$$= \frac{1}{6}(m+1)(m+2)(2m+3)$$

$$= \frac{1}{6}(m+1)((m+1)+1)(2(m+1)+1)$$

which is the formula with $n = m+1$.

Therefore, assuming that the result holds for $n = m$, we have proved that it also holds for $n = m + 1$. The principle of induction then allows the deduction that it is true for all $n \in \{1, 2, 3, \ldots\}$.

Note: The first step (proof for $n = 1$) is essential to the proof.

2. Show that:

$$\sum_{r=1}^{n} \frac{1}{r(r+1)} = \frac{n}{n+1} \text{ for } n = 1, 2, 3, \ldots$$

Answer

For $n = 1$, $\text{LHS} = \frac{1}{1(2)} = \frac{1}{2}$, $\text{RHS} = \frac{1}{1+1} = \frac{1}{2}$. Therefore, it is true for $n = 1$.

Now suppose that it holds for $n = m$

$$\Rightarrow \quad \sum_{r=1}^{m} \frac{1}{r(r+1)} \equiv \frac{1}{1\times 2} + \frac{1}{2\times 3} + \ldots + \frac{1}{m(m+1)} = \frac{m}{m+1}$$

$$\Rightarrow \quad \sum_{r=1}^{m+1} \frac{1}{r(r+1)} \equiv \left(\frac{1}{1\times 2} + \ldots + \frac{1}{m(m+1)}\right) + \frac{1}{(m+1)(m+2)}$$

$$= \frac{m}{m+1} + \frac{1}{(m+1)(m+2)} = \frac{m(m+2)+1}{(m+1)(m+2)}$$

$$= \frac{m^2+2m+1}{(m+1)(m+1)} = \frac{(m+1)^2}{(m+1)(m+2)} = \frac{m+1}{m+2}$$

which is the formula with $n = m+1$. Therefore, by the principle of induction, the formula is true for all $n \in \{1, 2, 3, \ldots\}$.

Section 6 Worked Examples: Sequences and Series

1. The 10th term of an arithmetic progression is 25 and the 15th term is 50. Find the 26th term.

Answer

Let $a =$ first term, $d =$ common difference — *define* all variables used.

10th term $\equiv a + 9d = 25$ (1) — nth term $= a + (n-1)d$

15th term $\equiv a + 14d = 50$ (2) — Simultaneous equations (see page 94)

Subtract term by term $-5d = -25$

$\Rightarrow \quad d = 5$

(1) $\Rightarrow \quad a + 45 = 25$

$\Rightarrow \quad a = -20$

$\Rightarrow \quad$ 26th term $= -20 + (25 \times 5) = 105$

2. The first term of a geometric sequence is $3k + 1$. The last term of this sequence is $3k^{11} + k^{10}$ and the common ratio is k. Calculate the number of terms in this sequence, and the sum of these terms.

Answer

The general term is ar^{n-1}, where $a =$ first term, $r =$ common ratio. Now page 42

$$3k^{11} + k^{10} = k^{10}(3k+1)$$

$$= (3k+1)k^{11-1}$$

Comparing with ar^{n-1}

$$a = 3k + 1, r = k, n = 11.$$

There are 11 terms in the sequence. The sum is

$$(3k+1)\left(\frac{k^{11}-1}{k-1}\right) \qquad\qquad S_n \equiv a\left(\frac{1-r^n}{1-r}\right)$$

$$\equiv a\left(\frac{r^n-1}{r-1}\right)$$

3. Express the recurring decimal $0{\cdot}\dot{3}\dot{0} \equiv 0{\cdot}303030\,30 \ldots$ as a rational number.

Answer

$$0{\cdot}303030\ldots = 0{\cdot}30 + 0{\cdot}0030 + 0{\cdot}000030 + \ldots$$

$$= 0{\cdot}30 + \frac{0{\cdot}30}{100} + \frac{0{\cdot}30}{100^2} + \ldots$$

$$= 0{\cdot}30 + 0{\cdot}30\left(\frac{1}{100}\right) + 0{\cdot}30\left(\frac{1}{100}\right)^2 + \ldots$$

This is an infinite geometric series with first term 0·30 and common ratio $\frac{1}{100}$. The sum is

$-1 < \frac{1}{100} < 1$ so that the series converges

$$\frac{0{\cdot}30}{1-\dfrac{1}{100}} = \frac{0{\cdot}30 \times 100}{99} \qquad\qquad \frac{a}{1-r}$$

$$= \frac{10}{33}$$

dividing out common factor 3

4. The sequence $\{u_r\}$ is defined *iteratively* by $u_{r+1} = u_r^2 - 3$, $r = 1, 2, \ldots$, and $u_1 = 0{\cdot}1$. Calculate u_4 to 2 decimal places.

Answer

$$u_2 = u_1^2 - 3 = 0{\cdot}1^2 - 3 = -2{\cdot}99 \qquad (r = 1)$$

$$u_3 = u_2^2 - 3 = (-2{\cdot}99)^2 - 3 = 5{\cdot}940 \qquad (r = 2), \text{ 3 decimal places}$$

$$u_4 = u_3^2 - 3 = (5{\cdot}940)^2 - 3 = 32{\cdot}28 \qquad (r = 3), \text{ 2 decimal places}$$

5. Find an expression for the sum of the first *n* *even* positive whole

numbers. Hence find an expression for the sum of the first *n odd* positive whole numbers.

Answer

$$2 + 4 + \ldots + (2n) = 2(1 + 2 + \ldots + n)$$ *n*th even number is $2n$

$$= 2\sum_{1}^{n} r = 2 \times \frac{1}{2}n(n+1)$$ page 52

$$= n(n+1)$$

Now,

$$1 + 2 + 3 + 4 + \ldots + (2n-1) + 2n$$ $2n - 1$ is *n*th odd number

$$= (1 + 3 + \ldots + (2n-1)) + (2 + 4 + \ldots + 2n)$$

$$= \text{odds} + \text{evens}$$

$$\Rightarrow \quad \text{odds} = \sum_{1}^{2n} r - \text{evens}$$ $\sum_{1}^{N} r = \frac{1}{2}N(N+1)$

$$= \frac{1}{2}(2n)(2n+1) - n(n+1)$$

$$= n(2n+1) - n(n+1) = n^2$$ *check:* $1 + 3 + 5 = 9 = 3^2$

6. A sequence is defined by $a_n = 3(5^n)$, $n = 0, 1, 2, \ldots$

A $\{a_n\}$ is geometric and Σa_n converges

B $\{a_n\}$ is geometric and Σa_n does not converge

C $\{a_n\}$ is arithmetic and Σa_n converges

D $\{a_n\}$ is arithmetic and Σa_n does not converge

E $\{a_n\}$ is neither geometric nor arithmetic

Answer

$$a_n = 3(5^n)$$

$$a_{n+1} = 3(5^{n+1})$$

$$\Rightarrow \quad \frac{a_{n+1}}{a_n} = \frac{3(5^{n+1})}{3(5^n)} = 5 \quad \text{which is constant}$$

and so $\{a_n\}$ is geometric with common ratio 5. Since $5 > 1$, the series does not converge.
The answer is B.

page 49, converges only if $-1 < r < 1$

7. A woman borrows £1000 and repays with monthly instalments. The interest is 20% per year, calculated on the amount owed after each monthly repayment. Show that after her second payment she owes a balance of £(1000) $(\frac{61}{20})^2 - x\ (\frac{61}{60} + (\frac{61}{60})^2)$ when £x is the monthly payment. After n monthly payments, the balance owed can be expressed in the form £(1000) $(\frac{61}{60})^n - x(\frac{61}{60} + (\frac{61}{60})^2 + \ldots + (\frac{61}{60})^n)$. If she pays off the debt after 24 monthly instalments, calculate, to the nearest penny, the amount of each repayment.

Answer

Monthly interest rate $= \frac{20}{12}\% = \frac{5}{3}\% = \frac{5}{300}$

Repaying £x per month, after first payment:

Interest $= £(1000 - x) \times \frac{5}{300}$

rate × balance

$$\text{New balance} = £(1000 - x) + (1000 - x) \times \frac{5}{300}$$

$$= £(1000 - x) \times \frac{61}{60}$$

After the second payment:

$$\text{Balance} = £((1000 - x)\tfrac{61}{60} - x)\tfrac{61}{60}$$

(new balance $- x$) × $\frac{61}{60}$

$$= £(1000)(\tfrac{61}{60})^2 - x(\tfrac{61}{60} + (\tfrac{61}{60})^2)$$

After n monthly payments:

$$\text{Balance} = £(1000)(\tfrac{61}{60})^n - x(\tfrac{61}{60} + (\tfrac{61}{60})^2 + \ldots + (\tfrac{61}{60})^n)$$

If the debt is repaid after 24 months

$$(1000)(\tfrac{61}{60})^{24} - x(\tfrac{61}{60} + (\tfrac{61}{60})^2 + \ldots + (\tfrac{61}{60})^{24}) = 0$$

$$\Rightarrow \quad x(\tfrac{61}{60} + \ldots + (\tfrac{61}{60})^{24}) = (1000)(\tfrac{61}{60})^{24}$$

$$\Rightarrow \quad x(\tfrac{61}{60})\left(\frac{(\frac{61}{60})^{24} - 1}{(\frac{61}{60}) - 1}\right) = 1000(\tfrac{61}{60})^{24}$$

geometric with $a = \frac{61}{60}, n = 24, r = \frac{61}{60}$

$$\Rightarrow \quad 29{\cdot}70x = 1000 \times (\tfrac{61}{60})^{24}$$

$\boxed{x^y}$ key of calculator

$$\Rightarrow \quad x = \frac{1000 \times 1{\cdot}487}{29{\cdot}70} = 50{\cdot}06$$

The monthly repayments are £50·06. to the nearest penny

8. Calculate $\sum_{r=3}^{16} r(r-1)$

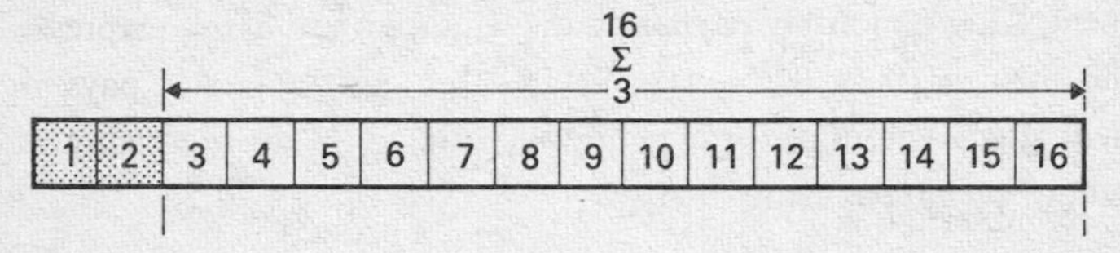

Answer

$$\sum_{r=3}^{16} r(r-1) = \sum_{3}^{16}(r^2 - r) = \sum_{3}^{16} r^2 - \sum_{3}^{16} r$$

$$= \left(\sum_{1}^{16} r^2 - \sum_{1}^{2} r^2\right) - \left(\sum_{1}^{16} r - \sum_{1}^{2} r\right)$$

$$= \left[\frac{1}{6}16(17)(33) - (1+4)\right]$$

$$- \left[\frac{1}{2}(16)(17) - (1+2)\right]$$

$$= 1358$$

9. The sum of the first n terms of a sequence is given by

$$S_n = 2n^2 - 3n + 1, \quad n = 1, 2, 3, \ldots$$

Find the first term, second term and 10th term. If the rth term of this sequence is denoted by a_r, calculate $\sum_{r=11}^{20} a_r$.

Answer

$$S_n = a_1 + a_2 + \ldots + a_n = 2n^2 - 3n + 1$$

the sequence starts at a_1 (*not* a_0)

Therefore,

$$S_1 = a_1 = 2(1^2) - 3(1) + 1 = 0$$

The first term is 0.

$$S_2 = a_1 + a_2$$

Therefore,

$$\begin{aligned} a_2 &= S_2 - a_1 \\ &= 2(2^2) - 3(2) + 1 - 0 \\ &= 3 \end{aligned}$$

The second term is 3.

S_{10}

1	2	3	4	5	6	7	8	9	10

S_9

The 10th term is

$$\begin{aligned} S_{10} - S_9 &= (2(10^2) - 3(10) + 1) - (2(9^2) - 3(9) + 1) \\ &= 35 \end{aligned}$$

$$\begin{aligned} \sum_{r=11}^{20} a_r &= \sum_{r=1}^{20} a_r - \sum_{r=1}^{10} a_r \\ &= S_{20} - S_{10} \\ &= 2(20)^2 - 3(20) + 1 - 171 \\ &= 570 \end{aligned}$$

10. Prove that $\sum_{r=1}^{n} r^3 = \frac{1}{4}n^2(n+1)^2$

Answer — by induction

For $n = 1$ — step 1

LHS $= 1^3 = 1$

RHS $= \frac{1}{4} \times 1 \times 4 = 1$

$\therefore$ it is true for $n = 1$.

Suppose it is true for $n = m$ — step 2

$\therefore \sum_{r=1}^{m} r^3 = \frac{1}{4}m^2(m+1)^2$ — $n = m$ in formula

$\therefore 1^3 + 2^3 + \ldots + m^3 = \frac{1}{4}m^2(m+1)^2$

$\therefore 1^3 + 2^3 + \ldots + (m+1)^3 = \frac{1}{4}m^2(m+1)^2 + (m+1)^3$ — add $(m+1)^3$

$$\therefore \sum_{1}^{m+1} r^3 = \tfrac{1}{4}(m+1)^2\,(m^2 + 4(m+1))$$
$$= \tfrac{1}{4}(m+1)^2\,(m^2 + 4m + 4)$$
$$= \tfrac{1}{4}(m+1)^2\,(m+2)^2$$

which is the formula with $n = m + 1$.

$\therefore$ it is also true for $n = m + 1$

$\therefore$ it is true for all $n \geqslant 1$

Section 7 Examination Questions

1. *The first term of an arithmetic series is $(3p + 5)$, where p is a positive integer. The last term is $(17p + 17)$ and the common difference is 2. Find, in terms of p, (i) the number of terms, (ii) the sum of the series. Show that the sum of the series is divisible by 14 only when p is odd.* [AEB]

2. *An arithmetic series has first term 6, common difference 8 and the sum of the first n terms is S_n. Express S_n in terms of n and show that it is the product of two consecutive integers.*

Deduce that S_n is not an integral power of 2.

The sum of the first n terms of a geometric series is $\frac{4}{3}(4^n - 1)$ and the nth term is u_n. Express u_n in terms of n and show that u_n is an integral power of 2. [AEB]

3. *A man invested £100 each year on the first of January and his money earned compound interest at 10% per annum. Determine the value, to the nearest £10, of his total investment immediately after his 20th investment of £100.* [LON]

4. *An arithmetic progression has first term a and common diffarence d. Its 10th term is 69 and the sum of its first 30 terms is four times the sum of its first 10 terms. Find the values of a and d.* [CAM]

(Hint: Use nth term $= a + (n-1)d$, $S_n = \frac{n}{2}(2a + (n-1)d)$ *to obtain two equations in a and d.)*

5. *A geometric series with first term 16 and third term 4 must 1. be convergent, 2. have common ratio* $\frac{1}{2}$, *3. have a sum to infinity 32.*

A 1, 2 and 3 B 1 and 2 only C 2 and 3 only D 1 only E 3 only

[LON]

6. *Find the least number of terms of the geometrical progression* $2 + 3 + 4{\cdot}5 + \ldots$ *that will have a sum in excess of 10000.*

[SUJB – part]

7. *The rth term of a sequence is* $5 - 3r$.

1. *The first term of the sequence is 5.*
2. *The terms of the sequence are in arithmetic progression.*
3. *The sum of the first n terms of the sequence is* $\frac{n}{2}(7 - 3n)$.

A 1, 2 and 3 are correct B 1 and 2 only C 2 and 3 only D 1 only E 3 only [LON]

8. *The series* $\sum_{r=1}^{n+1} u_r$ *is a geometric series with common ratio k, where* $k^2 \neq 1$.

Show that the series $\sum_{r=1}^{n} (u_r u_{r+1})$ *is a geometric series and that its sum is equal to*

$$\frac{u_1^2 k(1 - k^{2n})}{(1 - k^2)}$$

[LON]

(Hint: Let $v_r = u_r u_{r+1}$, *show that* $\{v_r\}$ *is geometric.)*

9. *Prove that* $\sum_{r=1}^{n} r(r+1) = \frac{1}{3}n(n+1)(n+2)$.

Evaluate $\sum_{r=1}^{20} r(r-1)$. [LON]

10. $\sum_{r=1}^{n} (n+2r+1) =$

A n^2+3n B n^2+2n+1 C $2n^2+2n$ D $2n^2+n+1$ E none of these

[LON]

11. *Using the iterative formula* $x_{r+1} = x_r(2-8x_r)$ *with* $x_1 = 0{\cdot}1$ *gives* $x_3 =$

A 1·248 B 1·2 C 0·1248 D 0·12 E 0·01248 [LON]

12. *(a) The positive integer k is given.*

(i) Find, in terms of k, an expression for S_1*, the sum of the integers from 2k to 4k, inclusive.*

(ii) Find, in terms of k, an expression for S_2*, the sum of the odd integers lying between 2k and 4k.*

(iii) Show that $\frac{S_1}{S_2} = 2 + \frac{1}{k}$.

(b) Prove that the sum of the first n terms of the geometrical progression having first term a and common ratio r $(r \neq 1)$ *is*

$$a\left(\frac{1-r^n}{1-r}\right)$$

By regarding the recurring decimal $0{\cdot}\dot{0}7\dot{5}$ $(=0{\cdot}075075\cdots$*, where the figures 075 repeat) as an infinite geometric progression, or otherwise, obtain the value of the decimal as a fraction in its lowest terms.* [CAM]

13. *Show by induction, or otherwise, that*

$$1\times3+3\times5\times7+\ldots+(2n-1)\times(2n+1)$$
$$=\tfrac{1}{6}(2n-1)(2n+1)(2n+3)+\tfrac{1}{2}$$

[OXF]

3 Polynomial Functions and Equations

Section 8

8.1 Introduction

Between any two real numbers, there are uncountably many other real numbers. For this reason, the real numbers cannot be written as an ordered sequence, and so it is not possible to form a sequence from the images of a function on $\mathbb{R}$.

Functions on $\mathbb{R}$ are usually defined in terms of formulae and may be represented by graphs (page 33). While the graph of a function of $\mathbb{N}$ (sequence) is composed of isolated points, the graph of a function of $\mathbb{R}$ is typically composed of continuous arcs.

Functions can be classified by the type of formula used. (We shall restrict attention to functions with *single* formulae in these sections.)

Type	*Example*
1. Polynomials	$3x^4 - 5x^2 + 6x - 2$
2. Other 'power' functions	$2x^{\frac{1}{2}} - 3x^{-2}$
3. Rational functions	$\dfrac{2x-3}{x^2+5x-7}$
4. Exponential functions	2^{3x+1}
5. Logarithmic functions	$\log_{10}(2x-3)$
6. Trigonometric functions	$\sin(3x)$

In this book, only functions of these types, and combinations of them, are considered.

The rest of this chapter concerns polynomial functions only. Later chapters deal with the other types.

8.2 Definitions

A **term** is formed by multiplying a power of the variable by a constant **coefficient**.

Examples

$$2x^3, \ -10a^{10}, \left(\frac{3}{5}\pi\right)y^4, \frac{1}{2}r^{-\frac{1}{2}}.$$

A **polynomial** is formed by adding terms in the *same* variable which have *positive* (*or* 0) *powers.*

Examples

$$f(x) = 3x^4 - 7x^3 + 5x^2 - 6x + 1$$

$$g(z) = z^5 - 6z^2 + z$$

are polynomial functions.

$h(x) = 2x^{\frac{1}{2}} - 3x^{-2}$ and $k(x, y) = 3x^2y + 2y$ do not satisfy the definition above. h involves fractional and negative powers, while k is a polynomial in *two* variables.

The terms of a polynomial are usually written with the powers in either ascending or descending order. Avoid starting with a $-$ sign, if possible (they can be too easily overlooked in a page of working).

Examples

1. Write $3x^4 + 5x^2 - 6x + 1$ and not $5x^2 + 3x^4 + 1 - 6x$.
2. Write $3 + 2x - x^2$ and not $-x^2 + 2x + 3$.

The highest power occurring is called the **order** or **degree** of the polynomial.

The coefficients of a polynomial *include* signs.

Example

The coefficient of x^2 in $3x^3 - x^2 + 2$ is -1.

8.3 Polynomial Types

Polynomials can be classified by their order (degree):

Order	*Name*	*Example*	*General Form* $f:x\mapsto$
0	Constant function	2	a
1	Linear	$3x-5$	$ax+b$
2	Quadratic	x^2-5x+1	ax^2+bx+c
3	Cubic	$1-2x+3x^2-x^3$	ax^3+bx^2+cx+d
4	Quartic	x^4-2x^3+1	$ax^4+bx^3+cx^2+dx+e$
5	Quintic	$2x^5+3x^3+x^2-2x$	$ax^5+bx^4+cx^3+dx^2+ex+f$

Notes

1. ax^n is called the **leading term** of the polynomial of order n.

2. $a, b, c, \ldots$ are constant. $a \neq 0$ but any of $b, c, d, \ldots$ may be zero (as in the quartic example where the coefficients of x^2 and x are zero).

3. $f:x\mapsto 2$, which assigns the same image to each value of x, is a special case of a polynomial. It is a **constant** function.

The next 5 subsections concern manipulation of polynomial expressions.

8.4 The Expansion of $(1+x)^n$: Pascal's Triangle

Expressions such as $(1+x)^2$, $(1+x)^3$ can be **expanded** by multiplying out the brackets:

$$(1+x)^2 = (1+x)(1+x) = 1+x+x+x^2 = 1+2x+x^2$$

$$(1+x)^3 = (1+x)(1+x)^2 = (1+x)(1+2x+x^2)$$

$$= 1+x+2x+2x^2+x^2+x^3$$
$$= 1+3x+3x^2+x^3$$

and so on.

With high powers, this calculation becomes much more tedious.

A more convenient method is to use **Pascal's triangle**:

1	1st row
1 1	2nd row
1 2 1	3rd row
↘ ↙	
1 3 3 1	4th row
↘ ↙	
1 4 6 4 1	5th row
↘ ↙	
1 5 10 10 5 1	6th row
↘ ↙	
1 6 15 20 15 6 1	7th row

A number in a row is obtained by adding the two numbers immediately above. The end numbers are always 1. Note that the numbers appear *symmetrically*.

The numbers of the 3rd row are the coefficients in the expansion $(1 + x)^2 = 1 + 2x + x^2$. The numbers in the 4th row are the coefficients in the expansion of $(1 + x)^3 = 1 + 3x + 3x^2 + (1)x^3$. This is true in general. The $(n + 1)^{\text{th}}$ row provides the coefficients in the expansion of $(1 + x)^n$. Thus,

$$(1 + x)^6 = 1 + 6x + 15x^2 + 20x^3 + 15x^4 + 6x^5 + x^6$$

Further rows can be easily obtained and the corresponding expansions derived. More complicated expansions can be found in the same way:

Examples

1. $(1 + 2x)^6 \equiv (1 + (2x))^6$
(regard $2x$ as a new variable)

$$\equiv 1 + 6(2x) + 15(2x)^2 + 20(2x)^3 + 15(2x)^4 + 6(2x)^5 + (2x)^6$$

(*replace* x by $2x$ in the expansion)

$$\equiv 1 + 12x + 60x^2 + 160x^3 + 240x^4 + 192x^5 + 64x^6$$

2. $$\left(1 + \frac{x}{2}\right)^6 \equiv 1 + 6\left(\frac{x}{2}\right) + 15\left(\frac{x}{2}\right)^2 + 20\left(\frac{x}{2}\right)^3 + 15\left(\frac{x}{2}\right)^4 + 6\left(\frac{x}{2}\right)^5 + \left(\frac{x}{2}\right)^6$$

$$= 1 + 3x + \frac{15x^2}{4} + \frac{5x^3}{2} + \frac{15x^4}{16} + \frac{3x^5}{16} + \frac{x^6}{64}$$

3. $(2 + x)^6 = \left[2(1 + \frac{x}{2})\right]^6 = 2^6\left(1 + \frac{x}{2}\right)^6$ first term inside the brackets must be 1

$$= 2^6\left(1 + 3x + \frac{15}{4}x^2 + \frac{5x^3}{2} + \frac{15x^4}{16} + \frac{3x^5}{16} + \frac{x^6}{64}\right)$$

$$= 64 + 192x + 240x^2 + 160x^3 + 60x^4 + 12x^5 + x^6$$

4. $(a + b)^6 = a^6\left(1 + \frac{b}{a}\right)^6 = a^6(1 + 6\left(\frac{b}{a}\right) + 15\left(\frac{b}{a}\right)^2 + 20\left(\frac{b}{a}\right)^3 + 15\left(\frac{b}{a}\right)^4$
$$+ 6\left(\frac{b}{a}\right)^5 + \left(\frac{b}{a}\right)^6\Bigg)$$

$$= a^6\left(1 + \frac{6b}{a} + \frac{15b^2}{a^2} + \frac{20b^3}{a^3} + \frac{15b^4}{a^4} + \frac{6b^5}{a^5} + \frac{b^6}{a^6}\right)$$

$$\therefore (a + b)^6 = a^6 + 6a^5b + 15a^4b^2 + 20a^3b^3 + 15a^2b^4 + 6ab^5 + b^6$$

Notice that in this expansion for each term the powers of a and b total 6.

In general,

$$(a + b)^n = a^n + \binom{n}{1}a^{n-1}b + \binom{n}{2}a^{n-2}b^2 + \ldots + \binom{n}{r}a^{n-r}b^r + \ldots + b^n$$

where $\binom{n}{1}$, $\binom{n}{2}$, ... $\binom{n}{r}$, ... are the **binomial coefficients** in the **binomial expansion** of $(a + b)^n$. They are just the numbers in Pascal's triangle. Thus,

$$\binom{2}{1} = \text{2nd number in the 3rd row} = 2$$

$$\binom{5}{2} = \text{3rd number in the 6th row} = 10$$

$$\binom{n}{r} = (r + 1)\text{th number in the } (n + 1)\text{th row}$$

Pascal's triangle is adequate for calculating these coefficients when n is small but soon becomes unwieldy for large n. Fortunately, a formula can be derived for $\binom{n}{r}$.

8.5 The Binomial Theorem

In the expansion $(1+x)^n = 1 + \binom{n}{1}x + \binom{n}{2}x^2 + \ldots + \binom{n}{r}x^r + \ldots + x^n$ the coefficients are given by the formula

$$\boxed{\binom{n}{r} = \frac{n!}{r!(n-r)!}}$$

where the **factorial notation** $n!$ means $n(n-1)(n-2) \ldots 2 \times 1$ (Multiply all positive numbers less than or equal to n.) Thus $3! = 3 \times 2 \times 1 = 6$, $5! = 5 \times 4 \times 3 \times 2 \times 1 = 120$.

PROPERTIES OF $n!$

Examples

1. $\dfrac{5!}{3!} = \dfrac{5 \times 4 \times 3 \times 2}{3 \times 2} = 5 \times 4 = 20$

2. $\dfrac{10!}{6!} = \dfrac{10 \times 9 \times 8 \times 7 \times 6 \times 5 \times 4 \times 3 \times 2}{6 \times 5 \times 4 \times 3 \times 2} = 10 \times 9 \times 8 \times 7$

In general,

$$\frac{n!}{r!} = n(n-1)(n-2) \ldots (r+1)$$

So,

$$\binom{n}{r} = \frac{n!}{r!(n-r)!} = \frac{n(n-1) \times \ldots \times (n-r)(n-r-1)\ldots 2 \times 1}{r!\,(n-r)(n-r-1)\ldots 2}$$

$$= \frac{n(n-1)\ldots(n-r+1)}{r!}$$

Thus,

$$\binom{n}{1} = \frac{n}{1}, \binom{n}{2} = \frac{n(n-1)}{2!}, \binom{n}{3} = \frac{n(n-1)(n-2)}{3!}$$

This formidable-looking formula is actually quite easy to use.

Example

$$(1+x)^7 = 1 + \frac{7}{1}x + \frac{7\times 6}{2!}x^2 + \frac{7\times 6\times 5}{3!}x^3 + \frac{7\times 6\times 5\times 4}{4!}x^4$$

$$+\frac{7\times 6\times 5\times 4\times 3}{5!}x^5 + \frac{7\times 6\times 5\times 4\times 3\times 2}{6!}x^6 + x^7$$

Note that the term $\frac{7\times 6\times 5}{3!}$ has 3 factors in the numerator, 3! in the denominator and x to the power 3. In the same way the coefficient of x^r has r factors in the numerator and $r!$ in the denominator.
Therefore, $(1+x)^7 = 1 + 7x + \frac{42x^2}{2} + \frac{210x^3}{6} + \frac{840x^4}{24} + \dots$
The *symmetry* of the coefficients can be used to finish off.

$$(1+x)^7 = 1 + 7x + 21x^2 + 35x^3 + 35x^4 + \dots$$

$$= 1 + 7x + 21x^2 + 35x^3 + 35x^4 + 21x^5 + 7x^6 + x^7$$

Since $\binom{7}{1} = \binom{7}{6}$, $\binom{7}{2} = \binom{7}{5}$, $\binom{7}{3} = \binom{7}{4}$. In general,

$$\boxed{\binom{n}{r} = \binom{n}{n-r}}$$

Proof

$$\binom{n}{r} = \frac{n!}{r!(n-r)!}$$

$$\binom{n}{n-r} = \frac{n!}{(n-r)!(n-(n-r))!} = \frac{n!}{(n-r)!(r)!} = \binom{n}{r}$$

Another example

$$(1-2x)^{10} = 1 + \binom{10}{1}(-2x) + \binom{10}{2}(-2x)^2 + \binom{10}{3}(-2x)^3$$

$$+\binom{10}{4}(-2x)^4 + \binom{10}{5}(-2x)^5 + \dots$$

$$= 1 + \frac{10}{1}(-2x) + \frac{10\times 9}{2}(-2x)^2 + \frac{10\times 9\times 8}{6}(-2x)^3$$

$$+\frac{10\times 9\times 8\times 7}{24}(-2x)^4+\frac{10\times 9\times 8\times 7\times 6}{120}(-2x)^5+\dots$$

$$=1-20x+180x^2-960x^3+3360x^4-8064x^5+\dots$$

where only terms as far as x^5 have been calculated (but note that the (-2) factor destroys the symmetry of the coefficients).

8.6 Permutations and Combinations

SEQUENCES OF OPERATIONS

If operation A can be performed in r ways and operation B in s ways, then the combination A followed by B can be performed in rs ways.

Example

How many 2-digit numbers can be formed by choosing digits from 1, 2, 3, 4, 5, where each digit may be chosen once only?

Answer

Operation A is the choice of first digit. This digit can be chosen in 5 ways. Operation B is the choice of second digit, for which there are now 4 choices.

The number of choices for the 2 digits is $5\times 4=20$.

PERMUTATIONS

Each distinguishable arrangement of a set of objects is called a **permutation**. The order of arrangement is important.

Example

The letters ABC have permutations ABC, ACB, BAC, BCA, CAB, CBA.

To find the permutations of n *distinguishable* objects, there are n choices for the first one, $n-1$ for the second, $n-2$ for the third and so on. Hence the number of permutations is $n(n-1)(n-2)\,\dots\,2\times 1\equiv n!$ (page 71).

n distinguishable objects have $n!$ permutations

Example

A 4-digit number is to be formed from the digits 1, 2, 3, 4. There are $4! = 24$ possible choices if each digit is used once only.

If digits may be repeated, there are 4 choices for each and so $4 \times 4 \times 4 \times 4 = 4^4 = 256$ numbers may be formed.

The set of objects to be permuted may contain repetitions.

Example

Find the number of permutations of the letters ALGEBRA.

Answer

Suppose first that the 2 As are distinguishable. There are 7! permutations of the letters $A_1LGEBRA_2$. The As can be swapped around in 2 ways, and so if the arrangements such as $A_1LGEBRA_2$ and $A_2LGEBRA_1$ are to be counted as the same there are only $\frac{7!}{2} = 2520$ distinguishable permutations of ALGEBRA.

If a set of n objects has a subset of r identical objects, another subset of s identical objects, and so on, there are $\frac{n!}{r!s!\ldots}$ permutations.

Example

LETTERS has $\frac{7!}{2!2!} = 1260$ permutations.

PARTIAL SELECTIONS

Suppose that r objects are selected and arranged *in order* from a set of n distinguishable objects.

There are n choices for the first one, $(n-1)$ for second, down to $(n-r+1)$ choices for the rth one.

There are $n(n-1)\ldots(n-r+1)$ ways to choose the r objects. This expression can be written as $\frac{n!}{(n-r)!}$ and is the number of permutations of r objects from a set of n distinguishable ones.

Example

I wish to read a different book each week for 3 weeks. There are 10 books to choose from. I can choose the 3 books in $10 \times 9 \times 8 = 720$ different ways.

The set may contain identical objects.

Example

In how many ways can 2 letters be chosen, in order from the letters ABRACADABRA?

Answer

We consider the number of repetitions in the pair:

1. 2 different letters. There are 5 different letters A, B, C, D, R and so $\frac{5!}{3!} = 20$ choices.

2. A pair of identical letters. The pair could be AA or BB so there are 2 choices.

Adding the numbers of choices gives a total of 22 selections.

CIRCULAR ARRANGEMENTS

When arranging objects in a circle, cyclic permutations are counted the same.

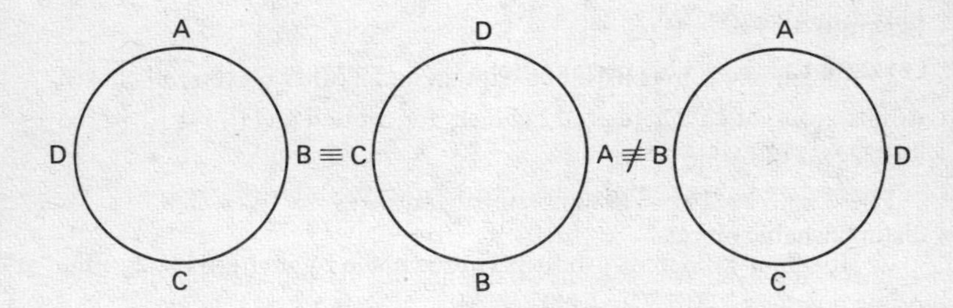

If n distinguishable objects are to be arranged in a circle, there is a free choice to place one anywhere round the circle. The remaining $(n - 1)$ can be arranged in $(n - 1)!$ ways around the remaining $(n - 1)$ places.

n distinguishable objects can be arranged in $(n-1)!$ ways around a circle, where cyclic permutations are considered equal.

Example

5 people can be seated in $4! = 24$ ways around a circular table.

COMBINATIONS

A selection in which order of arrangement is unimportant is called a **combination.**

A group of n objects clearly has only one combination taking all n of them.

Suppose that r out of n distinguishable objects are to be selected without order. Taken *in order* there are $\frac{n!}{(n-r)!}$ permutations. However, each selection is counted $r!$ times, since there are $r!$ permutations of r distinguishable objects. Dividing out

there are $\frac{n!}{r!(n-r)!}$ selections of r out of n distinguishable objects, order being unimportant.

(This is just the binomial coefficient $\binom{n}{r}$, page 71)

Examples

1. A team of 4 players is chosen from a group of 12 people. The number of possible teams is $\binom{12}{4} = \frac{12!}{4!8!} = 495$.

2. A team of 4 is to consist of a captain and 3 other players, all chosen from a group of 12. There are 12 choices for captain and $\binom{11}{3} = \frac{11!}{3!8!} = 165$ choices for the other 3.

   There are $12 \times 165 = 1980$ possible teams.

3. How many different products can be made by multiplying 3 of the prime numbers 2, 3, 5, 7 and 11?

Answer

There are $\binom{5}{3} = \frac{5!}{2!3!} = 10$ choices for the 3 numbers, and so 10 possible products.

4. A box contains 10 different small discs and 6 different large discs. In how many ways can 4 discs be chosen so that

(*a*) there are 2 small discs and 2 large discs,
(*b*) there is at least one large disc?

Answer

(*a*) The 2 small discs can be chosen in $\binom{10}{2} = 45$ ways, and the 2 large discs can be chosen in $\binom{6}{2} = 15$ ways.

There are $45 \times 15 = 675$ choices.

(*b*) There are $\binom{16}{4} = 1820$ ways to choose 4 discs, $\binom{10}{4} = 210$ of the selections have *no* large discs and so there are $1820 - 210 = 1610$ selections with at least one large disc.

8.7 Calculating and Rearranging

A formula such as $f(x) = 2x^3 - 3x^2 - 11x + 6$ is evaluated by substituting for values of the variable x. The formula can be rewritten in many ways. For example, $f(x) \equiv ((2x - 3)x - 11)x + 6$.

Values of the function can be calculated more easily using this expression as it only involves a sequence of multiplications and additions or subtractions. Thus,

$$\begin{aligned} f(2) &= ((4 - 3)2 - 11)2 + 6 \\ &= (2 - 11)2 + 6 \\ &= (-9)(2) + 6 = -18 + 6 = -12 \end{aligned}$$

(To see that this expression is easier, use both formulae to evaluate $f(9)$ on a calculator!)

Exercise

Rewrite $g(x) = 10x^4 - 6x^3 + 5x^2 - 9x + 2$ in a form similar to that above and calculate $g(-3)$.

Another useful way of rearranging a polynomial expression is to *factorize* it.

8.8 Factorization and Division of Polynomials

The function $f(x) = 2x^3 - 3x^2 - 11x + 6$ can be expressed as a product of linear factors; $f(x) \equiv (2x-1)(x+2)(x-3)$.

Exercise

Multiply out the brackets of this factorized form and verify that the original expression is obtained.

Using this form: $f(2) = (4-1)(2+2)(2-3) = 3 \times 4 \times -1 = -12$. Techniques for deriving factorized forms are introduced later (page 81).

Two expressions, one of which is obtained from the other by rearranging, are obviously equal for all values of the variable. An equality like

$$2x^3 - 3x^2 - 11x + 6 \equiv (2x-1)(x+2)(x-3)$$

is called an **identity**. (The $\equiv$ sign shows that both sides are equal for all values of x.)

An identity should not be confused with an *equation* such as $x^2 - 1 = 0$ in which both sides are equal *only* for a certain set of values of x; in this example $x = -1$ and $x = 1$ (see page 85).

Many careless mistakes can be made when rearranging formulae and expressions, particularly when multiplying out brackets. Always arrange your working neatly and methodically and *check* each step.

LONG DIVISION

The division

$$\begin{array}{r} 21 \\ 16\overline{)340} \\ -32\downarrow \\ \hline 20 \\ -16 \\ \hline 4 \end{array}$$

provides a **quotient** 21 and **remainder** 4 when 340 is divided by 16. We can then write

$$340 = 16 \times 21 + 4$$

(number = divisor × quotient + remainder).

In the same way, long division can be used with polynomial expressions.

Example

Divide $(x-2)$ into $2x^4 - x^3 + x^2 + x - 1$.

$$\begin{array}{r|l} & 2x^3 + 3x^2 + 7x + 15 \\ x-2 & 2x^4 - x^3 + x^2 + x - 1 \\ & 2x^4 - 4x^3 \\ & \quad 3x^3 + x^2 \\ & \quad 3x^3 - 6x^2 \\ & \qquad 7x^2 + x \\ & \qquad 7x^2 - 14x \\ & \qquad\quad 15x - 1 \\ & \qquad\quad 15x - 30 \\ & \qquad\qquad 29 \end{array}$$

Divide the *leading terms*
$2x^4 \div x = 2x^3$
Multiply divisor by $2x^3 \Rightarrow 2x^4 - 4x^3$ and *subtract* from first 2 terms.
Bring down next term to form a pair.
Repeat the process until a numerical remainder is left.

The quotient is $2x^3 + 3x^2 + 7x + 15$ and the remainder is 29. Thus, $2x^4 - x^3 + x^2 + x - 1 \equiv (x-2)(2x^3 + 3x^2 + 7x + 15) + 29$. *Check*: set $x = 1$, LHS $= 2 - 1 + 1 + 1 - 1 = 2$, RHS $= (-1)(2 + 3 + 7 + 15) + 29 = 2$.

In general, if a polynomial $f(x)$ of degree n is divided by a polynomial $g(x)$ of degree m, $(m \leqslant n)$, the quotient $q(x)$ has degree $n - m$ and the remainder $r(x)$ has degree at most $m - 1$.

$$f(x) \equiv g(x)q(x) + r(x).$$

In particular, if $g(x) = (x - a)$ (degree 1), then $r(x)$ has degree $1 - 1 = 0$ and so is a *constant*

$$f(x) \equiv (x - a)q(x) + r.$$

This leads to two useful results:

8.9 The Remainder and Factor Theorems

THE REMAINDER THEOREM

> When the polynomial $f(x)$ is divided by $(x - a)$ (a is a constant), the remainder is given by $f(a)$.

This follows directly from the identity

$$f(x) \equiv (x-a)q(x) + r$$

$$\Rightarrow f(a) = (a-a)q(a) + r$$

$$= 0 + r$$

$$= r.$$

Note: Division by the more general linear form $ax + b$ is equivalent to first dividing by a and then by $x + \frac{b}{a}$. The remainder is $f(-\frac{b}{a})$.

Examples

1. $f(x) \equiv 3x^4 - 2x^3 + 7x^2 - 5x + 2$. Division by $(x-3)$ produces a remainder $f(3) = 3(3^4) - 2(3^3) + 7(3^2) - 5(3) + 2 = 239$.

The **remainder theorem** provides a useful check on the accuracy of a long division. (As an exercise, check the remainder of the division above.)

2. The polynomial $f(x) \equiv 2x^3 - 3x^2 + ax + b$ has unknown coefficient of x and constant term. However, it is known that the remainder on division by $(x+2)$ is 2, and on division by $(x-2)$ it is -2. Calculate the values of a and b and hence find the remainder on division by $(x+1)$.

Answer

Using the remainder theorem:

$$\text{with } x + 2: f(-2) = -16 - 12 - 2a + b = 2 \Rightarrow -2a + b = 30 \quad (1)$$
$$\text{with } x - 2: f(2) = 16 - 12 + 2a + b = -2 \Rightarrow 2a + b = -6 \quad (2)$$

Adding thc simultancous cquations (pagc 94) (1) and (2)

$$\Rightarrow 2b = 24$$
$$\Rightarrow b = 12$$

From equation (1) $-2a + 12 = 30 \Rightarrow 2a = -18 \Rightarrow a = -9$. Hence, $f(x) \equiv 2x^3 - 3x^2 - 9x + 12$. The remainder on division by $(x+1)$ is $f(-1) = -2 - 3 + 9 + 12 = 16$.

A special case of the theorem arises when $f(a) = 0$; in this case, the remainder is zero:

THE FACTOR THEOREM

> If $f(x)$ is a polynomial and $f(a) = 0$ for a constant a, then $(x - a)$ is a factor of $f(x)$. In this case, $f(x) \equiv (x - a)q(x)$ for some polynomial $q(x)$.

This result can be used to factorize polynomial expressions.

Example

Express the polynomial $f(x) \equiv x^3 - 2x^2 - 5x + 6$ as the product of linear factors.

Answer

First find a value of x for which $f(x) = 0$. This can be done by **trial and error** (choose a value of x and see if it works). A good rule of thumb is to try factors of the constant term. 6 has factors ± 1, ± 2, ± 3, and ± 6.

$f(-1) = -1 - 2 + 5 + 6 = 8 \neq 0$. Therefore, $x + 1$ is not a factor. $f(1) = 1 - 2 - 5 + 6 = 0$. Therefore, $x - 1$ *is* a factor.

Now divide $f(x)$ by $(x - 1)$

$$\begin{array}{r@{}l} & x^2 - x - 6 \\ x - 1 \,\big)\! & \overline{x^3 - 2x^2 - 5x + 6} \\ & \underline{x^3 - x^2} \\ & \quad -x^2 - 5x \\ & \quad \underline{-x^2 + \ \ x} \\ & \qquad -6x + 6 \\ & \qquad \underline{-6x + 6} \\ & \qquad \quad \cdots \end{array} \qquad \text{(remainder is 0)}$$

Thus, $f(x) = (x - 1)(x^2 - x - 6)$.

The quadratic quotient $q(x) = x^2 - x - 6$ can be factorized 'by inspection' giving $(x + 2)(x - 3)$ (*check this!*) and so $f(x) \equiv (x - 1)(x + 2)(x - 3)$ in fully factorized form.

Note; not all quadratic expressions can be factorized (page 91). The values 1, -2 and 3 for which $f(x) = 0$ are called the **roots** or **solutions** of the equation $x^3 - 2x^2 - 5x + 6 = 0$. They form the **solution set** $\{1, -2, 3\}$. See pages 85–92 for a systematic treatment of polynomial equations.

Section 9 Graphs of Polynomial Functions

9.1 General Shapes

The general shape of the graph is largely determined by the degree of the polynomial

Degree	*Formula*	*Graph*
0	$f(x) = a$	

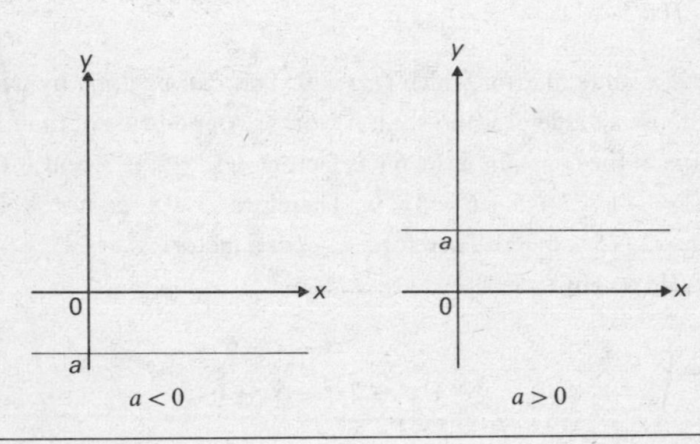

$a < 0$ $a > 0$

1	$f(x) = ax + b$	

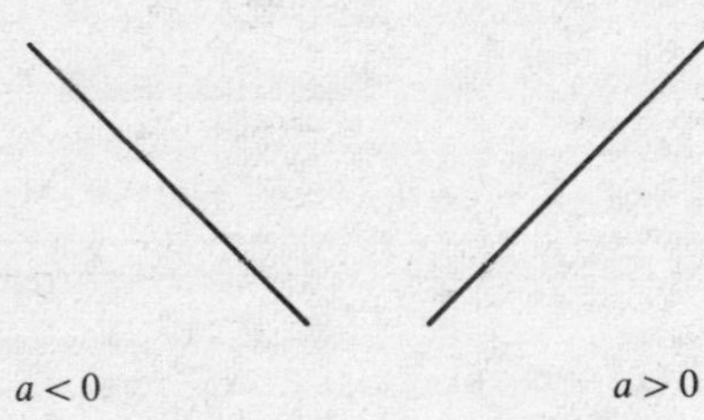

$a < 0$ $a > 0$

2	$f(x) = ax^2 + bx + c$	

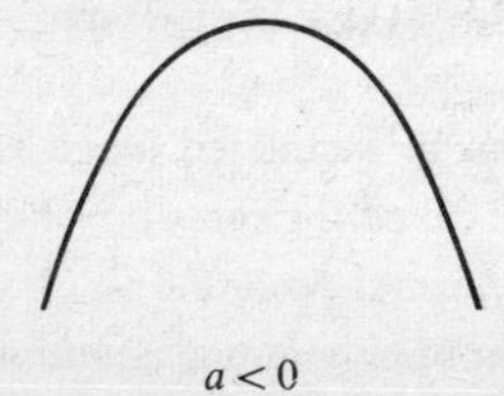

$a < 0$ $a > 0$

Degree	*Formula*	*Graph*	
3	$f(x) = ax^3 + bx^2 + cx + d$	$a < 0$	$a > 0$
4	$f(x) = ax^4 + bx^3 + cx^2 + dx + e$	$a < 0$	$a > 0$
5	$f(x) = ax^5 + bx^4 + cx^3 + dx^2 + ex + f$	$a < 0$	$a > 0$

Notes

1. The graphs for $a < 0$ are 'upside down' versions of the graphs for $a > 0$.

2. The graphs 'change directon' (up–down) at a **turning point**.

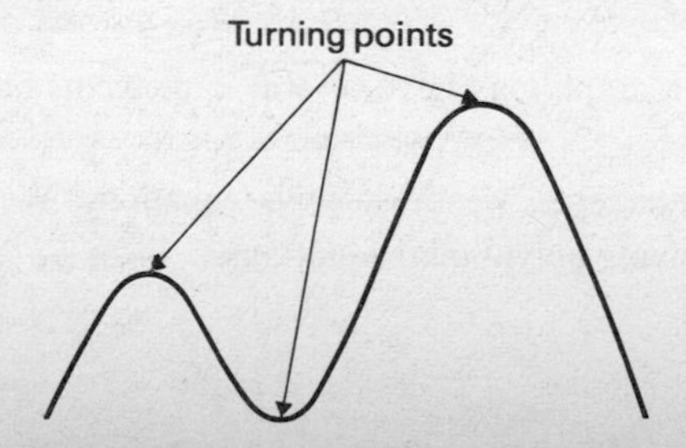

The diagrams in the table above show the *largest* number of turning points for polynomials of each degree.

The following examples show graphs which have fewer than this maximum number of turning points.

1. $y = x^3$ 2. $y = 2x^4 + 3x^2 + 1$

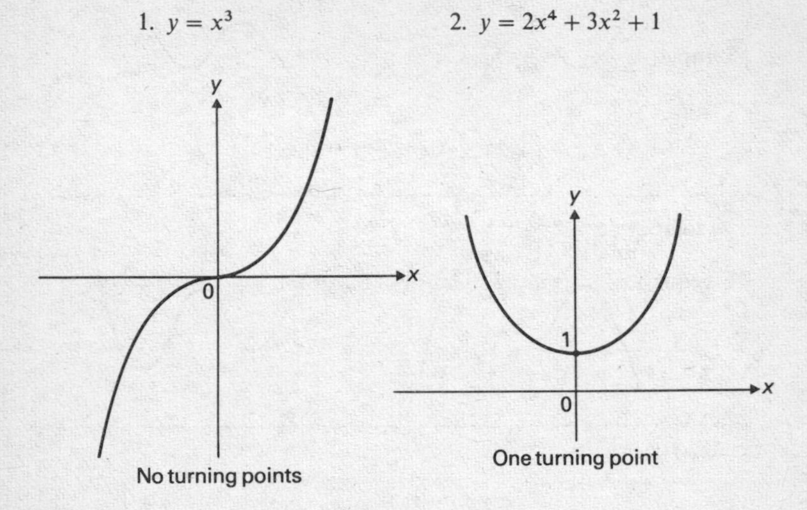

To determine the graph of a function more accurately, we need to know

1. the coordinates of points where the curve cuts the axes (called **intercepts**), and

2. the coordinates of any turning points.

A curve cuts the y-axis when $x = 0$. Thus, the coordinates of the y-intercept are $(0, f(0))$.

A curve cuts the x-axis when $y = 0$. These x-intercepts are found by solving the equation $f(x) = 0$.

Turning points can be found by the method of differentiation (see page 151).

Notice that a graph may have several x-intercepts but can only have one y-intercept.

To find x-intercepts, we must solve equations. We next introduce methods for solving polynomial equations.

9.2 Linear Equations and their Solutions

A linear equation of the form $ax + b = 0$ can be solved by a simple rearrangement to give the single solution $x = -\frac{b}{a}$ (a single solution since a straight line can only cut the x-axis once).

Example

$$3x - 2 = 0$$

$$\Rightarrow 3x = 2$$

$$\Rightarrow x = \frac{2}{3}$$

The solution set is $\{\frac{2}{3}\}$.

This equation gives the x-intercept of the graph $y = 3x - 2$.

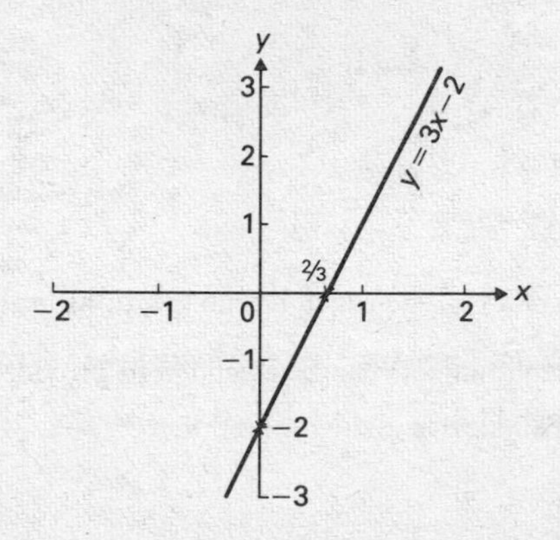

9.3 Quadratic Equations and Their Solutions

Any quadratic equation can be put in the form

$$ax^2 + bx + c = 0$$

where a, b and c are constants ($a \neq 0$).

TYPE 1 $(b = 0)$
Only x^2 and constant term present

$$ax^2 + c = 0$$

$$\Rightarrow x^2 = -\frac{c}{a}$$

$$\Rightarrow x = \pm\sqrt{-\frac{c}{a}} \text{ if } -\frac{c}{a} \text{ is negative.}$$

If $\frac{c}{a}$ is positive, there are no solutions in $\mathbb{R}$.
(Recall that a positive number has two square roots, a negative number has no square roots, and $\sqrt{0} = 0$.)

Examples

1. $4x^2 - 9 = 0$

$$\Rightarrow x^2 = \frac{9}{4}$$

$$\Rightarrow \quad x = -\frac{3}{2} \text{ or } x = +\frac{3}{2}$$

The solution set is $\{-\frac{3}{2}, \frac{3}{2}\}$.

2. $3x^2 + 1 = 0$

$$\Rightarrow x^2 = -\tfrac{1}{3} \text{ which has no solutions in } \mathbb{R}.$$

(However, the real numbers can be extended to provide solutions of this equation; see page 114)

TYPE 2 $(c = 0)$
There is no constant term

$$ax^2 + bx = 0$$

This can be factorized:

$$x(ax + b) = 0$$

A product of two quantities can only be zero if one of these quantities is itself zero. So, either $x = 0$ or $ax + b = 0$

$$\Rightarrow x = -\frac{b}{a}$$

Example

$$3x^2 + 5x = 0$$

$$\Rightarrow x(3x + 5) = 0$$

$$\Rightarrow x = 0 \text{ or } 3x + 5 = 0$$

$$\Rightarrow \text{solutions } x = 0 \text{ or } x = -\frac{5}{3}$$

The quadratic equation has been **factorized** to give two linear equations $x = 0$ and $3x + 5 = 0$.

TYPE 3

All terms present.

Example

$$6x^2 + 5x - 4 = 0$$

The quadratic expression can be factorized:

$$\Rightarrow (2x - 1)(3x + 4) = 0$$

$$\Rightarrow 2x - 1 = 0 \text{ or } 3x + 4 = 0$$

$$\Rightarrow x = \frac{1}{2} \text{ or } x = -\frac{4}{3}$$

Warning: It is only useful to factorize in this way when one side of the equation is zero. For example, $(x - 2)(x + 3) = 1$ does *not* imply that either $x - 2 = 1$ or $x + 3 = 1$!

It is not always possible to factorize a quadratic expression into simple linear expressions (for example, $2x^2 + 4x - 1$). A more general method follows.

COMPLETING THE SQUARE

Examples

1. The equation $x^2 - 4 = 0$ can be solved by:

$$\Rightarrow x^2 = 4$$

$$\Rightarrow x = \pm\sqrt{4}$$

$$\Rightarrow x = \pm 2$$

This is a model for more complicated cases.

2. $(x-1)^2 = 4$

$$\Rightarrow x - 1 = \pm 2$$

$$\Rightarrow x = 1 \pm 2$$

$$\Rightarrow x = 3 \text{ or } x = -1$$

3. $x^2 - 4x + 4 = 8$

The left side is a **perfect square**; it can be written in the form $(x-2)^2$ (check this!).

$$\Rightarrow (x-2)^2 = 8$$

$$\Rightarrow x - 2 = \pm\sqrt{8}$$

$$\Rightarrow x = 2 \pm \sqrt{8} = 2 \pm 2\sqrt{2} \qquad (\sqrt{8} = \sqrt{4 \times 2} = \sqrt{4}\sqrt{2} = 2\sqrt{2})$$

Therefore, $x = 2 - 2\sqrt{2}$ or $x = 2 + 2\sqrt{2}$.

4. $x^2 - 4x + 1 = 10$

The left side is *not* a perfect square. By comparison with example 3, we should add 3 to *both sides.*

$$x^2 - 4x + 4 = 13$$

$$\Rightarrow (x-2)^2 = 13$$

$$\Rightarrow x - 2 = \pm\sqrt{13}$$

$$\Rightarrow x = 2 \pm \sqrt{13}$$

5. $x^2 + 6x - 3 = 7$

Again, the left side is not a perfect square. We must find out what number should be added to make a perfect square. Comparing with $(x+a)^2 \equiv x^2 + 2ax + a^2$ provides the method.

Step 1 Move the constant term (add 3 to both sides)

$$x^2 + 6x = 10$$

Step 2 Divide the coefficient of x by 2, square and add to both sides

$$x^2 + 6x + 9 = 19 \qquad 6 \div 2 = 3, 3^2 = 9$$

$$\Rightarrow (x + 3)^2 = 19$$

$$\Rightarrow x + 3 = \pm\sqrt{19}$$

$$\Rightarrow x = -3 \pm \sqrt{19}$$

The solutions can then be found to any required accuracy, using a calculator. To 3 decimal places, $\sqrt{19} = 4{\cdot}359$, giving solution set $\{-7{\cdot}36, 1{\cdot}36\}$ (to 2 decimal places).

6. $2x^2 + 16x - 2 = 1$
First divide by the coefficient of x^2

$$x^2 + 8x - 1 = 0{\cdot}5$$

Add 1 to both sides

$$x^2 + 8x = 1{\cdot}5$$

$8 \div 2 = 4$, so add 16 to both sides

$$x^2 + 8x + 16 = 17{\cdot}5$$

The left side is now a perfect square

$$(x + 4)^2 = 17{\cdot}5$$

$$\Rightarrow x + 4 = \pm\sqrt{17{\cdot}5}$$

$$\Rightarrow x = -4 \pm \sqrt{17{\cdot}5}$$

To 2 decimal place accuracy, $x = -8{\cdot}18$ or $x = 0{\cdot}18$.

7. Using this method for the general case

$$ax^2 + bx + c = 0$$

gives the *general formula*

$ax^2 + bx + c = 0$ has solutions

$$x = \frac{-b \pm \sqrt{b^2 - 4ac}}{2a}$$

This formula can usually be quoted directly without proof. Just substitute for the values of a, b, and c.

Examples

1. $3x^2 - 5x + 1 = 0 \quad a = 3, b = -5, c = 1$

$$\Rightarrow x = \frac{-(-5) \pm \sqrt{(-5)^2 - 4(3)(1)}}{2(3)} = \frac{5 \pm \sqrt{13}}{6}$$

To three decimal place accuracy, the solutions are 0·232 and 1·432.

2. $4x^2 + 8x + 4 = 0$

First simplify the calculations by dividing out the common factor 4.

$$x^2 + 2x + 1 = 0 \qquad a = 1, b = 2, c = 1$$

$$x = \frac{-2 \pm \sqrt{4-4}}{2} = \frac{-2 \pm \sqrt{0}}{2} = \frac{-2 \pm 0}{2} = -1 \quad (\text{as } \sqrt{0} = 0)$$

$x = -1$ is the only solution. Note that $x^2 + 2x + 1$ is a perfect square.

3. $1 - 2x - 4x^2 = 0 \qquad \left.\begin{aligned} a &= -4 \\ b &= -2 \\ c &= 1 \end{aligned}\right\}$ Make sure you identify the coefficients correctly

$$x = \frac{-(-2) \pm \sqrt{(-2)^2 - 4(-4)(1)}}{2(-4)} = \frac{2 \pm \sqrt{20}}{-8}$$

$$\Rightarrow x = -\frac{1}{4} \pm \frac{1}{4}\sqrt{5}$$

4. $13x^2 - 17x + 10 = 0 \qquad a = 13, b = -17, c = 10$

$$x = \frac{17 \pm \sqrt{17^2 - 4(13)(10)}}{26} = \frac{17 \pm \sqrt{-231}}{26}$$

-231 has no real square root and so this equation has no real solutions. (However, see also page 114.)

These examples show equations with 2 roots, 1 root and 0 roots (in $\mathbb{R}$). The number of real roots of the equation $ax^2 + bx + c = 0$ is determined by the quantity $b^2 - 4ac$, called the **discriminant** of the equation.

> If $b^2 - 4ac > 0$, there are two real distinct roots.
> If $b^2 - 4ac = 0$, there is inly one root and the expression $ax^2 + bx + c$ is a perfect square.
> If $b^2 - 4ac < 0$, there are no real roots.

The case 1 real root only is often referred to as **two equal roots**.
If $b^2 - 4ac < 0$, the quadratic expression cannot be factorized.

9.4 Cubic and Higher-Order Equations

An equation of the form

$$(a_1x + b_1)(a_2x + b_2) \ldots (a_nx + b_n) = 0$$

separates into linear equations

$$a_1x + b_1 = 0, a_2x + b_2 = 0, \ldots, a_nx + b_n = 0$$

with the solutions

$$x = -\frac{b_1}{a_1}, x = -\frac{b_2}{a_2}, \ldots, x = -\frac{b_n}{a_n}$$

Examples

1. $$(2x - 3)(x + 1)(x - 5) = 0$$

$$\Rightarrow 2x - 3 = 0, x + 1 = 0 \text{ or } x - 5 = 0$$

$$\Rightarrow x = \frac{3}{2}, x = -1 \text{ or } x = 5$$

2. $$2x^3 - 9x^2 - 8x + 15 = 0.$$

Let $f(x) \equiv 2x^3 - 9x^2 - 8x + 15$. This cubic expression must be factorized.

First find a solution by trial and error (see Factor Theorem, page 81). Since $f(1) = 2 - 9 - 8 + 15 = 0$, $x - 1$ is a factor.

Dividing out $2x^3 - 9x^2 - 8x + 15 \equiv (x - 1)(2x^2 - 7x - 15)$
$\Rightarrow x = 1$ (as we already know) or $2x^2 - 7x - 15 = 0$, which factorizes to give $(2x + 3)(x - 5) = 0$ (or use the formula on page 90).

The roots of the cubic equation are $x = 1$, $x = -\frac{3}{2}$ and $x = 5$.

A cubic equation can have 1 real root only, 2 real roots or 3 real roots. Higher-order equations can be solved in the same way.

Example

$$x^4 - 2x^3 - 3x^2 + 8x - 4 = 0$$

Answer

Let $f(x) = x^4 - 2x^3 - 3x^2 + 8x - 4$. 4 has factors ± 1, ± 2, ± 4. $f(1) = 1 - 2 - 3 + 8 - 4 = 0$. Hence $(x - 1)$ is a factor (Factor Theorem, page 81). Dividing out, $f(x) = (x - 1)(x^3 - x^2 - 4x + 4)$ (*check* this). Now factorize $g(x) = x^3 - x^2 - 4x + 4$. $g(1) = 0$
$\therefore (x - 1)$ is a factor of $g(x)$.
$\Rightarrow x^3 - x^2 - 4x + 4 = (x - 1)(x^2 - 4)$
$\Rightarrow f(x) = (x - 1)(x - 1)(x^2 - 4)$
$\quad = (x - 1)^2(x - 2)(x + 2)$
The equation $x^4 - 2x^3 - 3x^2 + 8x - 4 = 0$ has the solution $x = 1$ (double root), $x = 2$ and $x = -2$.

Some equations can be simplified by a **change of variable**.

Example

$$3x^4 - 7x^2 + 4 = 0$$

Letting $z = x^2$, then $x^4 = (x^2)^2 = z^2$. The equation reduces to the quadratic $3z^2 - 7z + 4 = 0$.

$\Rightarrow (3z - 4)(z - 1) = 0$

$\Rightarrow z = \dfrac{4}{3}$ or $z = 1$

$\Rightarrow x^2 = \frac{4}{3}$ or $x^2 = 1$ since $z = x^2$

$\Rightarrow x = \pm\frac{2}{\sqrt{3}}$ or $x = \pm 1$

$\Rightarrow x = \pm\frac{2\sqrt{3}}{3}$ or $x = \pm 1$

since $\sqrt{3}\sqrt{3} = 3$, $\frac{2\sqrt{3}}{\sqrt{3}\sqrt{3}} = \frac{2\sqrt{3}}{3}$.

This is known as **rationalizing the denominator** to remove its $\sqrt{\ }$ sign

9.5 Simultaneous Equations and Graphs

If the graphs of $f(x)$ and $g(x)$ intersect, the coordinates of the points of intersection are found by solving the simultaneous equations

$y = f(x)$ (1)

$y = g(x)$ (2)

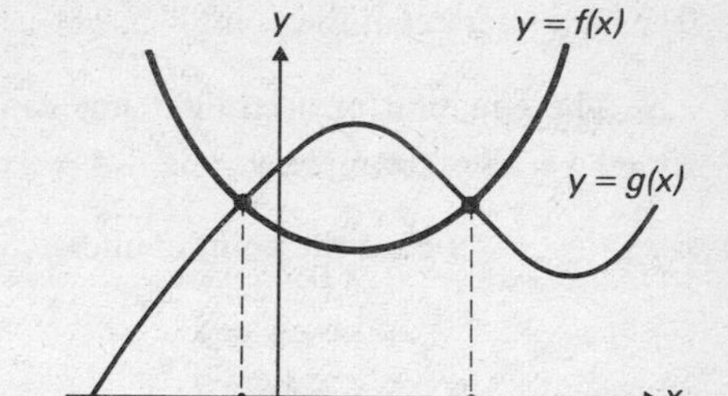

Since x and y must take the same values in each equation, we have the single equation $f(x) = g(x)$.

Examples

1. Find the coordinates of any points of intersection of the graphs of $y = x^2 + 3x - 6$ and $y = 2x - 4$.

Answer

The equation $x^2 + 3x - 6 = 2x - 4$

$$\Rightarrow x^2 + x - 2 = 0$$

$$\Rightarrow (x + 2)(x - 1) = 0$$

$$\Rightarrow x = -2 \text{ or } x = 1$$

When $x = -2$, $y = 2(-2) - 4 = -8$. When $x = 1$, $y = 2(1) - 4 = -2$.

The points of intersection are $(1, -2)$ and $(-2, -8)$.

2. Find the (single) point of intersection of the two lines

$$y = 3x - 4 \qquad (1)$$

and

$$y = x + 5 \qquad (2)$$

Answer

$$3x - 4 = x + 5 \Rightarrow 2x = 9 \Rightarrow x = 4{\cdot}5$$

$$(2) \Rightarrow y = 9{\cdot}5$$

The lines intersect at the point $(4{\cdot}5, 9{\cdot}5)$

3. The equation of a straight line can also be written in the form $ax + by = c$ (for example, $y = 3x - 4 \Rightarrow 3x - y = 4$).

Find the point of intersection of the lines

$$2x - y = 5 \qquad (1)$$
$$x + 4y = 7 \qquad (2)$$

Multiplying equation (2) by 2

$$\Rightarrow 2x + 8y = 14 \qquad (3)$$

Subtracting equation (1)

$$\frac{2x - 3y = 5}{11y = 9} \qquad (1)$$

$$\Rightarrow y = \frac{9}{11}$$

$$(2) \Rightarrow x + \frac{36}{11} = 7 \Rightarrow x = 7 - \frac{36}{11} = \frac{41}{11}$$

The lines intersect at the point $(\frac{41}{11}, \frac{9}{11})$.

4. Graphs may not intersect at all.

Points of intersection of

$$y = 2x^2 + 3 \qquad (1)$$

and

$$y = x - 1 \qquad (2)$$

are given by solutions of the equation

$$2x^2 + 3 = x - 1$$

$$\Rightarrow 2x^2 - x + 4 = 0$$

The discriminant $b^2 - 4ac = 1 - 32 < 0$, and so this equation has no real roots (page 91). The graphs do not intersect.

9.6 Quadratic Graphs, Equations and Inequalities

The graph of $y = ax^2 + bx + c$ cuts the x-axis twice if the equation $ax^2 + bc + c = 0$ has two distinct roots. The number of roots is determined by the discriminant $b^2 - 4ac$.

$b^2 - 4ac < 0$ The equation has no real roots. The graph does not cut the axis at all.

$b^2 - 4ac = 0$ The equation has equal roots. The graph touches the axis at a single point.

$b^2 - 4ac > 0$ The equation has two distinct real roots. The graph cuts the axis at two points.

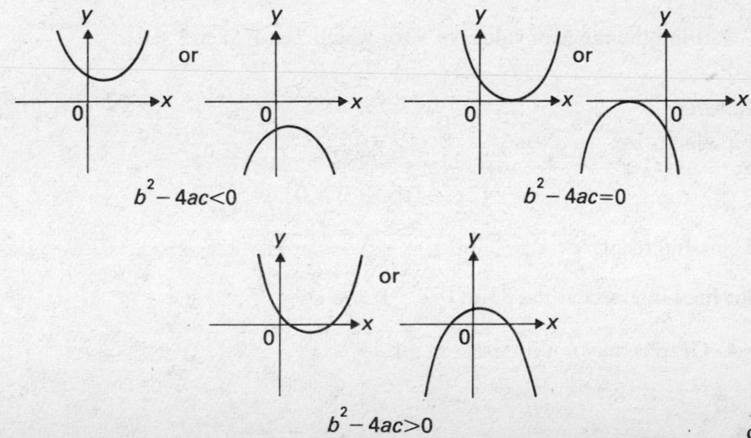

If the graph of $y = f(x)$ cuts the x-axis, it divides this axis into subsets. For x in each subset, the sign of $f(x)$ is constant.

Example

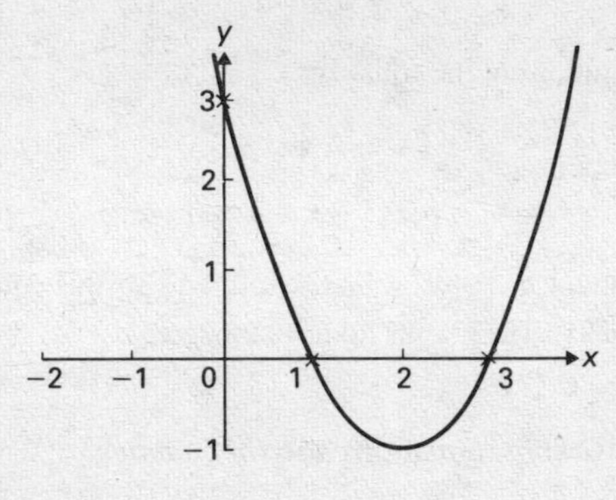

$$f(x) = (x - 1)(x - 3)$$

$f(x) > 0$ for $x < 1$ ($f(x) > 0$ if the graph is *above* the x-axis)
$f(x) < 0$ for $1 < x < 3$
and $f(x) > 0$ for $x > 3$

Thus, the **solution** of the **inequality** $(x - 1)(x - 3) < 0$ is the range of values $1 < x < 3$.

A quick sketch graph is invaluable for solving inequalities of this type.

Examples

1. Find the range of values of x for which $2x^2 + 5x - 3 \geqslant 0$.

Answer

First factorize:

$$(2x - 1)(x + 3) \geqslant 0$$

The x-intercepts are $x = \frac{1}{2}$ and $x = -3$.

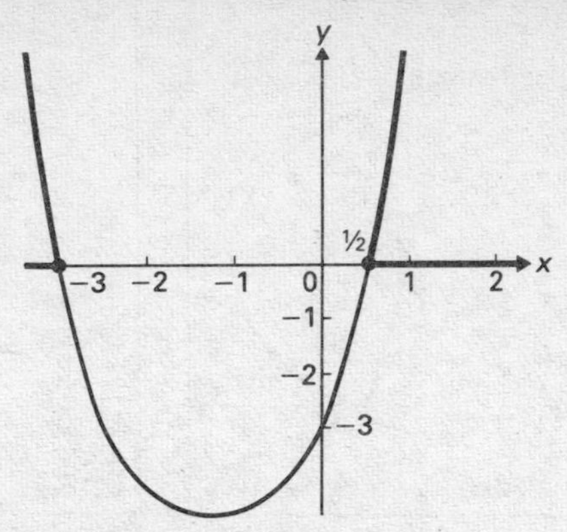

(Note that the coefficient of x^2 is 2, which is positive.)

The function is positive when $x \leqslant -3$ or $x \geqslant \frac{1}{2}$. The **solution set** of the inequality is

$$\{x : x \leqslant -3\} \cup \{x : x \geqslant \tfrac{1}{2}\}$$ page 25

2. State the set of values of x for which $x^2 + x + 1 > 0$.

Answer

$x^2 + x + 1$ will not factorize. In fact, the equation $x^2 + x + 1 = 0$ has no real roots because the discriminant $1^2 - 4(1)(1) = -3$ is negative.

The coefficient of x^2 is positive and so the graph is of the form

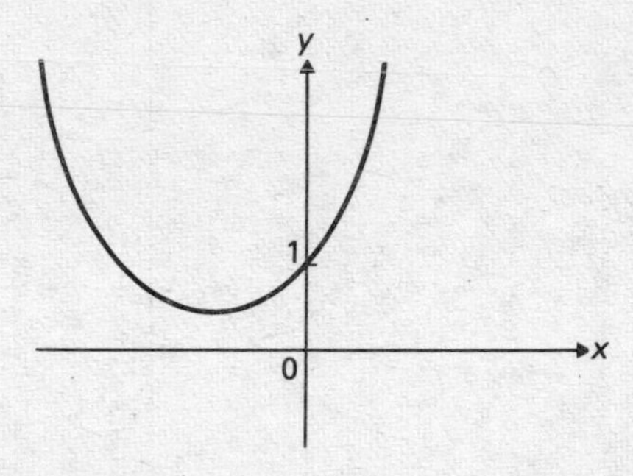

This graph does not cut or touch the x-axis. The inequality is satisfied by all $x \in \mathbb{R}$.

Summary

To solve an inequality of the form $f(x) > 0$, $\geqslant 0$, < 0 or $\leqslant 0$, where $f(x) = ax^2 + bx + c$:

	$b^2 - 4ac > 0$	$b^2 - 4ac = 0$	$b^2 - 4ac < 0$
	$ax^2 + bx + c = 0$ has 2 roots	$ax^2 + bx + c = 0$ has equal roots	$ax^2 + bx + c = 0$ has no real roots
$a > 0$	Graph cuts x-axis twice. $f(x) < 0$ between the intercepts 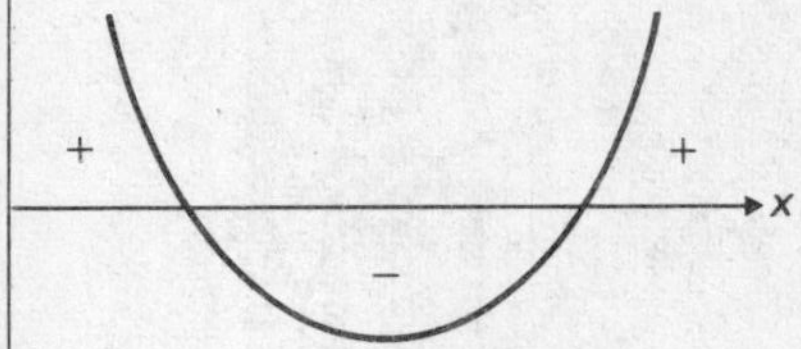	Graph touches x-axis $f(x) \geqslant 0$ for all x 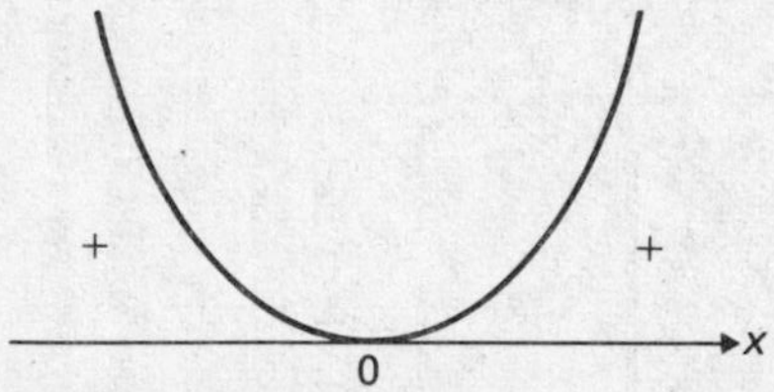	Graph lies above x-axis $f(x) > 0$ for all x 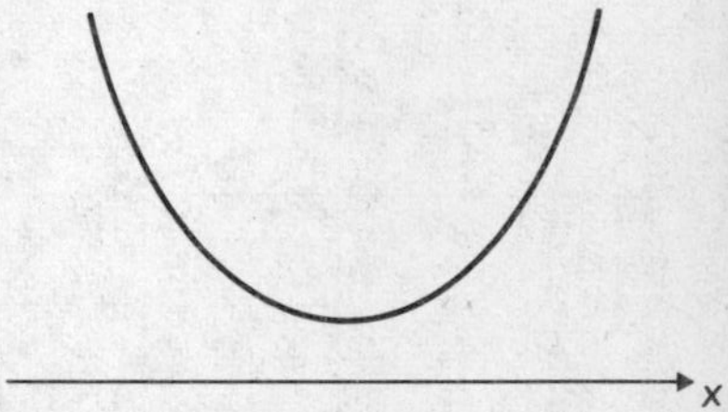
$a < 0$	Graph cuts x-axis twice. $f(x) > 0$ between the intercepts 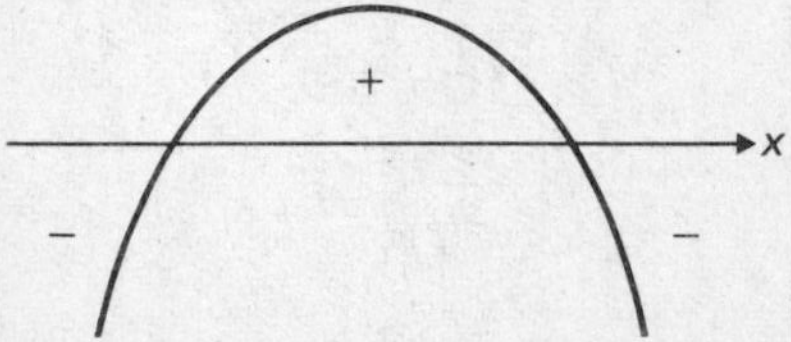	Graph touches x-axis $f(x) \leqslant 0$ for all x 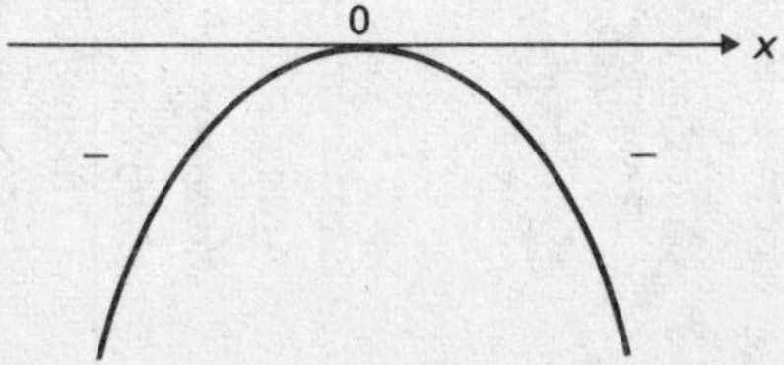	Graph lies below x-axis $f(x) < 0$ for all x 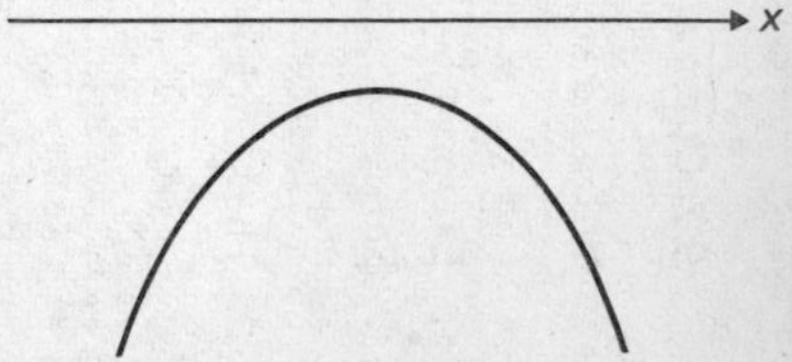

9.7 Cubic and Higher-Order Inequalities

We make use of sketch graphs again.

Example

Solve the inequality $(2x + 1)(x - 3)(x + 5) \geqslant 0$.

The equation $(2x + 1)(x - 3)(x + 5) = 0$ has roots $-\frac{1}{2}$, 3 and -5. The sketch graph is

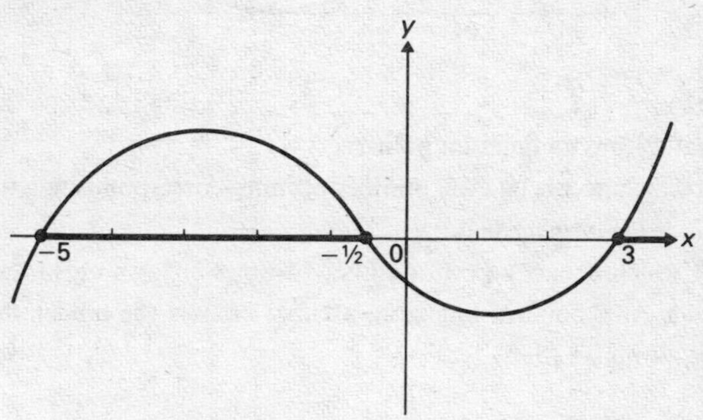

At this stage, we cannot calculate the coordinates of the turning points. However, we only need a very rough sketch to solve an inequality (for turning-point calculations, see page 151).

The graph lies above (or on) the x-axis for

$$-5 \leqslant x \leqslant -\frac{1}{2} \text{ and } x \geqslant 3$$

Note: An inequality with $\geqslant$ or $\leqslant$ will have $\geqslant$ and $\leqslant$ in the solution. A strict inequality $>$ or $<$ will correspond to $<$ and $>$ in the solution.

This method can be used for any inequality of the form $f(x) > 0$, $\geqslant 0$, < 0, $\leqslant 0$, where $f(x)$ is a polynomial in factorized form.

First find the roots of the equation $f(x) = 0$, then sketch the graph $y = f(x)$ and finally read off the solution sets from your diagram.

9.8 Repeated Roots

The function $f(x) \equiv (x - 2)^2 (x + 1)$ has a **repeated factor** $(x - 2)$. The corresponding equation $(x - 2)^2 (x + 1) = 0$ has a **repeated root** $x = 2$.

A repeated root corresponds to a point where the graph *touches* the x-axis.

The graph of $y = (x - 2)^2(x + 1)$

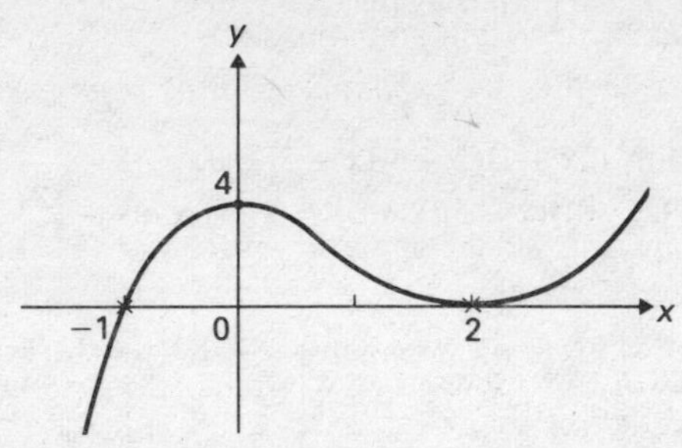

shows that (2, 0) is a minimum point.

A root which occurs an even number of times corresponds to a turning point (*maximum* or *minimum*).

A root which occurs an odd number of times corresponds to a **point of inflexion**. At a point of inflexion, a curve crosses the tangent at that point (see also page 158).

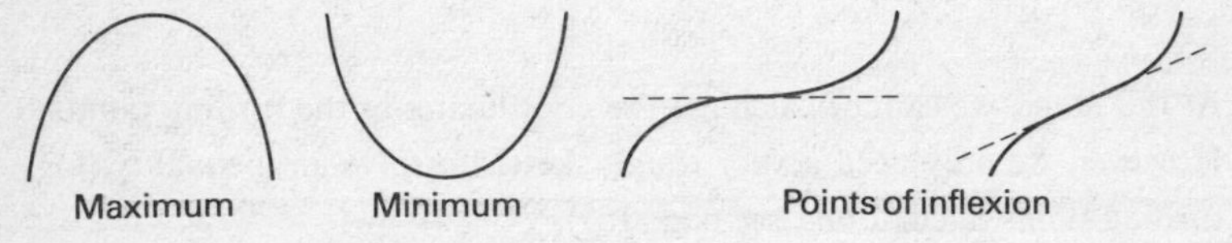

Example

Sketch the graph of $y = (x + 2)(x - 3)^2$.

Answer

$x = 3$ is a double root; $x = -2$ is a single root.

Knowing the general shape of a cubic curve (page 82), (3, 0) is a minimum point.

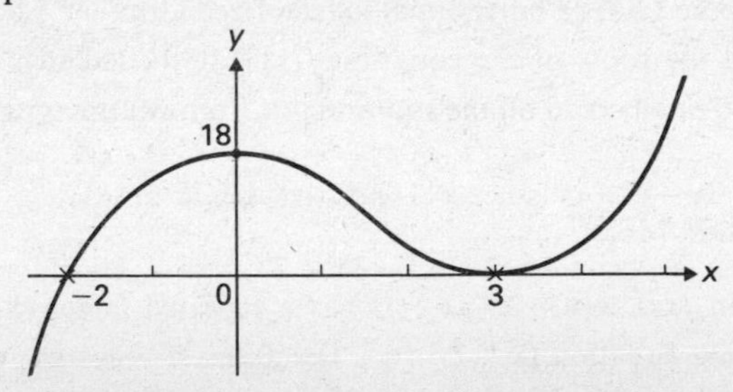

9.9 Manipulating Inequalities

Inequalities can be handled in much the same way as equations. However, care must be taken with certain operations:

1. Multiplying or dividing by a *negative* quantity reverses the inequality sign. For example, $x > 2 \Rightarrow -x < -2$.
2. Taking the reciprocal. For example, $x > 2 \Rightarrow \frac{1}{x} < \frac{1}{2}$.
3. Taking a square root. For example, $x^2 < 4 \Leftrightarrow -2 < x < 2$ (see example 4).
4. Squaring both sides of an inequality is permissible if both sides are known to be positive. For example, $2 < 4 \Rightarrow 4 < 16$ but $-4 < -2 \Rightarrow (-4)^2 > (-2)^2$.

Examples

1. $$3x^2 - 5x + 7 \geqslant 2x^2 + x - 1$$
$$\Rightarrow x^2 - 6x + 8 \geqslant 0$$
$$\Rightarrow (x-2)(x-4) \geqslant 0$$

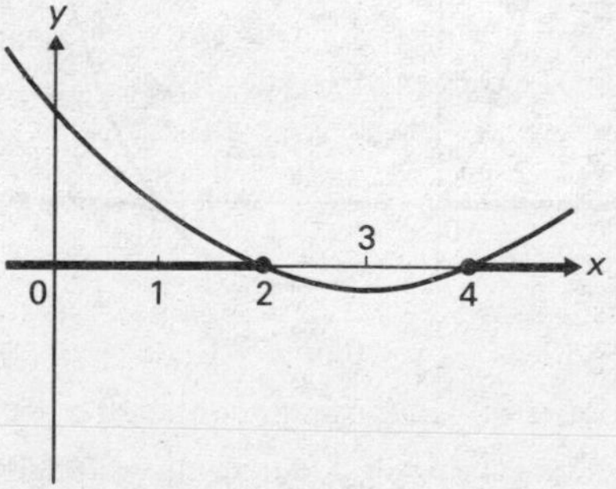

The solution is $x \leqslant 2$ or $x \geqslant 4$.

2. $$\frac{3x-2}{x^2} > 1$$

$3x - 2 > x^2$ (since x^2 is positive, this is allowed)

$$0 > x^2 - 3x + 2$$

$$x^2 - 3x + 2 < 0$$

$$(x-1)(x-2)<0$$

$$1<x<2$$

3. $\dfrac{3x-2}{x}>1.$

You *cannot* multiply through by x because you do not know whether it is positive or negative. However, x^2 is positive.

$$\Rightarrow x^2\frac{(3x-2)}{x}>x^2$$

$$\Rightarrow x(3x-2)>x^2$$

$$\Rightarrow 3x^2-2x>x^2$$
$$\Rightarrow 2x^2-2x>0$$
$$\Rightarrow x^2-x>0 \qquad \text{2 is positive}$$
$$\Rightarrow x(x-1)>0$$

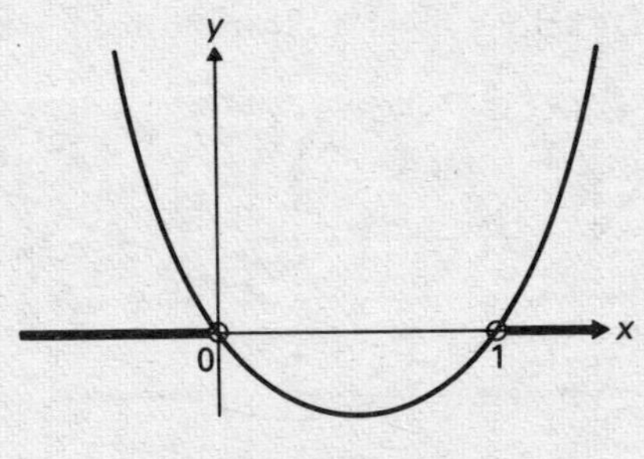

$$x<0 \text{ or } x>1$$

4. $x^2>4$

$$\Rightarrow x^2-4>0$$

$$\Rightarrow (x-2)(x+2)>0$$

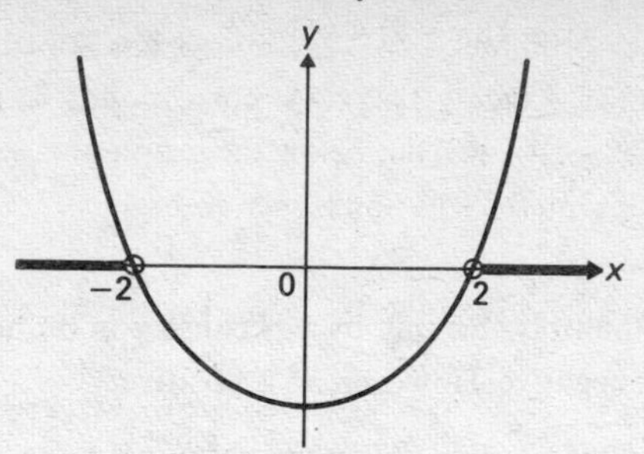

$$x < -2 \text{ or } x > 2$$

9.10 *Inequalities of the Form f (x) < g (x)*

These can be illustrated graphically.

Example

$$(2x - 1)(x + 3) < x + 4$$

First sketch the graphs $y = (2x - 1)(x + 3)$ and $y = x + 4$ on the same axes.

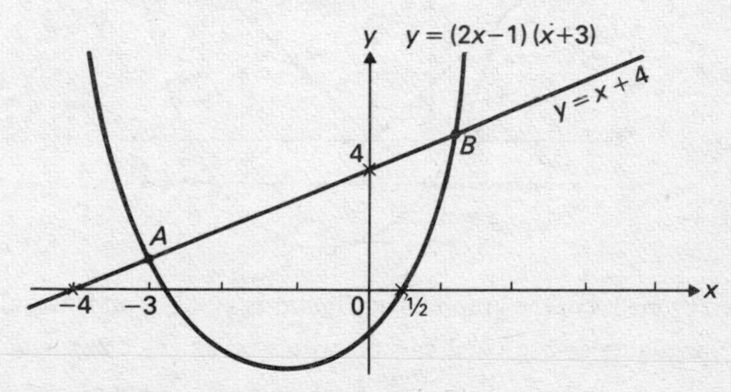

The graphs intersect at the points A and B. These points are found by solving the equation

$$(2x - 1)(x + 3) = x + 4$$ page 93

$$\Rightarrow 2x^2 + 5x - 3 = x + 4$$

$$\Rightarrow 2x^2 + 4x - 7 = 0$$

$$\Rightarrow x = \frac{-4 \pm \sqrt{72}}{4} = -1 \pm \frac{3\sqrt{2}}{2}$$ formula of page 90

Thus, A has x coordinate $-1-\frac{3\sqrt{2}}{2}$ and B has coordinate $-1+\frac{3\sqrt{2}}{2}$.
The inequality $(2x-1)(x+3) < x+4$ corresponds to points where the graph of $y=(2x-1)(x+3)$ lies below the graph of $y=(x+4)$.

From the diagram, the solution is seen to be

$$-1-\frac{3\sqrt{2}}{2} < x < -1+\frac{3\sqrt{2}}{2}$$

9.11 The Modulus Function $y = |x|$

The **modulus function** $f(x) = \begin{cases} x \text{ if } x \geqslant 0 \\ -x \text{ if } x < 0 \end{cases}$ is denoted by $|x|$.
It gives the **magnitude** of x. Thus, $|3| = 3$ while $|-2{\cdot}1| = 2{\cdot}1$.
The function has graph

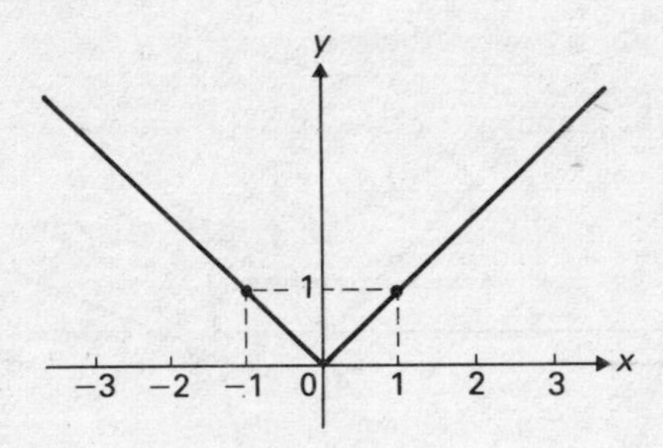

The two branches of the graph have equations $y = -x$ and $y = x$.

The inequality $-2 < x < 2$ can be expressed as $|x| < 2$. Thus, $x^2 < 4 \Leftrightarrow |x| < 2$.

MODULUS EQUATIONS

Examples

1. $|x+2| = 3 - \dfrac{x}{2}$.

First sketch the graphs of $y = |x+2|$ and $y = 3-\frac{x}{2}$ on the same diagram. To sketch $y = |x+2|$, just draw $y = x+2$ and then *reflect the part below the x-axis through this axis.*

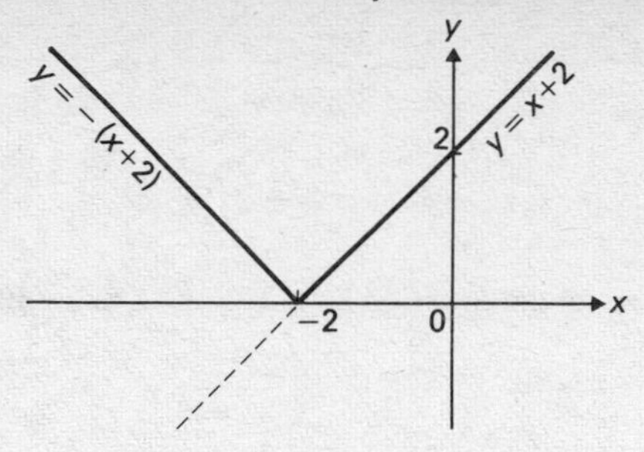

The part of this graph which was *not* reflected corresponds to equation $y = x + 2$. The reflected part corresponds to $y = -(x + 2)$. Adding the graph of $y = 3 - \frac{x}{2}$

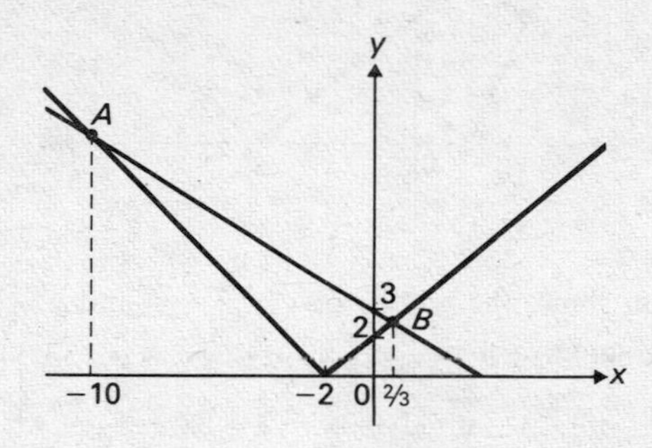

The graphs intersect at the two points A and B.

Point A is the intersection of $y = -(x + 2)$ and $y = 3 - \frac{x}{2}$

$$\Rightarrow -x - 2 = 3 - \frac{x}{2}$$

$$\Rightarrow -\frac{x}{2} = 5$$

$$\Rightarrow x = -10$$

Point B is the intersection of $y = x + 2$ and $y = 3 - \frac{x}{2}$

$$\Rightarrow x + 2 = 3 - \frac{x}{2}$$

$$\Rightarrow \frac{3x}{2} = 1$$

$$\Rightarrow x = \frac{2}{3}$$

The solution set of the equation $|x + 2| = 3 - \frac{x}{2}$ is $\{-10, \frac{2}{3}\}$.

2. $|3 - x| = |2 + 2x|$

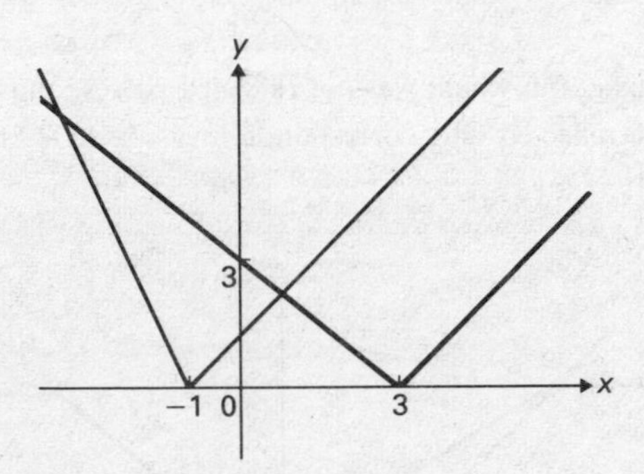

The diagram shows the graphs of $y = |3 - x|$ and $y = |2 + 2x|$. The solutions are found by solving

$$(a) \quad 3 - x = 2 + 2x \Rightarrow 1 = 3x \Rightarrow x = \tfrac{1}{3}$$

and

$$(b) \quad 3 - x = -(2 + 2x) \Rightarrow x = -5$$

The solution set is $\{-5, \frac{1}{3}\}$.

MODULUS INEQUALITIES

These can be solved by making use of these sketch graphs.

Examples

1. $|3 - x| < |2 + 2x|$

The diagram above shows that the solution set is

$$\{x : x > \tfrac{1}{3}\} \cup \{x : x < -5\}.$$

Alternatively, you can *square* both sides of the inequality.

2. $|2 + x| > |3 - 5x|$

$$\Rightarrow |2 + x|^2 > |3 - 5x|^2$$ but since $A^2 = (-A)^2$, then $|A|^2 = A^2$

$$\Rightarrow (2 + x)^2 > (3 - 5x)^2$$

$$\Rightarrow 4 + 4x + x^2 > 9 - 30x + 25x^2$$

$$\Rightarrow 0 > 24x^2 - 34x + 5$$

$$\Rightarrow 24x^2 - 34x + 5 < 0$$

The graph of $y = 24x^2 - 34x + 5$ cuts the x-axis at $x = \frac{5}{4}$ and $x = \frac{1}{6}$ (check!).

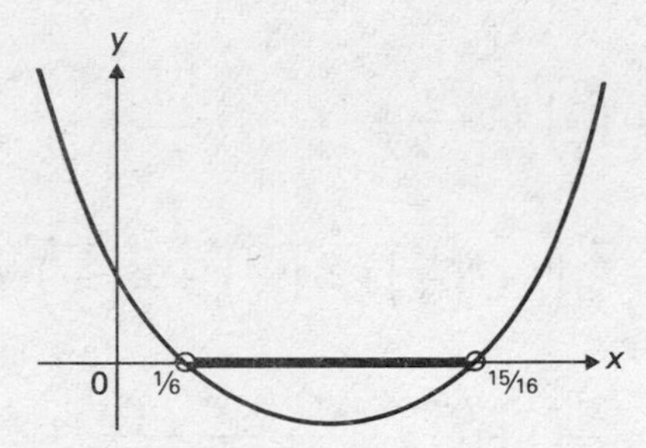

The solution is $\frac{1}{6} < x < \frac{5}{4}$.

Section 10 Worked Examples

1. Find a quadratic approximation to $(1 + 2x)^7$.

Answer

$(1 + 2x)^7 = 1 + 7(2x) + 21(2x)^2 + \ldots$ expand up to x^2 term in Pascal's Triangle

$= 1 + 14x + 84x^2 + \ldots$

2. Expand $f(x) = (1 + x)^3(2 - 5x)$ in ascending powers of x up to and including the term in x^2.

Answer

$$(1+x)^3 = 1 + 3x + 3x^2 + \dots$$ Pascal's Triangle up to x^2 term

$$(1+x)^3(2-5x) = (1+3x+3x^2)(2-5x)$$
$$= 2 + (6-5)x + (6-15)x^2 + \dots$$ Collecting terms in x, x^2,
$$= 2 + x - 9x^2 + \dots$$

3. Find the coefficient of x in the expansion of $\left(x + \frac{2}{x}\right)^7$

Answer

$$\left(x+\frac{2}{x}\right)^7 = \left(\frac{2}{x}\left(1+\frac{x^2}{2}\right)\right)^7$$

$$= \left(\frac{2}{x}\right)^7\left(1+\frac{x^2}{2}\right)^7$$

$$= \frac{2^7}{x^7}\left(1 + 7\left(\frac{x^2}{2}\right) + 21\left(\frac{x^2}{2}\right)^2 + 35\left(\frac{x^2}{2}\right)^3 + 35\left(\frac{x^2}{2}\right)^4 + \dots\right.$$

binomial expansion

$$= \frac{2^7}{x^7}\left(1 + \frac{7x^2}{2} + \frac{21x^4}{4} + \frac{35x^6}{8} + \frac{35x^8}{16} + \dots\right)$$

$$= 2^7 + \frac{7\times 2^6}{x^5} + \frac{2^5\times 21}{x^3} + \frac{2^4\times 35}{x} + 2^3\times 35x + \dots$$

The coefficient of x is $2^3 \times 35 = 280$.

4. (*a*) Find the range of values of k for which the equation $2x^2 + kx + 2 = 0$ has no real roots.

(*b*) By expressing $f(x) = 2x^2 + x + 2$ in the form $a(x + \frac{1}{4})^2 + b$, show that the minimum value of $f(x)$ is $\frac{15}{8}$, occurring when $x = -\frac{1}{4}$. Sketch the graph of $y = f(x)$.

Answer

(*a*) $2x^2 + kx + 2$ has no real roots if $\qquad a = 2, b = k, c = 2$

$k^2 - 4(2)(2) < 0 \qquad b^2 - 4ac < 0$

$k^2 < 16$

$-4 < k < 4$

(*b*) $2x^2 + x + 2 = 2(x^2 + \frac{1}{2}x + 1)$

$= 2(x^2 + \frac{1}{2}x + \frac{1}{16} + \frac{15}{16})$ page 87

$= 2(x + \frac{1}{4})^2 + 2(\frac{15}{16})$

$= 2(x + \frac{1}{4})^2 + \frac{15}{8}$

$(x + \frac{1}{4})^2$ has least value 0 when $x = -\frac{1}{4}$. Hence the least value of $f(x)$ is $0 + \frac{15}{8} = \frac{15}{8}$.

The curve cuts the y-axis at $y = 2$.

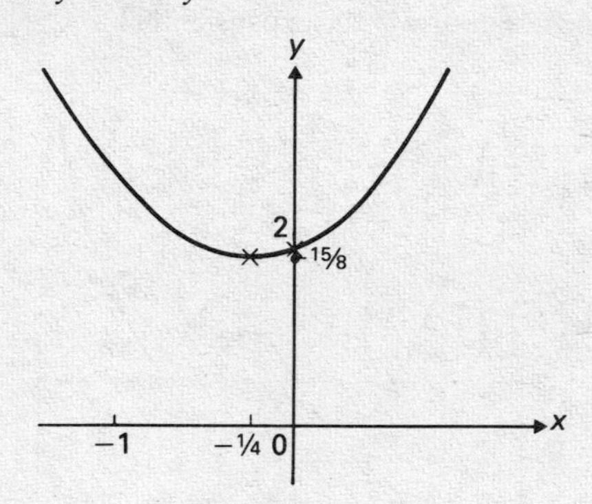

5. Sketch the graph of the function

$$f(x) = (x + 3)^2(x - 5)$$

Answer

$x = -3$ is a double root. $(-3, 0)$ is a turning point. page 99

$x = 5$ is a single root. $f(x) \equiv (x^2 + 6x + 9)(x - 5) \equiv x^3 + x^2 - 21x - 45$ cuts the y-axis at $f(0) = -45$.

The graph is

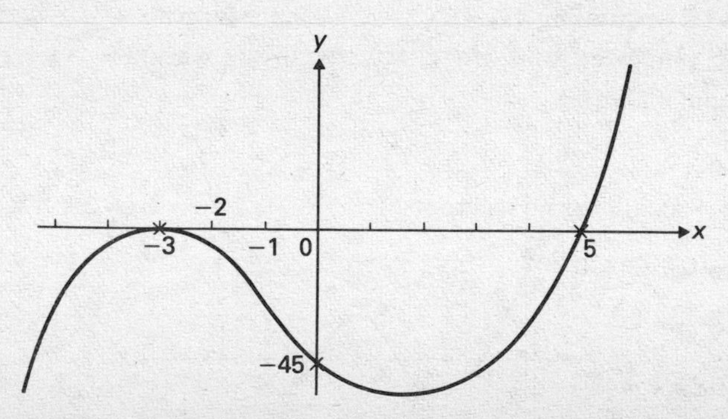

6. A quartic function $f(x)$ cuts the y-axis at $y = 2$, crosses the x-axis at $x = 1$, $x = 3$ and touches the x-axis at $x = 5$. Sketch the graph of this function and find an expression for $f(x)$. Using your graph, show that $f(x) = 2$ has at least two real roots. State whether these roots are positive or negative.

Answer

The graph is

see table of page 82

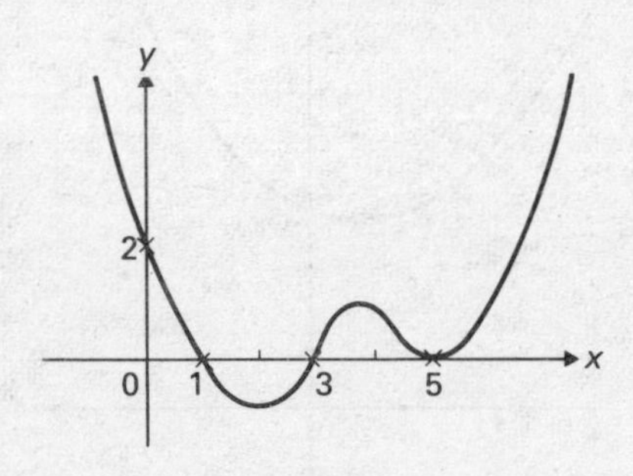

$x = 1$, $x = 3$ are single roots, $x = 5$ is a double root.

$f(x)$ has factors $(x - 1)(x - 3)(x - 5)^2$

page 99

$\Rightarrow f(x) = k(x - 1)(x - 3)(x - 5)^2$, where k is constant. But

$f(x)$ is quartic

$$f(0) = k(-1)(-3)(-5)^2 = 75k = 2$$

cuts y-axis at $y = f(0) = 2$

$$\Rightarrow k = \frac{2}{75}$$

$$\Rightarrow f(x) = \frac{2}{75}(x - 1)(x - 3)(x - 5)^2.$$

The line $y = 2$ cuts the curve at least twice

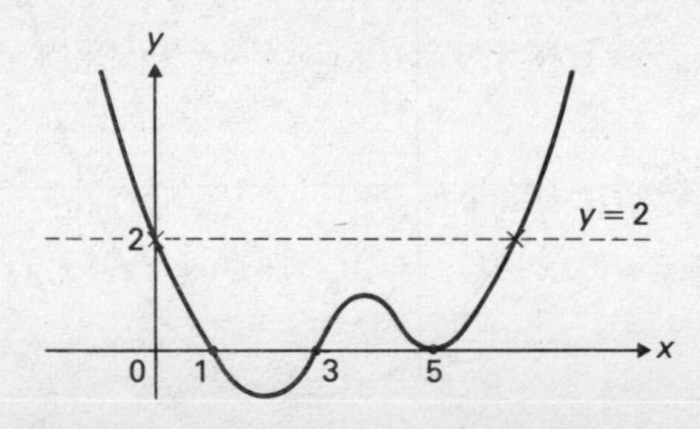

The number of intersections depends on the height of the maximum point between $x = 3$ and $x = 5$. In any case, one root is $x = 0$ and the other(s) positive.

Section II Examination Questions

1. *Show that* $(x-2)$ *is a factor of* $6x^4 - 7x^3 - 27x^2 + 28x + 12$ *and hence solve the equation* $6x^4 - 7x^3 - 27x^2 + 28x + 12 = 0$. [AEB]

2. *Given that* $f(x) \equiv 3 - 7x + 5x^2 - x^3$, *show that* $3 - x$ *is a factor of* $f(x)$. *Factorize* $f(x)$ *completely and hence state the set of values of* x *for which* $f(x) \leqslant 0$. [LON]

3. *Find the constants* p *and* r *so that the polynomial* $x^3 + px + r$ *has a remainder* -9 *when it is divided by* $(x+1)$ *and a remainder* -1 *when it is divided by* $(x-1)$. [LON]

4. *The set of all values of* x *for which* $(x+2)(x-2)(x-4) > 0$ *is:*

A $\{x:|x|<2\}$ B $\{x:x>4\}$ C $\{x:|x|<2\} \cup \{x:x>4\}$

D $\{x:x<-2\} \cup \{x:2<x<4\}$ E $\{x:x<2\} \cup \{x:x>4\}$ [LON]

5. *Given that* $2 < x < 3$, *then*

1. $|x-3| < |x-2|$ 2. $(x-3) < (x-2)$ 3. $(x-3)(x-2) < 0$

A 1, 2, 3 correct B 1 and 2 only are correct
C only 2 and 3 are correct D only 1 is correct
E only 3 is correct [LON]

6. *Given that* $f(x) \equiv x^2 - 6x + 10$, *show that* $f(x) > 0$ *for all real values of* x. [LON-part]

7. *Sketch separately the graphs of*

(i) $y = 2(x+2)(x-1)(x-2)$; (ii) $y = (x-1)(x-3)^2$

showing the coordinates of the points where they cross or touch the axes. Find a cubic function $f(x)$ *such that the graph of* $y = f(x)$ *crosses the* *x-axis at $x = 1$, touches the x-axis at $x = 3$ and crosses the y-axis at $y = 18$. From consideration of the sketch graph of $y = f(x)$, show that, if the roots of the equation $f(x) = k$ are all real, then k must be negative. Give the sign of each root in this case. Show, also, that, if $k > 0$, then the equation $f(x) = k$ has just one real root and give the range of values of k for which this root is negative.* [SUJB]

8. *Find the set of values of x for which $|x - 1| - |2x + 1| > 0$.* [LON]

9. *The equation $2x^4 - 4x^2 + 1 = 0$ has*

A no real roots B no positive roots C 2 of its roots lying between -1 and 1 D 2 of its roots lying between 0 and 1 E 4 positive roots.

[LON]

10. *Find the term independent of x in the binomial expansion of $(x^2 - \frac{1}{2x})^{12}$ expressing the answer as a fraction in its lowest terms.*

[CAM]

11. *It is given that $f(x) = (x - 2)^2 - \lambda(x + 1)(x + 2)$.*

(i) *Find the values of λ for which the equation $f(x) = 0$ has two equal roots.*

(ii) *Show that, when $\lambda = 2$, $f(x)$ has a maximum value of 25.*

(iii) *Given that the curve $y = f(x)$* has a turning point when $x = \frac{1}{4}$, *find the value of λ and sketch the curve for this value of λ.*

[CAM]

12. *Solve the simultaneous equations,*

$$x^2 + 2xy = 3$$

$$2x - y = 1$$

[OXF]

13. *The number of ways 6 persons can be seated at a round table facing inwards, if two arrangements are said to be indistinguishable when they are in the same clockwise order is*

A5 B6 C120 D240 E none of these [LON]

14. *There are 3 post-boxes marked P, Q and R. Find the number of ways in which 8 different letters can be posted so that 4 of them are in box P, 2 of them are in box Q, and 2 of them are in box R.* [LON]

15. *A committee of 4 people is to be selected from a group consisting of 8 men and 4 women. Determine the number of ways in which the committee may be formed if it is to contain*

(a) exactly one woman,

(b) at least one woman. [LON]

16. *A student must answer exactly 7 out of 10 questions in an examination. Given that she must answer* at least *3 of the first 5 questions, determine the number of ways in which she may select the 7 questions.* [LON]

4 Further Results for Quadratic Equations and their Roots

Section 12 Complex Numbers

12.1 Imaginary Numbers

On page 91, we met the result that the equation $ax^2 + bx + c = 0$ has no solutions in the set $\mathbb{R}$ if $b^2 - 4ac < 0$. For example, the equation $x^2 + 1 = 0$ has no real solutions.

The number of solutions an equation has depends on the number set that they are to be in.

Examples

$x - 3 = 0$ has the solution $3 \in \mathbb{N}$.

$x + 3 = 0$ has no solution in $\mathbb{N}$, but when the set is extended to include negative integers to form $\mathbb{Z}$, the equation has solution $x = -3$.

$2x - 1 = 0$ has no solution in $\mathbb{Z}$, but has the solution $x = \frac{1}{2}$ in the larger set $\mathbb{Q}$.

$x^2 - 2 = 0$ has no solutions in $\mathbb{Q}$, but has roots $x = \sqrt{2}$, $x = -\sqrt{2}$ in $\mathbb{R}$ (see page 26).

Thus, to enable solutions to be found for these equations, we first enlarge $\mathbb{N}$ to form $\mathbb{Z}$, then include the fractions to form $\mathbb{Q}$ and finally add in irrationals, such as $\sqrt{2}$, to form $\mathbb{R}$.

We now wish to enlarge $\mathbb{R}$ to enable us to solve the equation $x^2 + 1 = 0$.

Since this equation has no *real* solutions, the solution cannot represent the result of a *measurement* – it must be a completely new type of number. The situation is similar to that of introducing irrational numbers. A length representing an irrational number (e.g. $\sqrt{2}$) cannot be measured exactly since all exact (decimal) measurements correspond to rational numbers. You have become familiar with numbers like $\sqrt{2}$, $\sqrt{3}$ although they cannot be determined exactly! We accept them in calculations because we can *approximate* to them as closely as we like.

With this as motivation, we now **define** the **imaginary number** denoted i (or j in some texts) to be the square root of -1. In symbols, $i = \sqrt{-1}$ and so $i^2 = -1$. Clearly, $i \notin \mathbb{R}$, since the square of a real number must be positive.

The square root of any negative real number can now be expressed as a multiple of i. For example,

$$\sqrt{-4} = \sqrt{(-1)(4)} = \sqrt{-1}\sqrt{4} = i\sqrt{4} = 2i$$

A general imaginary number is of the form λi, *where* $\lambda \in \mathbb{R}$.

12.2 Quadratic Equations and Complex Numbers

We can now solve an equation like

$$x^2 + 10 = 0$$

$$\Rightarrow \qquad x^2 = -10$$

$$\Rightarrow \qquad x = i\sqrt{10} \text{ or } x = -i\sqrt{10}$$

(We must still allow a + or − root.)

More complicated quadratic equations can also be solved.

Example

$$x^2 + x + 1 = 0$$

Assuming that we can still use the formula of page 90

$$x = \frac{-1 \pm \sqrt{1^2 - 4(1)(1)}}{2} = \frac{-1 \pm \sqrt{-3}}{2}$$

$$x = -\frac{1}{2} \pm \frac{i\sqrt{3}}{2}$$

are the two solutions. A number like $-\frac{1}{2} + \frac{i\sqrt{3}}{2}$ is called a **complex number**. A general complex number is of the form $a + ib$, where $a, b \in \mathbb{R}$. The set of all complex numbers is denoted by $\mathbb{C}$.

We are assuming here that complex numbers obey the usual rules of arithmetic and algebra. This can be justified but is beyond the scope of A-level. The important point is that complex numbers can be manipulated in much the same way as real numbers, but with the new rule that $i^2 = -1$.

Any quadratic equation has solutions in $\mathbb{C}$. (Note that $\mathbb{R}$ is a subset of $\mathbb{C}$. For example, the real number 2 can be written as $2 + 0i$, which has the general form of a complex number.)

SUMMARY

The equation $ax^2 + bx + c = 0$ ($a \neq 0$) has

2 *real*, distinct roots when $b^2 - 4ac > 0$

2 *real*, *equal* roots when $b^2 - 4ac = 0$

2 *complex roots when* $b^2 - 4ac < 0$

The letter z is commonly used to denote a complex number. If $z \equiv a + bi$, a is called the **real part** of z (denoted $\text{Re}(z)$) and b is called the **imaginary part** of z (denoted $\text{Im}(z)$). Note that $\text{Re}(z)$ and $\text{Im}(z)$ are *both* real numbers. Two complex numbers are equal *only* if their respective real and imaginary parts are equal. Thus, $a + bi = x + yi \Rightarrow a = x$ and $b = y$.

12.3 Arithmetic with Complex Numbers

ADDITION AND SUBTRACTION

Combine real and imaginary parts separately.

Examples

1. $(2 + 3i) + (5 - i) = (2 + 5) + (3i - i) = 7 + 2i$

2. $(2 + 3i) - (6 + 7{\cdot}5i) = -4 - 4{\cdot}5i$

MULTIPLICATION

Multiply out the brackets and use $i^2 = -1$.

Examples

1. $(2 + 3i)(5 - i) = 10 + 15i - 2i - 3i^2$

$$= 10 + 13i + 3 \qquad \text{as } i^2 = -1$$

$$= 13 + 13i$$

2. $(-1 + \frac{1}{2}i)(2i) = -2i + i^2$

$$= -1 - 2i$$

POWERS

Repeated multiplication.

Examples

1. $(3 + i)^3 \quad = (3 + i)(3 + i)^2$

$$= (3 + i)(9 + 6i + i^2)$$

$$= (3 + i)(8 + 6i) \qquad i^2 = -1$$

$$= 24 + 8i + 18i + 6i^2$$

$$= 24 + 26i - 6 = 18 + 26i$$

2. $i^3 = ii^2 = -i$

3. $i^4 = (i^2)^2 = (-1)^2 = 1$, etc.

DIVISION

More complicated!

Example

$$\frac{2 + i}{1 - i}$$

This must be expressed in the form $a + bi$; $a, b \in \mathbb{R}$.
Multiply top and bottom by $1 + i$

$$\equiv \frac{(2 + i)(1 + i)}{(1 - i)(1 + i)} \equiv \frac{2 + i + 2i + i^2}{1^2 - i^2} \qquad \text{as } (a-b)(a+b) = a^2 - b^2$$

$$= \frac{1 + 3i}{1 + 1} \qquad i^2 = -1$$

$$= \frac{1+3i}{2}$$

$$= \frac{1}{2} + \frac{3}{2}i$$

In general, if the denominator is $a + bi$, multiply top and bottom by $a - bi$.

The product $(a + bi)(a - bi)$

$$= a^2 - (bi)^2$$

$$= a^2 - b^2 i^2$$

$$= a^2 + b^2$$

giving a real denominator, so that the calculation can be completed.

Example

$$\frac{3-i}{2-4i} \equiv \frac{(3-i)(2+4i)}{(2-4i)(2+4i)}$$

$$= \frac{6 - 2i + 12i - 4i^2}{4 - (4i)^2} = \frac{6 + 10i + 4}{4 + 16}$$

$$= \frac{10 + 10i}{20} = \frac{10}{20} + \frac{10}{20}i$$

$$= \frac{1}{2} + \frac{1}{2}i$$

12.4 Conjugate and Modulus

If $z = a + bi$, the number $a - bi$ is called the **conjugate** of z, denoted by z^*, or by $\bar{z}$ in older texts.

Example

$$z = -2 + 5i \Rightarrow z^* = -2 - 5i$$

(Do not alter the sign of the real part!)

Let $z = x + iy$ with conjugate $z^* = x - iy$. Then

$$zz^* = (x + iy)(x - iy)$$
$$= x^2 + y^2$$

which is a *real positive number*. Since $x^2 + y^2 \geqslant 0$, it has a real square root.

DEFINITION

The **modulus** of $z = x + iy$ is defined as

$$|z| = \sqrt{zz^*} \equiv \sqrt{x^2 + y^2}$$

take the positive square root

Example

If $z = 3 - 4i$, then $|z| = \sqrt{3^2 + (-4)^2} = \sqrt{9 + 16} = \sqrt{25} = 5$. If z is a real number, then $|z|$ is just the positive part of z, as defined on page 104. The definition of $|\quad|$ on $\mathbb{C}$ is an **extension** of the definition of $|\quad|$ on $\mathbb{R}$.

Examples

1. $z = 3 \quad \Rightarrow \quad z \equiv 3 + 0i$

$$\Rightarrow \quad |z| = \sqrt{9 + 0} = \sqrt{9} = 3$$

2. $z = -3 \quad \Rightarrow \quad z \equiv -3 + 0i$

$$\Rightarrow \quad |z| = \sqrt{(-3)^2 + 0} = \sqrt{9} = 3$$

3. $z = 5i \quad \Rightarrow \quad z \equiv 0 + 5i$

$$\Rightarrow \quad |z| = \sqrt{0^2 + 5^2} = \sqrt{25} = 5$$

PROPERTIES OF CONJUGATE AND MODULUS

1. $(z_1 + z_2)^* = z_1{}^* + z_2{}^*$ for all $z_1, z_2 \in \mathbb{C}$.

2. $(z_1 z_2)^* = z_1{}^* z_2{}^*$ for all $z_1, z_2 \in \mathbb{C}$.

3. $\left(\dfrac{z_1}{z_2}\right)^* = \dfrac{z_1{}^*}{z_2{}^*}$ for all $z_1, z_2 \in \mathbb{C}$.

In particular, $(z^*)^2 = (z^2)^*$ and $(\frac{1}{z})^* = 1/z^*$.

4. (*a*) If z is a *real number*, then $z^* = z$.

   (*b*) *Conversely* given that $z = z^*$, then z must be real.

Proof

Let $z = x + iy, \quad z^* = x - iy$ $\qquad x, y \in \mathbb{R}$

$$\begin{aligned} z = z^* \quad &\Rightarrow \quad x + iy = x - iy \\ &\Rightarrow \quad iy = -iy \\ &\Rightarrow \quad 2iy = 0 \\ &\Rightarrow \quad y = 0 \qquad \text{since } 2i \neq 0 \\ &\Rightarrow \quad z = x \in \mathbb{R} \end{aligned}$$

5. $|z_1 z_2| = |z_1||z_2|$

6. $|\frac{z_1}{z_2}| = \frac{|z_1|}{|z_2|}$

As an exercise, verify for $z_1 = 2 + i$, $z_2 = 3 - 2i$ that $(z_1 + z_2)^* = z_1^* + z_2^*$, $(z_1 z_2)^* = z_1^* z_2^*$ and $|z_1 z_2| = |z_1||z_2|$.

However, in general $|z_1 + z_2|$ is *not* equal to $|z_1| + |z_2|$.

Example

$$\begin{aligned} z_1 = 1 - i \quad &\Rightarrow \quad |z_1| = \sqrt{2} \\ z_2 = 1 + i \quad &\Rightarrow \quad |z_2| = \sqrt{2} \\ \therefore z_1 + z_2 = 2 \quad &\Rightarrow \quad |z_1 + z_2| = 2 \end{aligned}$$

and $\sqrt{2} + \sqrt{2} \neq 2$

In fact, $|z_1 + z_2| \leqslant |z_1| + |z_2|$ for all z_1, z_2. see page 383

Examples

1. Find all three roots of the equation $z^3 + 1 = 0$.

As on page 81, we first find any root. Now

$$z^3 = -1$$
$$\Rightarrow \quad z = \sqrt[3]{-1} = -1$$

is a root. There are more roots to find. The root $z = -1$ corresponds to the factor $z + 1$ of $z^3 + 1$.

Factor Theorem, page 80

$$z^3 + 1 = (z + 1)(z^2 - z + 1)$$

check by multiplying out

Now solving

$$z^2 - z + 1 = 0$$

$$z = \frac{1 \pm \sqrt{1-4}}{2} = \frac{1}{2} \pm i\frac{\sqrt{3}}{2}$$

The equation $z^3 + 1 = 0$ has the real root $z = -1$ and the two complex roots $z = \frac{1}{2} + i\frac{\sqrt{3}}{2}$ and $z = \frac{1}{2} - i\frac{\sqrt{3}}{2}$. These are the complex cube roots of 1.

2. Find the complex square roots of $2i$.

Answer

Let a square root be $a + ib$. Then

$$(a + ib)^2 = 2i$$
$$\Rightarrow \quad a^2 + 2abi - b^2 = 2i$$
$$\Rightarrow \quad (a^2 - b^2) + 2abi = 2i$$

Equating real and imaginary parts leads to the simultaneous equations

$$a^2 - b^2 = 0 \qquad (1)$$

$$ab = 1 \qquad (2)$$

$$(2) \quad \Rightarrow \quad b = \frac{1}{a}$$

Substituting in (1)

$$(1) \quad \Rightarrow \quad a^2 - \frac{1}{a^2} = 0$$

$$\Rightarrow \quad a^4 = 1$$

$$\Rightarrow \quad a = \pm 1 \qquad a \text{ is real}$$

If $a = 1$, $\quad (2) \Rightarrow b = 1$. $\quad$ If $a = -1$, $\quad (2) \Rightarrow b = -1$.

The square roots of $2i$ are $1 + i$ and $-(1 + i)$.

For a polynomial equation with real coefficients the roots occur in *conjugate pairs* (as in example 2 above). That is, if α is a root, then so also is α^*. We prove this for a cubic equation $az^3 + bz^2 + cz + d = 0$, where a, b $c, d \in \mathbb{R}$.

If α is a root, then

$$a\alpha^3 + b\alpha^2 + c\alpha + d = 0$$
$$\Rightarrow (a\alpha^3 + b\alpha^2 + c\alpha + d)^* = 0^*$$
$$\Rightarrow (a\alpha^3)^* + (b\alpha^2)^* + (c\alpha)^* + d^* = 0^*$$
$$\Rightarrow a^*(\alpha^3)^* + b^*(\alpha^2)^* + c^*\alpha^* + d^* = 0^*$$
$$\Rightarrow a^*(\alpha^*)^3 + b^*(\alpha^*)^2 + c^*\alpha^* + d^* = 0^*$$
$$\Rightarrow a(\alpha^*)^3 + b(\alpha^*)^2 + c\alpha^* + d = 0$$

since $a, b, c, d, 0 \in \mathbb{R}$.

$\Rightarrow \alpha^*$ is also a root.

Example

Find the value of the constant k for which $z = i$ is a root of the equation $z^3 - 2z^2 + z + k = 0$. Find the other 2 roots of this equation.

Answer

$z = i$ is a root

$$\Rightarrow \quad i^3 - 2i^2 + i + k = 0$$

$$\Rightarrow \quad -i + 2 + i + k = 0$$

$$\Rightarrow \quad k = -2$$

The equation is $z^3 - 2z^2 + z - 2 = 0$.

Since i is a root, so is $i^* = -i$. The roots i, $-i$ correspond to factors $(z - i)$ and $(z + i)$. Thus, $z^3 - 2z^2 + z - 2$ has the quadratic factor

$$(z - i)(z + i) \equiv z^2 - i^2 \equiv z^2 + 1$$

Factorizing

$$z^3 - 2z^2 + z - 2 = 0$$

$$\Rightarrow \quad (z^2 + 1)(z - 2) = 0 \qquad \text{check!}$$

$$\Rightarrow \quad z^2 + 1 = 0 \quad \text{or} \quad z - 2 = 0$$

$z^2 + 1 = 0$ corresponds to the two known roots $\pm i$. $z - 2 = 0$ has root $z = 2$.

The cubic equation has the three roots $-i$, i, 2.

Note: A cubic equation always has at least one *real* root.

Note: The general result is only true when the coefficients are *real*. For example, in 2 above the roots are $1 + i$ and $-1 - i$, which are not conjugates.

Section 13 Symmetric Properties of the Roots of a Quadratic Equation

13.1 Sum and Product of Roots

The factor theorem (page 80) shows how the roots of an equation correspond to factors of a polynomial.

A quadratic equation can be found with given roots α and β. These roots correspond to factors $(x - \alpha)$ and $(x - \beta)$ and so the required equation is $(x - \alpha)(x - \beta) = 0$. This simplifies to

$$x^2 - (\alpha + \beta)x + \alpha\beta = 0 \qquad (*)$$

Example

Write down a quadratic equation with roots $x = 1$ and $x = -5$.

Answer

$\alpha = 1, \beta = -5$ so $\alpha + \beta = -4$ and $\alpha\beta = -5$. The equation is

$$x^2 + 4x - 5 = 0$$

Now consider a general quadratic equation $ax^2 + bx + c = 0$ with roots α and β. Dividing each term by a, the equation becomes

$$x^2 + \frac{b}{a}x + \frac{c}{a} = 0$$

Comparing with the equation (*) above, the coefficients of x^2 match and so too must the other coefficients. Thus,

$$\boxed{\alpha + \beta = -\frac{b}{a}}$$

and

$$\boxed{\alpha\beta = \frac{c}{a}}$$

These two relations are known as the **symmetric properties** of the roots of a quadratic equation. (Note that α and β could be complex roots.)

Example

Write down the sum and product of the roots of the equation $3x^2 - 5x - 7 = 0$.

Answer

$$\text{sum} = \alpha + \beta = -\frac{b}{a} = -\frac{(-5)}{3} = \frac{5}{3}$$

$$\text{product} = \alpha\beta = \frac{c}{a} = -\frac{7}{3}$$

Note that we did not need to calculate the values of the roots themselves.

Example

The sum of the roots of a quadratic equation with integer coefficients is -3 and the product is $\frac{5}{2}$. Write down the quadratic equation.

Answer

$$\alpha + \beta = -3$$

$$\alpha\beta = \frac{5}{2}$$

An equation is

$$x^2 - (-3)x + \frac{5}{2} = 0$$

$$\Rightarrow \quad 2x^2 + 6x + 5 = 0$$

with integer coefficients

13.2 Related Quadratic Equations

Examples

1. The roots of the equation $2x^2 - 3x - 5 = 0$ are α and β. Calculate
   (*a*) $\alpha + \beta$, (*b*) $\alpha\beta$, (*c*) $\frac{1}{\alpha} + \frac{1}{\beta}$ (*d*) $\alpha^2 + \beta^2$

Answer

(*a*) $\alpha + \beta = -\frac{b}{a} = \frac{3}{2}$

(*b*) $\alpha\beta = \frac{c}{a} = -\frac{5}{2}$

(*c*) $\frac{1}{\alpha} + \frac{1}{\beta} = \frac{\alpha + \beta}{\alpha\beta} = \frac{\frac{3}{2}}{-\frac{5}{2}} = -\frac{3}{5}$

(*d*) $\alpha^2 + \beta^2 \equiv (\alpha + \beta)^2 - 2\alpha\beta$

important identity to remember

$$= (\tfrac{3}{2})^2 - 2(-\tfrac{5}{2})$$

$$= \tfrac{9}{4} + 5 = \tfrac{29}{4}$$

2. The quadratic equation $2x^2 + 5x + 1 = 0$ has roots α and β.
   (*a*) Evaluate $\frac{1}{\alpha} + \frac{1}{\beta}$ and $\frac{1}{\alpha\beta}$, (*b*) hence find a quadratic equation with integer coefficients having roots $\frac{1}{\alpha}$ and $\frac{1}{\beta}$.

Answer

(*a*) $\alpha + \beta = -\frac{5}{2}, \alpha\beta = \frac{1}{2}$ so $\frac{1}{\alpha} + \frac{1}{\beta} \equiv \frac{\alpha+\beta}{\alpha\beta} = \frac{-\frac{5}{2}}{\frac{1}{2}} = -5$ and $\frac{1}{\alpha\beta} = 2$.

(*b*) Let $\alpha' = \frac{1}{\alpha}, \beta' = \frac{1}{\beta}$. The equation with roots α', β' is

$$x^2 - (\alpha' + \beta')x + \alpha'\beta' = 0$$

$$\alpha' + \beta' = \frac{1}{\alpha} + \frac{1}{\beta} = -5, \quad \alpha'\beta' = \frac{1}{\alpha\beta} = 2 \quad \text{(from part (a))}$$

$x^2 + 5x + 2 = 0$ is the required equation.

Section 14 Worked Examples

1. $z = x + iy$. Solve the equation $z^* + 2z + 3 - \frac{2}{i} = 0$ for z.

Answer

$$\begin{aligned}
(x + iy)^* + 2(x + iy) + 3 - \tfrac{2}{i} &= 0 \\
(x - iy) + 2x + 2iy + 3 - \tfrac{2}{i} &= 0 \\
x - iy + 2x + 2iy + 3 + 2i &= 0 \\
(3x + 3) + i(y + 2) &= 0 \\
\Rightarrow 3x + 3 &= 0 \text{ and } y + 2 = 0 \\
\Rightarrow x &= -1 \text{ and } y = -2 \\
\Rightarrow z &= -1 - 2i
\end{aligned}$$

2. Solve the equation $z^4 - 16 = 0$

Answer

$$z^4 - 16 = (z^2 - 4)(z^2 + 4) = 0$$

$$\Rightarrow \quad z^2 + 4 = 0 \text{ or } z^2 - 4 = 0$$

$$\Rightarrow \quad z^2 = -4 \text{ or } z^2 = 4$$

$$\Rightarrow \quad z = \pm\sqrt{-4} = \pm 2i \text{ or } z = \pm 2 \qquad \sqrt{4} = \sqrt{(-1)4} = \sqrt{-1}\sqrt{4} = 2i$$

The four roots are $-2, 2, -2i, 2i$.

3. $z_1 = 3 + 4i, z_2 = 1 + i$. Express z_1z_2, $z_1^* + z_2^*$ in the form $a + bi$.

Answer

$$z_1 z_2 = (3 + 4i)(1 + i) = 3 + 4i + 3i - 4$$
$$= -1 + 7i$$
$$z_1^* + z_2^* = (3 - 4i) + (1 - i) = 4 - 5i$$

4. The equation $x^2 + px - 2p^2 = 0$, for $p > 0$, has roots α and β, where $\alpha > \beta$. Find $(\alpha + \beta)^2$, $\alpha^2 + \beta^2$, $(\alpha - \beta)^2$, $(\alpha - \beta)$ and $\alpha^2 - \beta^2$ in terms of p. Find a quadratic equation with roots $\alpha^3\beta$ and $\alpha\beta^3$.

Answer

$$x^2 + px - 2p^2 = 0 \quad \text{has roots } \alpha, \beta$$

Therefore

$$\alpha + \beta = -p$$
$$\alpha\beta = -2p^2$$

$\alpha + \beta = -\frac{b}{a}$

$\alpha\beta = \frac{c}{a}$

Therefore

$$(\alpha + \beta)^2 = (-p)^2 = p^2$$
$$\alpha^2 + \beta^2 \equiv (\alpha + \beta)^2 - 2\alpha\beta$$
$$= p^2 + 4p^2 = 5p^2$$

as $(\alpha + \beta)^2 = \alpha^2 + 2\alpha\beta + \beta^2$

$$(\alpha - \beta)^2 = \alpha^2 + \beta^2 - 2\alpha\beta$$
$$= 5p^2 + 4p^2 = 9p^2$$

Therefore

$$(\alpha - \beta) = \sqrt{(\alpha - \beta)^2} = 3p \quad (\text{since } \alpha > \beta)$$

taking positive root

$$\alpha^2 - \beta^2 = (\alpha - \beta)(\alpha + \beta)$$
$$= 3p(-p) = -3p^2$$

Now let $\alpha' = \alpha^3\beta$, $\beta' = \alpha\beta^3$.

$$\Rightarrow \quad \alpha' + \beta' = \alpha^3\beta + \alpha\beta^3 = \alpha\beta(\alpha^2 + \beta^2)$$
$$= (-2p^2)(5p^2) = -10p^4$$

and

$$\alpha'\beta' = \alpha^4\beta^4 = (\alpha\beta)^4 = 16p^8$$

The quadratic equation with roots $\alpha^3\beta$, $\alpha\beta^3$ is

$$x^2 + 10p^4x + 16p^8 = 0 \qquad x^2-(\alpha'+\beta')x+\alpha'\beta' = 0$$

5. Find the value of q for which one of the roots of $x^2 - q^2x + 6q = 0$ is double the other root, given that $q \neq 0$.

Answer

Let the roots be α and 2α. one double the other

Then

$$\alpha + 2\alpha \equiv 3\alpha = q^2 \qquad (1) \quad \alpha+\beta = -\tfrac{b}{a}$$

$$\alpha \times 2\alpha \equiv 2\alpha^2 = 6q \qquad (2) \quad \alpha\beta = \tfrac{c}{a}$$

$$(1) \Rightarrow \quad \alpha = \frac{q^2}{3} \Rightarrow \alpha^2 = \frac{q^4}{9}$$

$$(2) \Rightarrow \quad 2\left(\frac{q^4}{9}\right) = 6q$$

$$\Rightarrow \quad 2q^4 = 54q$$

$$\Rightarrow \quad q^3 = 27 \qquad (q \neq 0)$$

$$\Rightarrow \quad q = 3$$

Section 15 Examination Questions

1. $z = 3 - 4i$

1. $z - z^* = -8$ 2. $\frac{1}{z} = z^*$ 3. $z^2 = -7 - 24i$

A 1, 2, and 3 are all correct B 1 and 2 only C 2 and 3 only
D only 1 is correct E only 3 is correct [LON]

2. *Given that* $z_1 = 3 + 2i$ *and* $z_2 = 4 - 3i$,

(i) find z_1z_2 *and* $\frac{z_1}{z_2}$ *in the form* $a + ib$;
(ii) verify that $|z_1z_2| = |z_1||z_2|$. [CAM]

3. *If* $z = x + iy$ *and* $\bar{z} = x - iy$, *solve (for* z*) the equation* $z + 5\bar{z} = 6 + 8i$. *(*$\bar{z} \equiv z^*$.*)* [SUJB – part]

4. $z_1 = 2 + i$ *and* $\frac{1}{z} = 1 + \frac{1}{z_1}$.

$z =$

A $\frac{1}{5}(7 - i)$ B $\frac{1}{10}(7 + i)$ C $\frac{1}{10}(3 - i)$ D $\frac{1}{10}(3 + i)$ E $3 - i$

[LON]

5. *For all* z_1, z_2

$$1.\ |z_1 - z_2| \geqslant |z_1| - |z_2|, \quad 2.\ |z_1 z_2| = |z_1||z_2|,$$

$$3.\ |z_1 + z_2| \leqslant |z_1| + |z_2|.$$

A 1, 2, 3 are all correct B 1 and 2 only C 2 and 3 only D 1 only E 3 only [LON]

6. *If the roots of the quadratic equation* $x^2 - 3px + p^2 = 0$ *are* α *and* β, *where* $\alpha > \beta$, *find the values of* $\alpha^2 + \beta^2$ *and* $\alpha - \beta$ *when* p *is positive. Find, in terms of* p, *a quadratic equation whose roots are* $\frac{\alpha^3}{\beta}$ *and* $\frac{-\beta^3}{\alpha}$.

[AEB]

7. *Given that* α *and* β *are the roots of the equation* $x^2 - bx + c = 0$,
(a) show that $(\alpha^2 + 1)(\beta^2 + 1) = (c - 1)^2 + b^2$,
(b) find, in terms of b *and* c, *a quadratic equation whose roots are* $\frac{\alpha}{\alpha^2+1}$ *and* $\frac{\beta}{\beta^2+1}$. [AEB]

8. *Given that* a_1 *and* a_2 *are the roots of the quadratic equation* $(x - b_1)(x - b_2) = c$, *write down expressions for* $a_1 + a_2$ *and* $a_1 a_2$ *in terms of the constants* b_1, b_2 *and* c.
Show that $-a_1$ *and* $-a_2$ *are the roots of the equation* $(x + b_1)(x + b_2) = c$.

[LON]

9. *The roots of* $3x^2 + 4x - 2 = 0$ *are* α *and* β.

1. $\alpha\beta = \frac{2}{3}$ 2. $\alpha + \beta = \frac{4}{3}$ 3. α *and* β *are both real.*

A 1, 2, 3 are all correct B 1 and 2 only C 2 and 3 only D 1 only E 3 only [LON]

10. *(a) The product of two numbers is 29 more than their sum, and the difference between the numbers is 1. Find the possible pairs of numbers.*

(b) Given that one root of the equation $x^3 + x^2 - 2x - 2 = 0$ *is an integer, find all of the roots.* [SUJB – part]

5 Gradients, Differentiation and Integration for Polynomial Functions

Section 16 Linear Forms

16.1 Straight-Line Equations

If $f(x) = ax + b$, where a and b are constants, then the graph is a straight line. A point $P(x, y)$ lies on the graph if the coordinates satisfy the equation $y = ax + b$.

Example

Determine whether the points $A(1, -3)$ and $B(-2, -8)$ lie on the straight line $y = 2x - 5$.

Answer

Let $f(x) = 2x - 5$. $f(1) = -3 \Rightarrow A(1, -3)$ is on the line. $f(-2) = -9 \neq -8$, so $B(-2, -8)$ is not on the line.

Given the coordinates of two points, you can find the equation of the straight line passing through them.

Example

Find the equation of the straight line passing through points $A(3, 4)$ and $B(-2, 1)$.

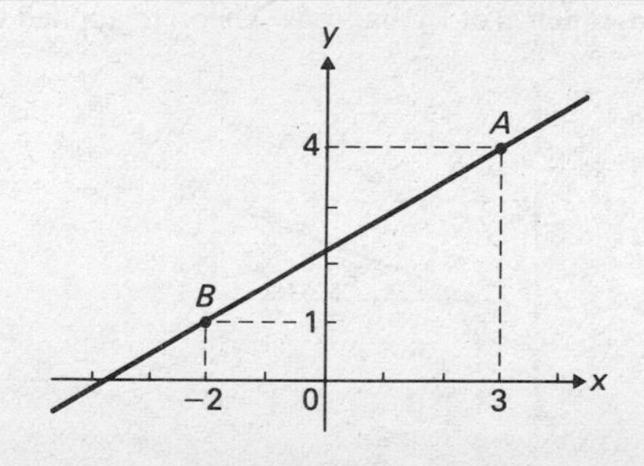

Answer

The equation must have the form $y = ax + b$.

$A(3, 4)$ is on the line, so $3a + b = 4$ (1)

$B(-2, 1)$ is on the line, so $-2a + b = 1$ (2)

These are simultaneous equations in a and b. Subtracting them

$$5a = 3$$

$$\Rightarrow \quad a = \frac{3}{5}$$

Substituting for a in equation (2)

$$-\frac{6}{5} + b = 1$$

$$\Rightarrow \quad b = \frac{11}{5}$$

The equation of the straight line is $y = \frac{3}{5}x + \frac{11}{5}$, which can also be expressed as $5y = 3x + 11$ or $3x - 5y + 11 = 0$.

Notice that the solutions for a and b are unique. There is exactly one straight line passing through two given points.

PYTHAGORAS' THEOREM

The distance between two points can be calculated from the following formula. If $A(x_1, y_1)$ and $B(x_2, y_2)$ are any two points in the plane, then distance

$$AB = \sqrt{(x_1 - x_2)^2 + (y_1 - y_2)^2}$$

It is a direct consequence of Pythagoras' Theorem applied to the triangle ABC below

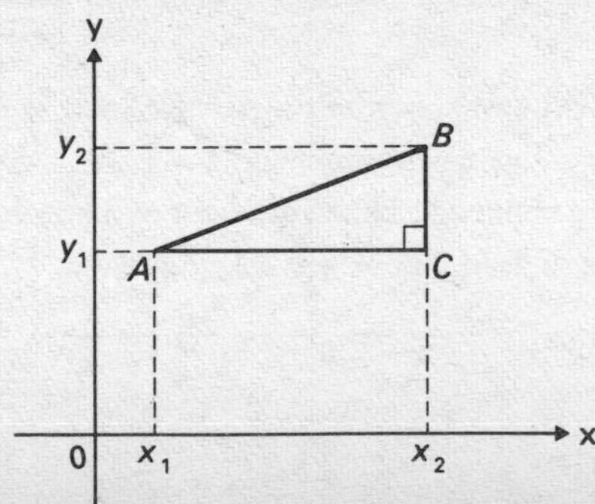

Example

The distance between points $P(-3, 2)$ and $Q(1, 7)$ is

$$\sqrt{(-3-1)^2+(2-7)^2} = \sqrt{16+25} = \sqrt{41}$$

16.2 Gradients

Let $P(x_1, y_1)$ and $Q(x_2, y_2)$ be two points in the plane.

> The *gradient* of the line segment PQ is defined as $\dfrac{y_2 - y_1}{x_2 - x_1}$

that is $\frac{\text{change in } y}{\text{change in } x}$.

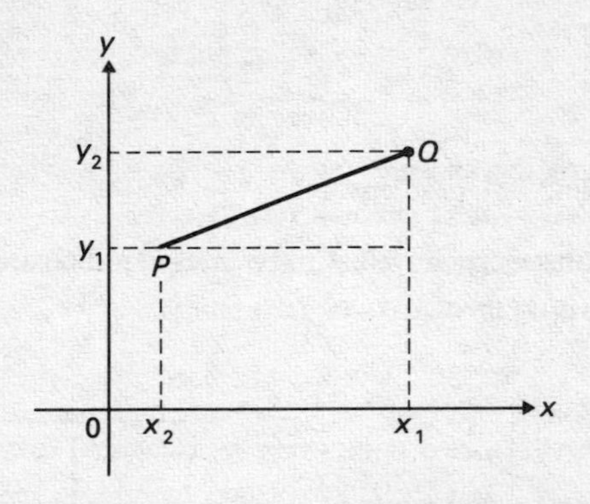

Suppose that the straight line passing through P and Q has equation $y = ax + b$. Then, $y_1 = ax_1 + b$ and $y_2 = ax_2 + b$.

Gradient of PQ

$$\frac{y_2 - y_1}{x_2 - x_1} = \frac{(ax_2 + b) - (ax_1 + b)}{x_2 - x_1} = \frac{a(x_2 - x_1)}{(x_2 - x_1)} = a$$

The gradient for any two points on the straight line $y = ax + b$ is the same no matter which two points are chosen.

This gradient is defined to be the gradient of the straight line.

The line with equation $y = ax + b$ has gradient a.

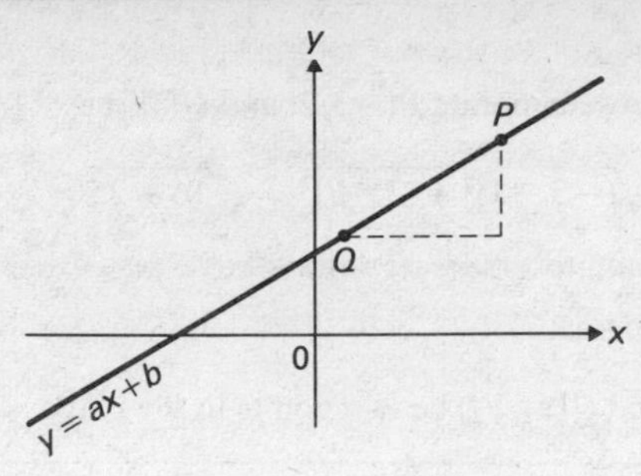

Examples

1. $y = 3x + 5$ represents a line with gradient 3.
2. $2x + 3y + 7 = 0$

$$\Rightarrow \quad 3y = -2x - 7$$

$$\Rightarrow \quad y = -\frac{2}{3}x - \frac{7}{3}$$

representing a line with gradient $-\frac{2}{3}$.

The gradient measures how fast y increases as x increases. It is the *rate of change* of y *with respect to* x.

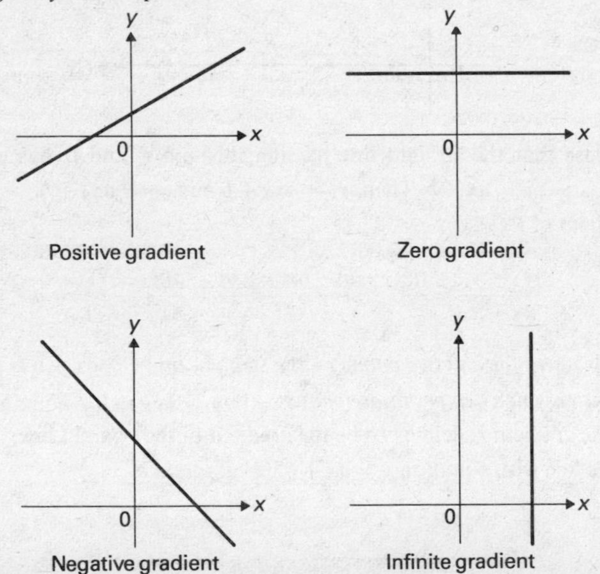

The larger the gradient, the steeper the graph.

A line sloping upwards (left to right x-increasing) has positive gradient.

A line parallel to the x-axis has zero gradient.

A line sloping downwards (left to right) has negative gradient.

A line with infinite gradient cannot have an equation of the form $y = ax + b$ (a cannot be ∞!) Such a line has an equation of the form, $x = \text{constant}$.

A line parallel to the x-axis has zero gradient and so has equation $y = \text{constant}$.

If $f(x) = ax + b$, then $b = f(0)$. b is the y-intercept of the graph (where the graph cuts the y-axis).

We have already seen how the equation of a straight line can be derived from the coordinates of two points on the line. From the above, it is sufficient to know the gradient and y-intercept.

It is also sufficient to know the gradient and one point on the line.

Example

Find the equation of the straight line passing through the point (1, 5) with gradient 3.

Answer

The equation is of the form $y = 3x + b$ (gradient = 3). The line passes through (1, 5). Therefore, $5 = 3 + b$, $\Rightarrow$ $b = 2$.

Therefore, the equation of the line is $y = 3x + 2$.

GENERAL FORMULAE

The straight line passing through points (x_1, y_1), (x_2, y_2) has equation

$$\boxed{y - y_1 = \left(\frac{y_2 - y_1}{x_2 - x_1}\right)(x - x_1)}$$

The line passing through point (x_1, y_1) with gradient m has equation

$$\boxed{y - y_1 = m(x - x_1)}$$

16.3 Parallel and Perpendicular Lines

Two straight lines in the plane that cannot meet, no matter how far they are extended, are said to be **parallel**.

Two lines are parallel if they have the same gradient.

Example

Find the equation of the straight line passing through the point $A(-1,5)$ and parallel to the line $y = 4x - 5$.

Answer

The gradient is 4 $\Rightarrow$ $y = 4x + b$.

The line passes through $(-1, 5)$

$$\Rightarrow \quad 5 = -4 + b$$

$$\Rightarrow \quad b = 9$$

$$\Rightarrow \quad y = 4x + 9$$

Two straight lines in the plane are **perpendicular** if they meet at right angles. The product of the gradients of two perpendicular lines is -1.

Summary

The two lines $y = a_1x + b_1$ and $y = a_2x + b_2$
are *parallel* $\Leftrightarrow a_1 = a_2$
are *perpendicular* $\Leftrightarrow a_1a_2 = -1$

Examples

1. Find the value of the constant k for which the line $y = kx - 3$ is perpendicular to the line through $A(1, -3)$ and $B(2, 7)$.

Answer

$y = kx - 3$ has gradient k.

AB has gradient $\frac{7-(-3)}{2-1} = 10$. The lines are perpendicular if $10k = -1$ $\Rightarrow k = -\frac{1}{10}$.

2. Find the equation of the line passing through the point $(3, 2)$ perpendicular to $3x - 5y + 9 = 0$.

Answer

$3x - 5y + 9 = 0$ has gradient $\frac{3}{5}$. The required line must have gradient $-\frac{-1}{\frac{3}{5}} = \frac{-5}{3}$. (*Check*: $\frac{3}{5} \times (-\frac{5}{3}) = -1$.) The equation of this line is

$$y = -\frac{5}{3}x + c$$

for a constant c. It passes through $(3, 2)$

$$\therefore \quad 2 = -5 + c$$

$$\therefore \quad c = 7$$

The line has equation $y = -\frac{5}{3}x + 7$

$$\Rightarrow \quad 3y = -5x + 21$$

$$\Rightarrow \quad 5x + 3y - 21 = 0$$

16.4 Fitting Straight Lines

Scientists and social scientists often have the problem of discovering relationships between variables. Such a relationship may be described by a formula connecting the variables.

Suppose that quantities x and y are thought to satisfy a linear relationship of the form $y = ax + b$ for some constants a and b. This relationship can be tested by plotting measured values of y and x on a graph. If the relationship is of the correct form, the graph should be a straight line. In practice, the measured values will be subject to inaccuracies and the graph will not be exactly straight. As long as a straight line can be drawn to fit the data reasonably well, it is safe to assume a linear relationship. Such a line is called a **best fit** line for the data.

Although there are statistical techniques for finding the best fit line of a set of data, for our purposes it is sufficient to draw the line 'by eye'. Draw a line so that as many of the plotted points lie above it as below.

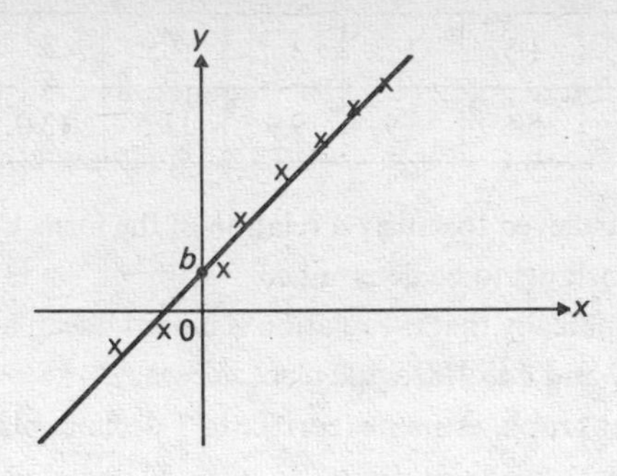

The values of the constants a and b can be estimated from the graph. a is the gradient and b is the y-intercept.

Note: Because the given pairs of values of x and y may be inaccurate, they cannot be substituted into the equation $y = ax + b$ to find a and b directly. These quantities *must* be found from the best fit line, so as to reduce errors.

Of course if the graph cannot be reasonably approximated by a straight line, then the relationship between x and y cannot be linear.

In some cases it will be apparent from the graph that some points do not fit at all closely to the line. This may be due to an error in the measured values, in which case such points should be ignored.

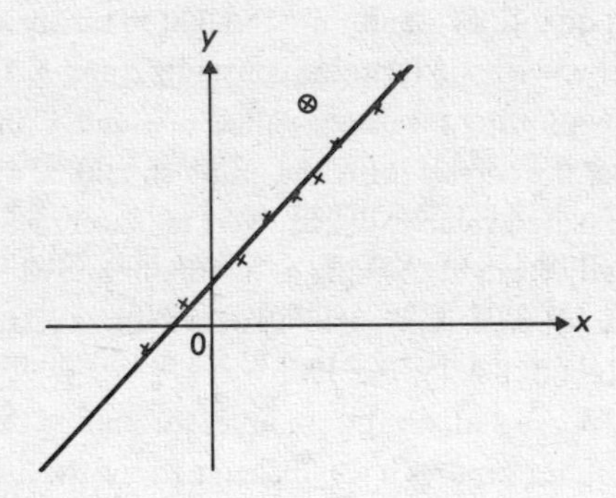

Example

Values of the quantities V and r are obtained by experiment. The data is given in the following table.

r	1	1·5	2	3	3·5	4	4·5	5
V	3·8	5·6	6·9	9·9	11·6	13·0	14·6	16·0

V and r are believed to satisfy a relation of the form $V = kr + c$, where k and c are constants to be determined.

Verify graphically that the relation is indeed linear, and use your graph to estimate k and c to 1 decimal place accuracy.

From your graph, estimate (correct to 1 decimal place) the value of V when $r = 2{\cdot}5$.

Answer

Plot the points (r, V) and draw the best fit line.

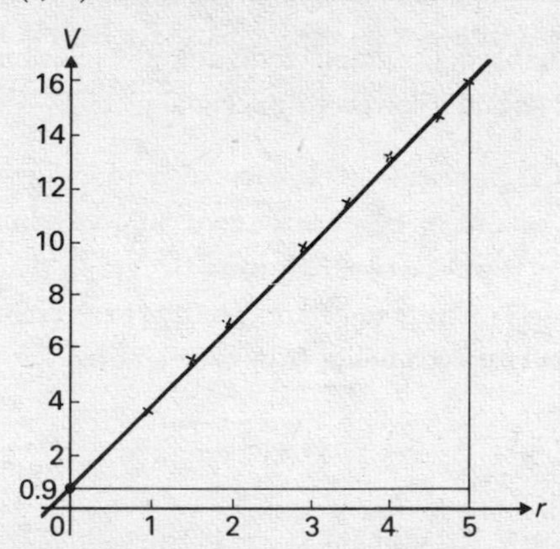

Using the points $(0, 0{\cdot}9)$ and $(5, 16)$ on the line, we obtain the gradient $k = \frac{16 - 0{\cdot}9}{5} = 3{\cdot}0$ (1 decimal place).

The line cuts the V-axis at $c = 0{\cdot}9$. The equation of the line is $V = 3r + 0{\cdot}9$. Using the equation with $r = 2{\cdot}5$, we estimate $V = 3(2{\cdot}5) + 0{\cdot}9 = 8{\cdot}4$. (*Check* that $(2{\cdot}5, 8{\cdot}4)$ is a point on the line in the figure.)

16.5 Testing Non-Linear Relations

The unknown constants can only be determined as above when the graph is a straight line.

When the relationship is *not* linear, changes of variable are necessary to produce a straight-line graph.

Example

Variables x and y are believed to satisfy an equation of the form

$$ax^2 + b\frac{x}{y} = 2$$

Values of x and y obtained by experiment are given in the following table.

x	1	1·5	2	2·5	3	3·5	4
y	0·79	0·69	0·57	0·48	0·41	0·36	0·33

By drawing a suitable *linear* graph, verify that the relation is correct and estimate values of a and b correct to 1 decimal place.

Answer

$$ax^2 + b\frac{x}{y} = 2$$

Divide throughout by $\frac{x}{y}$ (i.e. multiply by $\frac{y}{x}$).

$$\Rightarrow \quad axy + b = \frac{2y}{x}$$ isolate one constant

Letting $X = xy$, $Y = \frac{2y}{x}$

$$\Rightarrow \quad Y = aX + b$$

This represents a straight line graph of Y against X, with gradient a and Y-intercept b.

Calculating values of X and Y corresponding to the given values of x and y

$X = xy$	0·79	1·035	1·14	1·20	1·23	1·26	1·32
$Y = \frac{2y}{x}$	1·58	0·92	0·57	0·384	0·273	0·206	0·165

Plotting the points (X, Y) gives the graph

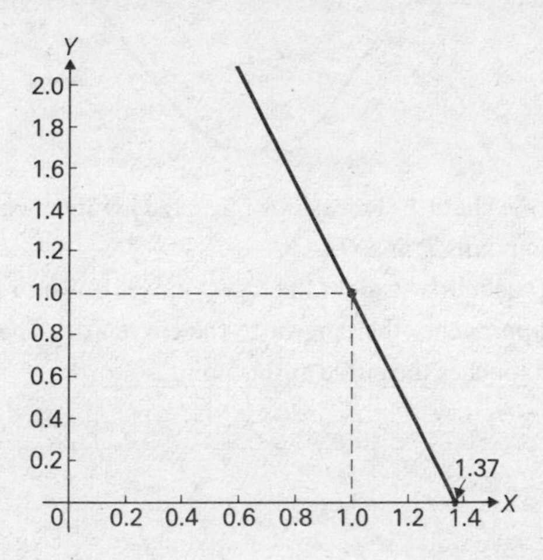

The graph is approximately a straight line, and so the relation $ax^2 + b\frac{x}{y} = 2$ can be reasonably assumed to be correct.

From the graph, a = gradient $= \frac{-2}{0{\cdot}69} \simeq -3$. The line does not cut the Y-axis on this diagram, and so we cannot read off the Y-intercept value. Take the coordinates of any point *on the line* and substitute into the equation $Y = -3X + b$. From the graph, $Y = 1{\cdot}0$ when $X = 1{\cdot}0$

$$\Rightarrow \quad 1 = -3 + b$$

$$\Rightarrow \quad b = 4$$

So $-3x^2 + \frac{4x}{y} = 2$

Section 17 Gradients of Curves – Differentiation

17.1 Gradients

Any two points P, Q on the curve define a line segment PQ with a corresponding gradient. Another choice of points P and Q may well give a different gradient.

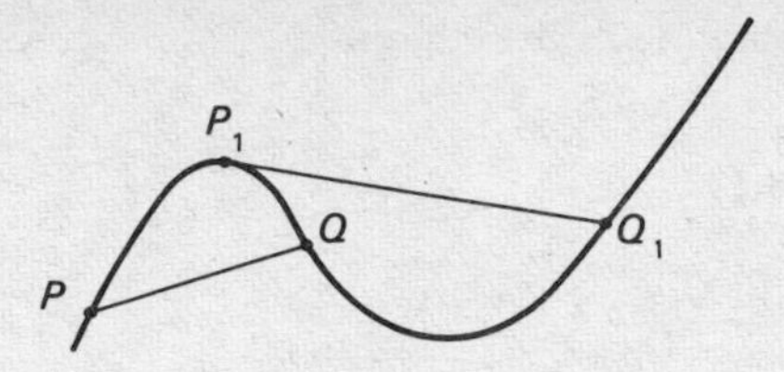

The gradient of the **chord** PQ measures the *average* rate of change of the function between points P and Q.

The chord PQ defines a straight line. As Q moves down to P along the curve, this line approaches the **tangent** to the curve at P. The tangent at P is a line which touches the curve at this point.

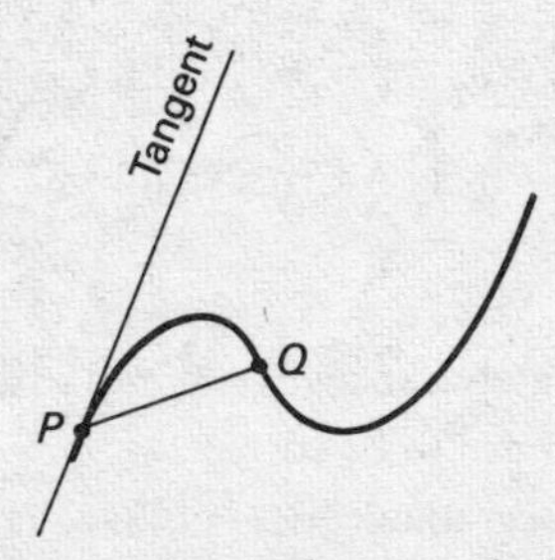

The gradient of a curve *at a point* on the curve is defined as the gradient of the tangent at that point. Notice that the gradient is only defined at a point where a tangent can be drawn. A curve is said to be **differentiable** at point P if it has a well-defined gradient at P. Not all graphs are differentiable at every point:

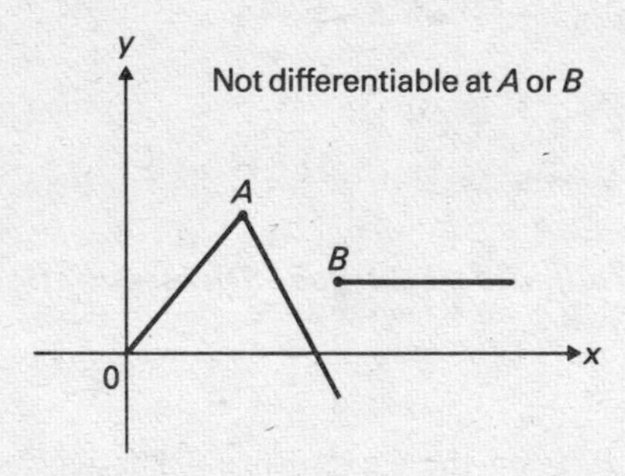

17.2 Tangents

A tangent meets the curve at a *repeated* point of intersection, called the point of contact.

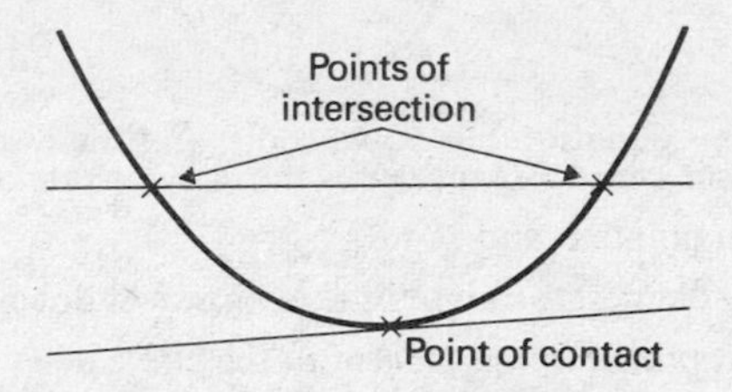

This property provides a test to determine whether a given line is tangent to a given curve.

Examples

1. Show that the line with equation $y = 4x - 2$ is a tangent to the curve $y = 3x^2 - 2x + 1$ and find the coordinates of the point of contact.

Answer

For points of intersection, solve the simultaneous equations

$y = 4x - 2 \quad (1) \qquad y = 3x^2 - 2x + 1 \quad (2)$ page 93

$$\Rightarrow \quad 4x - 2 = 3x^2 - 2x + 1$$

$$\Rightarrow \quad 3x^2 - 6x + 3 = 0$$

$$\Rightarrow \quad x^2 - 2x + 1 = 0$$

$$\Rightarrow \quad (x - 1)^2 = 0$$ perfect square

This equation has the **double root** $x = 1$, and so the line is a tangent. When $x = 1$, $y = 4 - 2 = 2$ (from (1)). The point of contact is $(1, 2)$.

2. Find the values of m for which the line $y = mx + 2$ is a tangent to the curve $y = x^2 + 6$. Find the coordinates of the point of contact in each case.

Answer

For points of intersection

$$x^2 + 6 = mx + 2$$

$$\Rightarrow \quad x^2 - mx + 4 = 0 \qquad (*)$$

For a tangent, this equation has equal roots, and the discriminant must be 0 (page 91)

$$\therefore \quad m^2 - 16 = 0$$

$$m^2 = 16$$

$$m = \pm 4$$

When $m = 4$, the tangent is $y = 4x + 2$. The point of contact is the solution of $x^2 - 4x + 4 = 0$ from (*)

$$\Rightarrow \quad (x-2)^2 = 0 \qquad \text{perfect square}$$

$$\Rightarrow \quad x = 2$$

$$\text{and } y = 4(2) + 2 = 10$$

The point of contact is (2, 10)

Similarly the other tangent is found to be $y = 2 - 4x$ with point of contact $(-2, 10)$.

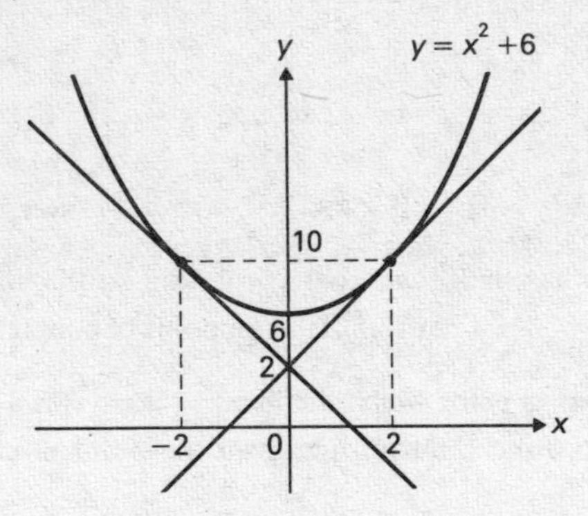

17.3 Calculating Gradients from First Principles

The gradient at a point on a curve can be estimated by plotting the graph accurately, drawing the tangent by eye and measuring its gradient.

This procedure is difficult to do accurately as it depends entirely on drawing and measuring. A calculation method is preferable. Such a calculational procedure is called **differentiation**.

DIFFERENTIATION FROM FIRST PRINCIPLES

Example

Find the gradient of the curve $y = x^2 + 1$ at the point $A(3, 10)$.

Answer

Suppose that an attempt to draw a tangent at the point $A(3, 10)$ in fact produces a line which cuts the curve again at the nearby point B. If B is near A, its coordinates will only differ by a small amount from those of A. Let B have x-coordinate $3 + h$ where h is a small quantity. Since B is on the curve $y = x^2 + 1$ it has y-coordinate $(3 + h)^2 + 1 = 10 + 6h + h^2$.

The chord AB has gradient

$$\frac{(10 + 6h + h^2) - 10}{(3 + h) - 3} = \frac{6h + h^2}{h} = 6 + h$$

As the attempt at a tangent becomes more and more accurate, the point B comes closer to A and h decreases in magnitude. Thus the gradient of the chord AB approaches more and more closely the gradient of the tangent at A. As $h = 0$, the gradient of AB tends to the limit 6. Symbolically

$$\underset{B \to A}{\text{limit}}\,(\text{gradient of } AB) = \lim_{h \to 0}(6 + h) = 6$$

We deduce that the gradient of the curve at the point A is *exactly* 6.

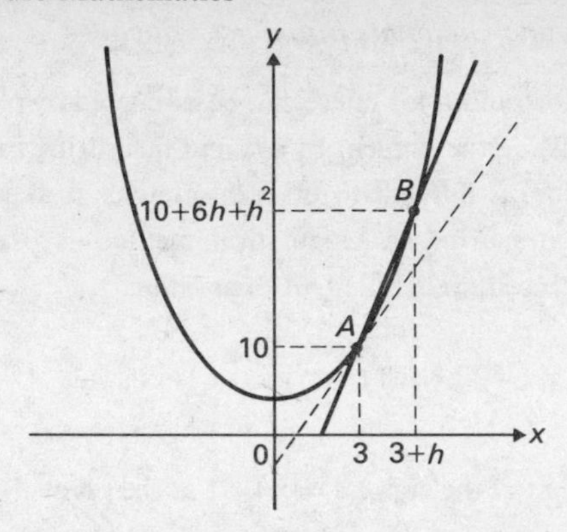

Notes

1. The gradient at A is the **limit** of a sequence of gradients of chords.
2. h can only be set to zero once the expression for the gradient of AB has been simplified. For example

$$\text{gradient} = \frac{(10 + 6h + h^2)}{(3 + h) - 3} \text{ would produce } \frac{0}{0}$$

when h is set to 0. $\frac{0}{0}$ is not a defined quantity. It is essential to simplify first: $\frac{6h+h^2}{h} = 6 + h$ which is well defined when h is set to zero.

Because a curve has a different value of gradient at each point, we refer to the **gradient function** of the curve.

We can use the method of first principles to find the value of the gradient function at a general point on the curve.

Example

Find the gradient function (in terms of x) of the function $y = x^2 + 1$.

Answer

Let $P(x, y)$ be a general point on the curve $y = x^2 + 1$. Let Q be a nearby point on the curve with x-coordinate $x + h$ where h is a small quantity.

The y coordinate of Q is $(x + h)^2 + 1$.

The gradient of line segment PQ is

$$\frac{((x+h)^2+1)-(x^2+1)}{(x+h)-x}$$

$$= \frac{x^2+2hx+h^2+1-x^2-1}{x+h-x}$$

$$= \frac{2hx+h^2}{h}$$

$$= 2x+h$$

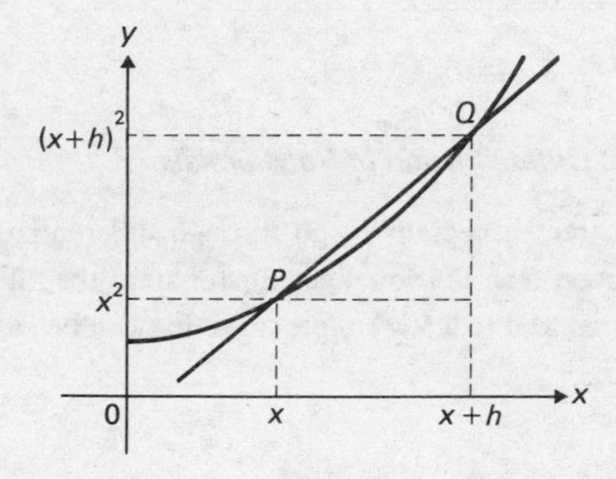

As Q moves down the curve to P, $h \to 0$ and the gradient of PQ tends to the limit $2x$.

The gradient function of $f(x) = x^2 + 1$ is $2x$.

The gradient function is often denoted by a 'prime', or dash $f'(x) = 2x$.

NOTATION

The quantity written as δa means a *small change* in quantity a. It is *not* a product of quantities δ and a and should *not* be separated into these two parts.

Thus δx and δy are small changes in x and y respectively. The gradient of line segment PQ is $\frac{\delta y}{\delta x}$. (Where δx was represented by h in the calculations above.)

The gradient of the tangent at P is the limit of this ratio as $\delta x \to 0$, and is denoted by $\frac{dy}{dx}$.

$$\frac{dy}{dx} = \underset{\delta x \to 0}{\text{limit}}\left(\frac{\delta y}{\delta x}\right) = \underset{\delta x \to 0}{\text{limit}}\left(\frac{f(x+\delta x)-f(x)}{\delta x}\right)$$

The notation $\frac{dy}{dx}$ for gradient function is in general use. However, you should always bear in mind that it is *not* a ratio of quantities dy and dx. It is the *limit* of ratios $\frac{\delta y}{\delta x}$.

Using this notation, if $y = x^2 + 1$ then $\frac{dy}{dx} = 2x$. This can also be expressed as $\frac{d}{dx}(x^2 + 1) = 2x$.

$f'(x) \equiv \frac{dy}{dx}$, the gradient function, is also called the **derived function**.

You should interpret the symbol $\frac{dy}{dx}$ as 'differentiate the function y with respect to the variable x'. In order to find $\frac{dy}{dx}$ you should be given a formula for y in terms of x.

17.4 General Differentiation of Polynomials

It would be extremely tedious to go through differentiation from first principles for every function you meet. Fortunately, the rules for differentiation can be reduced to a few simple steps that can be easily applied to any polynomial.

Rule 1

$$\text{If } y = x^n \text{ where } n \text{ is constant then } \frac{dy}{dx} = nx^{n-1}.$$

In this section we will consider the case when n is a positive integer, and the rule can be proved using the Binomial Expansion (page 71). However, the rule is in fact true for *any* value of n.

Examples

1. $\frac{d}{dx}(x^5) = 5x^4$
2. $\frac{d}{dx}(x) = \frac{d}{dx}(x^1) = 1x^{1-1} = 1x^0 = 1$
3. $\frac{d}{dx}(1) = \frac{d}{dx}(x^0) = 0x^{0-1} = 0$

Rule 2

For any two functions $y_1 = f(x)$, $y_2 = g(x)$,

$$\frac{d}{dx}(y_1 + y_2) = \frac{dy_1}{dx} + \frac{dy_2}{dx} \qquad \text{(additivity property)}$$

Example

$$\frac{d}{dx}(x^3 + x^5) = \frac{d}{dx}(x^3) + \frac{d}{dx}(x^5) = 3x^2 + 5x^4$$

Rule 3

For any function $y = f(x)$ and any *constant* k

$$\boxed{\frac{d}{dx}(ky) = k\frac{dy}{dx}}$$

Example

$$\frac{d}{dx}(3x^2) = 3\frac{d}{dx}(x^2) = 3(2x) = 6x$$

Note: This rule holds *only* when k is constant.

Applying these rules to a polynomial function:

Example

$$y = 2x^4 - 5x^3 + 6x^2 - 6x + 4$$

$$\frac{dy}{dx} = \frac{d}{dx}(2x^4 - 5x^3 + 6x^2 - 6x + 4)$$

$$= \frac{d}{dx}(2x^4) + \frac{d}{dx}(-5x^3) + \frac{d}{dx}(6x^2)$$

$$+ \frac{d}{dx}(-6x) + \frac{d}{dx}(4) \qquad \text{rule 2}$$

$$= 2\frac{d}{dx}(x^4) - 5\frac{d}{dx}(x^3) + 6\frac{d}{dx}(x^2)$$

$$-6\frac{d}{dx}(x) + 4\frac{d}{dx}(1) \qquad \text{rule 3}$$

$$= 2(4x^3) - 5(3x^2) + 6(2x) - 6(1) + 4(0) \qquad \text{rule 1}$$

$$= 8x^3 - 15x^2 + 12x - 6$$

Note: the constant term always vanishes when differentiated.

The gradient function can be used to find the value of the gradient at a given point. For example when $x = 1$ on the curve of the last example, $y = 2x^4 - 5x^3 + 6x^2 - 6x + 4$

$$\text{gradient} = \frac{dy}{dx} = 8(1) - 15(1) + 12(1) - 6 = -1$$

When $x = 1$, $y = 2 - 5 + 6 - 6 + 4 = 1$.

The equation of the tangent at the point $(1, 1)$ can now be found, since we have a point and the gradient (page 135).

Gradient $= -1 \quad \Rightarrow \quad y = -x + c$ for same constant c

Point $(1, 1) \quad \Rightarrow \quad 1 = -1 + c$

$\Rightarrow \quad c = 2$

$\therefore$ the equation of the tangent is $y = 2 - x$.

Warning: It only makes sense to find the equation of the tangent at a point *on the curve*. An isolated point has no tangent.

A related straight line is the **normal** to the curve at a given point. This line is perpendicular to the tangent.

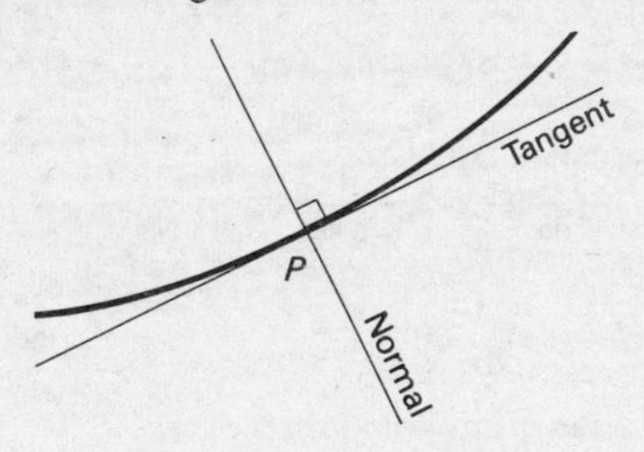

Example

Find the equation of the normal to the curve

$$y = 3x^2 - 5x + 2$$

at the point $(2, 4)$.

Answer

First check that (2, 4) *is* on the curve:

$$3(2^2) - 5(2) + 2 = 12 - 10 + 2 = 4$$

Gradient function $\frac{dy}{dx} = 6x - 5$. At (2, 4) the tangent has gradient

$$= 12 - 5$$

$$= 7$$

$\therefore$ gradient of *normal* $= -\frac{1}{7}$ (perpendicular lines, page 136).

The normal passes through (2, 4); using the formula of page 135 its equation is

$$y - 4 = -\frac{1}{7}(x - 2)$$

$$7y - 28 = -x + 2$$

$$x + 7y - 30 = 0$$

17.5 Applications of Differentiation

As in the example above, the gradient function can be used to find the gradient at a given point. Conversely we can find the coordinates of the point on the curve where the gradient takes a given value.

Example

Find the coordinates of any points on the curve

$$y = x^3 - 4x^2 - 5x - 2$$

at which the gradient is -2.

Answer

The gradient is found by differentiation:

$$\frac{dy}{dx} = 3x^2 - 8x - 5$$

$$\therefore 3x^2 - 8x - 5 = -2$$

at the required points.

$$\Rightarrow \quad 3x^2 - 8x - 3 = 0$$

$$\Rightarrow \quad (3x+1)(x-3) = 0$$

$$\Rightarrow \quad x = -\frac{1}{3} \text{ or } x = 3$$

When $x = -\frac{1}{3}$, $y = (-\frac{1}{3})^3 - 4(-\frac{1}{3})^2 - 5(-\frac{1}{3}) - 2 = -\frac{22}{27}$.
When $x = 3$, $y = 3^3 - 4(3^2) - 5(3) - 2 = -26$
The required points are $(-\frac{1}{3}, -\frac{22}{27})$ and $(3, -26)$.

Turning points can also be found by differentiation. Recall that at a turning point the graph changes direction from up to down (maximum point) or from down to up (minimum point) (page 99).

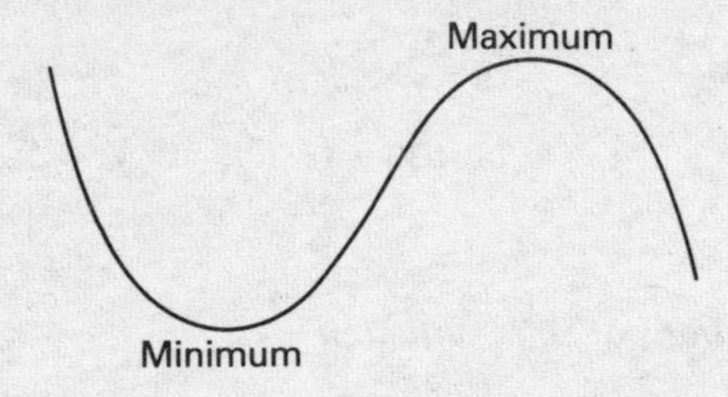

Since an upward slope has positive gradient, and a downward slope has negative gradient, *at a turning point the gradient is zero.*

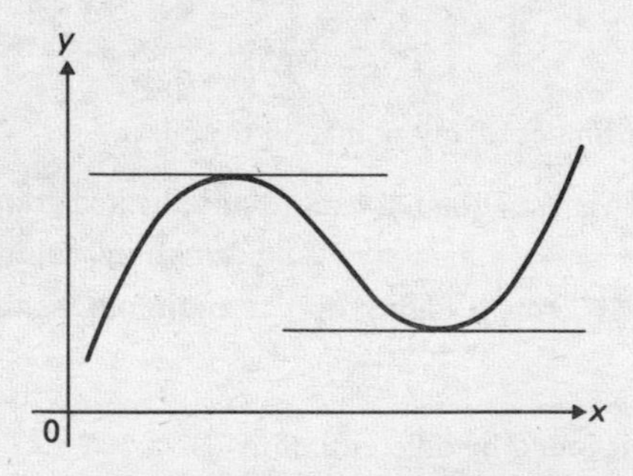

The tangent at a turning point is parallel to the x-axis. So, we can locate turning points by finding when $\frac{dy}{dx} = 0$.

Example

Determine the coordinates of any turning points on the graph of $y = x^3 + 3x^2 - 24x + 5$.

Answer

Gradient $\frac{dy}{dx} = 3x^2 + 6x - 24 = 0$ for turning points.

$\Rightarrow \quad x^2 + 2x - 8 = 0$ dividing by 3

$\Rightarrow \quad (x + 4)(x - 2) = 0$

$\Rightarrow \quad x = -4$ or $x = 2$

When $x = -4$, $y = -64 + 48 + 96 + 5 = 85$
When $x = 2$, $y = 8 + 12 - 48 + 5 = -23$
The turning points are $(-4, 85)$ and $(2, -23)$.

The table on page 82 provides the general shape of a cubic curve, with the positive coefficient of x^3. We deduce that $(-4, 85)$ is the maximum point and $(2, -23)$ is the minimum point.

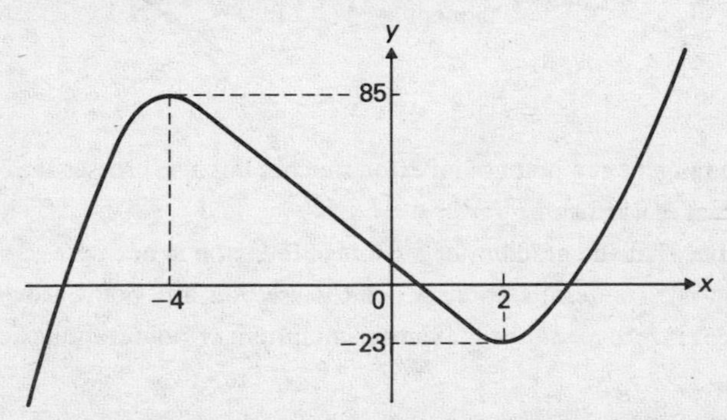

When the given function has a more complicated graph, it is not so easy to distinguish between maximum and minimum points. It is *not* always true that a maximum is higher than a minimum, as the sketches below illustrate.

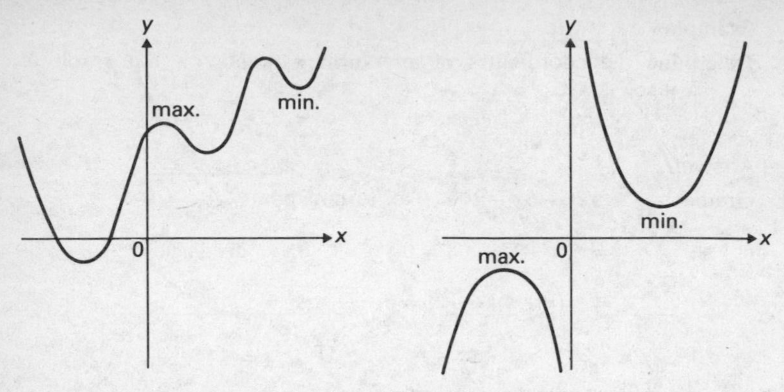

A further complication is that the gradient can be zero at a point which is neither a maximum nor a minimum. Such a point is an example of a point of inflexion.

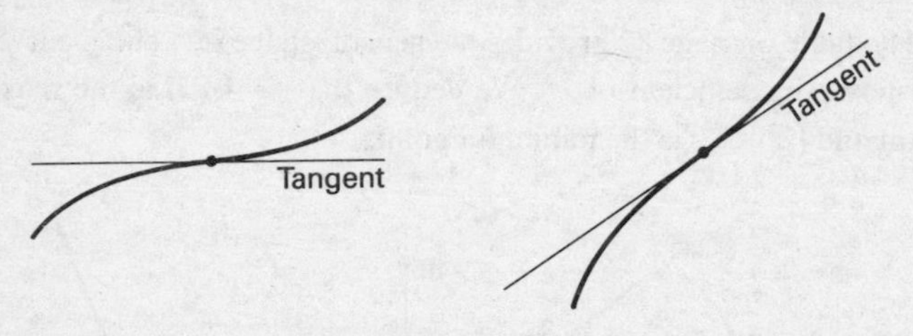

The tangent at a point of inflexion touches but also crosses the curve at the point of contact.

Notice that the gradient of a point of inflexion is not necessarily zero (page 158). The term **stationary point** is used for any point at which the gradient is zero (could be maximum, minimum *or* point of inflexion).

17.6 Tests to Distinguish between Stationary Points

We consider the gradient either side of a turning point.

At a maximum point, the gradient changes sign from + to −.

At a minimum point, the gradient changes sign from − to +.

At a point of inflexion, there is no sign change.

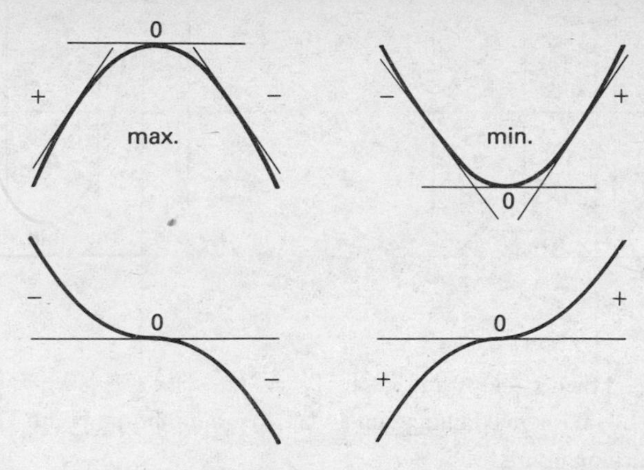

Example

Find any turning points on the curve $y = x^3 - 3x + 6$, distinguishing between them.

Answer

STEP 1

Differentiate and set the gradient equal to zero for a stationary point.

$$\frac{dy}{dx} = 3x^2 - 3 = 0$$

$$\Rightarrow \quad x^2 = 1$$

$$\Rightarrow \quad x = \pm 1$$

STEP 2

When $x = -1$, $y = -1 + 3 + 6 = 8$.

When $x = 1$, $y = 1 - 3 + 6 = 4$.

$(-1, 8)$ and $(1, 4)$ are **stationary points.**

STEP 3

Form tables of the sign of the gradient *near* these points.

$$\frac{dy}{dx} = 3(x - 1)(x + 1)$$

x	<-1	-1	>-1
$\frac{dy}{dx}$	+	0	−
		max	

x	<1	1	>1
$\frac{dy}{dx}$	−	0	+
		min	

(If $x < -1$ then $x - 1 < 0$ and $x + 1 < 0$, $\Rightarrow$ $(x-1)(x+1) > 0$, $\Rightarrow$ $\frac{dy}{dx} > 0$.)
Thus $(-1, 8)$ is a maximum point and $(1, 4)$ is a minimum point. They are both turning points.

Another useful test involves the **second derivative**, obtained by differentiating the gradient function.

Since the second derivative is $\frac{d}{dx}\left(\frac{dy}{dx}\right)$, we write $\frac{d^2y}{dx^2}$ for short.

Similarly $\frac{d^3y}{dx^3}$ is the result of differentiating y 3 times, and so on.

Example

$$y = 4x^4 - x^2 - 6$$

$$\frac{dy}{dx} = 16x^3 - 2x$$

$$\frac{d^2y}{dx^2} = 48x^2 - 2$$

$$\frac{d^3y}{dx^3} = 96x$$

$$\frac{d^4y}{dx^4} = 96$$

$$\frac{d^5y}{dx^5} = 0$$

The notation $y = f(x)$, $\frac{dy}{dx} = f'(x)$, $\frac{d^2y}{dx^2} = f''(x)$, and so on, is also used.

$\frac{d^2y}{dx^2}$ TEST FOR A TURNING POINT

$$\frac{dy}{dx} = 0 \textit{ and } \frac{d^2y}{dx^2} < 0$$

$$\Rightarrow \text{maximum}$$

$$\frac{dy}{dx} = 0 \textit{ and } \frac{d^2y}{dx^2} > 0$$

$$\Rightarrow \text{minimum}$$

$$\frac{dy}{dx} = 0 \textit{ and } \frac{d^2y}{dx^2} = 0$$

Inconclusive (use table of signs instead).

Example

$$y = x^4 - 2x^2 - 6$$

$$\frac{dy}{dx} = 4x^3 - 4x,$$

$$\frac{d^2y}{dx^2} = 12x^2 - 4$$

For a turning point, $\frac{dy}{dx} = 0$.

$\Rightarrow \quad 4x^3 - 4x = 0$

$\Rightarrow \quad 4x(x^2 - 1) = 0$

$\Rightarrow \quad x = 0, x = 1 \text{ or } x = -1$

The 3 points $(0, -6), (-1, -7), (1, -7)$ are stationary points.
When $x = 0, \frac{d^2y}{dx^2} = -4 \quad \Rightarrow \quad (0, -6)$ is a maximum point.

When $x = 1, \frac{d^2y}{dx^2} = 8 \quad \Rightarrow \quad (1, 7)$ is a minimum point.
Similarly $(-1, -7)$ is a minimum point.

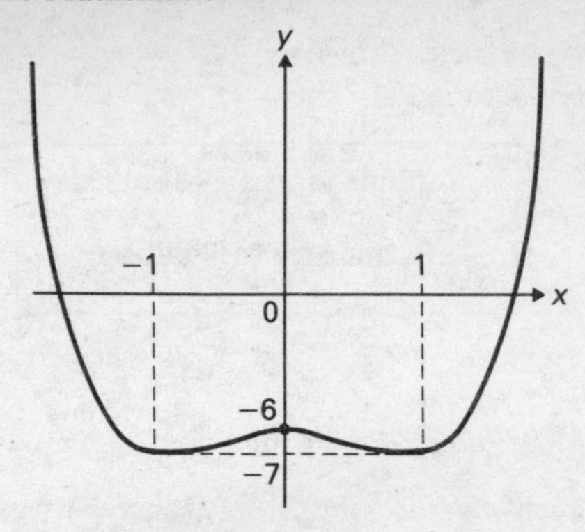

17.7 *Test for a Point of Inflexion*

$\frac{dy}{dx}$ may or may not be zero for a point of inflexion. However we *must* have $\frac{d^2y}{dx^2} = 0$ *and* $\frac{d^2y}{dx^2}$ changes sign either side of the point of inflexion.

Example

(2, 12) is a point of inflexion on the curve $y = x^3 - 6x^2 + 18x - 8$ at which the gradient is not zero (page 154).

Proof

$$\frac{dy}{dx} = 3x^2 - 12x + 18$$

$$\Rightarrow \quad \frac{d^2y}{dx^2} = 6x - 12 = 0 \text{ when } x = 2.$$

For $x = 2$, $y = 8 - 24 + 36 - 8 = 12$.

Now look for a sign change:

x	<2	2	>2
$\frac{d^2y}{dx^2}$	$-$	0	$+$

(when $x < 2$, $6x - 12 < 0$
when $x > 2$, $6x - 12 > 0$)

The sign of $\frac{d^2y}{dx^2}$ does change and so (2, 12) is a point of inflexion.
The gradient at this point is $\frac{dy}{dx} = 3(2^2) - 12(2) + 18 = 6$.

When evaluating y, $\frac{dy}{dx}$, $\frac{d^2y}{dx^2}$, make sure that you substitute the value of x into the *correct* formula!

y formula for the y-coordinate
$\frac{dy}{dx}$ formula for the gradient

17.8 Rate of Change Problems

Recall that gradient measures the rate of change of a function with respect to a variable. For example, velocity is the rate of change of position with time, acceleration is the rate of change of velocity with time.

$$v = \frac{dx}{dt}$$

$$a = \frac{dv}{dt}$$

Example

The graph shows how the position of a particle travelling in a straight line varies with time.

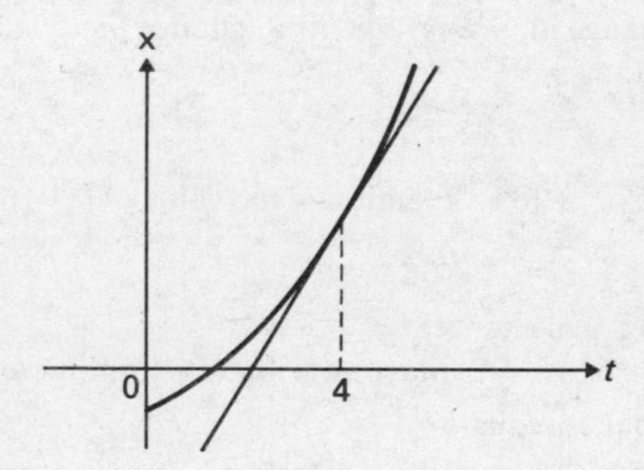

The velocity at time $t = 4$, say, can be found by drawing a tangent to the curve at the point where $t = 4$, and measuring the gradient.

If the position (x) is given as a formula in t (time), the velocity and acceleration can be found by differentiation.

Examples

1. If $x = 3t^2 - 2$, the velocity is given by the formula $v = \frac{dx}{dt} = 6t$. For example, when $t = 2$ the velocity is 12. Acceleration $a = \frac{dv}{dt} = 6$, which is constant.

2. A metal sphere is heated so that it expands. Calculate the rate of increase of the volume with respect to the radius, when the radius is 10 cm.

Answer

If V = volume in cm^3 and r = radius in cm, then $V = \frac{4}{3}\pi r^3$. Differentiating, $\frac{dV}{dr} = 4\pi r^2$.

When $r = 10$, $\frac{dV}{dr} = 4\pi(10)^2 = 400\pi$.

17.9 *Small Changes*

Differentiation can be used to estimate the change in the value of a function corresponding to a small change in the variable. Let $y = f(x)$ be a function of x. Let δx be a small change in x and δy the corresponding change in y. From the derivation of the gradient $\frac{dy}{dx}$ (page 145) it is clear that $\frac{dy}{dx} \approx \frac{\delta y}{\delta x}$, provided that δx is small enough.

Thus

$$\boxed{\delta y \approx \frac{dy}{dx}\delta x}$$

That is, (change in y) $\approx$ (gradient) $\times$ (change in x).

Example

$f(x) = 3x^3 - 5x^2 + 6x - 2$. Estimate the value of $f(1{\cdot}1)$.

Answer

$f(1) = 3 - 5 + 6 - 2 = 2$. Starting with $x = 1$, an increase of $\delta x = 0{\cdot}1$ is required to make x equal to $1{\cdot}1$.

If $y = f(x)$, then $\delta y \approx \frac{dy}{dx}\delta x = f'(x)\delta x$.

$$\frac{dy}{dx} = f'(x) = 9x^2 - 10x + 6$$

$$\Rightarrow \quad f'(1) = 9 - 10 + 6 = 5$$

So $\delta y \approx 5 \times 0{\cdot}1 = 0{\cdot}5$. Thus $f(1{\cdot}1)$

$$\begin{aligned} &= f(1) + \delta y \\ &\approx 2 + 0{\cdot}5 \\ &= 2{\cdot}5 \end{aligned}$$

Note: With the aid of a pocket calculator, $f(1{\cdot}1)$ can be easily evaluated and is found to be 2·543. The example illustrates the 'small change' technique which can be applied to more complicated examples (see page 197). It is also a useful estimation method when you do not have a calculator.

17.10 Change of Variable Rule

The function $f(x) = (2x - 3)^3$ could be differentiated by expanding out the brackets (page 68) and then using the methods of page 68. The same could theoretically be done for $f(x) = (2x - 3)^{100}$. However in practice this would be extremely tedious! (The expansion would have 101 terms.) Fortunately a quicker method can be used. The formula can be simplified by a **change of variable**.

Setting $z = 2x - 3$ gives $y = z^{100}$. We can now find $\frac{dy}{dz}$ by differentiating *y with respect to z*:

$$\frac{dy}{dz} = 100z^{99}$$

However we want $\frac{dy}{dx}$. This is obtained using the rule

$$\boxed{\frac{dy}{dx} = \frac{dy}{dz}\frac{dz}{dx}}$$

(known as **chain rule** or **function of a function rule**).

Since $z = 2x - 3$, then $\frac{dz}{dx} = 2$. From the rule,

$$\begin{aligned} \frac{dy}{dx} = 100z^{99} \times 2 &= 200z^{99} \\ &= 200(2x - 3)^{99} \end{aligned}$$

where we return to the old variable x.

Example

1. Find $\frac{dy}{dx}$ when $x = 1$ for $y = 4(2 - 3x)^7$

Answer

Let $z = 2 - 3x$, so that $y = 4z^7$ and $\frac{dz}{dx} = -3, \frac{dy}{dz} = 28z^6$.

$$\Rightarrow \frac{dy}{dx} = \frac{dy}{dz}\frac{dz}{dx} = -3 \times 28z^6$$
$$= -84(2 - 3x)^6$$
$$= -84(-1)^6 \text{ when } x = 1$$
$$= -84$$

17.11 Product Rule

The differentiation of more complicated functions can be made easier using this rule.

If a function $y = f(x)$ can be expressed as the product of two functions, $y = uv$, say, where u and v are functions of x, then

$$\boxed{\frac{d}{dx}(uv) = \frac{du}{dx}v + u\frac{dv}{dx}} \quad \text{(product rule).}$$

You should remember this formula. Avoid the mistake of calculating $\frac{du}{dx} \times \frac{dv}{dx}$!

Examples

1. $y = (2x + 1)(x^2 - 1)$

Let $u = 2x + 1$ and $v = x^2 - 1$

$$\therefore \quad \frac{du}{dx} = 2 \text{ and } \frac{dv}{dx} = 2x$$

So

$$\frac{dy}{dx} = 2(x^2 - 1) + (2x + 1)(2x)$$

which simplifies to

$$\frac{dy}{dx} = 6x^2 + 2x - 2$$

(You should always simplify your answer as much as possible.)

2. $y = (1-x)^{10}(2+x)^8 \quad u = (1-x)^{10} \quad v = (2+x)^8.$

These functions are differentiated using the change of variable rule (page 161).

Let $z = 1 - x$, so $u = z^{10}$

$$\frac{du}{dz} = 10z^9 = 10(1-x)^9$$

$$\Rightarrow \quad \frac{du}{dx} = \frac{du}{dz}\frac{dz}{dx} = 10(1-x)^9 \times (-1) = -10(1-x)^9$$
$$= 10(x-1)^9$$

(Noticing that $x - 1 = -(1-x)$ and $(-1)^9 = -1$.)

Similarly we find that $\frac{dv}{dx} = 8(2+x)^7$.

With simple functions like $(1-x)^{10}$ and $(2+x)^8$ it should not be necessary to go through the change of variable procedures in full. With practice you should be able to differentiate 'at sight',

$$\boxed{\frac{d}{dx}(f(x))^n = n(f(x))^{n-1}f'(x).}$$

Putting these results together:

$$\frac{dy}{dx} = 10(x-1)^9(2+x)^8 + (1-x)^{10}8(2+x)^7 \quad \text{product rule}$$

$$= 2(x-1)^9(2+x)^7(5(2+x) + 4(x-1)) \quad \text{taking common factors}$$

$$= 2(x-1)^9(2+x)^7(6+9x)$$

Section 18 Approximation Methods for Finding the Roots of Equations

18.1 Graphical Methods

It may be difficult, or impossible, to solve an equation of the form $f(x) = 0$ by purely algebraic manipulation. (For example, when $f(x)$ is a polynomial of degree >4, there is no *general* method to find the roots exactly.)

In such cases we must resort to graphical and numerical techniques.

By plotting a large number of points (x, y) on the graph of $y = f(x)$, a reasonably accurate curve can be drawn. The solutions of $f(x) = 0$ correspond to the x-intercepts of this graph.

This method is slow and difficult to use accurately. Also, without additional knowledge about the number of roots we cannot be sure that roots do not occur outside the range of values plotted (see Section 18.2).

Despite these drawbacks, graphical methods can be useful particularly for providing **first estimates** for roots. Numerical methods are then used to refine these estimates (Section 18.3).

The method can be generalized to equations of the form $f(x) = g(x)$. Plot the two graphs $y = f(x)$, $y = g(x)$ on the same diagram. Solutions correspond to points of intersection of the two graphs.

Example

$$2x^3 + 5x - 3 = 2x + 1$$

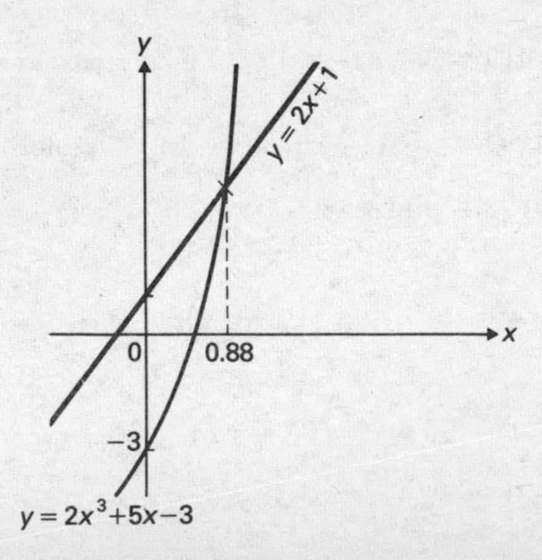

The equation has approximate solution 0·88.

Clearly the graphs should be drawn to as large a scale as possible to achieve the greatest accuracy. You should practise drawing smooth, clear graphs.

Exercise

Draw graphs of the functions

$$(a)\ f(x) \equiv 3x^3 - 2x^2 + 4x - 3$$

$$(b)\ g(x) \equiv x^4 + x^2 - 5$$

$$(c)\ h(x) \equiv x^5 - x^3 + x - 1$$

for $-5 \leqslant x \leqslant 5$ in each case. Find any solutions of the equations $f(x) = 0$, $g(x) = 0$, $h(x) = 0$ in this range, expressing your answers to 1 decimal place accuracy.

18.2 Determining the Number of (Real) Roots

As mentioned above, it is useful to know the number of roots of an equation, and also whether they are positive or negative. A sketch graph showing any turning points is often the easiest way to find this information.

Examples

1. Sketch the graphs of $y = x^3$ and $y = 1 - x^2$ to determine the number of real roots of the equation

$$x^3 + x^2 - 1 = 0$$

Answer

The graphs are

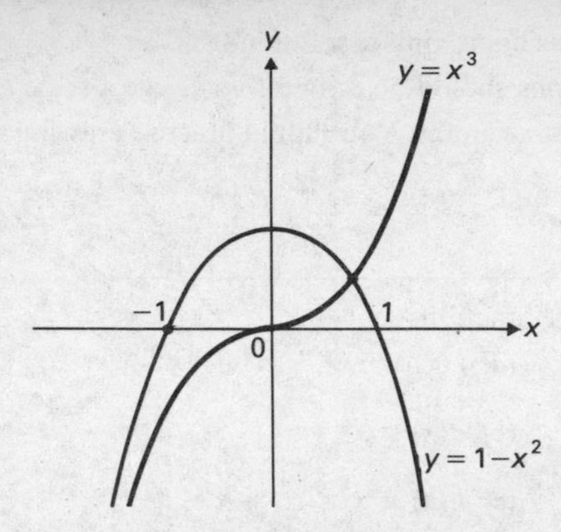

(Make sure that you can sketch graphs of simple functions like these, see page 82.)

$x^3 + x^2 - 1 = 0 \Rightarrow x^3 = 1 - x^2$. Solutions correspond to points of intersection of the graphs.

The graphs meet once only, and so the equation has one real root (which must be positive).

2. By considering stationary values of $f(x) \equiv 2x^3 + 3x^2 + 6x - 5$ show that the equation $f(x) = 0$ has only one real root.

Answer

For stationary values $f'(x) = 0$

$$f'(x) \equiv 6x^2 + 6x + 6 = 0$$

$$\Rightarrow \quad x^2 + x + 1 = 0$$

But this quadratic equation has no real roots (page 91). There are no stationary points on the graph.
The curve cuts the y-axis at $f(0) = -5$. The graph has shape

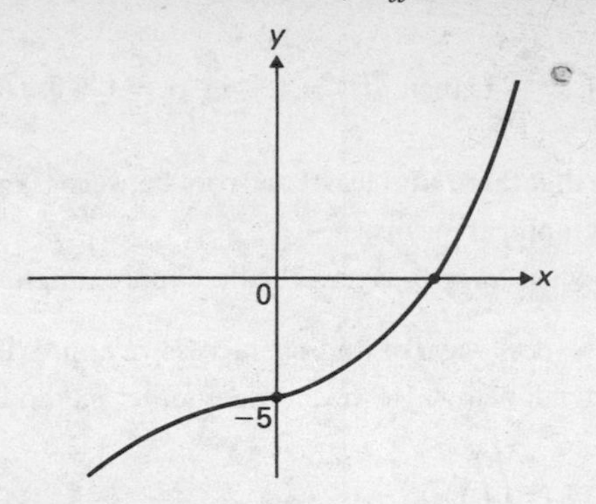

where we are making use of our knowledge of the general shape of a cubic curve (in this case with no turning points) (page 82).

The graph cuts the x-axis once only and so $f(x) = 0$ has one real root.

18.3 Numerical Methods

The idea is that we obtain closer and closer estimates to a root of an equation by applying some **iterative procedure**. That is, the result at each stage is used to determine the next approximation. In this way a sequence $x_0, x_1, x_2, \ldots$ of approximations is obtained. If the sequence approaches a limit, then the method **converges** (page 43). The required accuracy for a problem determines the number of steps needed. If 3·41, 3·415, 3·423, 3·428, 3·4287, 3·42875, for example, is a sequence of approximations, the root is 3·4 to 1 decimal place (1 term), 3·42 to 2 decimal places (2 terms), 3·429 to 3 decimal places (3 terms). In general, work to an accuracy of 2 decimal places more than that required for the answer.

We need a **first approximation** in order to start. One method is to draw graphs, as in Section 18.1. The estimate read off from the graph can then be used in the iterative process.

Another method relies on the fact that for a *continuous* graph (page 33), if $f(a) < 0$ and $f(b) > 0$, then for at least one value of x between a and b, $f(x) = 0$.

Example

If $f(x) = x^3 + x^2 - 1$, then $f(1) = 1 + 1 - 1 = 1 > 0$, $f(0) = 0 + 0 - 1 = -1 < 0$.

We deduce that there is (at least) one root between 0 and 1. (As found on page 166 by graphical means.)

We can now use $x_0 = 0$, say, as the first approximation.

There are several ways of finding successive approximations, we consider two in detail below. However, many other methods are available.

LINEAR INTERPOLATION

Suppose that a root has been located in the range $a < x < b$. An estimate for the root is found by joining points $(a, f(a))$ and $(b, f(b))$ with a straight line segment.

For the example above

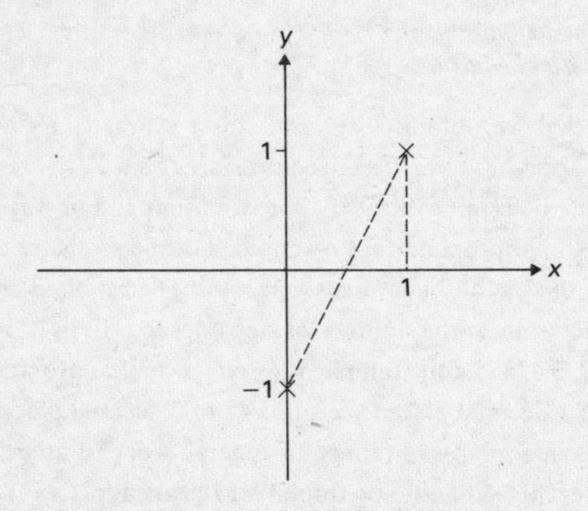

Two similar triangles are formed. The estimated root divides the interval $a \leqslant x \leqslant b$ in the same ratio as the heights of the triangles. This leads to the formula

$$\boxed{x_1 = a - \frac{f(a)(b-a)}{f(b) - f(a)}}$$

Thus $x_1 = 0 - \frac{-1(1-0)}{2} = 0{\cdot}5$, $f(0.5) = -0{\cdot}625$, <0. The root must lie in the interval $0{\cdot}5 < x < 1$.

Repeating the process, $x_2 = 0{\cdot}5 - \frac{f(0{\cdot}5)(1 - 0{\cdot}5)}{f(1) - f(0{\cdot}5)} = 0{\cdot}5 + \frac{0{\cdot}625 \times 0{\cdot}5}{1{\cdot}625}$

$= 0{\cdot}741$. $f(0{\cdot}741) = -0{\cdot}04405 < 0$. The root lies between $0{\cdot}741$ and 1. $x_3 = 0{\cdot}741 + \frac{0{\cdot}04405 \times 0{\cdot}259}{1{\cdot}04405} = 0{\cdot}752$, and so on.

A more efficient method follows.

THE NEWTON–RAPHSON METHOD

If x_n is an approximation to a root of $f(x) = 0$, then for 'well-behaved' functions

$$x_{n+1} = x_n - \frac{f(x_n)}{f'(x_n)}$$

is in general a closer approximation to the root.

Example

Find an approximation to a root of the equation

$$f(x) \equiv 3x^3 - 5x^2 + 6x - 2 = 0$$

$f(0) = -2 < 0, f(1) = 2 > 0$. There is a root between $x = 0$ and $x = 1$. As a first approximation, take $x_0 = 0{\cdot}5$ (midpoint of interval $(0, 1)$). Using Newton–Raphson

$$x_1 = x_0 - \frac{f(x_0)}{f'(x_0)}$$

$$= 0{\cdot}5 - \frac{f(0{\cdot}5)}{f'(0{\cdot}5)}$$

$$= 0{\cdot}5 - \frac{0{\cdot}125}{3{\cdot}25} = 0{\cdot}462 \quad \text{to 3 decimal places}$$

($f'(x) = 9x^2 - 10x + 6$.) The second approximation to the root is $0{\cdot}462$.

Further calculations give $x_2 = 0{\cdot}46181$, $x_3 = 0{\cdot}4618099$. (*Check* these!) To four decimal place accuracy the root is $0{\cdot}4618$.

The justification for the formula is seen in the following diagram

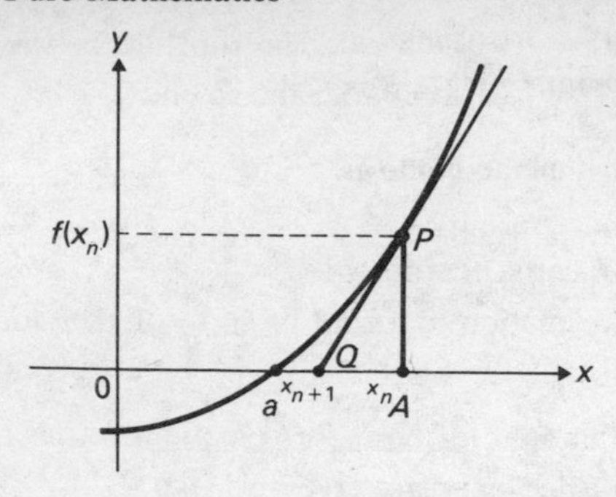

where x_n is an approximation to the true root $x = a$. A line is dropped through A on the x-axis, parallel to the y-axis. This line meets the graph at P. A tangent to the curve is drawn at P, to meet the x-axis at Q. Usually Q will be nearer to the root than A. A corresponds to x_n while Q corresponds to x_{n+1}. Since PQ is a tangent to the curve at $x = x_n$ then gradient of $PQ \equiv f'(x_n) = \frac{PN}{QN} = \frac{f(x_n)}{x_n - x_{n+1}}$

$$\Rightarrow \quad x_n - x_{n+1} = \frac{f(x_n)}{f'(x_n)}$$

$$\Rightarrow \quad x_{n+1} = x_n - \frac{f(x_n)}{f'(x_n)}$$

The following diagram shows how the method breaks down when the starting point is too far from the actual root.

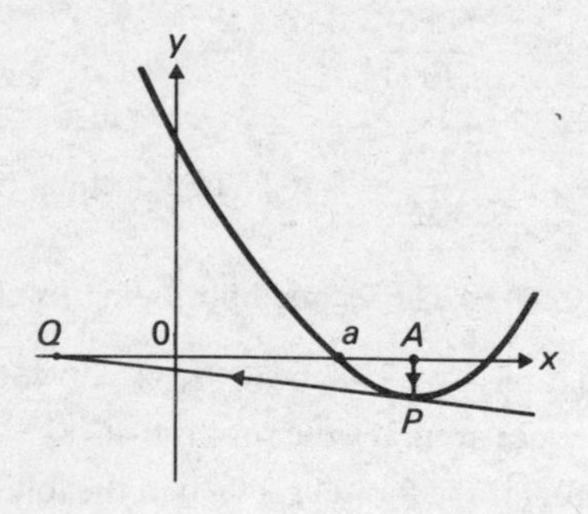

OTHER ITERATIVE METHODS

You may be given another relation which enables x_{n+1} to be calculated from the value of x_n (see iterative sequences, page 45).

Example

Show that the equation

$$x^3 - 2x - 5 = 0$$

has a root between $x = 2$ and $x = 3$.

Use the iterative formula

$$x_{n+1} = (2x_n + 5)^{1/3}$$

with $x_0 = 2$ to obtain four further approximations to this root. Express your working to five decimal place accuracy.

Answer

Let $f(x) = x^3 - 2x - 5$, then

$$f(2) = 8 - 4 - 5 = -1 < 0$$

$$f(3) = 27 - 6 - 5 = 16 > 0$$

$\therefore$ there is a root between $x = 2$ and $x = 3$.

$$x_0 = 2,\ x_1 = (2x_0 + 5)^{1/3} = 9^{1/3} = 2{\cdot}08008$$

$$x_2 = (2x_1 + 5)^{1/3} = 2{\cdot}09235,\ x_3 = 2{\cdot}09422,\ x_4 = 2{\cdot}09450$$

To two decimal places the root is 2·09.

This iterative formula corresponds to rearranging the equation in the form $x = F(x)$. The root corresponds to the point of intersection of the graphs of $y = F(x)$ and $y = x$.

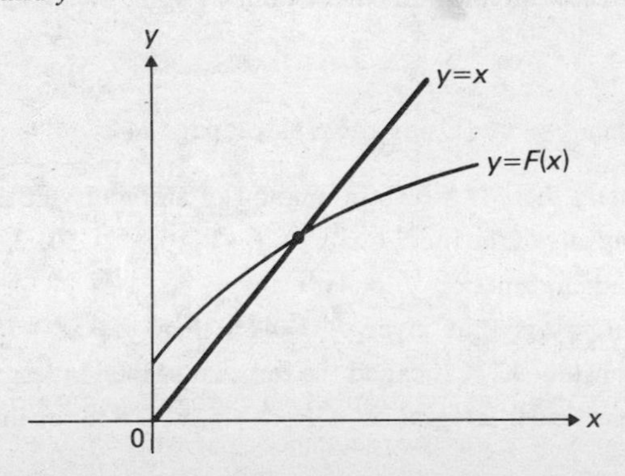

Example

Rearrange the equation $x^4 + 6x - 2 = 0$ into the form $x = F(x)$. Use the formula $x_{n+1} = F(x_n)$ with $x_0 = 0$ to calculate x_1, x_2, x_3 and x_4 to 5 decimal places. Hence determine one root of the equation to 3 decimal places.

Answer

$$x = \frac{2 - x^4}{6} = F(x)$$

$x_0 = 0$, $x_1 = F(0) = \frac{1}{3} = 0.33333$, $x_2 = F(x_1) = 0.33128$, $x_3 = F(x_2) = 0{\cdot}33133$, $x_4 = F(x_3) = 0{\cdot}33132$.

To 3 decimal places the root is 0·331.

There may be many ways to rearrange the equation in the form $x = F(x)$ For the sequence to converge we must have $|F'(x)| < 1$ for values of x considered. This will restrict the choices for $F(x)$.

Section 19 Integration of Polynomial Functions

19.1 Introduction

We have seen how to derive the gradient function $f'(x)$ for a given polynomial function $f(x)$. Conversely, given the gradient function we can often work backwards to find the original function. This process of reverse differentiation is called **integration.**

For simple cases integration can be done at sight.

Example

If $\frac{dy}{dx} = 4x^3$, then $y = x^4$. (Using the table on page 444.)

Unfortunately there is a certain amount of ambiguity in this process. Differentiating any of the functions $x^4 + 1$, $x^4 - 5$, $x^4 + 101{\cdot}3, \ldots$ will also result in a gradient function $\frac{dy}{dx} = 4x^3$.

All we can say is that given $\frac{dy}{dx} = 4x^3$, then $y = x^4 + K$ for some (unknown) constant K. K is called the **constant of integration.** Each value of K gives a **particular integral,** $x^4 + 1$, $x^4 + 6$, $x^4 - 8$ for example.

NOTATION

The statement 'integrate $4x^3$ with respect to variable x' is written symbolically as

$$\int 4x^3\,\mathrm{d}x$$

integrate ↗ (∫); function ↑ ($4x^3$); with respect to x ↑ (dx)

The dx is an *essential* part of this notation. It tells you what variable is involved. For example, $\int x^2\,\mathrm{d}z$ cannot be found unless x is expressed in terms of z.

$\int$, dx should be treated like a pair of brackets. The function to be integrated is placed between them; it is called the **integrand**.

19.2 Rules for Integrating Polynomials

1. The basic differentiation rule of page 148 states

$$\frac{\mathrm{d}}{\mathrm{d}x}(x^n) = nx^{n-1}$$

for any constant n.

$$\Rightarrow \quad \frac{1}{n}\frac{\mathrm{d}}{\mathrm{d}x}(x^n) = x^{n-1}$$

provided $n \neq 0$.

$$\Rightarrow \quad \frac{\mathrm{d}}{\mathrm{d}x}\left(\frac{x^n}{n}\right) = x^{n-1}$$

$$\Rightarrow \quad \frac{\mathrm{d}}{\mathrm{d}x}\left(\frac{x^{n+1}}{n+1}\right) = x^n$$

replacing n by $n+1$, provided $n \neq -1$.

Thus, the corresponding integration rule is

$$\boxed{\int x^n\,\mathrm{d}x = \frac{x^{n+1}}{n+1} + K \quad \text{for } n \neq -1}$$

The rule for $n = -1$ is more complicated, and requires logarithmic functions (see page 297).

2. Just as the terms of a polynomial can be differentiated separately, so they can be integrated separately.

(*a*) $\int(y_1 + y_2)\mathrm{d}x = \int y_1\,\mathrm{d}x + \int y_2\,\mathrm{d}x$
(*b*) $\int ky\,\mathrm{d}x = k\int y\,\mathrm{d}x$ for any *constant k*

Example

$$\int(x^3 - 5x^2 + 6x - 3)\mathrm{d}x = \frac{x^4}{4} - 5\left(\frac{x^3}{3}\right) + 6\left(\frac{x^2}{2}\right) - 3(x) + K$$

$$= \frac{x^4}{4} - \frac{5x^3}{3} + 3x^2 - 3x + K$$

NOTES

1. Only one constant of integration is required.

2. $\int x\,\mathrm{d}x = \int x^1\,\mathrm{d}x = \frac{x^2}{2} + K.$

3. $\int 1\,\mathrm{d}x = \int x^0\,\mathrm{d}x = \frac{x^1}{1} + K = x + K.$

4. $\int y_1 y_2\,\mathrm{d}x$ is *not* $\int y_1\,\mathrm{d}x \int y_2\,\mathrm{d}x$. Products are more complicated! (see page 306).

19.3 Evaluating the Constant

If the gradient function *and* the coordinates of a point on the graph are specified, then the particular integral can be found.

Example

$\frac{\mathrm{d}y}{\mathrm{d}x} = x^5 - 6x + 2$ and $y = 2$ when $x = -1$. Find y in terms of x.
(This is an example of a **differential equation**, involving x, $\frac{\mathrm{d}y}{\mathrm{d}x}$. Such equations can also involve y (page 309).)

Answer

$$y = \int(x^5 - 6x + 2)\mathrm{d}x = \frac{1}{6}x^6 - 3x^2 + 2x + K$$

$y = 2$ when $x = -1$

$$\Rightarrow \quad 2 = \frac{1}{6} - 3 - 2 + K$$

$$\Rightarrow \quad K = \frac{41}{6}$$

$$\Rightarrow \quad y = \frac{1}{6}x^6 - 3x^2 + 2x + \frac{41}{6}$$

19.4 General Integration

Remember that *any* two letters may be used as variables, not just x and y. Thus $\int t^2\,\mathrm{d}t = \frac{1}{3}t^3 + K$, etc.

An expression such as $(2x - 3)^{10}$ can be integrated by expanding out the brackets to obtain an 11-term polynomial. As for differentiation, the integration is simplified by a change of variable (page 161).

Example

$$\int (2x - 3)^{10}\,\mathrm{d}x$$

Let $u = 2x - 3$, $\Rightarrow$ $\int u^{10}\,\mathrm{d}x$. We now must replace $\mathrm{d}x$ by a $\mathrm{d}u$ term, in order that the integration can be done. To do this, differentiate the new variable:

$$u = 2x - 3$$

$$\Rightarrow \quad \frac{\mathrm{d}u}{\mathrm{d}x} = 2$$

If $\frac{\mathrm{d}u}{\mathrm{d}x}$ were a *fraction* (page 145) we could then write

$$\mathrm{d}x = \frac{1}{2}\mathrm{d}u$$

to obtain the integral $\int u^{10}\frac{1}{2}\mathrm{d}u =$

$$\frac{1}{2}\int u^{10}\,\mathrm{d}u = \frac{1}{2}\left(\frac{u^{11}}{11}\right) + K = \frac{u^{11}}{22} + K$$

$$\equiv \frac{(2x-3)^{11}}{22} + K$$

In fact the 'illegal' procedure of splitting $\frac{\mathrm{d}u}{\mathrm{d}x}$ does result in the correct answer. The more correct procedure is to use

$$\int y\,\mathrm{d}x = \int y\left(\frac{\mathrm{d}x}{\mathrm{d}u}\right)\mathrm{d}u$$

where x is regarded as a function of u.

However, splitting the $\mathrm{d}u$ and $\mathrm{d}x$ always results in the correct expression and is a useful aid to calculation. For this reason it is acceptable in your working.

Notice also that the final answer is written in terms of the original variable x.

Example

$$\int 3\left(\frac{1+5x}{2}\right)^{15}\mathrm{d}x$$

Let $u = \dfrac{1+5x}{2}$

$$\Rightarrow \quad \frac{\mathrm{d}u}{\mathrm{d}x} = \frac{5}{2}$$

$$\Rightarrow \quad \text{‘}\mathrm{d}x = \frac{2}{5}\mathrm{d}u\text{’}$$

$$\Rightarrow 3\int u^{15}\frac{2}{5}\mathrm{d}u$$

$$= \frac{6}{5}\int u^{15}\,\mathrm{d}u$$

$$= \frac{6}{5}\left(\frac{u^{16}}{16}\right) + K$$

$$= \frac{3u^{16}}{40} + K$$

$$= \frac{3}{40}\left(\frac{1+5x}{2}\right)^{15} + K$$

Notice that the *constant* 3 is brought outside the integral. This can *only* be done for constant terms.

19.5 Definite Integrals

The integrals considered above are **indefinite** – they contain the arbitrary constant K.

The integral of a function is also a function. Let

$$F(x) = \int f(x)\,dx$$

Define the **definite integral** as $\int_a^b f(x)\,dx = F(b) - F(a)$.

(Integrate the function, put in the top value of x, then the bottom value and then subtract.) a and b are called the **limits** of the integral.

Definite integrals are used for calculating areas and other quantities.

Examples

1. $$\int_{-3}^{5} (x^3 - 5x + 7)\,dx = \left[\frac{x^4}{4} - \frac{5x^2}{2} + 7x\right]_{-3}^{5}$$

$$= \left(\frac{5^4}{4} - \frac{5(5)^2}{2} + 7(5)\right) - \left(\frac{(-3)^4}{4} - \frac{5(-3)^2}{2} + 7(-3)\right)$$

$$= 152$$

Note the use of square brackets, also with limits.

Thus $\int_a^b f(x)\,dx = [F(x)]_a^b$ where $F(x) = \int f(x)\,dx$.

Note also that no constant of integration is required. For example:

$$\int_a^b x^2\,dx = \left[\frac{x^3+k}{3}\right]_a^b \equiv \left(\frac{b^3}{3}+K\right)-\left(\frac{a^3}{3}+K\right)$$

$$= \frac{b^3}{3} - \frac{a^3}{3}$$

The constants cancel out, and so are not necessary.

2. $$\int_3^0 (x^4+2x)\,dx = \left[\frac{x^5}{5}+x^2\right]_3^0 = (0) - \left(\frac{3^5}{5}+3^2\right) = -57{\cdot}6$$

The result of a definite integration is *a number.*

Definite integrals have the following useful properties

1. $$\int_a^b y_1\,dx + \int_a^b y_2\,dx = \int_a^b (y_1+y_2)\,dx$$

Example

$$\int_{-1}^2 (x^2+x+2)\,dx - \int_{-1}^2 (2x^2)\,dx = \int_{-1}^2 (x^2+x+2-2x^2)\,dx$$

$$= \int_{-1}^2 (-x^2+x+2)\,dx$$

$$= \left[-\frac{x^3}{3}+\frac{x^2}{2}+2x\right]_{-1}^2$$

$$= -\frac{8}{3}+2+4-\frac{1}{3}-\frac{1}{2}+2 = \frac{9}{2}$$

The limits must be the *same* in each integral.

2. $$\int_a^c y\,dx = \int_a^b y\,dx + \int_b^c y\,dx$$

(The range of integration can be split.)

Example

$$\int_1^4 x^2\,dx = \left[\frac{x^3}{3}\right]_1^4 = \frac{4^3}{3} - \frac{1^3}{3} = \frac{64}{3} - \frac{1}{3} = \frac{63}{3} = 21$$

and

$$\int_1^2 x^2\,dx + \int_2^4 x^2\,dx = \left[\frac{x^2}{3}\right]_1^2 + \left[\frac{x^2}{3}\right]_2^4$$

$$= \frac{8}{3} - \frac{1}{3} + \frac{64}{3} - \frac{8}{3} = \frac{63}{3} = 21$$

3. (Change of variable for definite integrals)

Example

$$\int_1^3 (3x-2)^5\,dx$$

Let

$$u = 3x - 2$$

$$\frac{du}{dx} = 3$$

$$\Rightarrow \quad dx = \frac{1}{3}du$$

The limits 1 and 3 are x values. New u-limits must be calculated for the u-integral, using the formula $u = 3x - 2$. Thus

x	1	3
u	1	7

$$\Rightarrow \quad \frac{1}{3}\int_1^7 u^5\,du = \frac{1}{3}\left[\frac{u^6}{6}\right]_1^7 = \frac{1}{3}\left(\frac{7^6}{6} - \frac{1}{6}\right) = 6\,536$$

You could also do this by replacing u by $3x - 2$ after integrating, and use the x-limits:

$$\int_1^3 (3x-2)^5\,dx = \frac{1}{3}\int_{x=1}^{x=3} u^5\,du = \frac{1}{3}\left[\frac{u^6}{6}\right]_{x=1}^{x=3} = \frac{1}{3}\left[\frac{(3x-2)^6}{6}\right]_1^3$$

$$= 6536$$

However, you may well forget that the limits are x-values and mistakenly calculate $\frac{1}{3}\left[\frac{u^6}{6}\right]_{u=1}^{u=3}$. It is far safer to rewrite the whole integral in terms of u, *including the limits.*

19.6 Applications of Define Integration to Areas

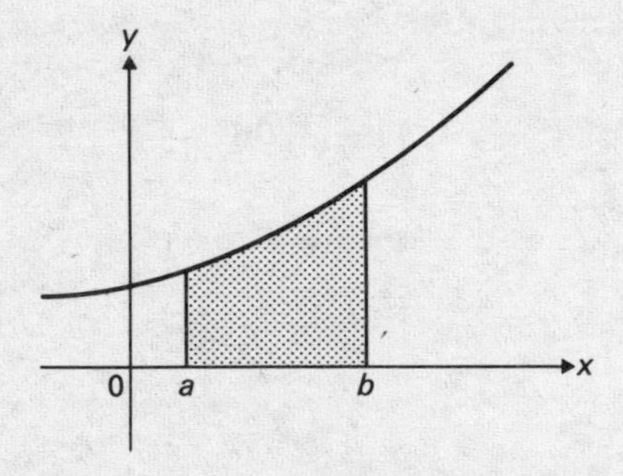

The diagram shows the area bounded by the curve $y = f(x)$, the x-axis and the lines $x = a$ and $x = b$. This area is found by evaluating the definite integral.

$$\boxed{\text{Area} = \int_a^b f(x)\,dx}$$

Note: The area can also be defined by the inequalities $0 \leqslant y \leqslant f(x)$, $a \leqslant x \leqslant b$.

This formula is correct as long as the section of the graph between $x = a$ and $x = b$ lies above the y-axis.

If the graph lies *below* the x-axis, the corresponding formula is

$$\text{Area} = -\int_a^b f(x)\,dx$$

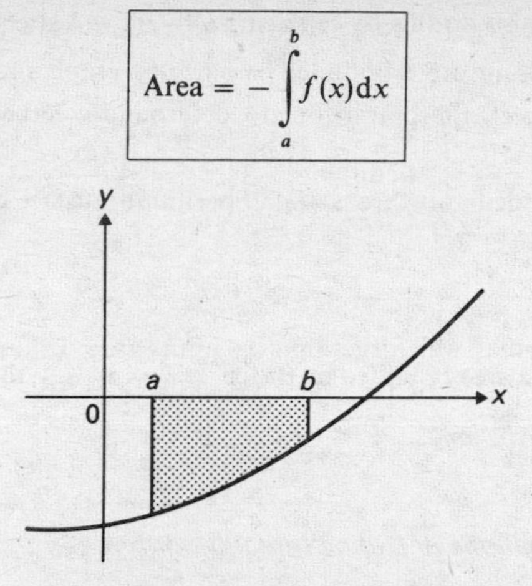

This is because the integral gives a negative answer, but an area must be positive.

If the curve crosses the x-axis, so that part is above and part below

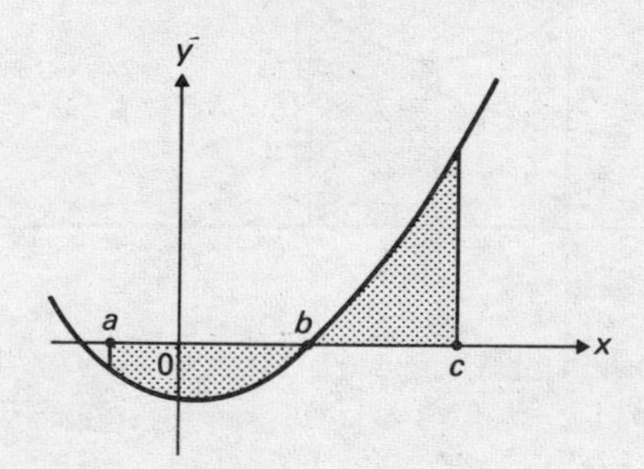

the integral must be split:

$$\text{Area} = -\int_a^b f(x)\,dx + \int_b^c f(x)\,dx$$

(Compare with result 2 on page 178)

This area is *not* given by $\int_a^b f(x)\,dx$. In this integral the negative and positive parts cancel to some extent and do not give the whole area.

When calculating areas bounded by part of a graph and the x-axis, it is essential to sketch the graph first to determine whether it crosses the x-axis.

Also, when calculating areas, the upper limit must be greater than the lower limit.

Examples

1. Calculate the area bounded by the curve $y = x^2 + 1$, the x-axis and the lines $x = 1$, $x = 2$.

Answer

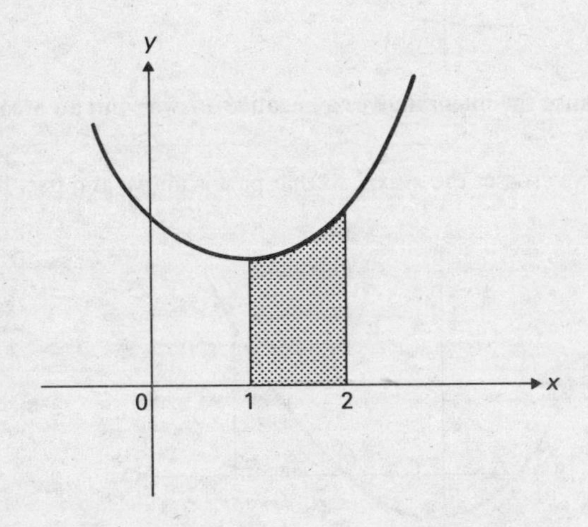

$$\text{The area is } \int_1^2 (x^2 + 1)\,dx = \left[\frac{x^3}{3} + x\right]_1^2$$

$$= \left(\frac{8}{3} + 2\right) - \left(\frac{1}{3} + 1\right)$$

$$= \frac{7}{3} + 1 = \frac{10}{3}$$

2. Calculate the area between $y = x(x + 1)(x - 2)$ and the x-axis.

Answer

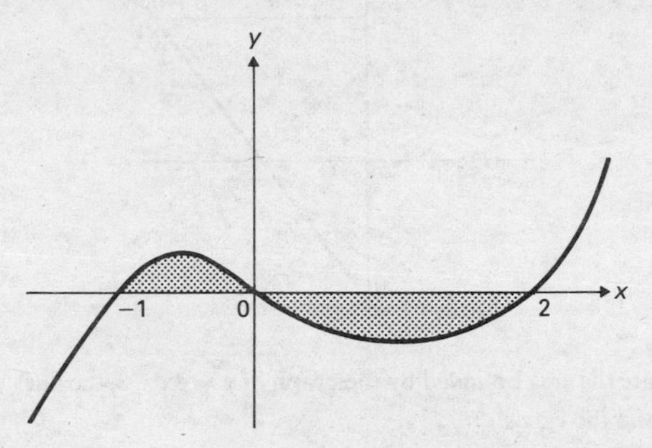

(The cubic curve cuts the x-axis when $x = 0, -1, 2$.)

$$\text{The area is } \int_{-1}^{0} y\,dx - \int_{0}^{2} y\,dx$$

$$= \int_{-1}^{0} (x^3 - x^2 - 2x)\,dx - \int_{0}^{2} (x^3 - x^2 - 2x)\,dx$$

$$= \left[\frac{x^4}{4} - \frac{x^3}{3} - x^2\right]_{-1}^{0} - \left[\frac{x^4}{4} - \frac{x^3}{3} - x^2\right]_{0}^{2}$$

$$= 0 - \left(\frac{1}{4} + \frac{1}{3} - 1\right) - \left(\frac{16}{4} - \frac{8}{3} - 4\right) + 0$$

$$= -\frac{17}{4} + \frac{7}{3} + 5 = \frac{37}{12}$$

We can find areas bounded by segments of the graph and the y-axis.

Example

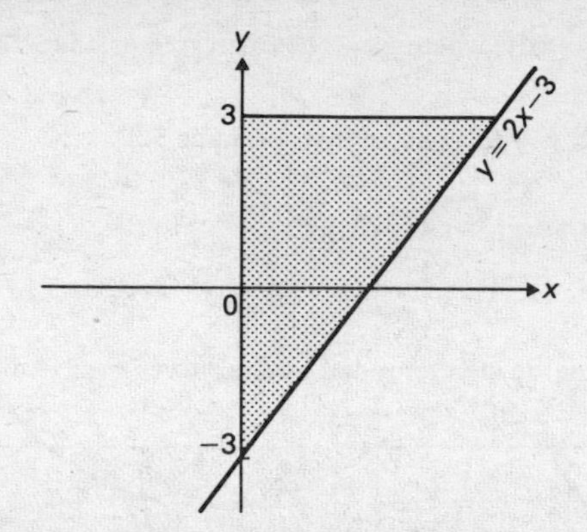

Calculate the area bounded by the graph of $y = 2x - 3$, the lines $y = -3$, $y = 3$ and the y-axis.

Answer

$$y = 2x - 3 \Rightarrow \quad x = \frac{y+3}{2}$$

The required area is

$$\int_{-3}^{3} \left(\frac{y+3}{2}\right) dy = \frac{1}{2}\left[\frac{1}{2}y^2 + 3y\right]_{-3}^{3}$$

$$= \frac{1}{2}\left[\left(\frac{9}{2}+9\right) - \left(\frac{9}{2}-9\right)\right] = 9 \text{ square units}$$

Notice how x and y have changed roles in the integration.

In general, the area shown in the following diagram

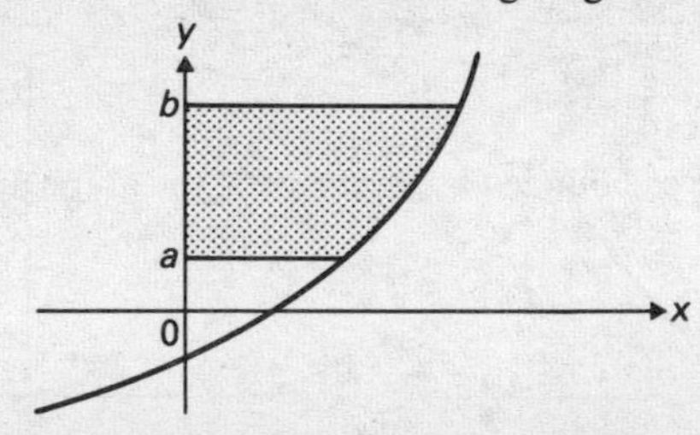

is given by $\int_{y=a}^{y=b} x\,dy$, where x can be expressed as a function of y (which is possible when $y = f(x)$ has an inverse, page 32).

THE AREA BETWEEN TWO CURVES

Example
Calculate the finite area bounded by the curves $y = 2x^2$ and $y = x^2 + x + 2$.

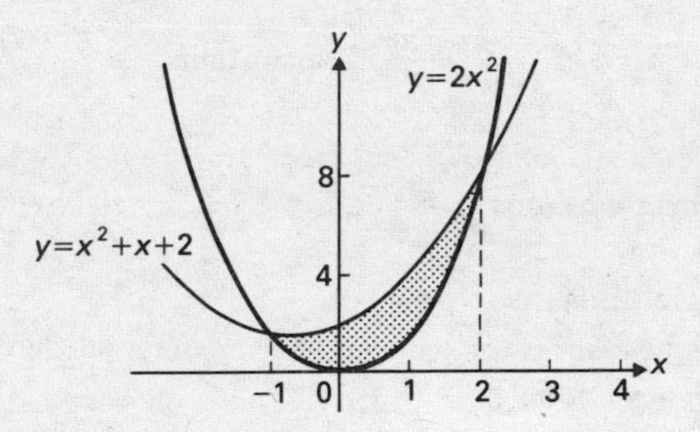

The curves intersect twice. We must calculate the x-coordinates of the points of intersection.

$$2x^2 = x^2 + x + 2$$ see page 93

$$\Rightarrow \quad x^2 - x - 2 = 0$$

$$\Rightarrow \quad (x - 2)(x + 1) = 0$$

$$\Rightarrow \quad x = 2 \text{ or } x = -1$$

The shaded area is found by *subtraction*.

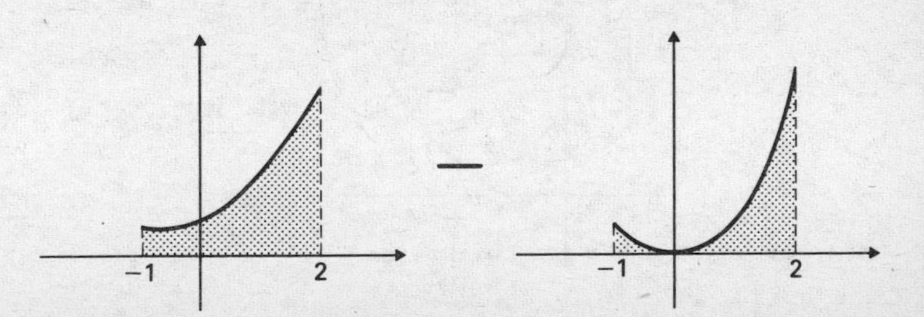

$$\text{Area} = \int_{-1}^{2} (x^2 + x + 2)\,dx - \int_{-1}^{2} (2x^2)\,dx$$

$$= \int_{-1}^{2} (-x^2 + x + 2)\,dx \qquad \text{property 1, page 178}$$

$$= \left[-\frac{x^3}{3} + \frac{x^2}{2} + 2x \right]_{-1}^{2} = \left(-\frac{8}{3} + 2 + 4 \right) - \left(\frac{1}{3} - \frac{1}{2} - 2 \right)$$

$$= 5{\cdot}5 \text{ square units}$$

19.7 Other Applications

SOLIDS OF REVOLUTION

If an area in the plane is rotated completely about a line in the plane, a **solid of revolution** is formed.

When the solid is formed by rotating the area bounded by the graph of $y = f(x)$, the lines $x = a$, $x = b$ and the x-axis, about the x-axis

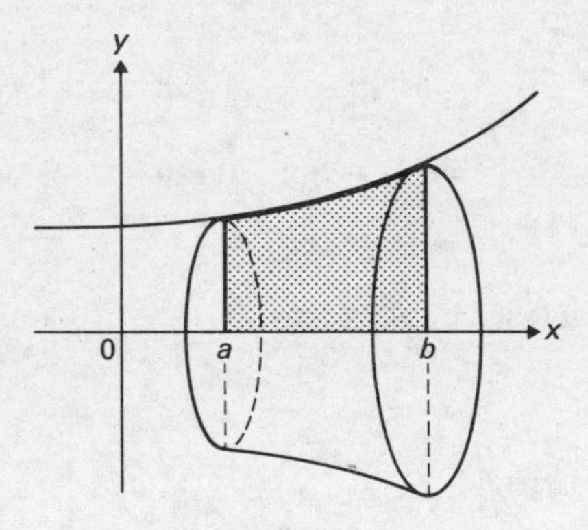

the volume of this solid is given by $\int_a^b \pi y^2\,dx$.

The corresponding formula for an area rotated about the y-axis is

$$\int_a^b \pi x^2 \, dy.$$

Example

The area defined by $0 \leqslant y \leqslant x^2 + 1$ and $1 \leqslant x \leqslant 2$ is rotated through 360° about the x-axis. Calculate the volume of the solid formed.

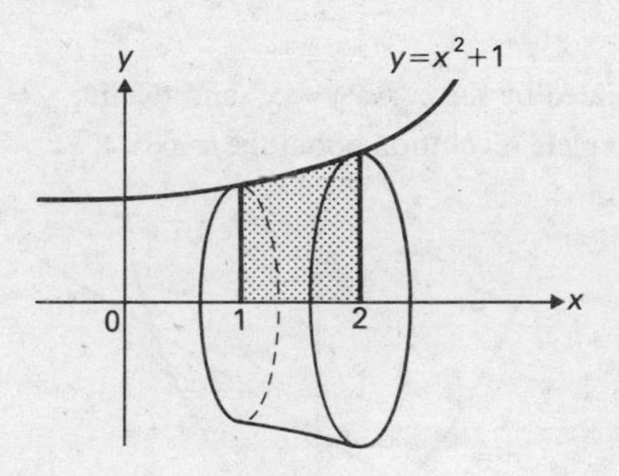

Answer

$$\text{Volume} = \pi \int_1^2 (x^2+1)^2 \, dx = \pi \int_1^2 (x^4 + 2x^2 + 1) dx$$

$$= \pi \left[\frac{x^5}{5} + \frac{2x^3}{3} + x \right]_1^2$$

$$= \pi \left(\frac{32}{5} + \frac{16}{3} + 2 - \frac{1}{5} - \frac{2}{3} - 1 \right)$$

$$= \pi \left(\frac{31}{5} + \frac{4}{3} + 1 \right) = \pi \left(\frac{93 + 70 + 15}{15} \right)$$

$$= \frac{178\pi}{15} \text{ cubic units}$$

A solid can be formed by rotating the area bounded by two curves $y = f(x)$ and $y = g(x)$ about the x-axis.

The volume of this solid is

$$\pi \int_a^b (f(x))^2 \, dx - \pi \int_a^b (g(x))^2 \, dx$$

$$= \pi \int_a^b \{(f(x))^2 - (g(x))^2\} \, dx$$

Example

The area bounded by the curve $y = x^2$ and the line $y = x + 2$ is rotated through a complete revolution about the x-axis.

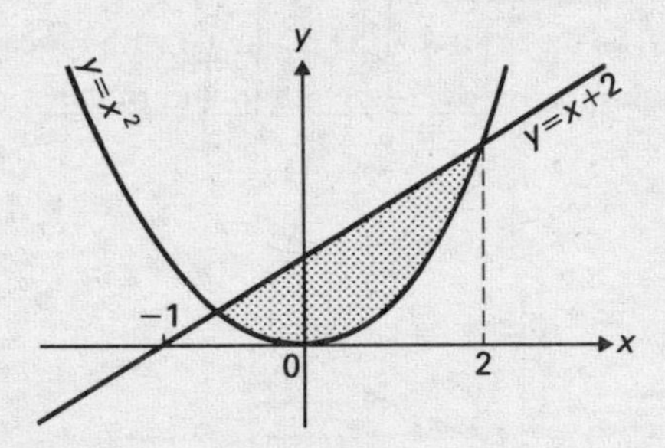

The curves intersect when

$$x^2 = x + 2$$

$$x^2 - x - 2 = 0$$

$$(x - 2)(x + 1) = 0$$

$$x = -1 \text{ or } x = 2$$

The required volume is

$$\pi \int_{-1}^{2} (x + 2)^2 - (x^2)^2 \, dx \equiv \pi \int_{-1}^{2} (x^2 + 4x + 4 - x^4) \, dx$$

$$= \pi \left[\frac{x^3}{3} + 2x^2 + 4x - \frac{x^5}{5} \right]_{-1}^{2}$$

$$= \left(\frac{8}{3} + 8 + 8 - \frac{32}{5}\right)\pi - \left(-\frac{1}{3} + 2 - 4 + \frac{1}{5}\right)\pi$$

$$= \left(\frac{8+1}{3} - \frac{33}{5} + 18\right)\pi = \left(\frac{105-33}{5}\right)\pi$$

$$= \frac{72\pi}{5} \text{ cubic units}$$

MEAN VALUES

The mean value of the function $y = f(x)$ over the interval $a \leqslant x \leqslant b$ is defined as $\bar{y} = \frac{1}{b-a}\int_a^b f(x)\mathrm{d}x$. If y is positive throughout this range, then $\bar{y}$ is interpreted as the height of the rectangle with base $(b - a)$ which has area equal to that bounded by the graph and the lines $x = a$, $x = b$ and the x-axis.

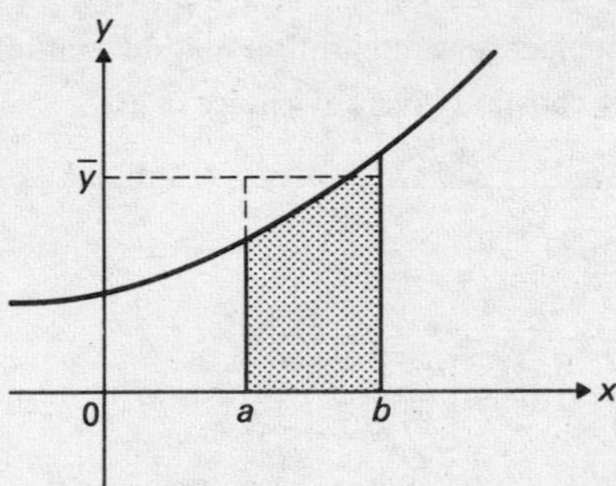

Example

Find the mean value of the function $y = x^3 - 2x + 1$ over the interval [1, 4].

Answer

$$\bar{y} = \frac{1}{4-1}\int_1^4 (x^3 - 2x + 1)\mathrm{d}x = \frac{1}{3}\left[\frac{x^4}{4} - x^2 + x\right]_1^4$$

$$= \frac{1}{3}\left\{\left(\frac{4^4}{4} - 4^2 + 4\right) - \left(\frac{1}{4} - 1 + 1\right)\right\} = \frac{1}{3}\left(52 - \frac{1}{4}\right) = \frac{69}{4}$$

19.8 The Fundamental Theorem of Calculus

The definite integral $\int_a^x f(t)\,\mathrm{d}t$ is a function of x, where a is a constant.

Example

$$\int_1^x t^2\,\mathrm{d}t = \left[\frac{t^3}{3}\right]_1^x = \frac{x^3}{3} - \frac{1}{3}$$

If the resulting function of x can be differentiated (true for all functions you are likely to meet at this level), then we have the result:

$$\frac{\mathrm{d}}{\mathrm{d}x}\left[\int_a^x f(t)\,\mathrm{d}t\right] = f(x)$$

which expresses the fact that integration and differentiation are inverses (up to an arbitrary constant given by choice of a).

Example

Let $f(t) = t^2$ so that

$$\int_a^x f(t)\mathrm{d}t = \left[\frac{t^3}{3}\right]_a^x = \frac{x^3 - a^3}{3}$$

$$\text{So } \frac{\mathrm{d}}{\mathrm{d}x}\int_a^x f(t)\mathrm{d}t = \frac{\mathrm{d}}{\mathrm{d}x}\left(\frac{x^3 - a^3}{3}\right)$$

$$= x^2 = f(x)$$

A similar result is

$$\int_a^b \frac{\mathrm{d}}{\mathrm{d}t}(f(t))\,\mathrm{d}t = f(b) - f(a).$$

INFORMAL PROOF OF THE FUNDAMENTAL THEOREM OF CALCULUS

Let $F(x) = \int_a^x f(t)\mathrm{d}t$. $F(x)$ is represented by the shaded area on the diagram. We have to prove that $F'(x) = f(x)$.

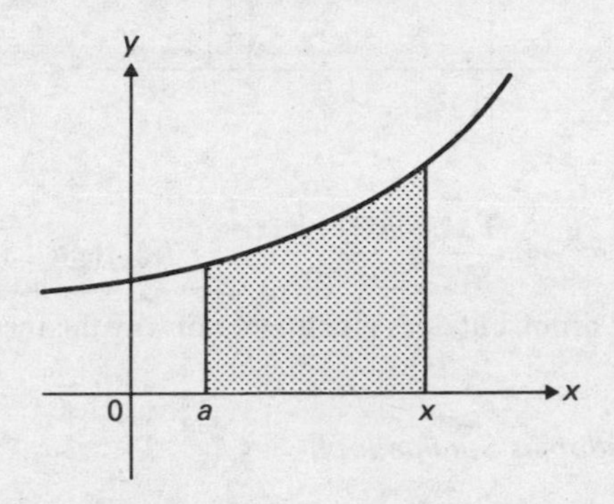

The method of first principles for differentiation (page 145) leads us to consider

$$\frac{F(x+\delta x) - F(x)}{\delta x} = \frac{\int_a^{x+\delta x} f(t)\mathrm{d}t - \int_a^x f(t)\mathrm{d}t}{\delta x}$$

$$= \frac{\int_x^{x+\delta x} f(t)\mathrm{d}t}{\delta x}$$

property 2, page 178

But this is just the mean value of $f(t)$ over the interval $x \leqslant t \leqq x + \delta x$. For 'reasonable' functions, the mean value approaches $f(x)$ as $\delta x \to 0$ (i.e. as the interval shrinks, the mean value tends to limit $f(x)$).

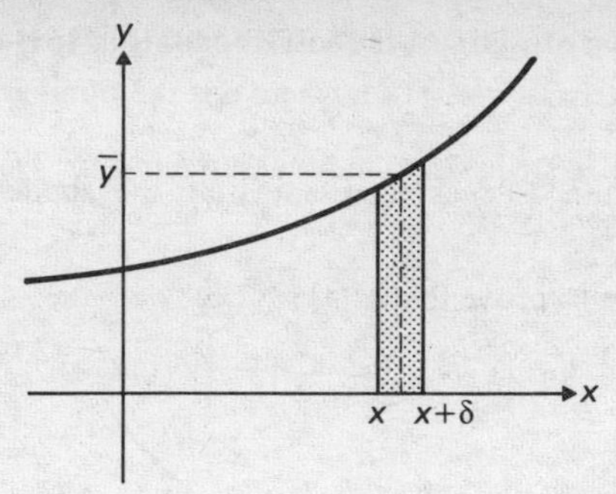

And since, as $\delta x \to 0$, $\dfrac{F(x+\delta x)-F(x)}{\delta x} \to F'(x)$, then $F'(x) = f(x)$. This is not a formal proof, but does give an idea of why the theorem is true.

19.9 Integration as Summation

The area between a segment of a graph and the x-axis can be approximated by dividing into strips as shown below, *where we suppose that the curve lies above the x-axis.*

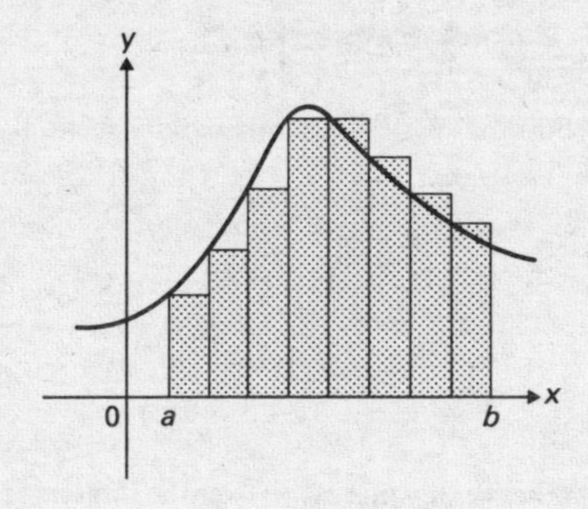

The more strips taken, the closer the area of the strips is to the true area beneath the graph.

For a given value of x, x_i say, the corresponding strip is of height $f(x_i)$. The area of this strip is $\frac{(b-a)}{n}f(x_i)$, where n is the number of strips. The total area for all n strips is found by summing $\sum_{i=1}^{n} f(x_i)\left(\frac{b-a}{n}\right)$. For reasonable functions

$$\lim_{n\to\infty} \sum_{i=1}^{n} f(x_i)\left(\frac{b-a}{n}\right) = \int_a^b f(x)\mathrm{d}x$$

The definite integral is thus the limit of a sequence of sums. Note that, in this correspondence, $\frac{b-a}{n}$ represents a small increase in x-value (the strip width), and so in the limit corresponds to the dx term. Thus

$$\int_a^b f(x)\mathrm{d}x \approx \sum_{i=1}^{n} f(x_i)\delta x$$

when many strips are taken, so that δx is small. The case when the graph lies below the x-axis can be treated similarly.

Section 20 Worked Examples

1. Find the coordinates of the point of intersection of the two lines $2x + 3y - 5 = 0$ (1) and $x + y + 2 = 0$ (2). Line (1) meets the x-axis at A, line (2) meets the y-axis at B. Find the equation of the line through A and B.

Answer

$$2x + 3y - 5 = 0 \ (1)$$

$$x + y + 2 = 0 \ (2)$$

$$(2) \times 2 \Rightarrow 2x + 2y + 4 = 0 \ (3)$$

$$(1) - (3) \Rightarrow y - 9 = 0$$

$$\Rightarrow y = 9$$

$$(2) \Rightarrow x + 9 + 2 = 0$$

$$\Rightarrow x = -11$$

The lines intersect at $(-11, 9)$.

$2x + 3y - 5 = 0$ meets the x-axis when $y = 0 \Rightarrow x = 2{\cdot}5$.

A is $(2{\cdot}5, 0)$.

$x + y + 2 = 0$ meets the y-axis when

$x = 0 \Rightarrow y = -2$.

B is $(0, -2)$.

The line through A and B has equation

$$y - 0 = \frac{-2 - 0}{0 - 2{\cdot}5}(x - 2{\cdot}5)$$

$$\Rightarrow 2{\cdot}5y = 2x - 5$$

$$\Rightarrow \quad 5y = 4x - 10$$

$$\Rightarrow 4x - 5y - 10 = 0$$

2.

s	8	15·8	25·8	38·7	54	70·8	91·5
t	1	1·5	2	2·5	3	3·5	4

The table shows pairs of values (s, t) believed to satisfy a relation of the form $s = at + bt^2$ where a and b are constants.

By drawing a suitable *linear* graph, show that the given values satisfy approximately a relation of this form, and estimate values of a and b. Express your answers to 1 decimal place.

Estimate the value of s when $t = 3{\cdot}4$, giving your answer to 1 decimal place.

Answer

$$s = at + bt^2$$ isolate a constant

$$\Rightarrow \quad \frac{s}{t} = a + bt$$ compare with $y = a + bx$

This equation represents a straight line with gradient b, cutting the $\frac{s}{t}$ axis at $\frac{s}{t} = a$.

t	1	1·5	2	2·5	3	3·5	4
$\frac{s}{t}$	8	10·5	12·9	15·5	18	20·2	22·9

compute values of $\frac{s}{t}$

The graph of $\frac{s}{t}$ against t is

show your working on a separate sheet, *not* on the graph paper

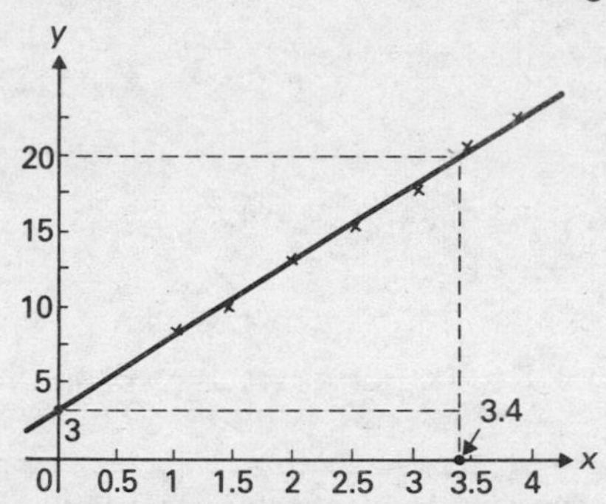

The graph is approximately a straight line, and so the relationship can be assumed correct.

Gradient $b = \frac{17}{3{\cdot}4} = 5{\cdot}0$ — 1 decimal place

The line cuts the $\frac{s}{t}$ axis at $a = 3{\cdot}0$, and so the relation is $\frac{s}{t} = 3 + 5t$, or $s = 3t + 5t^2$.

When $t = 3{\cdot}4$, $s = 3(3{\cdot}4) + 5(3{\cdot}4)^2 = 68{\cdot}0$.

3. Find the equations of the tangents to the curve $y = x^3 - 5x + 1$ which are parallel to the line $y = 7x + 2$.

Answer

$y = 7x + 2$ has gradient 7. The gradient of the curve is $\frac{dy}{dx} = 3x^2 - 5 = 7$ for tangents parallel to the given line

$$\Rightarrow \quad 3x^2 = 12$$
$$\Rightarrow \quad x^2 = 4$$
$$\Rightarrow \quad x = \pm 2$$

two roots

The points on the curve where the gradient is 7 are

$(-2, 3)$ and $(2, -1)$

when $x = -2$
$y = (-2)^3 - 5(-2) + 1$
$= 3$; when $x =$
2, $y = 2^3 - 5(2) + 1$
$= -1$

The tangents are

$$y - 3 = 7(x + 2)$$
$$y = 7x + 17$$

$y - y_1 = m(x - x_1)$

and

$$y + 1 = 7(x - 2)$$
$$y = 7x - 15$$

4. Calculate the coordinates of any turning points on the graph of $y = (x + 2)^2(x - 2)$, distinguishing between maximum and minimum. Find also any points of inflexion and *sketch* the graph of this function.

Answer

$$y = (x + 2)^2(x - 2)$$
$$\frac{dy}{dx} = 2(x + 2)(x - 2) + (x + 2)^2 \quad (1)$$

product rule, page 162

$$= (x + 2)(2x - 4 + x + 2)$$
$$= (x + 2)(3x - 2)$$

For a turning point

$(x + 2)(3x - 2) = 0$

$\frac{dy}{dx} = 0$

$$x = -2 \text{ or } x = \tfrac{2}{3}$$
$$y = 0 \qquad y = \frac{-256}{27}$$
$$\frac{d^2y}{dx^2} = 1(3x - 2) + (x + 2)(3)$$

product

$$= 6x + 4$$
$$x = -2 \Rightarrow \frac{d^2y}{dx^2} = -8 < 0, \text{ maximum}$$
$$x = \tfrac{2}{3} \Rightarrow \frac{d^2y}{dx^2} = 8 > 0, \text{ minimum}$$

For a point of inflexion

$$6x + 4 = 0$$

$\frac{d^2y}{dx^2} = 0$, page 158

$$\Rightarrow x = -\tfrac{4}{6} = -\tfrac{2}{3}, y = -\tfrac{128}{27}$$

$$x < -\frac{2}{3} \Rightarrow \frac{d^2y}{dx^2} < 0$$

$$x > -\frac{2}{3} \Rightarrow \frac{d^2y}{dx^2} > 0$$

$\therefore (-\frac{2}{3}, -\frac{128}{27})$ is a point of inflexion

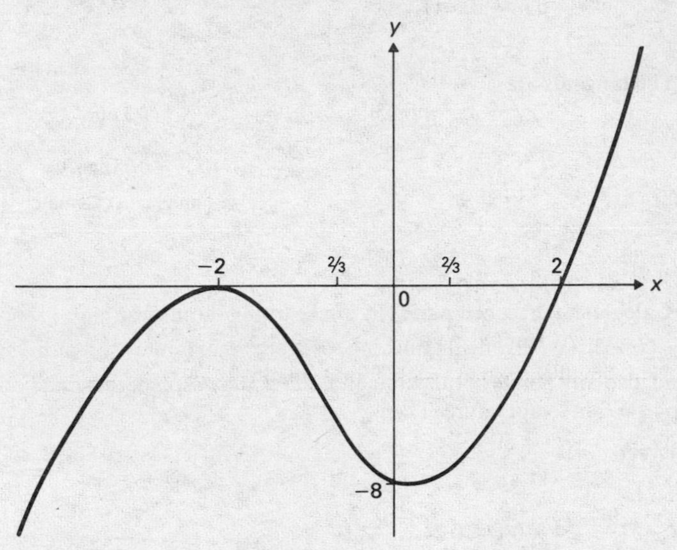

5. A metal block in the shape of a cube is heated so that it expands. Its linear dimensions increase uniformly at a rate of 0·5 mm per °C increase in temperature. Find the rate at which the volume increases with temperature at the instant when the surface area is 96 cm^2.

Hence estimate the percentage increase in volume when the temperature is then increased by a further 0·1 °C.

Answer

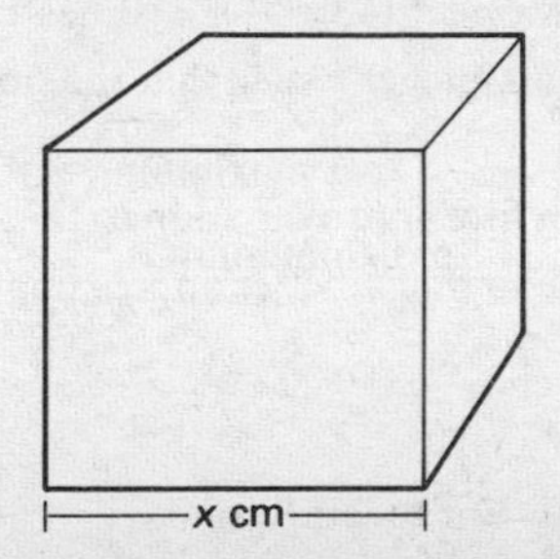

Let the cube have sides of x cm, and the temperature be T °C. Volume $= x^3$

$$\frac{dV}{dT} = \frac{dV}{dx}\frac{dx}{dT}$$ chain rule, page 161

$$= 3x^2\frac{dx}{dT}$$

$$= 3x^2 \times 0{\cdot}05$$ $\frac{dx}{dt} = 0{\cdot}5$ mm/°C

$= 0{\cdot}05$ cm/°C

Surface area $S = 6x^2 = 96$ units must all match

$\Rightarrow \quad x^2 = 16$

$$\Rightarrow \quad \frac{dV}{dt} = 3 \times 16 \times 0{\cdot}05 \text{ cm}^3/°\text{C}$$

$$= 2{\cdot}4 \text{ cm}^3/°\text{C}$$

Let δV = small change in volume for a small change, δT, in temperature. Then

$$\delta V \simeq \frac{dV}{dt}\delta T$$ page 160

$$\Rightarrow \quad \delta V \simeq 2{\cdot}4 \times 0{\cdot}1 = 0{\cdot}24.$$

$$\text{Percentage charge} = \frac{\delta V}{V} \times 100$$ since $x^2 = 16$ $\Rightarrow \quad x^3 = 64$

$$= \frac{0{\cdot}24 \times 100}{64}$$

$$= \frac{24}{64}\% = 0{\cdot}375\%$$

A 0·1 °C temperature increase produces a 0·375% increase in volume.

6. Show that the equation $x^4 - 3x^3 + 1 = 0$ has two positive roots and no negative root. Find an integer k such that the smaller root lies between k and $k + 1$.

Using $x_0 = k + 1$ as a first approximation to this root, use the Newton–Raphson Method twice to find a better approximation.

Answer

Let $f(x) = x^4 - 3x^3 + 1$. For turning points to sketch the graph

$$f'(x) \equiv 4x^3 - 9x^2 = 0$$

$$x^2(4x-9) = 0$$

$$\Rightarrow \quad x = 0 \text{ or } x = \frac{9}{4}$$

x	<0	0	>0
$f'(x)$	$-$	0	$-$

(point of inflexion)

$f''(x) = 12x^2 - 9x$

$\Rightarrow \quad f''(0) = 0$

the $f''(x)$ test of page 156 is inconclusive here

x	$<\frac{9}{4}$	$\frac{9}{4}$	$>\frac{9}{4}$
$f'(x)$	$-$	0	$+$

(minimum)

$\therefore \quad y = f(x)$ has one turning point only at

$x = \frac{9}{4}$, $y = f(\frac{9}{4}) = -\dfrac{1931}{256}$

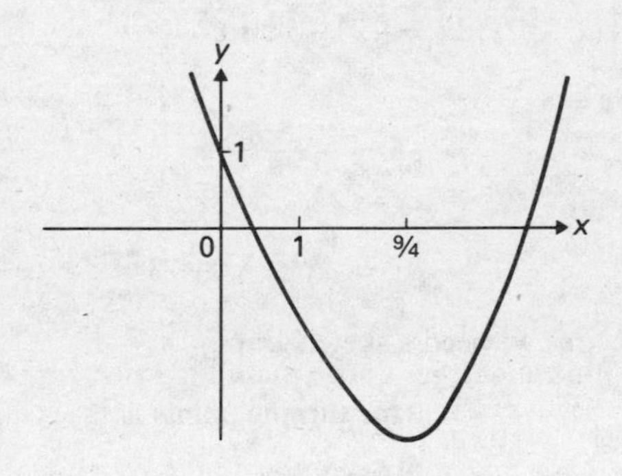

The graph cuts the x-axis twice. Both times on the positive side. The equation has two positive roots and no negative roots. Now

$$\left.\begin{array}{l} f(0) = 1 > 0 \\ f(1) = -1 < 0 \end{array}\right\}$$

$\Rightarrow$ a root lies between 0 and 1.

The second root is to the right of the minimum at $x = \frac{9}{4}$. The smaller root must lie between 0 and 1.

If $x_0 = 1$, Newton–Raphson gives $\qquad k = 0$

$$x_1 = 1 - \frac{f(1)}{f'(1)} = 1 - \frac{-1}{-5} = 0{\cdot}8 \qquad \Rightarrow \quad x_0 = k+1 = 0+1 = 1$$

$$x_2 = 0{\cdot}8 - \frac{f(0{\cdot}8)}{f'(0{\cdot}8)} = 0{\cdot}8 - \frac{-0{\cdot}1264}{-3{\cdot}712} = 0{\cdot}766$$

7. Find the equation of the curve which passes through the point $(-3, 5)$ and has gradient function $\frac{dy}{dx} = x(x-2)$.

Find the area of the finite region bounded by this curve and the line $y = 23$.

Answer

$$\frac{dy}{dx} = x(x-2) = x^2 - 2x \qquad \text{expand brackets before integrating}$$

$$\therefore \quad y = \int (x^2 - 2x)\,dx = \frac{1}{3}x^3 - x^2 + c$$

When $x = -3$, $y = 5$

$$\Rightarrow \quad 5 = -9 - 9 + c$$

$$\Rightarrow \quad c = 23$$

$$\Rightarrow \quad y = \frac{1}{3}x^3 - x^2 + 23$$

To calculate the area we need a sketch graph.

$$\frac{dy}{dx} = 0 \text{ for turning points}$$

$$\Rightarrow \quad x(x-2) = 0$$

$$\Rightarrow \quad x = 0 \text{ or } x = 2$$

$$y = 23 \text{ or } y = 21\tfrac{2}{3}$$

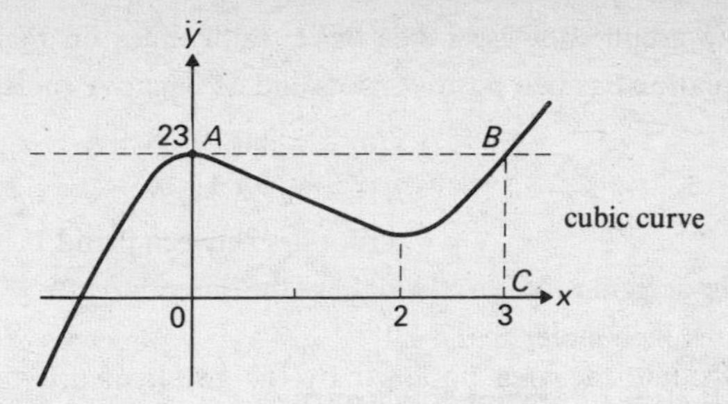

At A and B,

$$\frac{1}{3}x^3 - x^2 + 23 = 23$$ points of intersection

$$x^3 - 3x^2 = 0$$
$$x^2(x-3) = 0$$
$$x = 0 \text{ at } A,\ x = 3 \text{ at } B$$

Area of rectangle $ABCO = 3 \times 23 = 69$.

Area of

$$\left.\begin{aligned} &0 \leqslant y \leqslant \frac{1}{3}x^3 - x^2 + 23 \\ &0 \leqslant x \leqslant 3 \end{aligned}\right\}$$ area between curve and x-axis for $0 \leqslant x \leqslant 3$

is $$\int_0^3 \left(\frac{1}{3}x^3 - x^2 + 23\right)\mathrm{d}x = \left[\frac{1}{12}x^4 - \frac{1}{3}x^3 + 23x\right]_0^3$$

$$= \frac{81}{12} - \frac{27}{3} + 69$$

Required area $$= 69 - \left(\frac{81}{12} - \frac{27}{3} + 69\right)$$

$$= \frac{108 - 81}{12}$$

$$= \frac{27}{12} = \frac{9}{4} \text{ square units}$$

8. A function f is defined on $\mathbb{R}$ by:

$$f(x) = \begin{cases} x & \text{for } 0 \leqslant x \leqslant 1 \\ 2 - x^2 & \text{for } 1 < x < \sqrt{2} \\ 0 & \text{for } \sqrt{2} \leqslant x \leqslant 3 \end{cases}$$

and $f(x)$ is periodic with period 3.

Calculate the area bounded by the graph of this function and the x-axis for $0 \leqslant x \leqslant 4$.

Answer

The graph of $y = f(x)$ for $0 \leqslant x \leqslant 4$ is

drawing the graph using the formulae for the subsets $[0, 1]$, $[1, \sqrt{2}]$, $[\sqrt{2}, 3]$ of $\mathbb{R}$

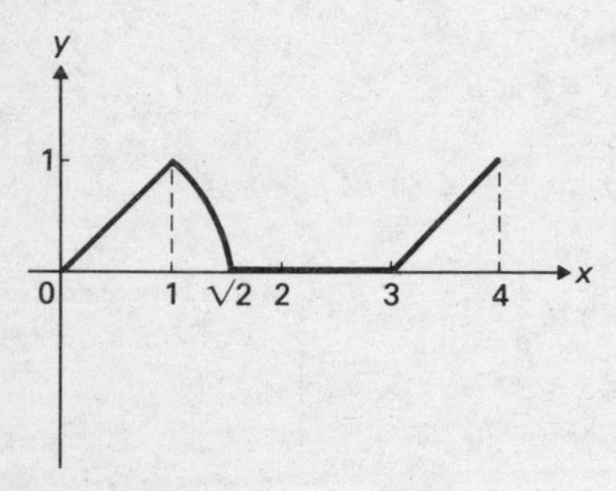

The required area is

$$2\int_0^1 x\,dx + \int_1^{\sqrt{2}} (2 - x^2)\,dx$$

the triangular regions for $0 \leqslant x \leqslant 1$ and $3 \leqslant x \leqslant 4$ have equal area

$$= 2\left[\frac{1}{2}x^2\right]_0^1 + \left[2x - \frac{1}{3}x^3\right]_1^{\sqrt{2}}$$

$$= 1 + 2\sqrt{2} - \frac{2}{3}\sqrt{2} - 2 + \frac{1}{3}$$

$$= \frac{4}{3}\sqrt{2} - \frac{2}{3} \text{ square units}$$

Section 21 Examination Questions

1. *$2x - 3y = 1$, $3x - 4y = 1$, $6x + 4y = 1$ represent three straight lines in the x–y plane which*
A are concurrent B are parallel C enclose a right-angled triangular region D enclose an acute angled triangular region E enclose an obtuse angled triangular region. [LON]

2. *Which one of the following equations does NOT give part of a straight line when y is plotted against x for $x > 0$?*
A $y - 3 = 7(x - 2)$ B $3(2x + y) = 2(3x + y)$ C $\frac{x}{2} + \frac{y}{3} = 1$
D $\frac{2}{x} + \frac{3}{y} = 1$ E $\frac{2}{x} + \frac{3}{y} = 0$

3.

v	5	10	15	20	25
R	149	175	219	280	359

The table shows corresponding values of variables R and v obtained in an experiment. By drawing a suitable linear graph, show that these pairs of values may be regarded as approximations to values satisfying a relation of the form $R = a + bv^2$ where a and b are constants.

Use your graph to estimate the values of a and b, giving your answers to 2 significant figures. [LON]

4. *Pairs of numerical values (x, y) are collected from an experiment and it is possible that the following equation may be applicable to these data:*

$$ax^2 + by^3 = 1$$

where a and b are constants. Explain carefully how you would use a graph to examine the validity of the equation. Explain how you would estimate the values of the constants if you found the equation to be approximately valid from your graph. [AEB – part]

5. *Given that $y = (x + 2)^2(3x - 1)^3$, find $\frac{dy}{dx}$, expressing the result as a product of factors.* [CAM]

6.

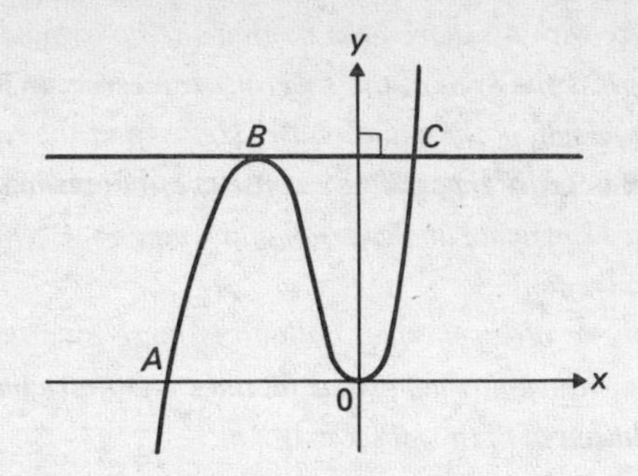

The graph of $y = x^2(x+3)$ is shown.

1. *The gradient at A is 9.*
2. *The equation of the tangent BC is $y = 4$.*
3. *C is the point $(1, 4)$.*

A 1, 2 and 3 are all true   B 1 and 2 only   C 2 and 3 only   D 1 only   E 3 only [LON]

7. *The equation $2x^4 - 4x^2 + 1 = 0$ has*
A no real roots   B no positive roots   C 2 of its roots lying between −1 and 1   D 2 of its roots lying berween 0 and 1   E 4 positive roots.

[LON]

8. *By considering the roots of the equation $f'(x) = 0$ or otherwise, prove that the equation $f(x) = 0$ where $f(x) = x^3 + 2x + 4$, has only one real root.*
Show that this root lies in the interval $-2 < x < 1$. Use the iterative formula $x_{n+1} = -\frac{1}{6}(x_n^3 - 4x_n + 4)$, $x_1 = -1$ to find two further approximations to the root of the equation giving your final answer to 2 decimal places.

[LON]

9. *Show that the equation $f(x) = 0$, where $f(x) = x^3 + x^2 - 2x - 1$ has a root in each of the intervals $x < -1$, $-1 < x < 0$, $x > 1$. Use the Newton–Raphson procedure, with initial value 1, to find two further approximations to the positive root of $f(x) = 0$, giving your final answer to 2 decimal places.*

[LON]

10. *From a large thin sheet of metal it is required to make an open rectangular box with a square base so that the box would contain a given volume V. Express the area of the sheet used in terms of V and x, where x is the length of a side of the square base. Hence find the ratio of the height of the box to x in order that the box consists of minimum area of the metal sheet.* [LON]

11. *The volume of a spherical balloon is increasing at a constant rate* $C\ m^3s^{-1}$. *Find, in* ms^{-1}, *the rate of increase of the radius of the balloon when the surface area of the balloon, is* $5\ m^2$. [LON]

12. *The equation of the curve which passes through the point (1,1) and for which* $\frac{dy}{dx} = 2x + 2$ *is*

A $y = x^2 + 2x$ B $y = 2x^2 + 2x - 3$ C $y = x^2 + 2x + 2$

D $y = x^2 + 2x - 2$ E *none of these* [LON]

13. *The area of the region for which* $0 < y < 3 - 2x - x^2$ *and* $x > 0$ *is*

A $\int_1^3 (3 - 2x - x^2)\,dx$ B $\int_{-3}^1 (3 - 2x - x^2)\,dx$ C $\int_0^1 (3 - 2x - x^2)\,dx$

D $\int_0^3 (3 - 2x - x^2)\,dx$ E $\int_{-1}^3 (3 - 2x - x^2)\,dx$ [LON]

14. *To find the numerical value of* $\int_{-2}^{2} (px^3 + qx + s)\,dx$ *it is necessary to know the values of the constants*

1. p 2. q 3. s

A *1, 2 and 3* B *1 and 2 only* C *2 and 3 only* D *1 only* E *3 only*

[LON]

15. *For the curve* $y = (3 - 2x)(x^2 - 36)$ *prove that* $\frac{dy}{dx} > 0$ *if and only if* $-3 < x < 4$.

Sketch the curve $y = (3 - 2x)(x^2 - 36)$, *clearly labelling with their co-ordinates:*

(a) the turning points,

(b) the points where the curve intersects the coordinate axes.

[AEB – part]

16. *Find the values of x for which the function* $f(x) = 4x^3 + 6x^2 - 9x + 2$ *has a maximum or minimum. Draw a rough sketch of the graph of the function* $f(x)$*, indicating clearly the positions of any maximum or minimum.*

[OXF]

6 Other Power Functions, Implicit Functions, Further Geometry, and Parametric Equations

Section 22 Other Powers (Rational and Negative Indices)

22.1 Introduction

By allowing fractional and negative powers we obtain functions more general than polynomials.

Examples

$$(x^2+1)^{2/3},\ 2x^{1/2}-3x^{-2},\ \sqrt{1+x^4}$$

(Recall that $\sqrt{a}=a^{1/2}$, $\sqrt[3]{a}=a^{1/3}$ and so on.)

Evaluation of these functions for a given value of x is straightforward with a calculator having an $\boxed{x^y}$ button.

Example

To evaluate $f(3.1)$ when $f:x\mapsto(x^2+1)^{2/3}$ the sequence of buttons to press is

$\boxed{3}\ \boxed{\cdot}\ \boxed{1}\ \boxed{x^2}\ \boxed{+}\ \boxed{1}\ \boxed{=}\ \boxed{x^y}\ \boxed{(}\ \boxed{2}\ \boxed{\div}\ \boxed{3}\ \boxed{)}\ \boxed{=}$

The displayed answer is then 4·828478.

There may be restrictions on the domains of such functions. Remember that you can only take the square root of a positive quantity, when considering functions: $\mathbb{R}\to\mathbb{R}$.

The domain of the function $f:x\mapsto\sqrt{1+x}$ could be $\{x\in\mathbb{R}:x\geqslant-1\}$.

Also, division by zero is undefined. $x=-2$ cannot belong to the domain of $f:x\mapsto\frac{1}{x+2}$.

22.2 Equations

Equations are often solved by manipulating them until they become polynomial equations.

Example

1. $$\sqrt{x^2+2} = 1 + x$$

$$\Rightarrow x^2 + 2 = (1+x)^2 \text{ (squaring both sides)}$$

$$\Rightarrow x^2 + 2 = 1 + 2x + x^2 \text{ (expanding the brackets)}$$

$$\Rightarrow 2x = 1$$

$$\Rightarrow x = \tfrac{1}{2}$$

This approach must be treated with caution, as the next example shows.

2. $$\sqrt{x} = x - 2$$

$$\Rightarrow x = (x-2)^2$$

$$\Rightarrow x = x^2 - 4x + 4$$

$$\Rightarrow x^2 - 5x + 4 = 0$$

$$\Rightarrow (x-1)(x-4) = 0$$

$$\Rightarrow x = 1 \textit{ or } x = 4$$

Checking in the original equation

$$\sqrt{1} \neq 1 - 2 \text{ but } \sqrt{4} = 4 - 2 = 2$$

Thus $x = 2$ is the only solution of $\sqrt{x} = x - 2$. $x = 1$ is the solution of the equation $\sqrt{x} = 2 - x$.

Squaring an equation very often produces 'spurious' solutions in this way. You should *always* check the answers in the *original* equation.

22.3 Extension of the Binomial Theorem

Recall the expansion

$$(1+x)^n = 1 + nx + \frac{n(n-1)}{2!}x^2 + \frac{n(n-1)(n-2)}{3!}x^3 + \dots$$

introduced on page 71, for $n \in \mathbb{N}$. It was found that the right-hand side was a polynomial with $n+1$ terms.

The result can be extended to the case when $n \notin \mathbb{N}$. The same rule is used for calculating the coefficients.

Example

$$(1+x)^{-1} = 1 + (-1)x + \frac{(-1)(-2)}{2!}x^2 + \frac{(-1)(-2)(-3)}{3!}x^3 + \dots$$

$$= 1 - x + x^2 - x^3 + \dots$$

Clearly the coefficients $\frac{n(n-1)(n-2)\cdots(n-r+1)}{r!}$ can never become zero when $n \notin \mathbb{N}$. The right-hand expression is a series with infinitely many terms. On page 49 we found that such series were meaningful when the terms were sufficiently small. It turns out that for the expansion

$$(1+x)^n \equiv 1 + nx + \frac{n(n-1)}{2!}x^2 + \frac{n(n-1)(n-2)}{3!}x^3 + \dots +$$

$$\frac{n(n-1)\dots(n-r-1)}{r!}x^r + \dots$$

1. If n is a non-zero positive integer, then the right-hand expression is a polynomial with $n+1$ terms. The identity is valid for all values of x.
2. If n is not a non-zero positive integer, the right-hand expression is an infinite series which converges when $-1 < x < 1$ (i.e. $|x| < 1$).

Examples

1. Find the first 4 non-zero terms in the expansion of $(1+x)^{\frac{1}{2}}$ and hence estimate $\sqrt{1 \cdot 1}$.

Answer

$$(1+x)^{\frac{1}{2}} = 1 + \tfrac{1}{2}x + \frac{\frac{1}{2}(\frac{1}{2}-1)}{2!}x^2 + \frac{\frac{1}{2}(\frac{1}{2}-1)(\frac{1}{2}-2)}{3!}x^3 + \ldots$$

$$= 1 + \tfrac{1}{2}x + \frac{\frac{1}{2}(-\frac{1}{2})}{2}x^2 + \frac{\frac{1}{2}(-\frac{1}{2})(-\frac{3}{2})}{6}x^3 + \ldots$$

$$\Rightarrow \quad (1+x)^{\frac{1}{2}} = 1 + \tfrac{1}{2}x - \tfrac{1}{8}x^2 + \tfrac{1}{16}x^3 + \ldots$$

This series converges for $-1 < x < 1$.

$$\sqrt{1{\cdot}1} = \sqrt{1 + 0{\cdot}1} = (1 + 0{\cdot}1)^{\frac{1}{2}}$$

Substituting $x = 0{\cdot}1$

$$\Rightarrow \sqrt{1{\cdot}1} \simeq 1 + \tfrac{1}{2}(0.1) - \frac{1}{8}(0{\cdot}01) + \frac{1}{16}(0{\cdot}001)$$

$$= 1 + 0{\cdot}05 - 0{\cdot}00125 + 0{\cdot}0000625$$

$$= 1{\cdot}0488 \text{ (4 decimal places)}$$

2. Show that the binomial series for $(2+x)^{-2}$ converges when $-2 < x < 2$ and find the first 3 non-zero terms of this expression.

Answer

$$(2+x)^{-2} = \left(2\left(1 + \frac{x}{2}\right)\right)^{-2}$$

$$= 2^{-2}\left(1 + \frac{x}{2}\right)^{-2}$$

The series for $(1 + \frac{x}{2})^{-2}$ converges if $-1 < \frac{x}{2} < 1$; that is $-2 < x < 2$ as stated.

$$2^{-2}\left(1 + \frac{x}{2}\right)^{-2} = 2^{-2}\left(1 + (-2)\left(\frac{x}{2}\right) + \frac{(-2)(-3)}{2\;!}\left(\frac{x}{2}\right)^2 + \ldots\right)$$

$$= \frac{1}{4}\left(1 - x + \frac{3}{4}x^2 + \ldots\right)$$

$$= \frac{1}{4} - \frac{1}{4}x + \frac{3}{16}x^2 + \ldots$$

22.4 Differentiation

The rule $\frac{d}{dx}(x^n) = nx^{n-1}$ of page 148 is valid for *any* constant n.

Examples

1. $$y = x^{\frac{1}{2}} + 2$$
$$\Rightarrow \frac{dy}{dx} = \tfrac{1}{2}x^{-\frac{1}{2}}$$

2. $$y = 3x^{-2} + 5x^{1\cdot 4}$$
$$\Rightarrow \frac{dy}{dx} = -6x^{-3} + 7x^{0\cdot 4}$$

The change of variable rule (page 161) can be used.

Example

If $f: x \mapsto \sqrt{x^3 + 2x}$, let $u = x^3 + 2x$ so that $y = f(x) = u^{\frac{1}{2}}$.

$$\frac{dy}{du} = \tfrac{1}{2}u^{-\frac{1}{2}} = \tfrac{1}{2}\frac{1}{u^{\frac{1}{2}}} = \frac{1}{2\sqrt{u}}$$

and

$$\frac{du}{dx} = 3x^2 + 2.$$

Thus

$$\frac{dy}{dx} = \frac{dy}{du}\frac{du}{dx} = \frac{1}{2\sqrt{u}} \times (3x^2 + 2)$$

$$= \frac{3x^2 + 2}{2\sqrt{(x^3 + 2x)}}$$

Turning points can be found (page 151).

Examples

1. The function $f(x) = x^{3/2}$ is defined on domain $\{x \in \mathbb{R} : x \geqslant 0\}$. Show that the graph of $y = f(x)$ has no turning points. Show further that y increases as x increases, and sketch the graph of $y = x^{3/2}$.

Answer

For a turning point $\frac{dy}{dx} = 0$.

$$y = x^{3/2} \Rightarrow \frac{dy}{dx} = \frac{3}{2}x^{\frac{1}{2}} = 0 \text{ for turning points.}$$

$$\Rightarrow x^{\frac{1}{2}} = 0$$

$$\Rightarrow x = 0$$

However, $f(x)$ is undefined for $x < 0$ and so $(0, 0)$ cannot be a turning point.

y is an increasing function of x if it has a positive gradient for all values of x.

Since the gradient is $\frac{dy}{dx} = \frac{3}{2}x^{\frac{1}{2}} > 0$ for all $x > 0$, then the function is increasing.

The graph is

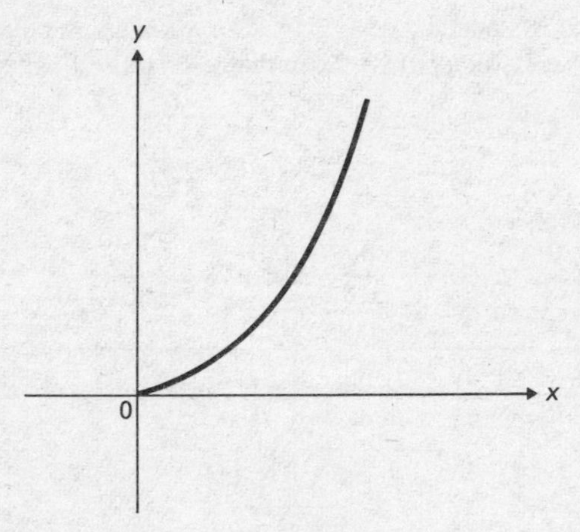

2. Find the turning points on the graph of $y = x + \frac{1}{x}$. Verify that the maximum value is *smaller* than the minimum value.

Answer

$$y = x + \frac{1}{x} = x + x^{-1}$$

$$\frac{dy}{dx} = 1 + (-1)(x^{-2}) = 0$$

for a turning point

$$\Rightarrow \frac{dy}{dx} = 1 - \frac{1}{x^2} = 0$$

$$\Rightarrow x^2 = 1$$

$$\Rightarrow x = \pm 1$$

$$\frac{d^2y}{dx^2} = \frac{d}{dx}(1 - x^{-2})$$

$$= -(-2)x^{-3} = 2x^{-3}$$

$x = -1$	$x = +1$
$y = -2$	$y = 2$
$\dfrac{d^2y}{dx^2} = -2 < 0$	$\dfrac{d^2y}{dx^2} = 2 > 0$

$\therefore$ $(-1, -2)$ is a maximum point. $(1, 2)$ is a minimum point. Maximum value $= -2$. Minimum value $= 2 > -2$.

The sketch graph of $x \mapsto x + \frac{1}{x}$ is

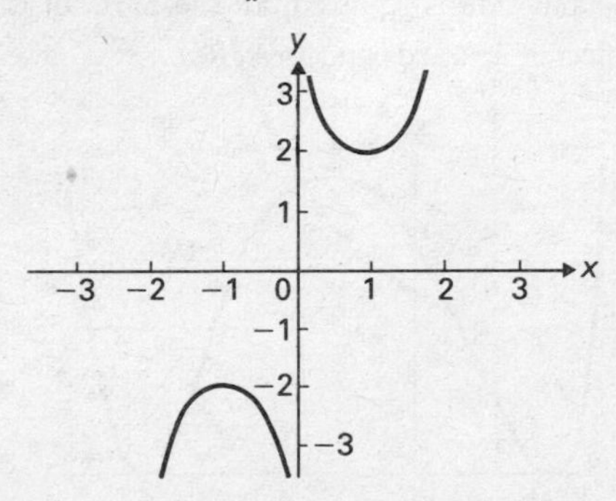

which shows how the minimum can be greater than the maximum. (See curve sketching for rational functions, page 268.)

From the graph we can see that the *range set* of this function is

$$\{y : y \geqslant 2\} \cup \{y : y \leqslant -2\}$$

22.5 Graphs of $y = (f(x))^2$ and $y^2 = f(x)$

Having sketched the graph of $y = f(x)$ you can then quickly sketch the two related graphs $y = (f(x))^2$ and $y^2 = f(x)$.

Example

$y = (x + 1)(x - 2)$ has graph

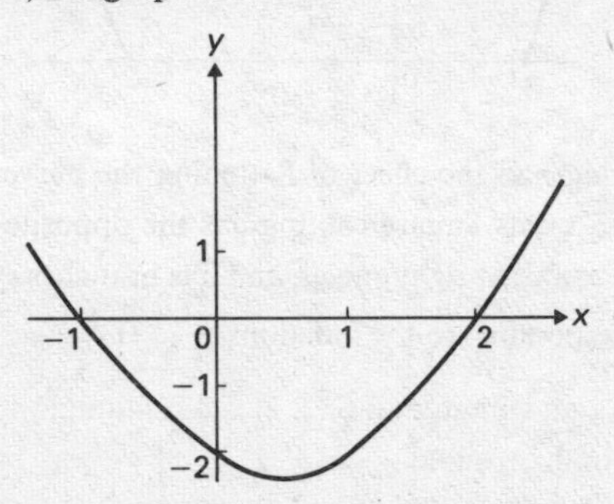

When the right-hand side is squared, all the parts of this curve below the x-axis are reflected upwards and *stretched.*

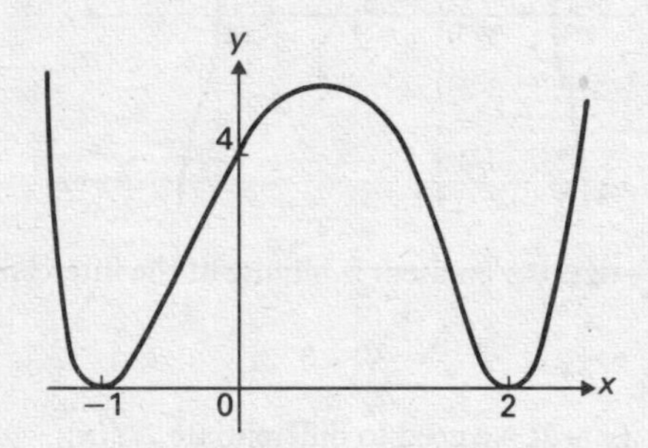

If $|a| < 1$ then $|a^2| < |a|$, so that points whose y-coordinates are between -1 and 1 move closer to the x-axis on squaring. Those points for which $|y| > 1$ move further away.

The x-intercepts on the original graph correspond to minima on the new graph.

$y^2 = f(x)$ corresponds to the two functions $y = \sqrt{f(x)}$ and $y = -\sqrt{f(x)}$ which are defined for $f(x) \geqslant 0$.

The first step is to *discard* parts of the graph which lie below the x-axis:

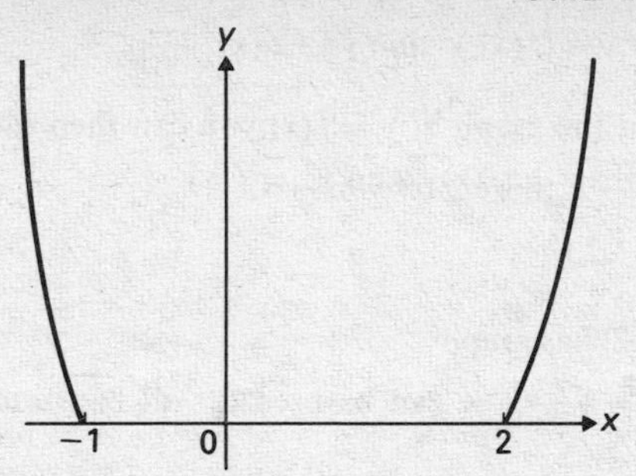

Whereas squaring had the effect of flattening the curve to a minimum where it met the x-axis, square rooting has the opposite effect. The new curve meets the x-axis at right angles, and has branches symmetric about the x-axis (corresponding to the functions $\pm\sqrt{f(x)}$).

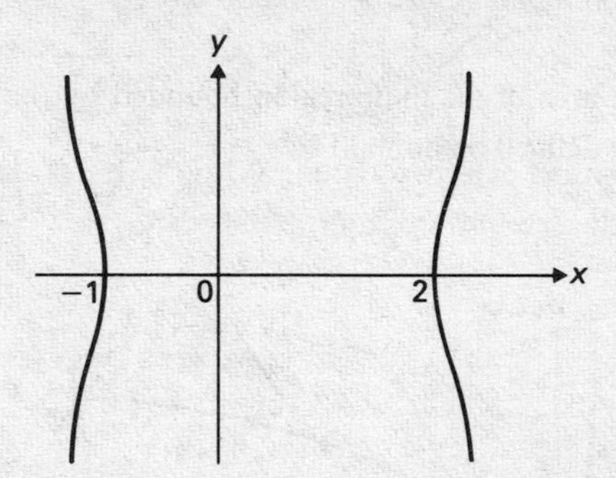

We can verify that the gradient is infinite at the intercepts.

Example

If $f(x) = (x + 1)(x - 2)$, we need to differentiate $\sqrt{f(x)}$

$$\equiv (f(x))^{\frac{1}{2}}$$

$$\equiv (x + 1)^{\frac{1}{2}}(x - 2)^{\frac{1}{2}}$$

$$\frac{d}{dx}((x + 1)^{\frac{1}{2}}(x - 2)^{\frac{1}{2}}) = \left(\frac{d}{dx}(x + 1)^{\frac{1}{2}}\right)(x - 2)^{\frac{1}{2}} + (x + 1)^{\frac{1}{2}}\frac{d}{dx}(x - 2)^{\frac{1}{2}}$$

product rule

$$= \tfrac{1}{2}(x + 1)^{-\frac{1}{2}}(x - 2)^{\frac{1}{2}} + \tfrac{1}{2}(x + 1)^{\frac{1}{2}}(x - 2)^{-\frac{1}{2}}$$

change of variable

$$= \frac{1}{2}\sqrt{\frac{x-2}{x+1}} + \frac{1}{2}\sqrt{\frac{x+1}{x-2}}$$

As $x \to -1$ or $x \to 2$, this expression $\to \infty$.

22.6 Integration

The rule $\int x^n \mathrm{d}x = \frac{x^{n+1}}{n+1} + K$ can be used for all constant powers except $n = -1$.

Examples

1.
$$\int (x^{\frac{1}{2}} - x^{-\frac{1}{2}})\mathrm{d}x = \frac{x^{\frac{1}{2}+1}}{\frac{1}{2}+1} - \frac{x^{-\frac{1}{2}+1}}{-\frac{1}{2}+1} + K$$
$$= \frac{2x^{3/2}}{3} - 2x^{\frac{1}{2}} + K$$

2. Calculate the area of the finite region bounded by the curves $y = x^2$ and $y = x^{\frac{1}{2}}$ both defined on domain $\mathbb{R}^+$.

Answer

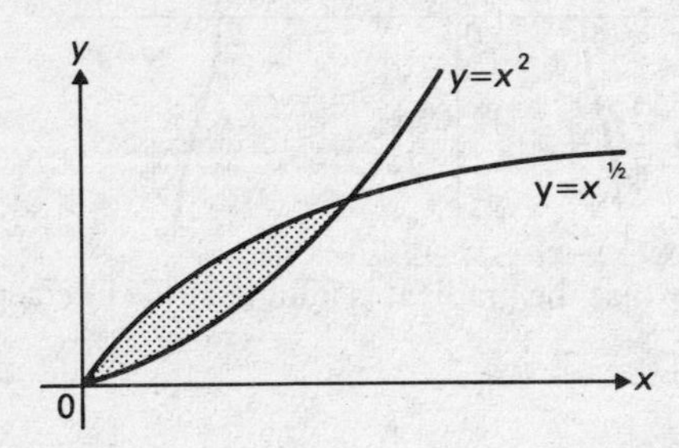

The curves intersect when

$$x^2 = x^{\frac{1}{2}}$$

$$\Rightarrow x^2 - x^{\frac{1}{2}} = 0$$
$$\Rightarrow x^{\frac{1}{2}}(x^{3/2} - 1) = 0$$

$$\Rightarrow x = 0 \text{ or } x^{3/2} = 1$$
$$\Rightarrow x = 1$$

The required area is

$$\int_0^1 (x^{\frac{1}{2}} - x^2)\mathrm{d}x$$ page 185

$$= \left[\frac{2x^{3/2}}{3} - \frac{x^3}{3}\right]_0^1 = \frac{2}{3} - \frac{1}{3} = \frac{1}{3} \text{ square units}$$

(Note: $f{:}x \mapsto x^2$ and $y{:}x \mapsto x^{\frac{1}{2}}$ are **inverse functions** on $\mathbb{R}^+$ (page 32).)

The change of variable rule is also useful (page 161).

Examples

1. $\int x\sqrt{1+x}\,\mathrm{d}x$ Let $u = 1 + x$ so that $x = u - 1$

$\Rightarrow \frac{\mathrm{d}u}{\mathrm{d}x} = 1$

$\Rightarrow$ '$\mathrm{d}u = \mathrm{d}x$'

$= \int (u-1)u^{\frac{1}{2}}\mathrm{d}u$ change to a u-integral

$= \int (u^{3/2} - u^{\frac{1}{2}})\mathrm{d}u$ expand brackets

$= \frac{2u^{5/2}}{5} - \frac{2u^{3/2}}{3} + K$

$= \frac{2}{5}(1+x)^{5/2} - \frac{2}{3}(1+x)^{3/2} + K$ back to x-variable

$= \frac{2}{15}(1+x)^{3/2}(3(1+x) - 5) + K$ factorize

$= \frac{2}{15}(1+x)^{3/2}(3x-2) + K$

2. $\int_0^1 3x(1-x^2)^{3/2}\mathrm{d}x$ Let $u = 1 - x^2$

$\Rightarrow \frac{\mathrm{d}u}{\mathrm{d}x} = -2x$

$= 3\int_0^1 (1-x^2)^{3/2}(x\mathrm{d}x)$ $\Rightarrow$ '$\mathrm{d}u = -2x\mathrm{d}x$'

$\Rightarrow$ '$x\mathrm{d}x = -\frac{1}{2}\mathrm{d}u$'

$$= 3\int_1^0 u^{3/2}(-\tfrac{1}{2}\mathrm{d}u) \qquad \begin{array}{c|cc} x & 0 & 1 \\ \hline u & 1 & 0 \end{array} \text{ change limits}$$

$$= -\frac{3}{2}\int_1^0 u^{3/2}\,\mathrm{d}u$$

$$= -\frac{3}{2}\left[\frac{2u^{5/2}}{5}\right]_1^0$$

$$= -\frac{3}{2}\left(0 - \frac{2}{5}\right)$$

$$= \frac{3}{5}$$

Notice how the x-factor combined with the $\mathrm{d}x$ to give $-\frac{1}{2}\mathrm{d}u$. This can be spotted by seeing that the expression *inside* the brackets when differentiated gives the term *outside* the brackets apart from a constant factor.

Section 23 Implicit Functions and Coordinate Geometry

23.1 Implicit Functions and Equations of Curves

We have so far considered curves in the x–y plane which are graphs of functions of the form $y = f(x)$. These are called **explicit** functions, since a value of y can be calculated directly given a value of x.

Now consider the relation $x^2 + y^2 = 1$. This represents a set of points in the x–y plane, since it is only satisfied by certain pairs of coordinates (x, y). Thus $(0, 1)$ and $\left(\frac{1}{\sqrt{2}}, -\frac{1}{\sqrt{2}}\right)$ belong to this set, while $(1, 1)$ does not.

The subset of the plane for which x and y satisfy the equation is called the **locus** of points with equation $x^2 + y^2 = 1$.

With a suitable choice of domain, y can be thought of as a function of x, since it must vary as x varies. We call y an **implicit** function of x as it is not in the form $y = f(x)$.

In general, any expression involving x and y determines a locus in the x–y plane.

Examples

1. $x^2 + 4x + y^2 - 6y + 1 = 0$

2. $y^2 = 4x$

3. $2x^3y - 3xy^4 + x^2y^2 - 2y + x - 3 = 0$

In some cases we can recognize what shape the locus of points (x, y) will be. One such example is $x^2 + y^2 = 1$ which can be written as $\sqrt{x^2 + y^2} = 1 \Rightarrow \sqrt{(x - 0)^2 + (y - 0)^2} = 1$.

The left-hand side represents the distance from the origin (0, 0) to the variable point $P(x, y)$(Pythagoras' Theorem, page 132).

Thus the equation $x^2 + y^2 = 1$ represents points which are all 1 unit away from the origin, in other words a circle centre (0, 0) and radius 1.

23.2 Equations of Circles

In general a circle in the x–y plane is specified by its centre and radius.

Suppose that a circle has centre (a, b) and radius r. Let $P(x, y)$ be a general point on this circle.

Using the distance formula on page 132

$$\sqrt{(x - a)^2 + (y - b)^2} = r$$

$$\Rightarrow (x - a)^2 + (y - b)^2 = r^2$$

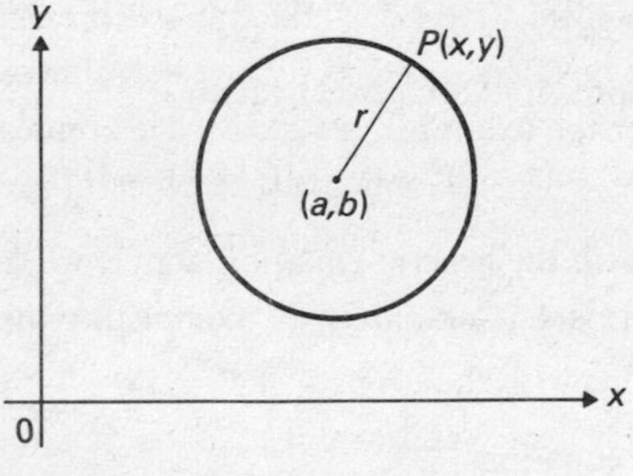

This is the general form for the equation of a circle in the x–y plane. It can be simplified by expanding the brackets.

$$x^2 + y^2 - 2ax - 2by + a^2 + b^2 - r^2 = 0$$

By comparison, the equation $x^2 + y^2 + 2gx + 2fy + c = 0$ represents a circle with centre $(-g, \; -f)$ and radius $\sqrt{g^2 + f^2 - c}$ provided $g^2 + f^2 - c > 0$.

Examples

1. Find the equation of the circle with centre (1, 1) and radius 3.

Answer

Using the general form above

$$(x-1)^2 + (y-1)^2 = 3^2$$

$$x^2 - 2x + 1 + y^2 - 2y + 1 = 9$$

$$x^2 + y^2 - 2x - 2y - 7 = 0$$

In the next example, we find the centre and radius of a given circle.

2.
$$x^2 + y^2 - 4x - 6y - 3 = 0$$
$$\Rightarrow x^2 - 4x + y^2 - 6y = 3$$

Now divide the x and y coefficients by 2 and add the squares of these quantities to both sides

$$x^2 - 4x + 4 + y^2 - 6y + 9 = 4 + 9 + 3$$
$$\Rightarrow (x^2 - 4x + 4) + (y^2 - 6y + 9) = 16$$

The bracketed expressions are perfect squares

$$(x-2)^2 + (y-3)^2 = 16 = 4^2$$

By comparison with the general equation above, we see that the centre is (2, 3) and radius is 4. (Compare with 'completing the square' on page 87.)

3. Show that the equations

$$(1)\;\; x^2 + y^2 - 2x + 4y - 4 = 0$$

and

$$(2)\;\; x^2 + y^2 + 2x - 2y - 2 = 0$$

represent circles. Determine the coordinates of the centres and the radii of these circles. Show that the circles intersect in two points.

Answer

$$x^2 + y^2 - 2x + 4y - 4 = 0$$

can be rewritten as

$$x^2 - 2x + y^2 + 4y = 4$$

$$\Rightarrow (x^2 - 2x + 1) + (y^2 + 4y + 4) = (4 + 1 + 4)$$

$$\Rightarrow (x - 1)^2 + (y + 2)^2 = 9$$

which represents a circle with centre $(1, -2)$ and radius 3.

Similarly

$$x^2 + y^2 + 2x - 2y - 2 = 0$$

$$\Rightarrow x^2 + 2x + y^2 - 2y = 2$$

$$\Rightarrow (x^2 + 2x + 1) + (y^2 - 2y + 1) = 2 + 1 + 1$$

$$\Rightarrow (x + 1)^2 + (y - 1)^2 = 4$$

which represents a circle with centre $(-1, 1)$ and radius 2.

For points of intersection we solve the simultaneous equations (1) and (2).

The first step is to subtract the equations, to cancel the x^2, y^2 terms,

$$\Rightarrow -4x + 6y - 2 = 0$$

$$\Rightarrow 2x - 3y + 1 = 0$$

This is the equation of a straight line.

$$(3) \Rightarrow y = \frac{2x + 1}{3}$$

Substitute into (1)

$$x^2 + \left(\frac{2x + 1}{3}\right)^2 - 2x + 4\left(\frac{2x + 1}{3}\right) - 4 = 0$$

$$9x^2 + 4x^2 + 4x + 1 - 18x + 24x + 12 - 36 = 0$$

$$13x^2 + 10x - 23 = 0$$

$$\Rightarrow (13x + 23)(x - 1) = 0$$

The equation has solutions

$$x = -\frac{23}{13} \text{ and } x = 1$$

using (3) to find

$$y = -\frac{11}{13} \text{ and } y = 1$$

The circles intersect at the points $A(-\frac{23}{13}, -\frac{11}{13})$ and $B(1, 1)$. (See also section 23.6, page 228.)

The equation $2x - 3y + 1 = 0$ (3) represents the line which passes through A and B. AB is the **common chord** of the circles.

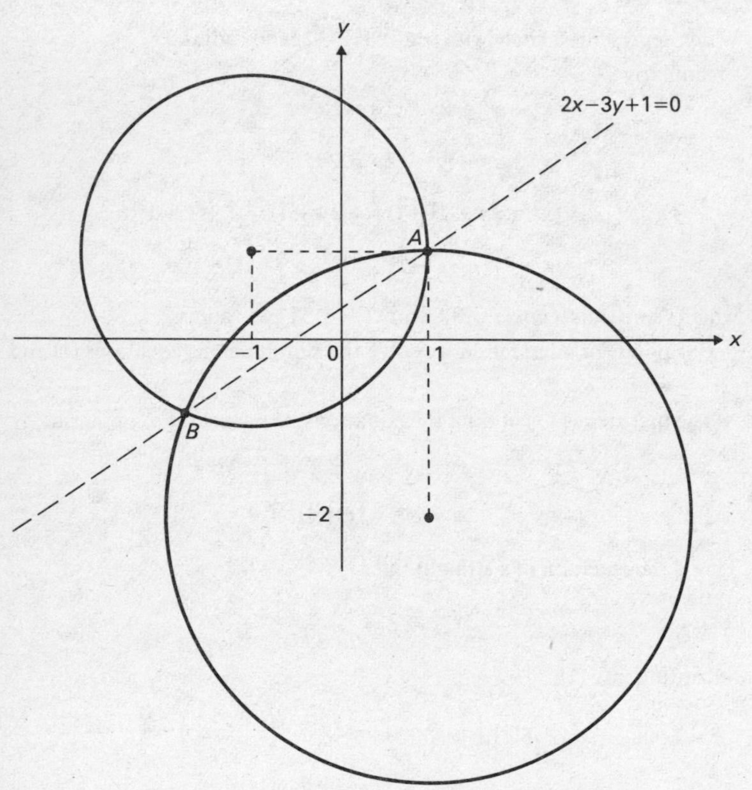

23.3 Regions Defined by Inequalities

An equation such as $x^2 + y^2 = 1$ defines a curve in the plane. If the coordinates of a point satisfy this equation then the point lies on the circle.

Suppose that the point $P(x, y)$ is *inside* the circle. Then the distance OP, from the centre to P, must be less than 1. The inequality $x^2 + y^2 < 1$ corresponds to the inside of the circle and the inequality $x^2 + y^2 > 1$ corresponds to the outside

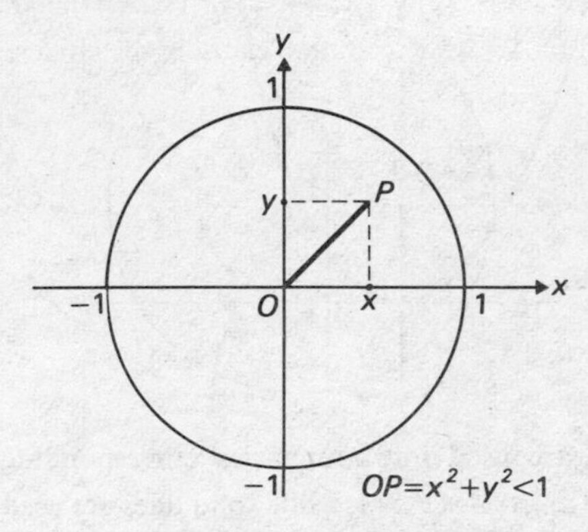

Example

Shade the region of the plane defined by the inequalities

$$(x-1)^2 + (y-1)^2 \leqslant 4,$$

$$(x-1)^2 + (y-1)^2 > 1,$$

and

$$x^2 - y \leqslant 0$$

Answer

The *boundaries* of this region are

$$(x-1)^2 + (y-1)^2 = 4 \text{ (circle centre (1, 1) radius 2)}$$

$$(x-1)^2 + (y-1)^2 = 1 \text{ (circle centre (1, 1) radius 1)}$$

$$y = x^2 \text{ (parabola)}$$

$(x-1)^2+(y-1)^2 \leqslant 4$ corresponds to the inside and circumference of the larger circle.

$(x-1)^2+(y-1)^2 > 1$ corresponds to the outside of the smaller circle.

$x^2 - y \leqslant 0$ corresponds to the 'inside' of the parabola.

See this by substituting, for example, $x = 0$, $y = 1$

$\Rightarrow x^2 - y = 0^2 - 1 < 0$, (0, 1) is known to be 'inside' the parabola.

The required region is

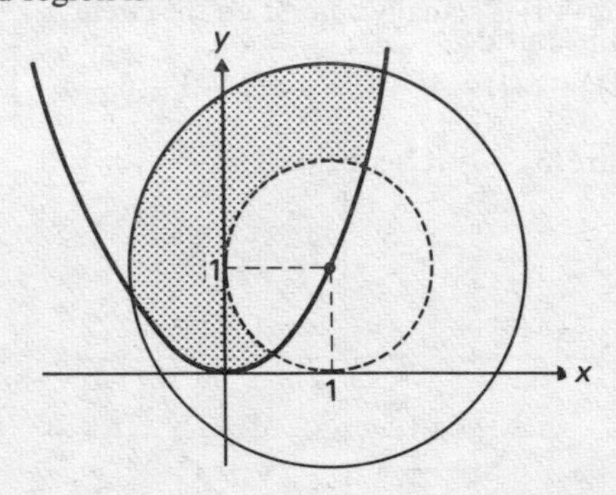

Dashed lines are used for boundaries corresponding to the *strict* inequality $(x-1)^2+(y-1)^2 > 1$, while solid lines are used for $(x-1)^2 + (y-1)^2 \leqslant 4$ and $x^2 - y \leqslant 0$.

23.4 Tangents and Circles

Given a point on a circle, the equation of the tangent can be found using the property that a radius is perpendicular to the tangent.

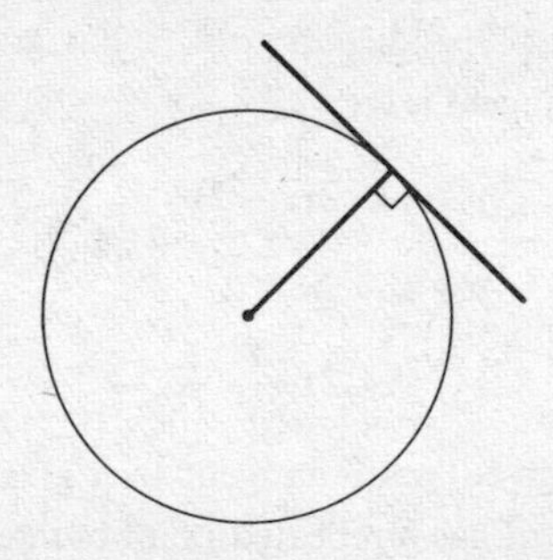

Example

Find the equation of the tangent to the circle

$$x^2 + y^2 - 6x + 4y + 8 = 0$$

at the point $(1, -1)$.

Answer

First check that $(1, -1)$ is actually a point on the circle.

$$1^2 + (-1)^2 - 6(1) + 4(-1) + 8 = 1 + 1 - 6 - 4 + 8 = 0$$

The circle has centre $(3, -2)$. (Check this !)

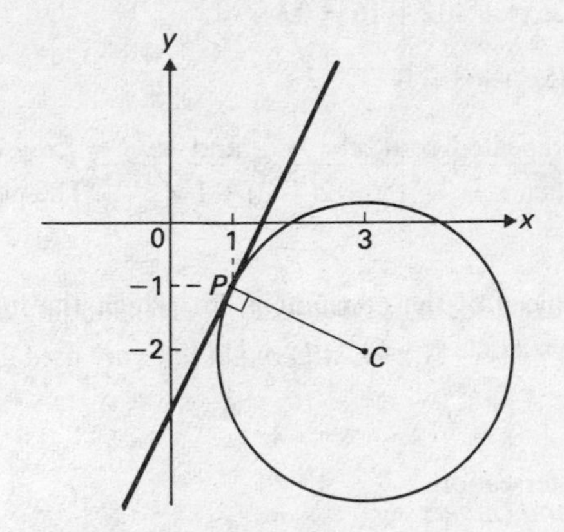

$$\text{Radius } CP \text{ has gradient } \frac{-1-(-2)}{1-3} = -\frac{1}{2}.$$

The tangent, which is perpendicular to CP, has gradient 2 (page 136). The equation of this tangent is

$$y + 1 = 2(x - 1) \qquad \text{formula on page 135}$$

$$y + 1 = 2x - 2$$

$$y = 2x - 3$$

We can test whether a given line is tangent to a given circle by using the property that a tangent has a repeated point of intersection with the circle (page 199).

Examples

1. Show that the line $y = 2x + 1$ is tangent to the circle $5x^2 + 5y^2 - 10x + 15y - 4 = 0$, and find the coordinates of the point of contact.

Answer

For points of intersection $y = 2x + 1$ and $5x^2 + 5y^2 - 10x + 15y - 4 = 0$

$$\therefore 5x^2 + 5(2x+1)^2 - 10x + 15(2x+1) - 4 = 0$$

$$\Rightarrow 5x^2 + 5(4x^2 + 4x + 1) - 10x + 30x + 15 - 4 = 0$$

$$\Rightarrow 5x^2 + 20x^2 + 20x + 5 - 10x + 30x + 15 - 4 = 0$$

$$\Rightarrow 25x^2 + 40x + 16 = 0$$

$$\Rightarrow (5x+4)^2 = 0$$

which has the repeated root $x = -\frac{4}{5}$, and so $y = 2x + 1$ is a tangent to the circle. When $x = -\frac{4}{5}$, $y = 2(-\frac{4}{5}) + 1 = -\frac{3}{5}$. The point of contact is $(-\frac{4}{5}, -\frac{3}{5})$.

2. Find the value(s) of the constant m for which the line $y = mx + 3$ is a tangent to the circle $(x-2)^2 + (y+1)^2 = 4$.

Answer

For points of intersection

$$(x-2)^2 + (mx+4)^2 = 4$$

$$x^2 - 4x + 4 + m^2x^2 + 8mx + 16 = 4$$

$$x^2(1+m^2) + (8m-4)x + 16 = 0$$

The line is a tangent when this equation has equal roots ($b^2 - 4ac = 0$, page 91).

$$\Rightarrow (8m-4)^2 - 4(1+m^2)16 = 0$$

$$16(2m-1)^2 - 16(4)(1+m^2) = 0$$

$$4m^2 - 4m + 1 - 4 - 4m^2 = 0 \quad \text{dividing out the factor 16}$$

$$4m = -3$$

$$m = -\frac{3}{4}$$

is the only solution.

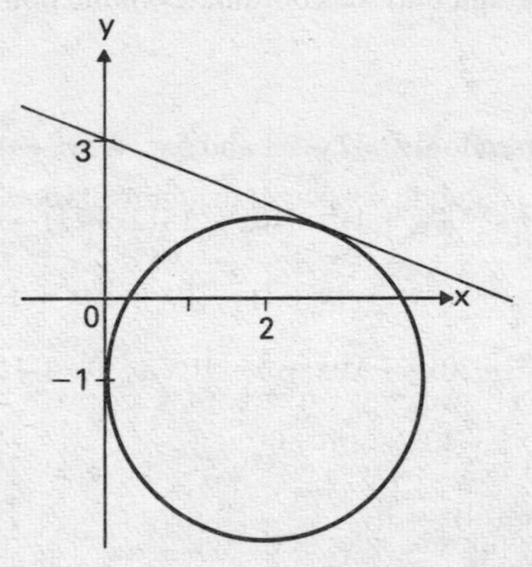

We expect *two* tangents. The diagram shows that the second tangent is the y-axis, which has infinite gradient and so cannot be derived from the equations above.

23.5 Distance from a Point to a Line

For a line to be a tangent, the perpendicular distance from the centre of the circle to this line must equal the radius.

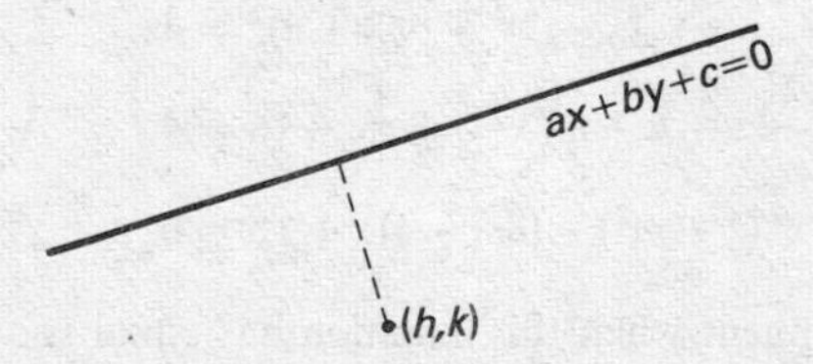

The formula for distance from a point (h, k) to a line $ax + by + c = 0$ is given by

$$\boxed{\left|\frac{ah + bk + c}{\sqrt{a^2 + b^2}}\right|}$$

The modulus signs are necessary since the quantity $ah + bk + c$ could be negative.

If points (h_1, k_1) and (h_2, k_2) are on the same side of a line $ax + by + c = 0$, then $ah_1 + bk_1 + c$ and $ah_2 + bk_2 + c$ have the same sign. Otherwise they have opposite signs.

Example

Show that the points (1, 1) and (– 3, – 5) are on opposite sides of the line $x + y + 6 = 0$ and calculate the perpendicular distances from these points to the line.

Answer

$$\text{For } (1, 1),\ x + y + 6 = 1 + 1 + 6 = +8 > 0.$$

$$\text{For } (-3, -5)\ x + y + 6 = -3 - 5 + 6 = -2 < 0.$$

The points are on opposite sides of the line.

The distance from (1, 1) to the line is $\dfrac{8}{\sqrt{1^2 + 1^2}} = \dfrac{8}{\sqrt{2}} = \dfrac{8\sqrt{2}}{2} = 4\sqrt{2}.$

The distance from (– 3, – 5) to the line is $\left|\dfrac{-2}{\sqrt{2}}\right| = \dfrac{2}{\sqrt{2}} = \sqrt{2}.$

23.6 Touching Circles and Orthogonal Circles

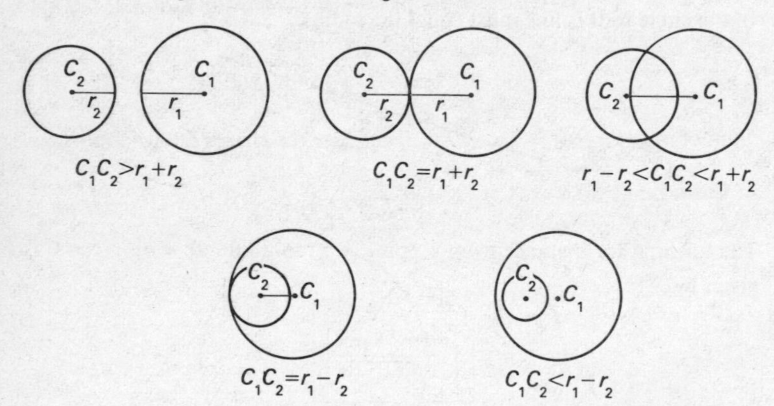

The diagrams above show the relations between the radii of the circles and the distance between the centres.

For the circles to touch externally, $r_1 + r_2 = C_1C_2$.

For the circles to touch internally, $r_1 - r_2 = C_1C_2$ (assuming r_1 is the radius of the larger circle).

Examples

1. Show that the circles $(x-1)^2 + (y-2)^2 = 9$ and $(x-5)^2 + (y-5)^2 = 4$ touch externally.

Answer

$$(x-1)^2 + (y-2)^2 = 9 \text{ has centre } (1, 2), \text{ radius } 3$$
$$(x-5)^2 + (y-5)^2 = 4 \text{ has centre } (5, 5), \text{ radius } 2.$$

Distances between the centres

$$C_1C_2 = \sqrt{(5-1)^2 + (5-2)^2} = \sqrt{16+9} = \sqrt{25} = 5$$

Sum of radii $r_1 + r_2 = 5 = C_1C_2$. $\therefore$ the circles touch externally.

2. Show that the circles $(x-2)^2 + (y-4)^2 = 9$ and $(x+1)^2 + (y+9)^2 = 1$ do not intersect.

Answer

$$(x-2)^2 + (y-4)^2 = 9 \text{ has centre } (2, 4), \text{ radius } 3.$$

$$(x+1)^2 + (y+9)^2 = \text{ has centre } (-1, -9), \text{ radius } 1.$$

Distance between centres

$$= \sqrt{3^2 + 13^2} = \sqrt{9+169} = \sqrt{178}$$

Sum of radii $r_1 + r_2 = 4 < \sqrt{178}$. Therefore the circles do not intersect.

Orthogonal circles cut at right angles

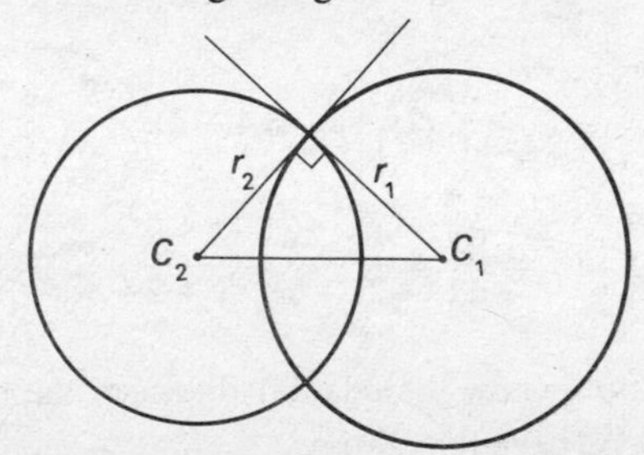

Using Pythogoras' Theorem and the fact that radii are normal to tangents, the circles are orthogonal if $C_1C_2 = \sqrt{r_1^2 + r_2^2}$. This relation can be used as a test for orthogonality.

23.7 Differentiation for Implicit Functions

An equation such as $x^2 + y^2 - 4x + 6y + 9 = 0$ represents a curve in the x–y plane. Tangents can be drawn at each point of this curve and so the curve has a well-defined gradient.

It is not always possible to rewrite such an equation in the form $y = f(x)$ where $f(x)$ is a function, and so a new method is required to calculate $\frac{dy}{dx}$. *Each* term of the equation is differentiated, regarding y as a function of x. y^2 can be differentiated using the change of variable rule. Letting $u = y^2$ we require

$$\frac{du}{dx} = \frac{du}{dy}\frac{dy}{dx}$$

page 161

$$= 2y\frac{dy}{dx}$$

The equation when differentiated becomes

$$2x + 2y\frac{dy}{dx} - 4 + 6\frac{dy}{dx} = 0$$

since

$$\frac{d}{dx}(9) = 0 \text{ and } \frac{d}{dx}(0) = 0$$

This can be rearranged to form an expression for $\frac{dy}{dx}$ *in terms of both x and y.*

$$\Rightarrow \frac{dy}{dx}(2y + 6) = 4 - 2x$$

$$\Rightarrow \frac{dy}{dx} = \frac{4 - 2x}{2y + 6} \equiv \frac{2 - x}{y + 3}$$

Values of both x and y are required to calculate the gradient (because y is not given as a formula in terms of x).

For example, the point (2, − 1) lies on the curve since

$$2^2 + (-1)^2 - 4(2) + 6(-1) + 9 = 4 + 1 - 8 - 6 + 9 = 0$$

The gradient at this point is $\frac{2-2}{-1+3} = 0$.

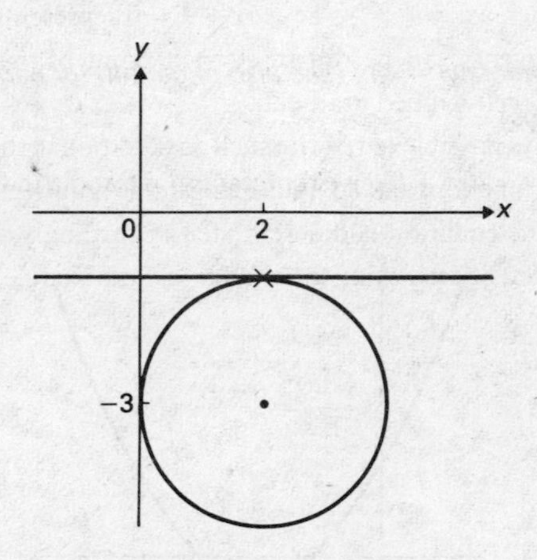

The equations of **tangents and normals** can be found.

Example

Find the equations of the tangent and normal to the curve $x^3 + y^3 - 3xy = 3$ at the point (2, 1).

Answer

Differentiating $\quad 3x^2 + 3y^2\frac{dy}{dy} - 3\left(y + x\frac{dy}{dx}\right) = 0$

$$\Rightarrow 3x^2 - 3y + \frac{dy}{dx}(3y^2 - 3x) = 0$$

$$\Rightarrow \frac{dy}{dx} = \frac{y - x^2}{y^2 - x}$$

At (2, 1) the gradient is $\frac{1-4}{1-2} = 3$. The tangent has equation

$$y - 1 = 3(x - 2) \Rightarrow y = 3x - 5$$

The normal has gradient $-\frac{1}{3}$ (page 136) and equation

$$y - 1 = -\tfrac{1}{3}(x - 2)$$
$$\Rightarrow 3y - 3 = -x + 2$$
$$\Rightarrow x + 3y - 5 = 0$$

23.8 The Parabola $y^2 = 4ax$ (see also page 240 for parametric equations)

The equation $y = ax^2 + bx + c$ represents a parabola in the x–y plane.

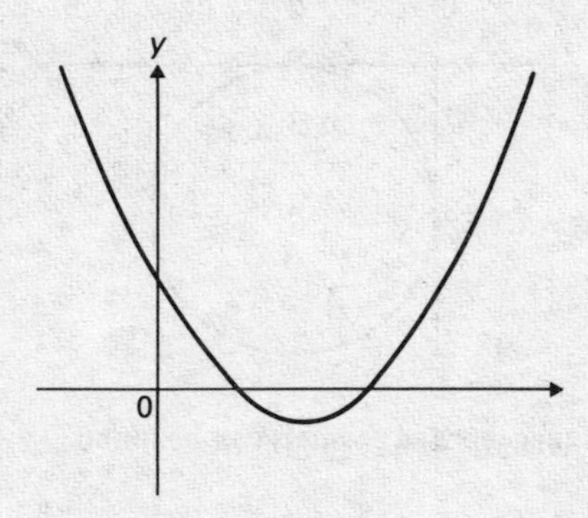

For a constant a, $y^2 = 4ax$ also represents a parabola, but this one is symmetric about the x-axis.

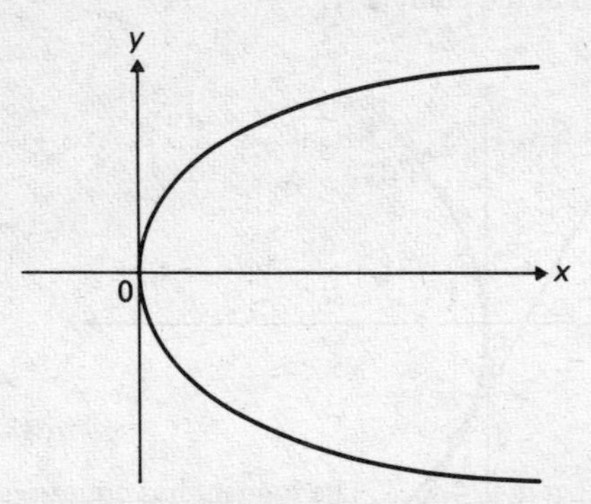

It corresponds to the two functions $y = 2\sqrt{ax}$, $y = -2\sqrt{ax}$. The **vertex** of this parabola is at the origin.

If $a < 0$, these two functions are defined for $x \leqslant 0$, if $a > 0$ they are defined for $x \geqslant 0$.

Examples

1. Find the equations of the tangent and normal to the parabola $y^2 = 16x$ at the point $(1, -4)$.

Answer

$$y^2 = 16x$$

$$\Rightarrow 2y\frac{dy}{dx} = 16$$

$$\Rightarrow \frac{dy}{dx} = \frac{8}{y} = -2 \text{ at the point } (1, -4)$$

The tangent has equation

$$y + 4 = -2(x - 1)$$

$$y = -2x - 2 \qquad (1)$$

The normal has gradient $\frac{1}{2}$, it has equation

$$y + 4 = \tfrac{1}{2}(x - 1)$$

$$2y + 8 = x - 1$$

$$2y = x - 9 \qquad (2)$$

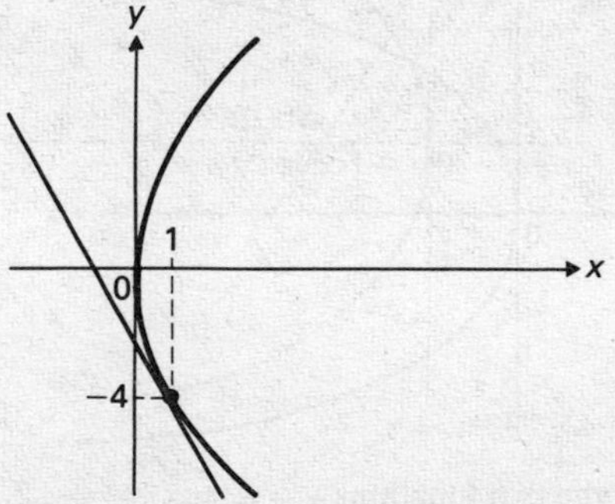

This can be generalized.

2. Find the equation of the tangent to the parabola $y^2 = 4ax$ at the point $P(x_1,y_1)$.

Answer

$$2y\frac{dy}{dx} = 4a \Rightarrow \frac{dy}{dx} = \frac{2a}{y}$$

At $P(x_1,y_1)$, the gradient is $\frac{2a}{y_1}$ and the tangent has equation

$$y - y_1 = \frac{2a}{y_1}(x - x_1)$$

$$\Rightarrow yy_1 - y_1{}^2 = 2ax - 2ax_1$$

However, as (x_1, y_1) lies on the parabola, $y_1{}^2 = 4ax_1$. The tangent equation reduces to

$$yy_1 - 4ax_1 = 2ax - 2ax_1$$

$$\Rightarrow y_1y - 2ax = 2ax_1$$

FOCUS AND DIRECTRIX

The parabola $y^2 = 4ax$ has as **focus** the point $S(a, 0)$ on the x-axis and as **directrix** the line $x = -a$.

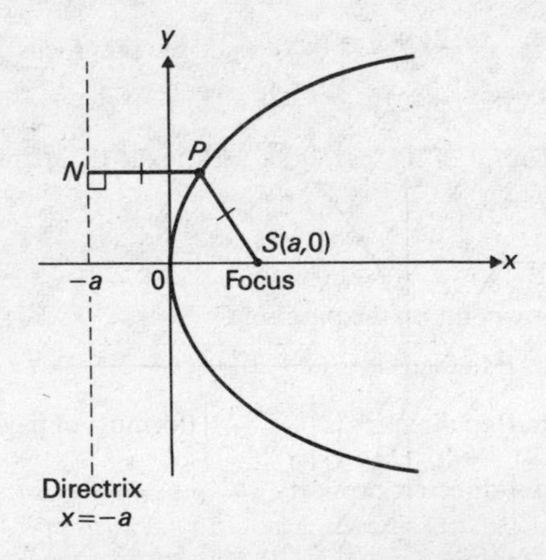

Any point $P(x, y)$ on the parabola has the property that it is equidistant from the focus and directrix (focus–directrix property).

To see this, calculate the distances PS and PN.

$$PS = \sqrt{(x-a)^2 + y^2} \qquad \text{Pythagoras}$$

$$PN = |x + a|$$

So

$$PS = \sqrt{(x-a)^2 + y^2} = \sqrt{x^2 - 2ax + a^2 + y^2}$$

$$= \sqrt{x^2 - 2ax + a^2 + 4ax} \qquad \text{on the curve } y^2 = 4ax$$

$$= \sqrt{x^2 + 2ax + a^2}$$

$$= \sqrt{(x+a)^2}$$

$$= |x + a|$$

$$= PN$$

A parabola is the locus of points equidistant from a fixed straight line and a fixed point.

Examples

1. Find the focus and directrix of the parabola $y^2 = 16x$.

Answer

Comparing with $y^2 = 4ax \Rightarrow a = 4$, and so the focus is (4, 0) and directrix is $x = -4$.

2. Find the equation of the parabola with focus (2, 3) and directrix the line $3x - 4y + 7 = 0$.

Answer

Let $P(x, y)$ be any point on the parabola.

Distance from P to focus is $\sqrt{(x-2)^2 + (y-3)^2}$.

Distance from P to directrix is $\left|\frac{3x - 4y + 7}{\sqrt{3^2 + 4^2}}\right|$ (formula of page 227).

From the focus–directrix property

$$\sqrt{(x-2)^2 + (y-3)^2} = \left|\frac{3x - 4y + 7}{5}\right|$$

$$\Rightarrow (x-2)^2 + (y-3)^2 = \frac{(3x-4y+7)^2}{25}$$

$$\Rightarrow 25(x^2 + y^2 - 4x - 6y + 13) =$$
$$9x^2 - 24xy + 16y^2 + 42x - 56y + 49$$

$$\Rightarrow 16x^2 + 9y^2 + 24xy - 142x - 94y + 276 = 0$$

3. Find the focus and directrix of the parabola $x^2 = 28y$.

Answer

This parabola has the y-axis as axis of symmetry. The general form is $x^2 = 4ay$ with focus $(0, a)$ and directrix the line $y = -a$.

Thus the focus is $(0, 7)$, directrix $y = -7$.

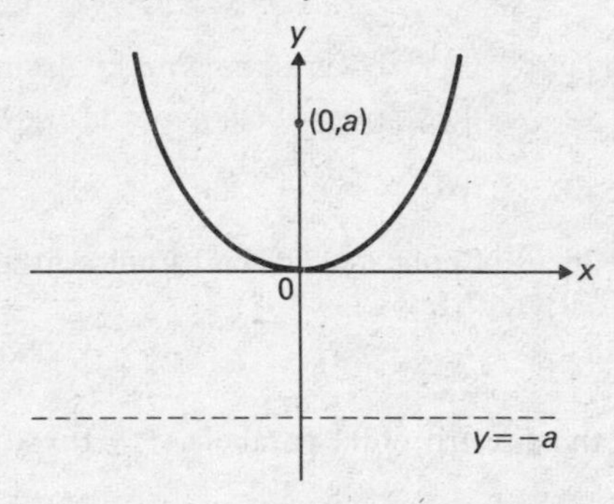

4. Find the foci and directrices of the parabolae (i) $y^2 = 16(x+1)$ and (ii) $y^2 = 4(2-x)$.

Answer

(i) Letting $X = x + 1$, the equation becomes $y^2 = 16X$, which has focus at $X = 4$, $y = 0$ and directrix $X = -4$. Transforming back to x, y co-ordinates using $x = X - 1$, the focus is $x = 4 - 1 = 3$, $y = 0$, the point $(3, 0)$. The directrix is the line $x = -5$.

(ii) In the same way, using $X = 2 - x$, the focus is found to be $(1, 0)$ and the directrix $x = 3$.

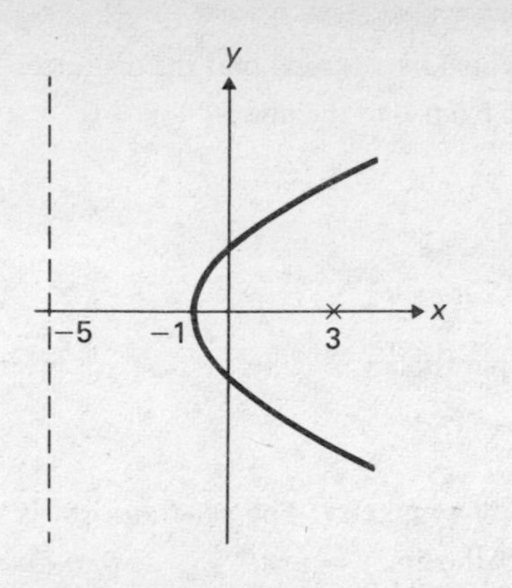

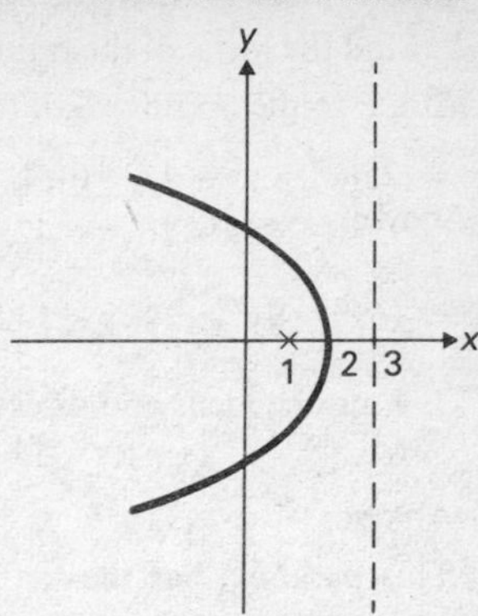

23.9 Other Loci

The parabola and circle are loci defined in terms of distances. Equations of other loci can also be found from geometrical constraints.

Examples

1. Find the locus of the variable point $P(x, y)$ which is equidistant from the points $A(-2, 3)$ and $B(1, 5)$.

Answer

$$PA^2 = (x+2)^2 + (y-3) \text{ and } PB^2 = (x-1)^2 + (y-5)^2$$

$$\Rightarrow x^2 + 4x + 4 + y^2 - 6y + 9 = x^2 - 2x + 1 + y^2 - 10y + 25$$

$$\Rightarrow 6x + 4y - 13 = 0$$

The locus is a straight line, the perpendicular bisector of line segment AB.

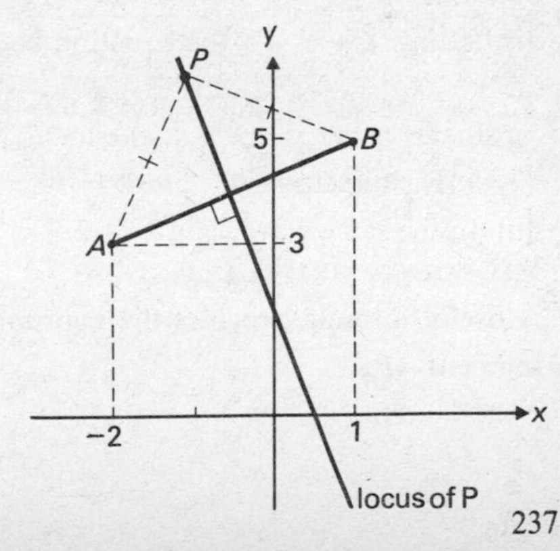

2. Find the locus of the point $P(x, y)$ which moves such that the distance from P to the origin is half the distance from P to the line $3x + y = 6$.

Answer

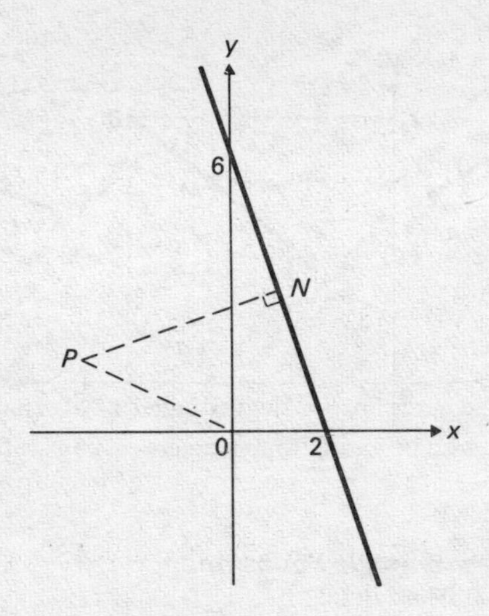

$$OP = \sqrt{x^2 + y^2}$$

$$PN = \left|\frac{3x + y - 6}{\sqrt{10}}\right|$$ page 227

$$\therefore \sqrt{x^2 + y^2} = \frac{1}{2}\left|\frac{3x + y - 6}{\sqrt{10}}\right|$$

$$\Rightarrow x^2 + y^2 = \frac{1}{4}\frac{(3x + y - 6)^2}{10}$$

$$\Rightarrow 40x^2 + 40y^2 = 9x^2 + 6xy + y^2 - 36x - 12y + 36$$

$$\Rightarrow 31x^2 + 39y^2 - 6xy + 36x + 12y - 36 = 0$$

MIDPOINT FORMULA

A useful formula provides the coordinates of the midpoint of the line segment AB.

If A is (x_1, y_1) and B is (x_2, y_2) then the midpoint is

$$M\left(\frac{x_1 + x_2}{2}, \frac{y_1 + y_2}{2}\right)$$

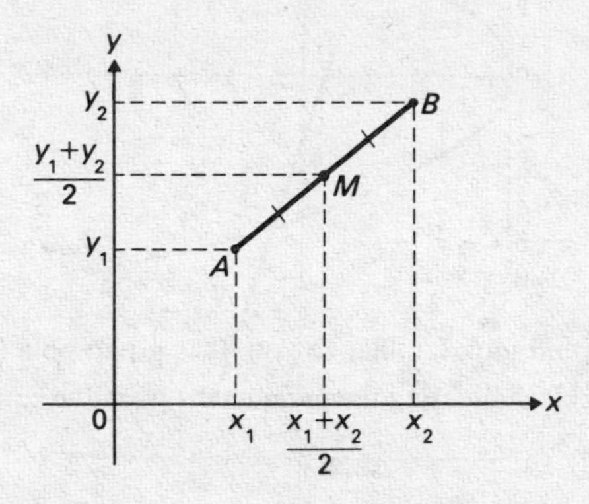

Section 24 Parametric Equations

24.1 Curves Defined by Parametric Equations

A curve in the plane can be defined by any rule which allows pairs of values (x, y) to be calculated.

Parametric equations give expressions for x and y in terms of a third variable or **parameter**.

Example

$x = t^2$, $y = 2t$ for $-\infty < t < \infty$ defines a curve in the x–y plane. For each value of t a pair of coordinates (x, y) is obtained.

t	-3	-2	-1	0	1	2	3
x	9	4	1	0	1	4	9
y	-6	-4	-2	0	2	4	6

Plotting the points $(9, -6)$, $(4, -4)$, $(1, -2)$, $(0, 0)$, $(1, 2)$, $(4, 4)$ and $(9, 6)$ enables a section of the graph to be sketched.

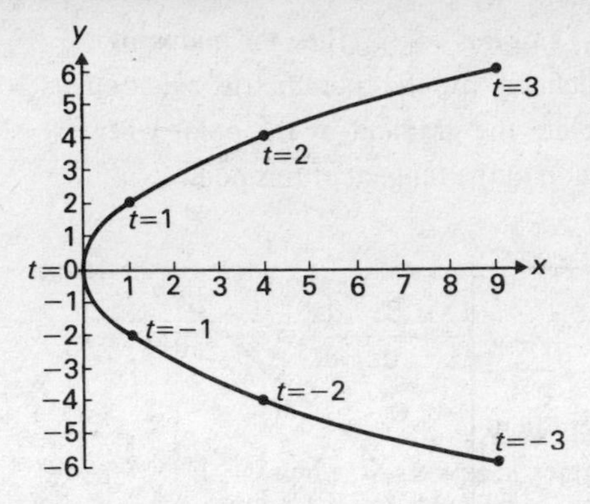

This shape should look familiar to you. It is a parabola (page 232). We can prove this by eliminating the parameter t from the equations

$$x = t^2 \qquad (1)$$

$$y = 2t \qquad (2)$$

From (2) $t = \frac{y}{2}$. Substituting in (1) gives $x = (\frac{y}{2})^2$ or $y^2 = 4x$, a parabola. This means that the coordinates of a general point on this parabola can be expressed in the form $(t^2, 2t)$. Elimination of the parameter results in a single x–y equation for the curve.

It should not be necessary to resort to plotting many points to obtain the graph. The general features of the curve can be deduced by examining the parametric equations.

24.2 Differentiation and Curve Sketching for Parametric Equations

The differentiation rule is similar to the change of variable rule of page 161.

The change of variable rule states that

$$\frac{dy}{dt} = \frac{dy}{dx}\frac{dx}{dt}$$

so that

$$\boxed{\frac{dy}{dx} = \frac{dy}{dt} \bigg/ \frac{dx}{dt}}$$

Examples

1. A curve is defined by the parametric equations $x = t^2 + 2t - 3$, $y = t - t^3$. Calculate the gradient at the point where $t = 2$ and hence deduce the equation of the tangent at this point.

Answer

$$\frac{dy}{dx} = \frac{dy}{dt}\bigg/\frac{dx}{dt} \equiv \frac{1 - 3t^2}{2t + 2}$$

When $t = 2$ the gradient is $\frac{1-12}{4+2} = -\frac{11}{6}$.

From the parametric equations, when $t = 2$

$$x = 4 + 4 - 3 = 5$$

$$y = 2 - 8 = -6$$

The equation of the tangent at this point is

$$y + 6 = -\frac{11}{6}(x - 5)$$

$$\Rightarrow 6y + 36 = -11x + 55$$

$$\Rightarrow 11x + 6y - 19 = 0$$

2. Calculate the coordinates of any points on the curve defined by the equations

$$x = t + 4$$

$$y = 1 - t^2$$

at which the gradient is -3.

Answer

Gradient $= \frac{dy}{dx} = \frac{dy}{dt}\big/\frac{dx}{dt} = \frac{-2t}{1} = -2t$.

At the required point $-2t = -3$.

$$\Rightarrow t = 3/2$$

$$\Rightarrow x = \frac{3}{2} + 4 = \frac{11}{2}$$

and

$$y = 1 - \frac{9}{4} = \frac{-5}{4}$$

The gradient is -3 at the point $(\frac{11}{2}, \frac{-5}{4})$.

THE EQUATION OF THE TANGENT TO THE PARABOLA $y^2 = 4ax$ AT THE POINT $(at^2, 2at)$

$$x = at^2, y = 2at, \text{ so that } \frac{dy}{dx} = \frac{dy}{dt} \bigg/ \frac{dx}{dt} = \frac{2a}{2at} = \frac{1}{t}.$$

The tangent has gradient $\frac{1}{t}$. The equation is

$$y - 2at = \frac{1}{t}(x - at^2)$$

$$\Rightarrow y - 2at = \frac{1}{t}x - at$$

$$\Rightarrow \qquad y = \frac{1}{t}x + at$$

The equation of the normal at (at^2, at) is similarly found to be

$$tx + y = 2at + at^3$$

with gradient $-t$.

TURNING POINTS

Turning points can be found by determining when $\frac{dy}{dx} = 0$. Since $\frac{dy}{dx} = \frac{dy}{dt} / \frac{dx}{dt}$ this occurs when $\frac{dy}{dt} = 0$ (but $\frac{dx}{dt} \neq 0$).

Examples

1. Find any turning points on the curve with parametric equations

$$x = t^2$$

$$y = t^3 - 3t \; (-\infty < t < \infty).$$

Examine the behaviour of the curve at the origin and as $t \to \infty$. From the information you obtain, sketch the curve defined by these equations.

Answer

$$\frac{dy}{dx} = \frac{dy}{dt}\bigg/\frac{dx}{dt} = \frac{3t^2 - 3}{2t} = \frac{3(t^2 - 1)}{2t}$$

This is zero when $t^2 - 1 = 0 \Rightarrow t = \pm 1$. ($\frac{dx}{dt} = \pm 2 \neq 0$)

When $t = 1, x = 1, y = -2$.

When $t = -1, x = 1, y = 2$.

To determine whether these are maximum or minimum points we look at the gradient as t varies.

x	$<+1$	$=1$	$>+1$
t	>-1	-1	<-1
$\frac{dy}{dx}$	$+$	0	$-$
		maximum	

x	<1	$=1$	>1
t	<1	1	>1
$\frac{dy}{dx}$	$-$	0	$+$
		minimum	

Notice how the behaviour differs depending on whether t is positive or negative. The tables above *must* show the sign of the gradient as x increases from left to right.

At the origin, $x = 0$ (and $y = 0$) $\Rightarrow t^2 = 0 \Rightarrow t = 0$. Gradient when $t \equiv 0$ is $-\frac{3}{0}$ which is **undefined**.

However, gradient $\rightarrow \pm \infty$ as $t \rightarrow 0$. The y-axis is a tangent at the origin.

As $t \rightarrow +\infty$	As $t \rightarrow -\infty$
$x \rightarrow +\infty$	$x \rightarrow +\infty$
$y \rightarrow +\infty$ (cubic in t)	$y \rightarrow -\infty$ (cubic in t)

Note also that the curve is only defined for *positive* values of x. The curve cuts the x-axis when $y = t^3 - 3t = 0 \Rightarrow t(t^2 - 3) = 0 \Rightarrow t = 0$ or $t = \pm\sqrt{3}$. When $t = 0$, $x = 0$, when $t = \pm\sqrt{3}$, $x = 3$. Putting this together

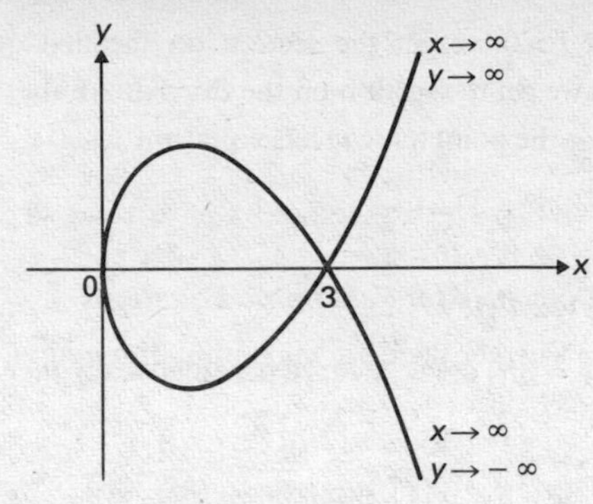

The curve forms a loop. Hence it cannot represent the graph of a single function (as it is not one–one). The cartesian equation is $y^2 = x(x-3)^2$.

2. Investigate the curve defined by the parametric equations $x = ct$, $y = \frac{c}{t}$ when c is a positive constant.

Answer

For turning points $\frac{dy}{dx} = 0$. Now, $\frac{dy}{dx} = \frac{dy}{dt} / \frac{dy}{dt} = \frac{-c}{t^2} / c = \frac{-1}{t^2} < 0$ for all values of t. There are no turning points, moreover the curve slopes downwards at all points.

As $t \to 0$, $x \to 0$ and $y \to \infty$. We say that the y-axis is a **vertical asymptote**; that is, the curve approaches more and more closely to the y-axis but does not cross it. As $t \to +\infty$, $x \to \infty$ and $y \to 0$. As $t \to -\infty$, $x \to -\infty$ and $y \to 0$. The curve approaches the x-axis for large values of x. We say that the x-axis is a **horizontal asymptote**.

Since $x = 0 \Rightarrow t = 0 \Rightarrow y = \infty$, the curve does not cross the x-axis. The curve is

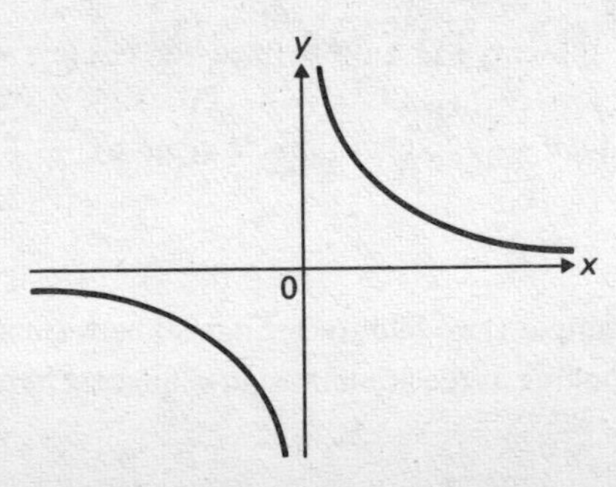

Notice that for $t > 0$ we get the section on the first quadrant ($x > 0$, $y > 0$), for $t < 0$ we get the section on the third quadrant ($x < 0$, $y < 0$).

The tangent at the point $(ct, c/t)$ has equation $x + t^2y = 2ct$.

24.3 Second Derivative for Parametric Equations

If $x = f(t)$ and $y = g(t)$ define a curve parametrically then

$$\frac{dy}{dx} = \frac{dy}{dt}\bigg/\frac{dx}{dt} = \frac{g'(t)}{f'(t)}$$

Thus $\frac{d}{dx}(\quad) = \frac{d}{dt}(\quad)/\frac{dx}{dt}$, where *any* function of t can be placed inside the brackets ( ).

So $\frac{d}{dx}(\frac{dy}{dx}) = \frac{d}{dt}(\frac{dy}{dx})/\frac{dx}{dt}$, since $\frac{dy}{dx}$ is itself a function of t.

$$\Rightarrow \boxed{\frac{d^2y}{dx^2} = \frac{d}{dt}\left(\frac{dy}{dx}\right)\bigg/\frac{dx}{dt}}.$$

Example

$$x = 3t^2, \qquad y = 5t$$

$$\Rightarrow \frac{dx}{dt} = 6t, \qquad \frac{dy}{dt} = 5$$

So

$$\frac{dy}{dx} = \frac{5}{6t}$$

and hence

$$\frac{d^2y}{dx^2} = \frac{-5}{6t^2}\bigg/6t = \frac{-5}{36t^3}$$

$$\left(\textit{not } \frac{-5}{6t^2}, \text{ you } \textit{must} \text{ divide again by } \frac{dx}{dt}.\right)$$

Example

On page 242, example 1, we had to distinguish between a maximum and a minimum by looking at the gradient sign changes. Alternatively, $x = t^2$, $y = t^3 - 3t$, $\frac{dy}{dx} = \frac{3(t^2-1)}{2t} = \frac{3t}{2} - \frac{1}{2t}$.

So

$$\frac{d^2y}{dx^2} = \left(\frac{3}{2} + \frac{1}{2t^2}\right)\Big/ 2t = \frac{3}{4t} + \frac{1}{4t^3}$$

When $t = 1$, $\frac{d^2y}{dx^2} = \frac{3}{4} + \frac{1}{4} > 0$ for a minimum.

When $t = -1$, $\frac{d^2y}{dx^2} = -\frac{3}{4} - \frac{1}{4} < 0$ for a maximum.

24.4 Integration and Areas

Example

Find the area bounded by the loop of the curve defined by $x = t^2$, $y = t^3 - 3t$ (Example 1, page 242).

Answer

See figure on page 244.

The curve crosses itself when $t = \pm\sqrt{3}$. The area is given by the formula

$$\boxed{\text{Area} = \left| \int_{t_1}^{t_2} y^2 \frac{dx}{dt} dt \right|}$$

which is obtained by using the change of variable rule (page 244).

$$\int_{-\sqrt{3}}^{\sqrt{3}} (t^3 - 3t)2t dt = \int_{-\sqrt{3}}^{\sqrt{3}} (2t^4 - 6t^2) dt$$

$$= \left[\frac{2t^5}{5} - 2t^3\right]_{-\sqrt{3}}^{\sqrt{3}}$$

$$= \left(\frac{18\sqrt{3}}{5} - 6\sqrt{3}\right) - \left(-\frac{18\sqrt{3}}{5} + 6\sqrt{3}\right)$$

$$= \frac{36\sqrt{3}}{5} - 12\sqrt{3}$$

$$= -\frac{24\sqrt{3}}{5}$$

The area must be *positive*, and is equal to $\frac{24\sqrt{3}}{5}$ square units.

While many curve sketching, differentiating and integration problems can be solved by reverting to x–y forms, it is usually preferable to work with the parametric forms directly.

Section 25 Approximate Methods for Integration

Integration of the more general functions in this chapter can be difficult or even impossible! In such cases we resort to numerical methods of integration.

25.1 Use of the Binomial Expansion

Example

Estimate $\int_0^{0.1} \frac{1}{(1+x^2)^2}\,dx$.

Answer

Express $\frac{1}{(1+x^2)^2}$ as a binomial expansion.

$$\frac{1}{(1+x^2)^2} = (1+x^2)^{-2} = 1 + (-2)(x^2) + \frac{(-2)(-3)}{2!}(x^2)^2 + \dots$$

$$= 1 - 2x^2 + 3x^4 + \dots$$ page 209

which is a convergent series provided $-1 < x < 1$. Since the values of x are taken between the limits 0 and 0·1, we can be sure that this series converges. Also, since the range of values of x is small, only a few terms of the series are required for a reasonable approximation.

Assuming that the series can be integrated term by term:

$$\int_0^{0\cdot1} \frac{1}{(1+x^2)^2}\,dx \approx \int_0^{0\cdot1} (1-2x^2+3x^4)\,dx$$

$$\approx \left[x - \frac{2}{3}x^3 + \frac{3}{5}x^5\right]_0^{0.1}$$

$$= 0\cdot1 - \frac{2}{3}(0\cdot001) + \frac{3}{5}(0\cdot00001)$$

$$= 0\cdot1 - 0\cdot000667 + 0\cdot000006 = 0\cdot09939$$

(to 5 decimal places)

It is *essential* that the limits for x are small in magnitude. $\int_2^5 \frac{1}{(1+x^2)^2}\,dx$ *cannot* be evaluated in this way.

25.2 The Trapezium Rule

Since an integral corresponds to an area between part of a curve and the x-axis, we can approximate to this area by splitting it into trapezia:

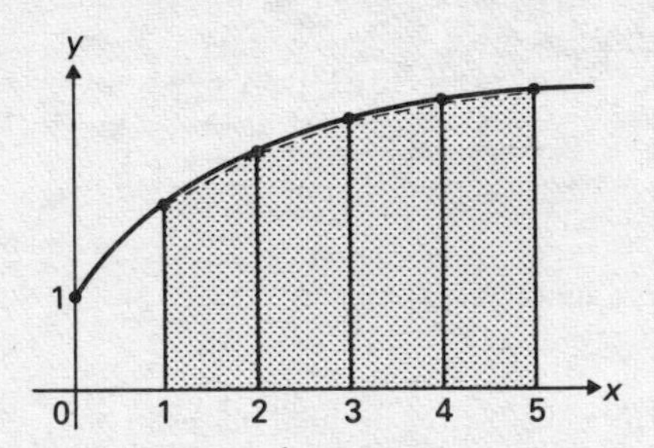

The figure shows the area bounded by the curve $y = \sqrt{1+x^2}$, the x-axis and the lines $x = 1$ and $x = 5$. It is split into 4 trapezia of equal widths.

By adding the areas of the trapezia we find an approximation to the integral $\int_1^5 \sqrt{1+x^2}\,dx$.

The area of a trapezium is given by the formula $\frac{1}{2} \times$ (sum of parallel sides) $\times$ distance between parallel sides.

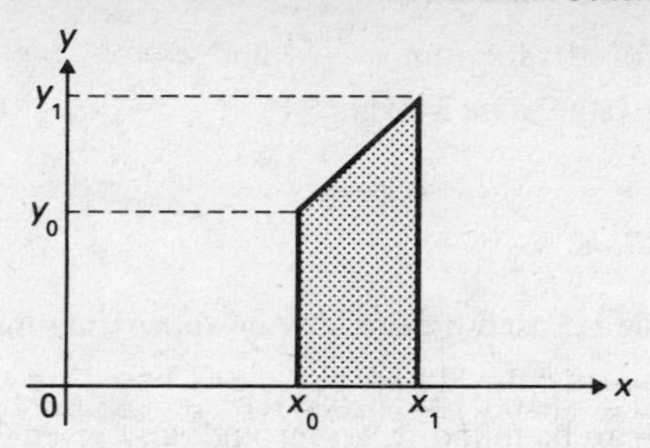

If a trapezium is is formed by the x-axis, the lines $x = x_0$ and $x = x_1$, and the curve $y = f(x)$, then it has area $\frac{h}{2}(y_0 + y_1)$ where $h = x_1 - x_0 =$ width of trapezium and $y_0 = f(x_0)$, $y_1 = f(x_1)$.

For the function of $y = \sqrt{1 + x^2}$ with $1 \leqslant x \leqslant 5$ and 4 strips, we need to evaluate y for the values 1, 2, 3, 4, 5 of x. Set this out in a table.

x	1	2	3	4	5
y	1·4142	2·2361	3·1623	4·1231	5·0990

using a calculator to 4 decimal places

The corresponding trapezia have areas

$$\tfrac{1}{2}(1{\cdot}4142 + 2{\cdot}2361) = 1{\cdot}8252$$

$$\tfrac{1}{2}(2{\cdot}2361 + 3{\cdot}1623) = 2{\cdot}6992$$

$$\tfrac{1}{2}(3{\cdot}1623 + 4{\cdot}1231) = 3{\cdot}6427$$

and

$$\tfrac{1}{2}(4{\cdot}1231 + 5{\cdot}0990) = 4{\cdot}6111$$

giving a total of 12·7782.

Thus $\int_1^5 \sqrt{1 + x^2}\,dx \simeq 12{\cdot}78$ (to 2 decimal places).

In general, if the area is split into n trapezia corresponding to the $(n + 1)$ values of x coordinates $x_0, x_1, \ldots x_n$ with corresponding y values $y_0, y_1, \ldots, y_n$, then

$$\boxed{\int_a^b y\,dx \approx \frac{h}{2}(y_0 + 2(y_1 + \ldots + y_{n-1}) + y_n)}$$

where h = width of a trapezium = $\frac{b-a}{n}$ and $a = x_0$, $b = x_n$. (assuming the trapezia all have the same width).

25.3 Simpson's Rule

The trapezium rule is based on the idea of approximating to the curve with straight line segments. Simpson's rule is based on the fact that a parabolic section can be found to go through any given 3 points. Thus *quadratic* approximations are found to fit the curve.

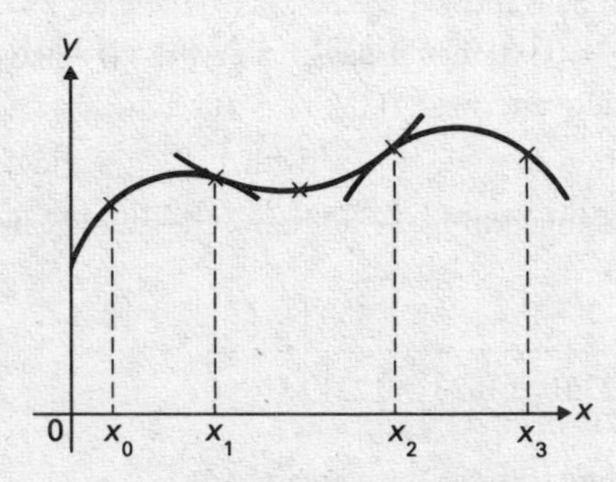

If the interval $a \leqslant x \leqslant b$ is split into n equal pieces (where n must be *even* now) $(n+1)$ x-values are obtained $a = x_0, x_1, x_2, \ldots x_n = b$. The corresponding values of the functions are $y_0 = f(x_0), \ldots, y_n = f(x_n)$.

$$\text{If } h = \frac{b-a}{n} = \text{(constant) strip width then}$$

$$\int_a^b f(x)\,dx \simeq \frac{h}{3}(y_0 + y_n + 4(y_1 + y_3 + \ldots) + 2(y_2 + y_4 + \ldots))$$

Example

Use Simpson's rule to find an approximation to $\int_1^5 \sqrt{1+x^2}\,dx$ with 4 strips.

Answer

The x values are 1, 2, 3, 4, 5.

x	1	2	3	4	5
y	1·4142	2·2361	3·1623	4·1231	5·0990

as in the last example

$$h = \frac{b-a}{n} = \frac{5-1}{4} = 1$$

$$\int_1^5 \sqrt{1+x^2}\,dx \simeq \frac{1}{3}(1{\cdot}4142 + 5{\cdot}0990 + 4(2{\cdot}2361 + 4{\cdot}1231) + 2(3{\cdot}1623))$$

$$= 12{\cdot}7582$$

More advanced integration methods give the *exact* answer 12·75597 to 5 decimal places.

Section 26 Worked Examples

1. Show that if x is small enough for terms in x^3 and higher powers of x to be ignored, then

$$\frac{(1+2x)^{-\frac{1}{2}}}{1-x} = 1 + \frac{3}{2}x^2 + \ldots$$

State the range of values of x for which the expansions converge.

Answer

$$(1+2x)^{-\frac{1}{2}} = 1 + (-\tfrac{1}{2})(2x) + \frac{(-\frac{1}{2})(-\frac{3}{2})}{2}(2x)^2 + \ldots$$

binomial expanions, page 209

$$= 1 - x + \frac{3}{2}x^2 + \ldots$$

up to x^2 term

$$\frac{1}{1-x} \equiv (1-x)^{-1} = 1 + x + x^2 + \ldots$$

Thus

$$\frac{(1+2x)^{-\frac{1}{2}}}{(1-x)} = (1 - x + \frac{3}{2}x^2)(1 + x + x^2) \qquad \text{up to } x^2 \text{ term}$$

$$= 1 - x + \frac{3}{2}x^2 + x - x^2 + x^2 \qquad \text{ignoring } x^3 \text{ and higher}$$

$$= 1 + \frac{3}{2}x^2 + \ldots$$

The series for $(1 + 2x)^{-\frac{1}{2}}$ converges if $-1 < 2x < 1$.

The series for $(1 - x)^{-1}$ converges if $-1 < x < 1$.

The inequalities $-\frac{1}{2} < x < \frac{1}{2}, -1 < x < 1$ must both be satisfied. Thus $-\frac{1}{2} < x < \frac{1}{2}$.

2. Find the values of a for which $y = a(x + 1)$ is a tangent to the parabola $y^2 = 16x$. Find the values of b for which $y = 2x + b$ is a tangent to the curve $2x^2 - y^2 = 4$. Hence write down the equation of a common tangent to the two curves.

Answer

For points of intersection

$$a^2(x + 1)^2 = 16x$$

$$\Rightarrow a^2(x^2 + 2x + 1) = 16x$$

$$\Rightarrow a^2x^2 + (2a^2 - 16)x + a^2 = 0$$

For a tangent

$$(2a^2 - 16)^2 - 4a^2 \cdot a^2 = 0 \qquad \text{equal roots}$$

$$4a^4 - 64a^2 + 256 - 4a^4 = 0$$

$$\Rightarrow 64a^2 = 256$$

$$\Rightarrow \quad a^2 = 4$$

$$\Rightarrow \quad a = \pm 2$$

For the line $y = 2x + b$ and the curve $2x^2 - y^2 = 4$

$$2x^2 - (2x + b)^2 = 4$$

$$2x^2 - 4x^2 - 4bx - b^2 = 4$$

$$-2x^2 - 4bx - b^2 = 4$$

$$2x^2 + 4bx + (b^2 + 4) = 0$$

For a tangent

$$16b^2 - 4(2)(b^2 + 4) = 0$$

$$\Rightarrow 16b^2 - 8b^2 - 32 = 0$$
$$\Rightarrow 8b^2 = 32$$
$$\Rightarrow b^2 = 4$$
$$\Rightarrow b = \pm 2$$

The common tangent is

$$y = 2x + 2 \ (a = 2, b = 2)$$

3. A curve is defined by the parametric equation

$$x = t^2, y = t^3$$

Sketch the graph of this curve, showing the behaviour at the origin. Calculate the area bounded by the curve and the line $x = 4$.

Answer

$x = t^2 \Rightarrow x$ is positive for all t.

$x = 0 \Leftrightarrow t = 0 \Leftrightarrow y = 0$ find intercepts

The curve meets either axis only at the origin.

Gradient $= \frac{dy}{dx} = \frac{dy}{dt} / \frac{dx}{dt}$

$$\frac{3t^2}{2t} = \frac{3t}{2}$$

At (0, 0), $t = 0$ and so $\frac{dy}{dx} = 0$

As t increases to $+\infty$, x, y and $\frac{dy}{dx}$ increase. the curve gets steeper

If $t < 0$, $y < 0$ and $\frac{dy}{dx} < 0$.

The graph is

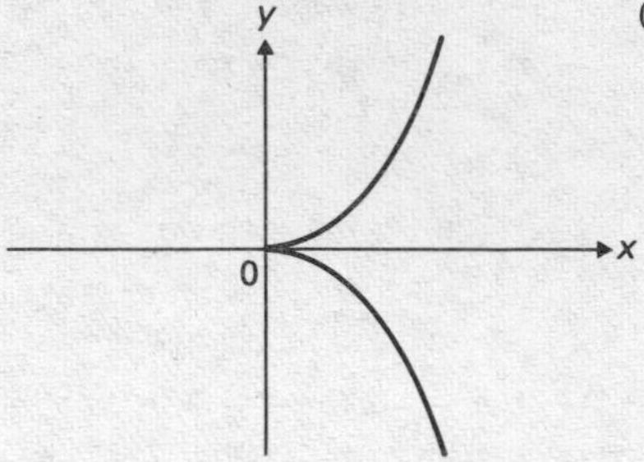

gradient is zero at (0, 0)

The curve is symmetric about the x-axis, since $y \to -y \Rightarrow t - t \Rightarrow x \to x$, i.e. for each value of x there are two points (x, y) and $(x, -y)$ on the curve.

When $x = 4$, $t^2 = 4 \Rightarrow t = 2$ (or -2).

The area required is

$$2\int_0^2 y\frac{dx}{dt}dt = 2\int_0^2 t^3 2t\,dt$$

double the top area

$$= 4\int_0^2 t^4 dt = \frac{4}{5}[t^5]_0^2 = \frac{128}{5} \text{ square units}$$

4. (*a*) Evaluate $\int \frac{1}{\sqrt{x}(1+\sqrt{x})^3}dx$ by using the substitution $u = 1 + \sqrt{x}$.

(*b*) Use Simpson's rule to estimate $\int_0^1 \frac{1}{(1+\sqrt{x})^3}dx$ using 5 ordinates. Express your working to 3 decimal place accuracy.

Answer

(*a*) $$\int \frac{1}{\sqrt{x}(1+\sqrt{x})^3}dx$$

change to a u-integration

using the substitution $u = 1 + \sqrt{x}$, so that $\frac{du}{dx} = \frac{1}{2}x^{-\frac{1}{2}} \Rightarrow 2du = \frac{1}{\sqrt{x}\,dx}$.

The integral becomes $\int \frac{1}{u^3} 2\mathrm{d}u$

$$2\int \frac{1}{u^3}\,\mathrm{d}u$$

$$= 2\left(\frac{u^{-2}}{-2}\right) + K \qquad \int x^n \mathrm{d}x = \frac{x^{n+1}}{n+1} + K$$

$$= -u^{-2} + K$$

$$= -(1 + x^{\frac{1}{2}})^{-2} + K \qquad \text{revert to } x\text{-variable, } x^{\frac{1}{2}} = \sqrt{x}$$

$$= K - \frac{1}{(1+\sqrt{x})^2}$$

(b) $y = \dfrac{1}{(1+\sqrt{x})^3}$

The 5 ordinates are 0, 0.25, 0.5, 0.75, 1.0

x	0	0·25	0·5	0·75	1·0
y	1·0	0·296	0·201	0·154	0·125

Interval width = 0·25

By Simpson's rule

$$\int_0^1 \frac{1}{(1+x)^3}\mathrm{d}x \simeq \frac{0{\cdot}25}{3}(1{\cdot}0 + 0{\cdot}125 + 4(0{\cdot}296 + 0{\cdot}154) + 2(0{\cdot}201))$$

$$= 0{\cdot}277 \text{ (to 3 decimal places)}$$

5. A point $P(x, y)$ moves in the plane so that its distance from the point $A\,(-3, 0)$ is always 3 times the distance from the point $B(4, 0)$. Find an equation for the locus of P and describe it geometrically.

Answer

$$AP = \sqrt{(x+3)^2 + y^2} \qquad \text{Pythagoras, page 132}$$

$$= \sqrt{x^2 + 6x + 9 + y^2}$$

$$BP = \sqrt{(x-4)^2 + y^2} = \sqrt{x^2 - 8x + 16 + y^2}$$

Given $AP = 3BP$

$$\sqrt{x^2 + 6x + 9 + y^2} = 3\sqrt{x^2 - 8x + 16 + y^2}$$

$$\Rightarrow x^2 + 6x + 9 + y^2 = 9(x^2 - 8x + 16 + y^2) \qquad \text{squaring both sides}$$

$$\Rightarrow 8x^2 + 8y^2 - 78x + 135 = 0 \quad (1) \qquad \text{locus of } P$$

$$\Rightarrow x^2 + y^2 - \frac{39}{4}x + \frac{135}{8} = 0$$

$$\Rightarrow \left(x - \frac{39}{8}\right)^2 + (y - 0)^2 = -\frac{135}{8} + \left(\frac{39}{8}\right)^2 = \frac{441}{64}$$

This is a circle with centre $(\frac{39}{8}, 0)$ and radius $\frac{\sqrt{441}}{8}$ (page 219).

6. $P(ap^2, 2ap)$ and $Q(aq^2, 2aq)$ are two different points on the parabola $y^2 = 4ax$. The chord PQ passes through the focus $S(a, 0)$.
(i) Show that $pq = -1$, (ii) find the equations of the tangents at P and Q and show that they are perpendicular.
(iii) Show that these two tangents intersect on the line $x = -a$.
(iv) Find the locus of the midpoint of PQ as p varies.

Answer

(i) PQ has equation

$$y - 2ap = \frac{(2aq - 2ap)}{(aq^2 - ap^2)}(x - ap^2)$$

$$y - 2ap = \frac{2(q - p)}{(q^2 - p^2)}(x - ap^2)$$

$$y - 2ap = \frac{2}{(q + p)}(x - ap^2)$$

$(a, 0)$ lies on this line, so that

$$-2ap = \frac{2}{(q + p)(a - ap^2)}$$

$$-p(p + q) = 1 - p^2$$

$$-pq - p^2 = 1 - p^2$$

$$pq = -1$$

(ii) At the point $(at^2, 2at)$, $y^2 = 4ax$ has gradient $\frac{dy}{dt}/\frac{dx}{dt} = \frac{2a}{2at} = \frac{1}{t}$. The tangent at $(at^2, 2at)$ is

$$y - 2at = \frac{1}{t}(x - at^2)$$

$$ty - 2at^2 = x - at^2$$

$$ty = x + at^2$$

The tangents at P and Q are

$$py = x + ap^2 \text{ and } qy = x + aq^2$$

with gradients $\frac{1}{p}$ and $\frac{1}{q}$ respectively. The product of the gradients is $\frac{1}{p} \times \frac{1}{q} = \frac{1}{pq} = -1$, since $pq = -1$. The tangents are perpendicular (page 136).

(iii) For points of intersection

$$\frac{(x + ap^2)}{p} = \frac{(x + aq^2)}{q}$$

$$qx + ap^2q = px + apq^2$$

$$x(q - p) = apq(q - p)$$

$$x = apq \qquad p \neq q$$

$$x = -a \qquad pq = -1$$

(iv) PQ has midpoint $M\left(\frac{(ap^2 + aq^2)}{2}, \frac{(2ap + 2aq)}{2}\right)$

$$M\left(\frac{a(p^2 + q^2)}{2}, a(p + q)\right)$$

So

$$x = \frac{a(p^2 + q^2)}{2} \quad y = a(p + q)$$

$$\therefore y^2 = a^2(p + q)^2 = a^2(p^2 + q^2 + 2pq)$$

$$= a^2(p^2 + q^2 - 2) \text{ since } pq = 1.$$

But

$$x = \frac{a(p^2 + q^2)}{2} \Rightarrow p^2 + q^2 = \frac{2x}{a}$$

Thus

$$y^2 = a^2\left(\frac{2x}{a} - 2\right)$$

$$y^2 = 2a(x - a)$$

which is the locus of M.

Section 27 Examination Questions

1. *Given that* $|x| < 1$, *find in ascending powers of* x, *up to and including the terms in* x^3, *series expansions in which the coefficients are simplified for (a)* $(1 + x)^{\frac{1}{2}}$, *(b)* $(1 + \frac{x}{4})^{-1}$.

Prove that if x *were sufficiently small for terms in* x^4 *and higher powers of* x *to be neglected, then* $(1 + x)^{\frac{1}{2}} - \frac{4 + 3x}{4 + x} = \frac{1}{32}x^3$. [AEB]

2. *Prove that for all values of* m, *the line* $y = mx - 2m^2$ *is a tangent to the parabola* $8y = x^2$.

Find the value of m *for which the line* $y = mx - 2m^2$ *is also a tangent to the parabola* $y^2 = x$.

The line PQ *is a tangent to* $8y = x^2$ *at* P *and a tangent to* $y^2 = x$ *at* Q. *Find the coordinates of* P *and* Q. [AEB]

3. *Obtain the first three non-zero terms in the expansion of* $(1+y)^{\frac{1}{2}}$, $|y|<1$, *as a series of ascending powers of* y. *Given that* $f(x) \equiv (1+x^{\frac{1}{2}})^{\frac{1}{2}}$, *write down the coefficients* a_0, a_1, a_2 *in the expansion* $a_0 + a_1x^{\frac{1}{2}} + a_2x + \ldots$ *of* $f(x)$ *as a series of ascending powers of* $x^{\frac{1}{2}}$.

Using this expansion, or otherwise, estimate the value of $\int_0^{0\cdot 01} f(x)\,dx$, *giving your answer to 4 decimal places.* [LON]

4. *A curve is given parametrically by the equations*

$$x = 1 + t^2, y = 2t - 1$$

Show that an equation of the tangent to the curve at the point with parameter t *is*

$$ty = x + t^2 - t - 1$$

Verify that the tangent at $A(2, 1)$ *passes through the point* $C(6, 5)$. *Show the line* $5y = x + 19$ *passes through* C *and is also a tangent to the curve.*

Find also the coordinates of the point of contact of this line with the given curve. [LON]

5. *A point* P *moves in the* x–y *plane so that its distance from the origin,* O, *is twice its distance from the point with coordinates* $(3a, 0)$. *Show that the locus of* P *is a circle and obtain the coordinates of its centre and its radius. If the circle meets the x-axis in* A *and* B *where* $OA < OB$, *find the coordinates of* A *and* B. *If the tangents from* O *to the circle are* OL *and* OM, *find the angle* LOM *and the equations of* OL *and* OM. *Calculate the area of the triangle enclosed by the lines* OL, OM, *and the tangent to the circle at* A. [SUJB]

6. $P(ap^2, 2ap)$ *and* $Q(aq^2, 2aq)$ *are points on the parabola* $y^2 = 4ax$. *that the equation of the chord* PQ *can be written in the form* $(p+q)y - 2x = 2apq$ *and that the gradient of the normal to the parabola at* P *is* $-p$.

The gradient of the normal at P *is six times the gradient of the tangent at* Q. *Prove (i) that* PQ *passes through a fixed point on the axis of the parabola; (ii) that the midpoint of* PQ *lies on the parabola* $y^2 = 2a(x - 6a)$. *Sketch the graphs of the two parabolae on the same axes and give the coordinates of the focus of each.* [SUJB]

7. *A curve is defined by the equations*

$$x = t^2 - 1, y = t^3 - t$$

where t is a parameter. Sketch the curve for all real values of t.

Find the area of the region enclosed by the loop of the curve. [LON]

8. *Find* $\int \frac{x}{\sqrt{(x-2)}} dx$ [LON–part]

9. *Show that the area of the finite region enclosed by the line* $y = 4x$ *and the curve* $y^2 = 16x$ *is* $\frac{2}{3}$. [LON]

10. *A curve is defined with parameter t by the equations* $x = at^2$, $y = 2at$. *The tangent and normal at the point P, with parameter* t_1, *meet the x-axis at T and N respectively. Prove that* $PT/PN = |t_1|$. [LON]

11. *The equation of the tangent to the curve* $xy = 2$ *at the point* $(2, 1)$ *is*

A $x - 2y = 0$ B $x + 2y = 4$ C $2x + y = 5$ D $2x - y = 3$ E $y = 2$

[LON]

12. $2x^2 - xy - y^2 = 0$. *When* $x = 1$ *and* $y = -2$, $\frac{dy}{dx} =$

A -2 B $-\frac{3}{2}$ C $\frac{4}{3}$ D $\frac{3}{2}$ E 2 [LON]

13. *The gradient of the normal at the point* (t^2, t^{-3}) *on the curve* $y^2 = x^{-3}$ *is*

A $-2t^5/3$ B $-3t/2$ C $-3/(2t^5)$ D $2/(3t)$ E $2t^5/3$

[LON]

14. *The circles*

$$x^2 + y^2 + 2x - 4y + 1 = 0$$

$$x^2 + y^2 + 2x + 2y - 2 = 0$$

1. *have their centres on the line* $x = 1$,
2. *intersect on the line* $y = \frac{1}{2}$,
3. *have equal radii.*

A 1, 2 and 3 are all true B 1 and 2 only C 2 and 3 only D 1 only E 3 only [LON]

15. *An approximate value of* $\int_0^{0 \cdot 2} \frac{1}{1+x^3} dx$, *obtained by expanding* $1/(1+x^3)$ *as a series in ascending powers of* x *as far as the term in* x^3, *is*

A 0·992 B 0·1920 C 0·1996 D 0·2004 E 1·008 [LON]

16. $\frac{1}{5-3x}$ *can be expanded as a series of ascending powers of* x *when*

$$1.\ x = -2 \quad 2.\ x = -1 \quad 3.\ x = 1.$$

A 1, 2 and 3 are all true B 1 and 2 only C 2 and 3 only D 1 only E 3 only [LON]

17. *Find the area of the region bounded by the curve* $y = 1 + x^{3/2}$, *the tangent to the curve at the point where* $x = 4$, *and the axis* Oy. *Find also the volume of the solid obtained by revolving this area through one complete revolution round the axis* Oy. [OXF]

18. *Find the equation of the normal to the parabola* $y^2 = 4ax$ *at the point* $(at^2, 2at)$. *The straight line* $4x - 9y + 8a = 0$ *meets the parabola at the points* P *and* Q; *the normals to the parabola at the points* P *and* Q *meet at* R. *Find the coordinates of* R, *and verify that it lies on the parabola.* [OXF]

7 Rational, Exponential and Logarithmic Functions

Section 28 Rational Functions

28.1 Introduction

A *rational function* has the form $y = \frac{f(x)}{g(x)}$ where $f(x)$ and $g(x)$ are polynomials.

If the order of $f(x)$ is strictly less than that of $g(x)$, we call the rational function a **proper fraction**, otherwise it is **improper**.

The values of x for which the denominator is zero must be excluded from the domain of the function. (Division by 0 is not permitted.)

Example

$$f: x \mapsto \frac{2x-1}{(x+3)(x-5)} \text{ on domain } \{x \in \mathbb{R} : x \neq -3, x \neq 5\}.$$

Equations involving rational functions can be solved by rearranging to form polynomial equations. It is useful to recall that a fraction can only take the value zero when its numerator is zero.

Example

$$\frac{2-x}{1+x} + \frac{3+2x}{5-x} = \frac{7}{3}$$

Answer

Take all terms to the left and put over a common denominator.

$$\frac{2-x}{1+x} + \frac{3+2x}{5-x} - \frac{7}{3} = 0$$

$$\frac{3(2-x)(5-x) + 3(3+2x)(1+x) - 7(1+x)(5-x)}{(1+x)(5-x)3} = 0$$

$$\Rightarrow 3(2-x)(5-x) + 3(3+2x)(1+x) - 7(1+x)(5-x) = 0$$

$$\Rightarrow 3(10 - 7x + x^2) + 3(3 + 5x + 2x^2) - 7(5 + 4x - x^2) = 0$$

$$\Rightarrow 16x^2 - 34x + 4 = 0$$

$$\Rightarrow 8x^2 - 17x + 2 = 0$$

This can be solved by factorizing

$$(x - 2)(8x - 1) = 0$$

$$\Rightarrow x = 2 \text{ or } x = \frac{1}{8}$$

28.2 Determining the Range

The graph of a rational function is often complicated, and so using the graph to find the range of a rational function may be tedious. (See Section 28.5 below.)

Fortunately some rational functions can be handled using our knowledge of quadratic functions (page 95).

Example

Find the range of the function

$$f: x \mapsto \frac{2x}{x^2 + 4}$$

defined on $\mathbb{R}$.

Answer

Let $y = \frac{2x}{x^2+4}$. If y is in the range set of f then it corresponds to at least one value of x. To find such values of x, we must solve the equation

$$y = \frac{2x}{x^2 + 4} \quad \text{for } x \qquad \text{regarding } y \text{ as a constant}$$

$$\Rightarrow x^2y + 4y = 2x$$

$$\Rightarrow yx^2 - 2x + 4y = 0$$

This is a quadratic equation in x, and can be solved to give *real* roots provided the discriminant is not negative (page 91).

$$4 - 4(y)(4y) \geqslant 0$$

$$\Rightarrow 1 - 4y^2 \geqslant 0$$

$$\Rightarrow \quad y^2 \leqslant \tfrac{1}{4}$$

$$\Rightarrow -\tfrac{1}{2} \leqslant y \leqslant \tfrac{1}{2}$$

INVERSE FUNCTIONS

The range of a function can sometimes be found by calculating the formula for the inverse function (page 32).

Example

$$f: x \mapsto \frac{2x+1}{x-3} \text{ on domain } \{x \in \mathbb{R}: x \neq 3\}.$$

Let $y = \dfrac{2x+1}{x-3}$

$$\Rightarrow xy - 3y = 2x + 1$$

$$\Rightarrow x(y-2) = 3y + 1$$

$$\Rightarrow x = \frac{3y+1}{y-2}$$

Thus $f^{-1}: y \mapsto \frac{3y+1}{y-2}$. This formula is valid provided that $y \neq 2$, and so the range of f is $\{y \in \mathbb{R}: y \neq 2\}$.

The inverse function is $f^{-1}: x \mapsto \frac{3x+1}{x-2}$.

28.3 Differentiating Rational Functions (Quotient Rule)

If $f(x) = \frac{u}{v}$ where u and v are (any) functions of x, then

$$f'(x) = \frac{v\dfrac{du}{dx} - u\dfrac{dv}{dx}}{[v]^2}$$

(Compare with product rule of page 162.)

Example

If $y = \frac{2x}{x^2+4}$, $u = 2x$ and $v = x^2 + 4$, $\frac{du}{dx} = 2$, $\frac{dv}{dx} = 2x$.

$$\Rightarrow \frac{dy}{dx} = \frac{(x^2+4)2 - 2x(2x)}{(x^2+4)^2}$$

$$= \frac{2x^2 + 8 - 4x^2}{(x^2+4)^2}$$

$$= \frac{8 - 2x^2}{(x^2+4)^2}$$

This result can be used to locate any turning points on the graph of $y = \frac{2x}{x^2+4}$.

For a turning point $\frac{dy}{dx} = 0 \Rightarrow \frac{8-2x^2}{(x^2+4)^2} = 0$

$$\Rightarrow 8 - 2x^2 = 0$$

$$\Rightarrow x^2 = 4$$

$$\Rightarrow x = \pm 2$$

When $x = -2$, $y = -\frac{4}{8} = -\frac{1}{2}$. When $x = 2$, $y = \frac{4}{8} = \frac{1}{2}$.

To distinguish maximum from minimum, consider

$$\frac{d^2y}{dx^2} = \frac{(x^2+4)^2(-4x) - (8-2x^2)(2)(x^2+4)(2x)}{(x^2+4)^4}$$

quotient rule again

$$= \frac{(x^2+4)(-4x) - 4x(8-2x^2)}{(x^2+4)^3}$$

$$= \frac{-4x^3 - 16x - 32x + 8x^3}{(x^2+4)^3}$$

notice that $\frac{d}{dx}[x^2+4)^2] = 2(x^2+4)(2x)$

$$= \frac{4x^3 - 48x}{(x^2+4)^3}$$

When $x = -2$, $\frac{d^2y}{dx^2} = \frac{-32+96}{8^2} > 0$

$\therefore (-2, -\frac{1}{2})$ is a minimum point.

page 156

When $x = 2$, $\frac{d^2y}{dx^2} = \frac{-32-96}{8^3} < 0$

$\therefore (2, \frac{1}{2})$ is a maximum point.

28.4 Inequalities with Rational Functions

Recall that you should not multiply an inequality by a quantity unless you know its sign.

Examples

1. $\dfrac{2x+1}{x^2+1} < 0$

$\Rightarrow 2x + 1 < 0$

Multiplying by $x^2 + 1$ is allowed because we know that $x^2 + 1 > 0$.

$\Rightarrow x < -\frac{1}{2}$

2. $\dfrac{2x+1}{x-1} < 0$

We cannot multiply by $x - 1$, since it could be negative. Instead we multiply by $(x-1)^2$, which is definitely positive.

$$\frac{(x-1)^2(2x+1)}{(x-1)} < 0$$

$\Rightarrow (x-1)(2x+1) < 0$

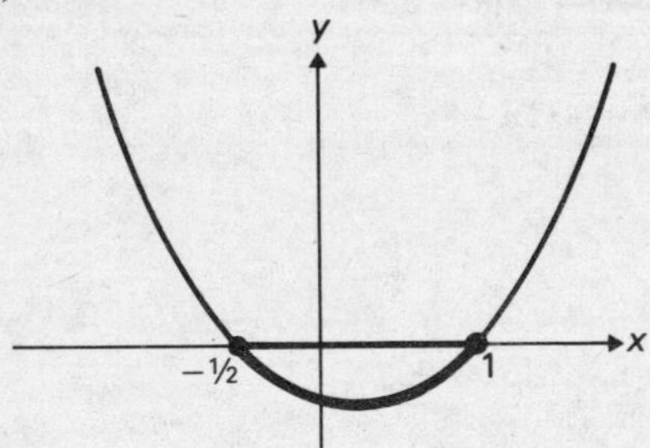

which has solution $-\frac{1}{2} < x < 1$,

see page 101

3. $\dfrac{2x+1}{x-1} < 1$

$\Rightarrow \dfrac{(x-1)^2(2x+1)}{(x-1)} < (x-1)^2$ multiplying by $(x-1)^2$

$\Rightarrow (x-1)(2x+1) < (x-1)^2$

$\Rightarrow (x-1)(2x+1) - (x-1)^2 < 0$ do not 'cancel' $(x-1)$ from both sides, it corresponds to *division*

$\Rightarrow (x-1)((2x+1)-(x-1)) < 0$ factorize

$\Rightarrow (x-1)(x+2) < 0$

$\Rightarrow -2 < x < 1$

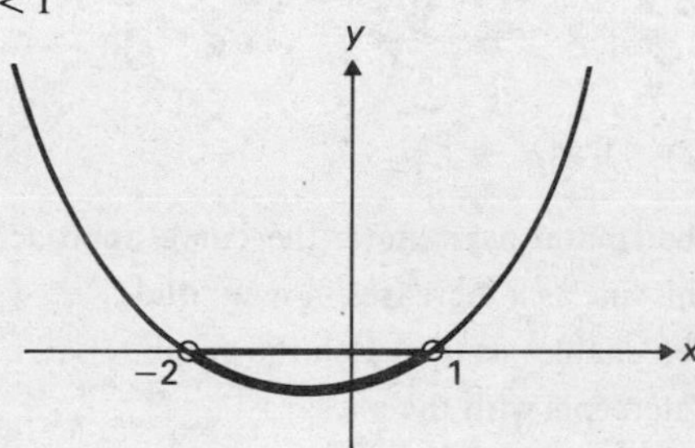

4. $\dfrac{x+3}{x^2-4} \geqslant 0$

$\Rightarrow (x^2-4)^2 \dfrac{(x+3)}{(x^2-4)} \geqslant 0$ multiply by $(x^2-4)^2$

$\Rightarrow (x^2-4)(x+3) \geqslant 0$

$\Rightarrow (x-2)(x+2)(x+3) \geqslant 0$

The cubic expression $(x-2)(x+2)(x+3)$ has graph

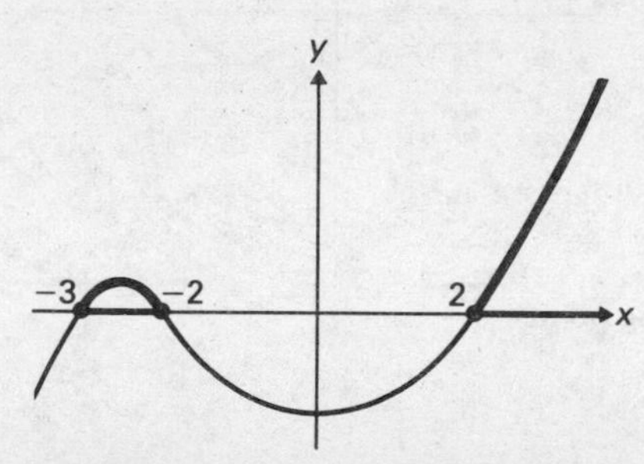

$\Rightarrow -3 \leqslant x < -2$ or $x > 2$

28.5 Curve Sketching

In section 28.3 we found the turning points on the curve $y = \frac{2x}{x^2+4}$. From section 28.2 we know that $\frac{2x}{x^2+4} \geqslant 0$ when $x \geqslant 0$. The graph cuts the x-axis when $y = 0 \Rightarrow x = 0$. The graph crosses the x-axis only through O (0, 0).

$$\text{As } x \to \pm\infty, \; y = \frac{2x}{x^2+4}$$

$$= \frac{\frac{2}{x}}{1 + \frac{4}{x^2}} \qquad \text{divide throughout by } x^2$$

$$\to \frac{0}{1+0} \qquad \frac{1}{x}, \frac{1}{x^2} \to 0$$

$$\therefore y \to 0 \text{ as } x \to \pm\infty$$

The x-axis is a **horizontal asymptote**: the curve approaches more and more closely to this line as x increases in magnitude.

This information enables us to sketch the graph.

First plot the intercepts with the axes.

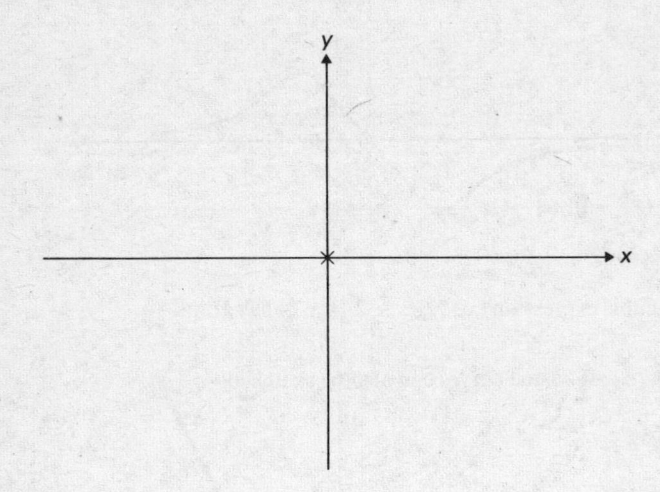

Then the turning points

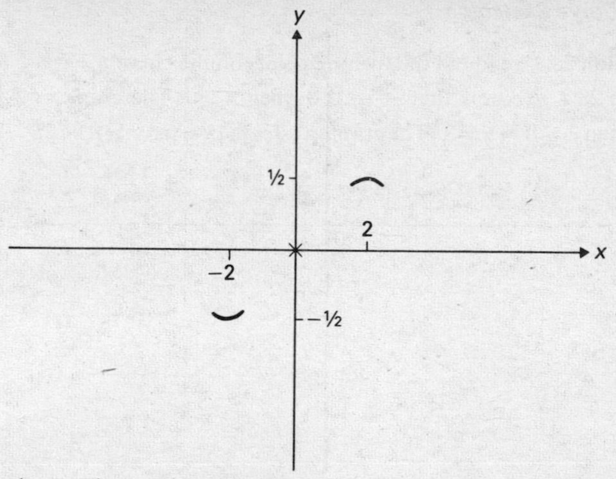

Join up these points and indicate the curve approaching the asymptote.

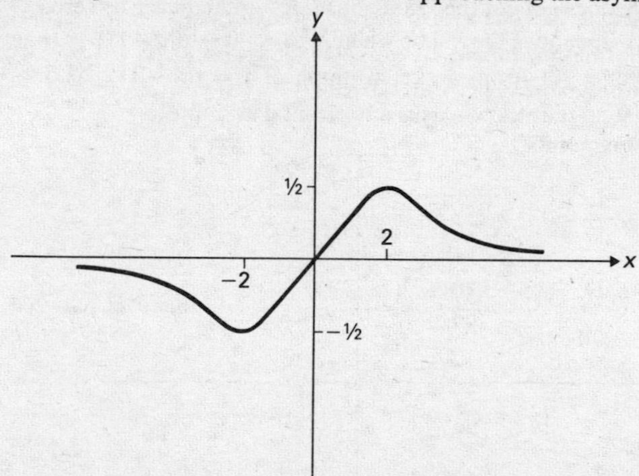

More complicated curves can also be sketched.

Example

$$y = \frac{2}{x(x-1)}$$

This function is not defined for all values of x. The denominator would be zero for $x = 0$ and $x = 1$. The lines $x = 0$ and $x = 1$ are **vertical asymptotes**, shown as dotted lines on the figure.

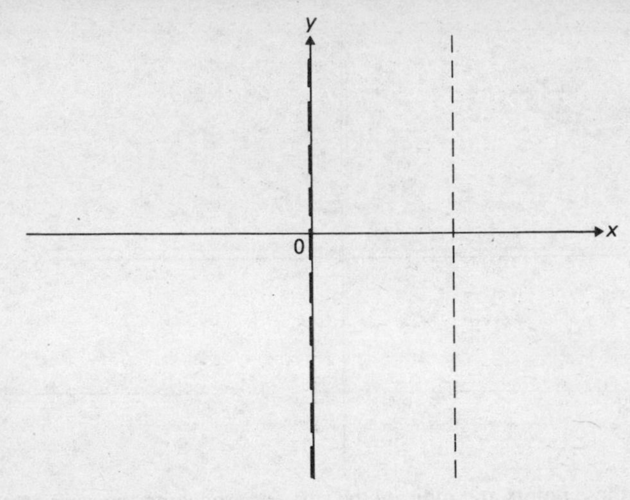

The curve does not cut the x-axis since $\frac{2}{x(x-1)}$ can never be zero. The curve lies above the x-axis when $\frac{2}{x(x-1)} > 0 \Rightarrow x(x-1) > 0$ (page 266) $\Rightarrow x < 0$ or $x > 1$ (from a sketch graph of $y = x(x-1)$). As $x \to \pm\infty$, $\frac{2}{x(x-1)} \to 0$, so that the x-axis is a horizontal asymptote.
For turning points,

$$\frac{dy}{dx} = 0.$$

$$\frac{dy}{dx} = \frac{(x^2 - x)(0) - 2(2x-1)}{(x^2-x)^2}$$ quotient, page 264

$$= \frac{2-4x}{(x^2-x)^2}$$

$$= 0 \text{ when } x = \tfrac{1}{2}$$

$$x = \tfrac{1}{2} \Rightarrow y = \frac{2}{\frac{1}{2}(-\frac{1}{2})} = -8$$

x	$<\frac{1}{2}$	$=\frac{1}{2}$	$>\frac{1}{2}$
$\frac{dy}{dx}$	+	0	−

page 154

$\Rightarrow (\frac{1}{2}, -8)$ is a maximum point.

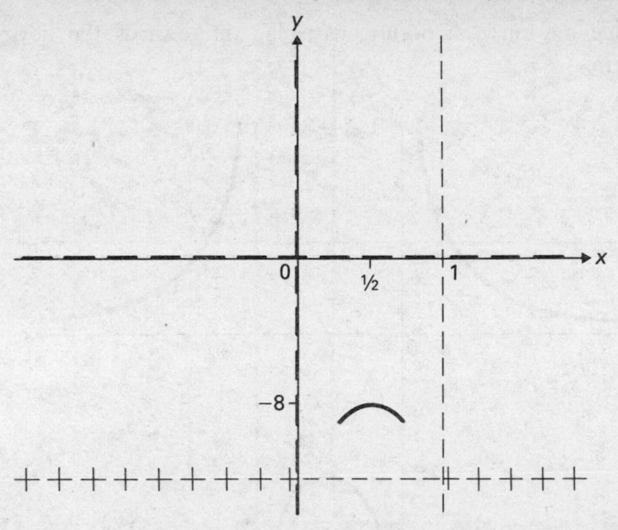

Near the vertical asymptote, the sign of y determines whether the curve turns upward (+) or downwards (−).

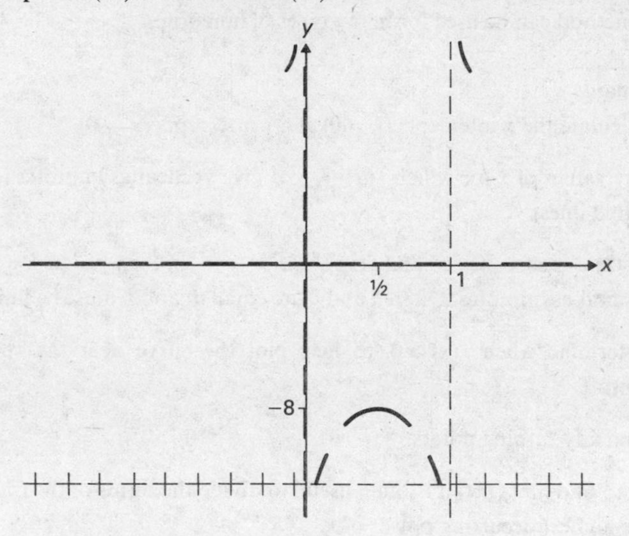

Continue the curve smoothly, flattening off towards the horizontal asymptote

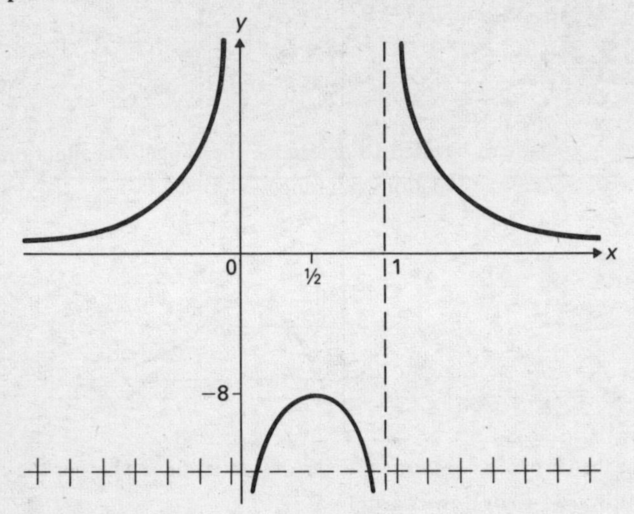

This method can be used for many types of function.

Summary

1. Calculate the x intercepts ($y = 0$) and y intercepts ($x = 0$).

2. Any values of x for which $f(x) \to \pm\infty$ give vertical asymptotes (show as dotted lines).

3. If $f(x) \to a$ as $x \to +\infty$ and $f(x) \to b$ as $x \to -\infty$, then $y = a$, $y = b$ are horizontal asymptotes. Often a and b are equal (a and b must be finite).

4. Determine when $f(x) \geqslant 0$, to help plot the curve near the vertical asymptote.

5. Find any turning points.

Note: to find $\lim(f(x))$ it is often useful to divide the terms of the fraction by the highest occurring power of x.

Examples

1. $y = \dfrac{x^2 - 3}{x^3 + 4} = \dfrac{\frac{1}{x} - \frac{3}{x^3}}{1 + \frac{4}{x^3}} \to \dfrac{0 - 0}{1 + 0} = 0$ as $x \to \pm\infty$

2. $y = \dfrac{x + 3}{2x - 5} = \dfrac{1 + \frac{3}{x}}{2 - \frac{5}{x}} \to \dfrac{1 + 0}{2 - 0} = \dfrac{1}{2}$ as $x \to \pm\infty$

A sketch graph can be used to determine the range of a function. The figure below shows a function with range $-1 \leqslant y \leqslant 1$.

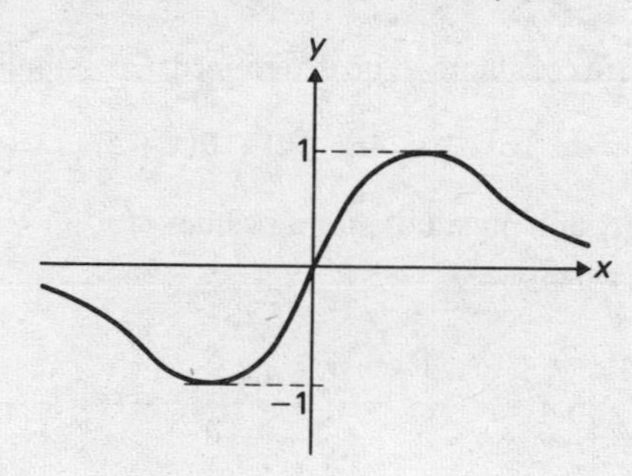

28.6 Partial Fractions

We are used to combining two or more functions to form a single fraction.

Example

$$\frac{2}{1-x} + \frac{3x}{2+x} \equiv \frac{2(2+x) + 3x(1-x)}{(1-x)(2+x)}$$

$$\equiv \frac{4 + 2x + 3x - 3x^2}{(1-x)(2+x)}$$

$$\equiv \frac{4 + 5x - 3x^2}{(1-x)(2+x)}$$

The reverse procedure is to split a fraction into simpler **partial fractions**. The method depends on how complicated the fraction is.

Examples

1. $\dfrac{3x-2}{(x+5)(x-2)}$

Proper fraction with factorized denominator. The factors are *linear* and *not repeated.* We can split this fraction in the form

$$\frac{3x-2}{(x+5)(x-2)}=\frac{A}{x+5}+\frac{B}{x-2}$$

where A and B are constants to be determined. Cross-multiplying:

$$3x-2\equiv A(x-2)+B(x+5)$$

This is an identity and must hold for all values of x.

In particular, when $x=2$

$$4=7B\Rightarrow B=\frac{4}{7}.$$

and when $x=-5$

$$-17=-7A\Rightarrow A=\frac{17}{7}$$

Thus

$$\frac{3x-2}{(x+5)(x-2)}=\frac{17}{7(x+5)}+\frac{4}{7(x-2)}$$

Notice the trick of choosing values of x for which one of the right-hand terms vanishes.

This type can also be handled using the so-called **'cover up' rule.**

2. $\dfrac{2x+1}{(x-1)(x-3)}\equiv\dfrac{A}{x-1}+\dfrac{B}{x-3}$ (A and B constants)

First 'cover up' the $x-1$ factor in the expression $\frac{2x+1}{(x-1)(x-3)}$ and then set $x=1$. This gives the value of A. So $A=\frac{3}{-2}=-\frac{3}{2}$.

Then cover up the $x-3$ factor and set $x=3$ to obtain B. So $B=\frac{7}{2}$.

Thus

$$\frac{2x+1}{(x-1)(x-3)} \equiv \frac{-3}{2(x-1)} + \frac{7}{2(x-3)}$$

Exercise

Check this result by finding A and B by the long method of example 1.

3. $\dfrac{3x+1}{(x+1)^2(x-2)}$

Proper fraction with linear factors, some *repeated*. This must be split as

$$\frac{3x+1}{(x+1)^2(x-2)} \equiv \frac{A}{(x+1)} + \frac{B}{(x+1)^2} + \frac{C}{(x-2)}$$

with *both* $(x+1)$ and $(x+1)^2$ as denominators on the right.

Cross-multiplying by $(x+1)^2(x-2)$

$$3x+1 \equiv A(x+1)(x-2) + B(x-2) + C(x+1)^2$$

Let $x = 2, 7 = 9C \Rightarrow C = 7/9$.

Let $x = -1, -2 = -3B, \Rightarrow B = 2/3$.

No other value of x will make a term on the right vanish. Choose any value of x. $x = 0$ is simplest:

$$1 = -2A - 2B + C$$

$$\Rightarrow 1 = -2A - \frac{4}{3} + \frac{7}{9}$$

$$\Rightarrow 2A = \frac{7}{9} - \frac{4}{3} - 1 = \frac{-14}{9} \Rightarrow A = -\frac{7}{9}$$

Hence

$$\frac{3x+1}{(x+1)^2(x-2)} \equiv -\frac{7}{9(x+1)} + \frac{2}{3(x+1)^2} + \frac{7}{9(x-2)}$$

4. $\dfrac{2x+3}{(x^2+1)(x-2)}$

Proper fractions. The denominator has a quadratic factor which will not factorize into linear expressions.

$$\frac{2x+3}{(x^2+1)(x-2)} \equiv \frac{Ax+B}{x^2+1} + \frac{C}{x-2}$$

Note that the numerator for the first term on the right is a general polynomial of degree 1 *less* than the denominator.

$$\Rightarrow 2x+3 \equiv (Ax+B)(x-2) + C(x^2+1)$$

$x = 2 \Rightarrow 7 = 5C \Rightarrow C = 7/5$

$$x = 0 \Rightarrow 3 = -2B + C \Rightarrow 3 = -2B + \frac{7}{5}$$

$$\Rightarrow 2B = \frac{-8}{5} \Rightarrow B = \frac{-4}{5}$$

$$x = 1 \Rightarrow 5 = -A - B + 2C$$

$$\Rightarrow 5 = -A + \frac{4}{5} + \frac{14}{5}$$

$$\Rightarrow A = -\frac{7}{5}$$

Thus

$$\frac{2x+3}{(x^2+1)(x-2)} \equiv \frac{\frac{-7x}{5} - \frac{4}{5}}{x^2+1} + \frac{7}{5(x-2)}$$

$$\equiv \frac{7}{5(x-2)} - \frac{(7x+4)}{5(x^2+1)}$$

Note: 1. $\frac{2x+3}{(x^2+1)(x-2)}$ *cannot* be put in the form $\frac{A}{x^2+1} + \frac{B}{x-2}$. 2. The cover up rule can *only* be used for fractions of the type in examples 1 and 2.

5. $\dfrac{3x^2-5}{(x-1)(x+3)}$

Not a proper fraction. First use long division to obtain an expression of the form polynomial + proper fraction. The proper fraction can then be split into partial fractions as in the examples above. By long division

$$\frac{3x^2 - 5}{(x-1)(x+3)} \equiv 3 + \frac{4 - 6x}{(x-1)(x+3)}$$ see page 78

Now,

$$\frac{4-6x}{(x-1)(x+3)} \equiv \frac{A}{x-1} + \frac{B}{x+3}$$

$$\equiv -\frac{1}{2(x-1)} - \frac{11}{2(x+3)} \quad \text{cover up rule}$$

$$\therefore \frac{3x^2 - 5}{(x-1)(x+3)} \equiv 3 - \frac{1}{2(x-1)} - \frac{11}{2(x+3)}$$

Summary

Example	Split as
$\frac{2x}{(x-1)(x+2)}$	$\frac{A}{(x-1)} + \frac{B}{(x+2)}$
$\frac{x^2+1}{(x-1)(x+2)}$	$A + \frac{B}{(x-1)} + \frac{C}{(x+2)}$
$\frac{x^3-2}{(x-1)(x+2)}$	$Ax + B + \frac{C}{(x-1)} + \frac{D}{(x-2)}$
$\frac{2x}{(x-1)^2(x+2)}$	$\frac{A}{(x+1)} + \frac{B}{(x-1)^2} + \frac{C}{(x+2)}$
$\frac{2x}{(x^2+1)(x-2)}$	$\frac{Ax+B}{(x^2+1)} + \frac{C}{(x-2)}$

28.7 Partial Fractions and Differentiation

Rational functions are more easily differentiated when split into partial functions. The example of page 270 illustrated how tedious the quotient rule can be in practice!

Example

If $f(x) = \frac{3x^2-5}{x^2+2x-3}$ find expressions for $f'(x)$ and $f''(x)$.

Answer

We saw above that

$$f(x) = \frac{3x^2 - 5}{(x-1)(x+3)} \equiv 3 - \frac{1}{2(x-1)} - \frac{11}{2(x+3)}$$

$$\Rightarrow f'(x) = \frac{11}{2(x+3)^2} + \frac{1}{2(x-1)^2}$$

and

$$f''(x) = -\frac{11}{(x+3)^3} - \frac{1}{(x-1)^3}$$

These were done 'at sight' but really involved the change of variable rule; for example:

$$y = \frac{11}{2(x+3)} = \frac{11}{2}(x+3)^{-1}$$

Let $u = x + 3$

$$\Rightarrow y = \frac{11}{2}u^{-1} \qquad \frac{du}{dx} = 1$$

$$\Rightarrow \frac{dy}{du} = -\frac{11}{2}u^{-2} = -\frac{11}{2u^2}$$

$$\Rightarrow \frac{dy}{dx} = \frac{dy}{du}\frac{du}{dx} = -\frac{11}{2u^2} \times 1 = -\frac{11}{2(x+3)^2}$$

Differentiating again

$$\frac{d}{du}\left(\frac{dy}{dx}\right) = \frac{d}{du}\left(-\frac{11}{2}u^{-2}\right) = 11u^{-3} = \frac{11}{(x+3)^3}$$

$$\Rightarrow \frac{d^2y}{dx^2} = \frac{d}{dx}\left(\frac{dy}{dx}\right) = \left(\frac{d}{du}\left(\frac{dy}{dx}\right)\right)\frac{du}{dx} = \frac{11}{(x+3)^3}\left(\text{as } \frac{du}{dx} = 1\right)$$

28.8 Integration and Rational Functions

The change of variable rule can be used to simplify some of these integrals.

Examples

1. $\int \frac{1}{(3x-2)^2} dx$ let $u = 3x - 2$

$\Rightarrow \frac{du}{dx} = 3$

$\Rightarrow \frac{1}{3} du = dx$

$$= \frac{1}{3} \int \frac{1}{u^2} du = \frac{1}{3} \int u^{-2} du$$

$$= \frac{1}{3}[-u^{-1}] + K$$

$$= -\frac{1}{3u} + K = -\frac{1}{3(3x-2)} + K$$

2. $\int \frac{x+3}{x^3} dx = \int \frac{1}{x^2} + \frac{3}{x^3} dx$ dividing out

$$= \int x^{-2} + 3x^{-3} dx$$

$$= \frac{x^{-1}}{-1} + \frac{3x^{-2}}{-2} + K$$

$$= -\frac{1}{x} - \frac{3}{2x^2} + K$$

3. $\int \frac{x^2 + 2x}{(x+1)^2} dx$

First use long division to obtain a proper fraction:

$\Rightarrow \int 1 - \frac{1}{(x+1)^2} dx$ see page 78

$= x + \frac{1}{x+1} + K$ change of variable $u = x + 1$, say

4. $\displaystyle\int \frac{3+x}{x}\,dx = \int 1 + \frac{3}{x}\,dx$

We cannot integrate this yet, it corresponds to the value $n = -1$ for which the rule $\int x^n dx = \frac{x^{n+1}}{n+1}$ does not hold. This type of integral is covered on page 303.

28.9 The graph of $y = \frac{1}{f(x)}$

Given the graph of $y = f(x)$ we can deduce the shape of $y = \frac{1}{f(x)}$ by noting that when the reciprocal is taken the following correspondences are set up.

$y = f(x)$		$y = \dfrac{1}{f(x)}$
0	$\leftrightarrow$	∞
∞	$\leftrightarrow$	0
maximum	$\leftrightarrow$	minimum
minimum	$\leftrightarrow$	maximum
+	$\leftrightarrow$	+
−	$\leftrightarrow$	−

Example

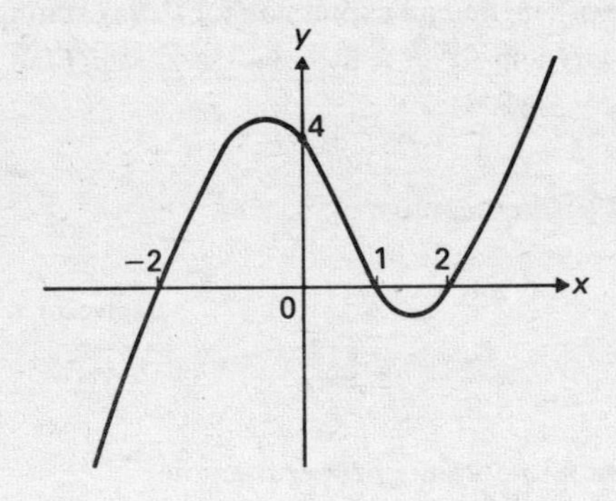

The diagram shows the graph of $y = (x-1)(x^2-4)$. Sketch the graph of $y = \frac{1}{(x-1)(x^2-4)}$.

Answer

The zeros $-2, 1, 2$ become vertical asymptotes. The maximum point becomes a minimum. The minimum point becomes a maximum. The y-intercept $y = 4$ becomes a y-intercept $y = \frac{1}{4}$.

The graph of $y = \frac{1}{(x-1)(x^2-4)}$ is

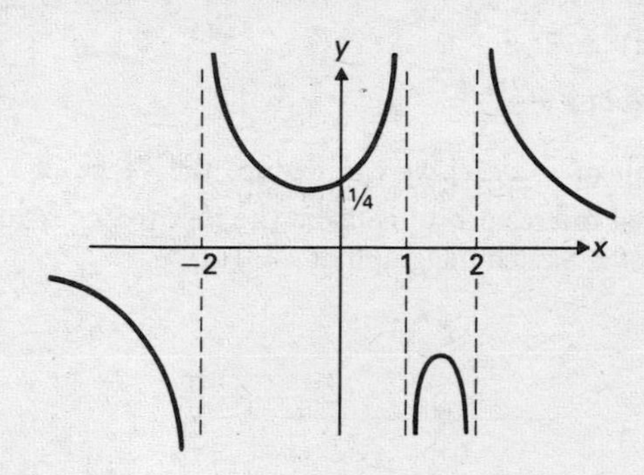

Section 29 Worked Examples

1. The function f is defined by $f: x \mapsto \frac{2x}{x+5}$, $x \in \mathbb{R}$, $x \neq -5$.
(*a*) Find the range of f, (*b*) find an expression for $f^{-1}(x)$, stating its domain. Another function g is defined on $\mathbb{R}$ by $g: x \mapsto x^2 + 1$. (*c*) Find $fg(x)$.

Answer

(*a*) Let $y = \frac{2x}{x+5}$. If y is in the range of f then

$xy + 5y = 2x$ solve for x

$x(y-2) = -5y$

$$x = \frac{5y}{2-y}$$

This expression is defined for all $y \in \mathbb{R}$ except $y = 2$.

The range of f is $\{y \in \mathbb{R}, y \neq 2\}$.

(*b*) $f: x \mapsto y$

$f^{-1}: y \mapsto x$ page 32

$$\Rightarrow f^{-1}: y \mapsto \frac{5y}{2-y}$$

$$\Rightarrow f^{-1}(x) = \frac{5x}{2-x}$$

The domain of f^{-1} is $\{x \in \mathbb{R}, x \neq 2\}$. — i.e. range of f

(*c*) $fg(x) = f(x^2 + 1)$ — page 30

$$= \frac{2(x^2+1)}{(x^2+1)+5} = \frac{2(x^2+1)}{x^2+6}$$

2. $f(x) = 1 - \dfrac{2}{x^2+3}$, $x \in \mathbb{R}$. Show that $f(x) \geqslant \frac{1}{3}$ for all values of x. Sketch the graph of $y = f(x)$.

Answer

$$fx = 1 - \frac{2}{x^2+3}$$

$x^2 + 3 \geqslant 3$, for all x, as $x^2 \geqslant 0$

$$\therefore \frac{1}{x^2+3} \leqslant \frac{1}{3}$$

$$\therefore 1 - \frac{2}{x^2+3} \geqslant 1 - \frac{2}{3} = \frac{1}{3}$$

$$f'(x) = \frac{4x}{(x^2+3)^2} = 0$$

set $u = x^2 + 3$ and use

$$\frac{dy}{dx} = \frac{dy}{du}\frac{du}{dx}$$

For a turning point

$$\left.\begin{aligned} \Rightarrow x &= 0 \\ y &= \frac{1}{3} \end{aligned}\right\}$$

x	<0	0	>0
$f'(x)$	$-$	0	$+$

$\therefore$ (0, 1/3) is a minimum point.

As $x \to \pm\infty, f(x) \to 1$. — $f(x) = 1 - \dfrac{2}{x^2+3} \to 1 - 0 = 1$ as $x \to \infty$

$\therefore y = 1$ is a horizontal asymptote.

The graph is

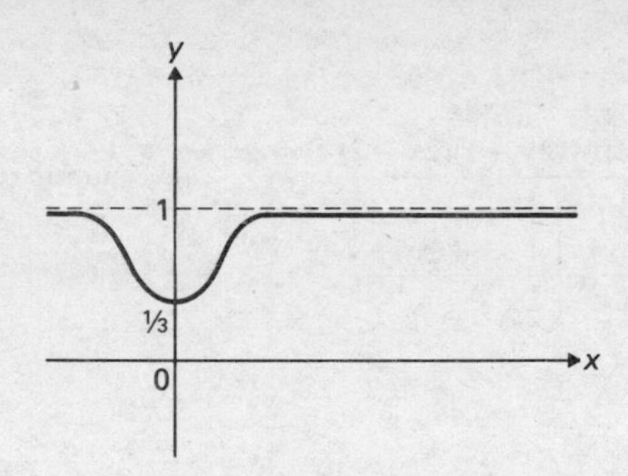

3. Express $\frac{1}{x(x-1)}$ in partial fractions and hence evaluate $\sum_{r=2}^{n} \frac{1}{r(r-1)}$ and find $\sum_{r=2}^{\infty} \frac{1}{r(r-1)}$.

Answer

$$\frac{1}{x(x-1)} = \frac{A}{x} + \frac{B}{x-1}$$

$A = -1, B = 1$ — cover up role, page 274

$$\therefore \frac{1}{x(x-1)} = \frac{1}{x-1} - \frac{1}{x}$$

Hence

$$\sum_{r=2}^{n} \frac{1}{r(r-1)} = \sum_{r=2}^{n} \left(\frac{1}{r-1} - \frac{1}{r}\right)$$

$$= \left(\frac{1}{1} - \frac{1}{2}\right) + \left(\frac{1}{2} - \frac{1}{3}\right) + \ldots + \left(\frac{1}{n-1} - \frac{1}{n}\right)$$

method of differences, page 53

$$= 1 - \frac{1}{n}$$

As $n \to \infty$, $1 - \frac{1}{n} \to 1$. Hence $\sum_{r=2}^{\infty} \frac{1}{r(r-1)} = 1$

4. If $y = \frac{2x-1}{x(x-2)}$, show that $\frac{dy}{dx}$ is negative for all x. Find the greatest value of y in the interval $\frac{1}{2} \leqslant x \leqslant \frac{3}{4}$.

Answer

$$y = \frac{2x - 1}{x^2 - 2x}$$

$$\frac{dy}{dx} = \frac{(x^2 - 2x)(2) - (2x - 1)(2x - 2)}{(x^2 - 2x)^2}$$

quotient rule

$$= \frac{2x^2 - 4x - 4x^2 + 2x + 4x - 2}{(x^2 - 2x)^2}$$

$$= \frac{-2x^2 + 2x - 2}{(x^2 - 2x)^2}$$

$$\frac{dy}{dx} = \frac{-2(x^2 - x + 1)}{(x^2 - 2x)^2}$$

The quantity $x^2 - x + 1$ is always positive as its discriminant $1 - 4 = -3$ is negative.

page 95

Thus $\frac{dy}{dx} < 0$ for all x, and so the graph slopes downwards.

$$\frac{(-)(+)}{(+)} = -$$

The greatest value of $f(x)$ for $\frac{1}{2} \leqslant x \leqslant \frac{3}{4}$ is $f(\frac{1}{2}) = \frac{1-1}{\frac{1}{4}-1} = 0$.

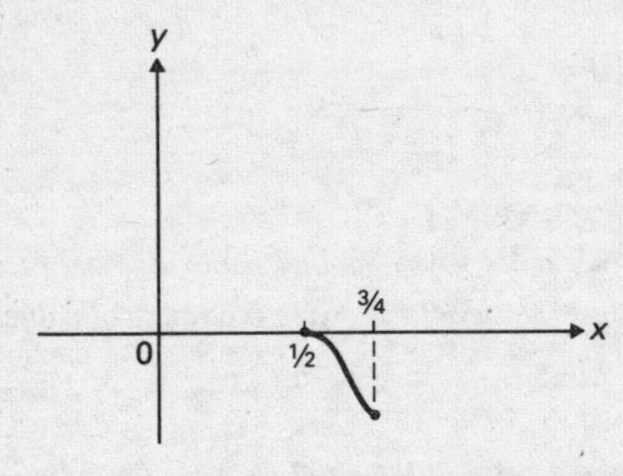

A curve which always slopes downwards is called **monotonic decreasing.**
A curve which always slopes upwards is called **monotonic increasing.**

Section 30
Examination Questions – Rational Functions

1. *The function f is defined by*

$$f: x \mapsto \frac{x+3}{x-1}, \ (x \in \mathbb{R}, x \neq 1)$$

Find (a) the range of f, (b) ff(x), (c) $f^{-1}(x)$. [LON]

2. *Given that $f(x) = 2 - \frac{3}{x^2 - 2x + 4}$ show that f(x) is always positive. Sketch the graph of the curve y = f(x), stating the equations of any asymptotes and the coordinates of any points of intersection with the coordinate axes.*

[LON]

3. *Why cannot f(x), where*

$$f(x) = \frac{x^2}{(x-1)(x-2)}$$

be expressed in the form

$$\frac{a}{x-1} + \frac{b}{x-2}$$

where a and b are constants?

Express f(x) in partial fractions and hence expand f(x) in ascending powers of x as far as the term in x^3. Give the range of values of x for which the expansion is valid. [SUJB]

4. *The gradient of a curve at the point (x, y) is given by $\frac{dy}{dx} = \frac{x^4 - 16}{x^2}$. Find the equation of the curve given that it passes through the point (2, 4). Find the coordinates of the two stationary points on the curve and determine whether they are maximum or minimum points. State, with reason, whether or not the curve has a point of inflexion. Give a rough sketch of the curve.*

[SUJB]

5. $\dfrac{2x}{(1-x)(1+x^2)} \equiv \dfrac{R}{1-x} + \dfrac{Sx+T}{1+x^2}$

where R, S and T are constants.

1. $R = 1$ 2. $S = -1$ 3. $T = 1$

A 1, 2 and 3 B 1 and 2 only C 2 and 3 only D 1 only E 3 only

[LON]

6. *The substitution $x^2 + 1 = u$ gives* $\int_1^2 \frac{x}{(x^2+1)^2}\,dx =$

A $-0{\cdot}75$ B $-0{\cdot}35$ C $-0{\cdot}15$ D $0{\cdot}15$ E $0{\cdot}35$ [LON]

7. *Express* $\frac{1}{r(r+2)}$ *in partial fractions. Hence find* $\sum_{r=1}^{n} \frac{1}{r(r+2)}$. [LON]

8. *Given that* $y = \frac{x^2-1}{2x^2+1}$, *find* $\frac{dy}{dx}$ *and state the set of values of x for which* $\frac{dy}{dx}$ *is positive.*

Find the greatest and least values of y for $0 \leqslant x \leqslant 1$. [LON]

9. *The function g is defined by*

$$g: x \mapsto \frac{2x+5}{x-3} \quad (x \in \mathbb{R}, x \neq 3)$$

Sketch the graph of the function g. Find an expression for $g^{-1}(x)$, specifying its domain.

10. *Using the same axes sketch the curves*

$$y = \frac{1}{x-1}, \quad y = \frac{x}{x+3}$$

giving the equations of the asymptotes. Hence, or otherwise, find the set of values of x for which $\frac{1}{x-1} > \frac{x}{x+3}$. [LON]

11. *Evaluate the integral* $\int_0^1 \frac{2x-1}{(x-3)^3}\,dx$ *(by substitution or otherwise)*

[OXF–part]

12. *Show that, if* $f(x) = \dfrac{ax+b}{x^2+c}$, then

$$(x^2+c)\frac{d^2f}{dx^2} + 4x\frac{df}{dx} + 2f = 0$$

Show that when $b = 0$ *and* $a > 0$ *the graph of the function* $f(x)$ *has three points of inflexion if* c *is positive, and one point of inflexion if* c *is negative.*

[OXF]

Section 31 Exponential and Logarithmic Functions

31.1 Introduction

The variables appear in the index of an exponential function.

Examples

$$f(x) = 2^x,\ g(z) = 5^{z^2+2},\ h(t) = 2e^{-3t}$$

We shall be looking mainly at functions of the form $f(x) = a^x$ where a is a constant ($a > 0$). The other exponential functions can be obtained by a change of variable.

The graph of $y = a^x$ has the general shape

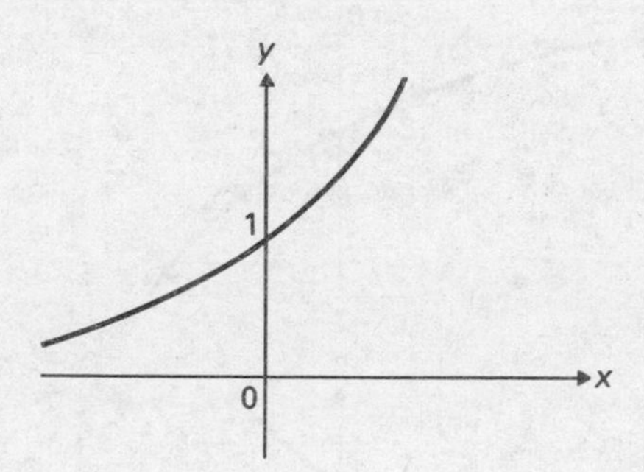

It is monotonic increasing (page 284).

Since $a^0 = 1$ for any $a \neq 0$, the graph cuts the y-axis at $y = 1$.

$a^x > 0$ for all values of x. The x-axis is a horizontal asymptote (on the left), that is $\lim_{x \to -\infty} (a^x) = 0$.

Notice that a^x is not real valued when a is negative. For example, if $f(x) = (-1)^x$ then $f(\frac{1}{2}) = (-1)^{\frac{1}{2}} = \sqrt{-1}$ is not a real number.

Exercise

Using the x^y key of a calculator if necessary, *plot* an accurate graph of $y = 2^x$ for $-3 \leqslant x \leqslant 4$.

Related functions are

1. $y = a^{-x}$

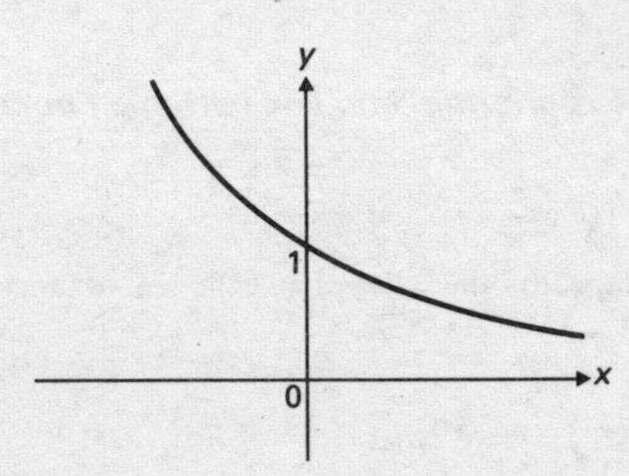

which is the reciprocal function of a^x, since $a^{-x} \equiv \frac{1}{a^x}$.

2. $y = -a^x$

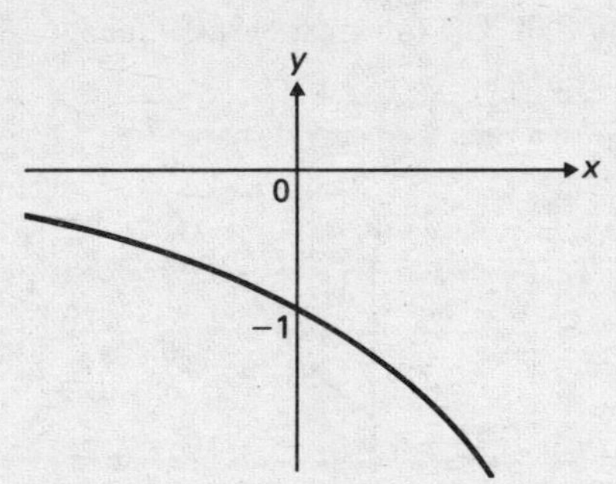

3. $y = a^x + 1$

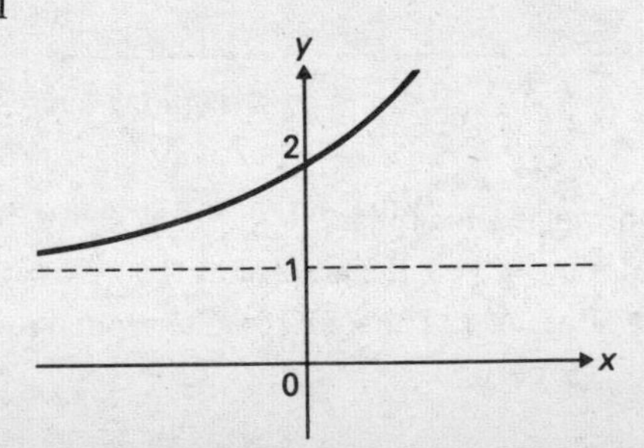

31.2 The Logarithmic Function

$f(x) = a^x$ is monotonic increasing and hence a one–one function (as can be seen from its graph). It has an inverse function $f^{-1}(x)$ denoted by $\log_a x$. It is called the **logarithmic function** with base a, and is defined on the domain $\{x \in \mathbb{R} : x > 0\}$.

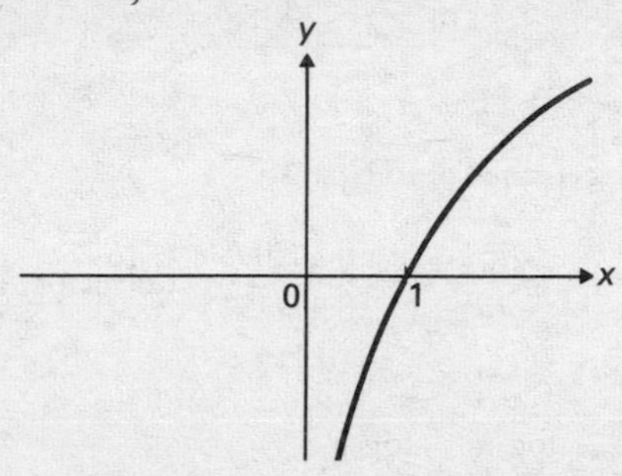

The graph is obtained from that of $y = a^x$ by reflection in the line $y = x$. Notice that the y-axis is a vertical asymptote.

From the definition of inverse functions:

$$\log_a (a^x) = x \text{ for any } x \in \mathbb{R},\ a > 0$$

and

$$a^{\log_a x} = x \text{ for any } x \geqslant 0,\ a > 0$$

Notice that for a to be a logarithm base it must be strictly positive.

Examples

1. $\log_{10}(1000) \equiv \log_{10}(10^3) = 3$
2. $3^{\log_3(4)} = 4$
3. If $a = \log_b c$ then $c = b^a$
4. $\log_a 1 \equiv \log_a(a^0) = 0$
5. $\log_a a = \log_a(a^1) = 1$

Logarithms to base 10 can be found by using four-figure tables or the log key of a calculator. Conventionally, base 10 logarithms are simply denoted by log. All other logarithms must have a specified base, as in $\log_b$.

Exercise

Plot an accurate graph of $y = \log x$ for $0{\cdot}2 \leqslant x \leqslant 2{\cdot}0$.

31.3 Change of Base Formula

The log key of a calculator can also be used to find logarithms to any other base, by using the formula

$$\boxed{\log_a b = \frac{\log_c b}{\log_c a}}$$

Examples

1. To calculate $\log_3 7$, change to base 10

$$\Rightarrow \frac{\log_{10} 7}{\log_{10} 3} = \frac{0{\cdot}845098}{0{\cdot}477121} \quad \text{calculator (to 6 decimal places)}$$

$$= 1{\cdot}7712 \quad \text{to 5 significant figures}$$

2. $\log_4 x \equiv \dfrac{\log_2 x}{\log_2 4} = \dfrac{\log_2 x}{\log_2 2^2} = \dfrac{\log_2 x}{2}$

PROOF OF CHANGE OF BASE FORMULA

Let $\log_a b = x$, $\log_c b = y$ and $\log_c a = z$. Then

$a^x = b \quad (1)$

$c^y = b \quad (2)$ — from example 3 above

and

$c^z = a \quad (3)$

(1) and (2) $\Rightarrow a^x = c^y$

from (3) $(c^z)^x = c^y$

$\Rightarrow c^{zx} = c^y$ — index rules, page 19

$\Rightarrow zx = y$

$x = \dfrac{y}{z}$

$$\Rightarrow \log_a b = \frac{\log_c b}{\log_c a}$$

31.4 Manipulating Logs

The rules of indices

$$a^x a^y = a^{x+y} \quad \text{(i)}$$
$$a^x \div a^y = a^{x-y} \quad \text{(ii)}$$
$$(a^x)^n = a^{nx} \quad \text{(iii)}$$

can be written in terms of logarithms.
From (i)

$$\log_a(a^x a^y) = x + y \text{ (definition of log)}$$

Let $x = \log_a p$ and $y = \log_a q$ for some p and q. So $a^x = p$, $a^y = q$.

Then $\log_a(pq) = \log_a p + \log_a q$
Similarly from (ii)
$\log_a(p \div q) = \log_a p - \log_a q$
and (iii)
$\log_a(p^n) = n \log_a p$

Examples

1. $\log_{10}5 + \log_{10}2 \equiv \log_{10}(5 \times 2) = \log_{10}10 = 1$
2. $2\log_3 x - 3\log_3 y + \log_3(xy) \equiv \log_3 x^2 - \log_3 y^3 + \log_3(xy)$

$$= \log_3\left(\frac{x^2(xy)}{y^3}\right)$$
$$= \log_3\left(\frac{x^3}{y^2}\right)$$

3. $2\log_2 x + \log_4 y \equiv \log_2(x^2) + \dfrac{\log_2 y}{2}$ change of base

$$= \log_2 x^2 + \log_2 y^{\frac{1}{2}}$$
$$= \log_2(x^2 y^{\frac{1}{2}})$$

31.5 Exponential and Log Equations

Examples

1. $2^{3x-5} = 4$

Answer

Write both sides as powers of 2.

$$2^{3x-5} = 2^2$$

$$\Rightarrow 3x - 5 = 2 \Rightarrow x = \frac{7}{3}$$

This uses the 'Balance and Match' approach to equations. Write the equation so that both sides have the same form (*for balance*) and then *match* the corresponding parts.

The solution can also be found by taking logs of both sides:

2. $3^{2x+4} = 5$
   $\Rightarrow \log_{10}(3^{2x+4}) = \log_{10}5$
   $\Rightarrow (2x+4)\log_{10}3 = \log_{10}5$
   $\Rightarrow 2x + 4 = \dfrac{\log_{10}5}{\log_{10}3} = \dfrac{0{\cdot}69897}{0{\cdot}47712} = 1{\cdot}465$ (to 3 decimal places)
   $\Rightarrow 2x = 1{\cdot}465 - 4$
   $\Rightarrow x = -1{\cdot}268$

3. $2^x3^{x+1} = 10$
   $\Rightarrow 2^x3^x3^1 = 10$
   $\Rightarrow 3(2 \times 3)^x = 10$ rules of indices
   $\Rightarrow 3(6^x) = 10$
   $\Rightarrow 6^x = \dfrac{10}{3}$
   $\Rightarrow x \log_{10}6 = \log_{10}\left(\dfrac{10}{3}\right)$ taking $\log_{10}$ of both sides
   $\Rightarrow x \log_{10}6 = \log_{10}10 - \log_{10}3$
   $= 1 - \log_{10}3$
   $\Rightarrow x = \dfrac{1 - \log_{10}3}{\log_{10}6}$
   $= 0{\cdot}672$ calculator

4. $\log_4(5x - 3) = 2$
   $\Rightarrow 5x - 3 = 4^2$ definition of log
   $\Rightarrow 5x = 19$
   $\Rightarrow x = \dfrac{19}{5} = 3.8$

5. $\log_x 5 = 4$

$\Rightarrow x^4 = 5$

$\Rightarrow x = 5^{1/4}$

$x = 1{\cdot}495$ (to 3 decimal places)

Note: although $5^{1/4} = \pm 1{\cdot}495$, we can only take the *positive* root here. x is a logarithm base and so must be positive.

6. $\log_2(3x) + \log_4(x^2) = 2$

$\Rightarrow \log_2(3x) + \dfrac{\log_2(x^2)}{2} = 2$ change of base

$\Rightarrow \log_2(3x) + \log_2 x = 2$ $\frac{1}{2}\log_2 x^2 = \log_2 (x^2)^{\frac{1}{2}} = \log_2 x$

$\Rightarrow \log_2(3x^2) = 2$ log rules, page 291

$\Rightarrow 3x^2 = 2^2 = 4$

$\Rightarrow x^2 = 4/3$

$\Rightarrow x = \sqrt{\dfrac{4}{3}}$

Only the positive root is allowed as $\log_2(3x)$ is only defined for positive values of x.

7. $2^{2x+1} - 3(2^x) + 1 = 0$

Notice that $2^{2x} = (2^x)^2$. Change variable to $y = 2^x$.

Since $2^{2x+1} = 2^1 2^{2x} = 2y^2$ then the equation becomes

$2y^2 - 3y + 1 = 0$

$\Rightarrow (2y - 1)(y - 1) = 0$

$\Rightarrow y = \frac{1}{2}$ or $y = 1$

$\Rightarrow 2^x = 2^{-1}$ or $2^x = 1$

$\Rightarrow x = -1$ or $x = 0$

8. $\log_x 4 + 3 \log_4 x = 4$

Change the base of one term so that only one base is used in the equation. Since

$$\log_x 4 = \frac{\log_4 4}{\log_4 x} = \frac{1}{\log_4 x}$$

the equation becomes

$$\frac{1}{\log_4 x} + 3\log_4 x = 4$$

Change to variable $y = \log_4 x$:

$$\frac{1}{y} + 3y = 4$$
$$\Rightarrow 1 + 3y^2 = 4y$$
$$\Rightarrow 3y^2 - 4y + 1 = 0$$
$$\Rightarrow (3y - 1)(y - 1) = 0$$
$$\Rightarrow y = 1/3 \text{ or } y = 1$$
$$\Rightarrow \log_4 x = 1/3 \text{ or } \log_4 x = 1$$
$$\Rightarrow x = 4^{1/3} \text{ or } x = 4^1$$
$$\Rightarrow x = 1{\cdot}587 \text{ or } x = 4{\cdot}0 \qquad \text{(to 3 decimal places)}$$

Notice the special case of the change of base formula

$$\boxed{\log_a b = \frac{1}{\log_b a}}$$

31.6 Differentiation of Exponential Functions

$f(x) = a^x$ cannot be differentiated by any rule so far introduced. You *cannot* use $\frac{d}{dx}(x^n) = nx^{n-1}$, since this only works when the power is *constant*. We must go back to first principles (page 145).

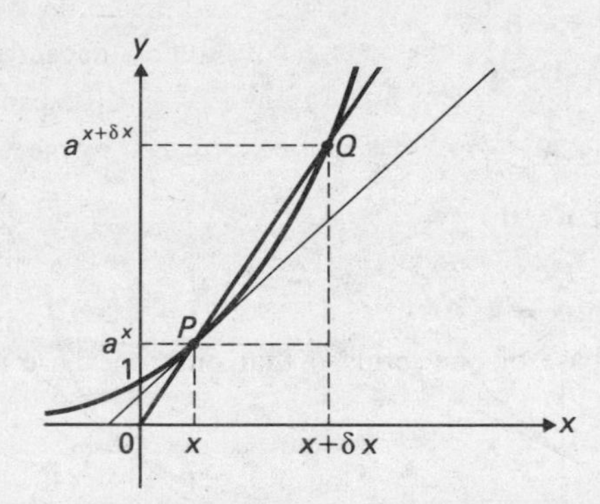

P is the point (x, a^x) and Q the nearby point $(x + \delta x, a^{x+\delta x})$, both on the curve $y = a^x$.

The gradient of PQ is

$$\frac{a^{x+\delta x} - a^x}{\delta x} = \frac{a^x a^{\delta x} - a^x}{\delta x} = a^x\left(\frac{a^{\delta x} - 1}{\delta x}\right)$$

We require the limit of this gradient as $\delta x \to 0$. The expression $(\frac{a^{\delta x} - 1}{\delta x})$ is actually the gradient of the line segment AB where A is (0, 1) (y-intercept) and B is $(\delta x, a^{\delta x})$.

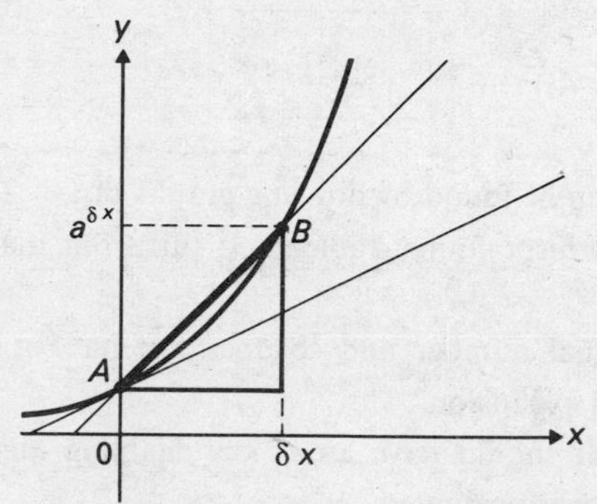

As $\delta \to 0$, $(\frac{a^{\delta x} - 1}{\delta x}) \to$ the gradient of the tangent at A (assuming this limiting process is valid, which it is!). Denote this (unknown) gradient by m_a. Then gradient at P is

$$\lim_{\delta x \to 0} a^x\left(\frac{a^{\delta x} - 1}{\delta x}\right) = a^x \lim_{\delta x \to 0}\left(\frac{a^{\delta x} - 1}{\delta x}\right)$$
$$= m_a a^x$$

Thus for $y = a^x$, $\frac{dy}{dx} = m_a a^x$ for some constant m_a (dependent on a).

We can find the gradient function at $P(x, y)$ if we can determine the gradient at the y-intercept. This can be *estimated* by measurement on an accurate graph.

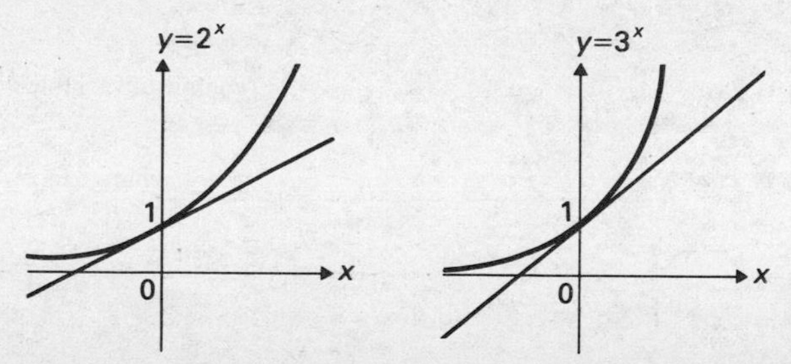

The graphs of $y = 2^x$, $y = 3^x$ above give values $m_2 = 0{\cdot}7$ and $m_3 = 1{\cdot}1$. Noticing that $m_2 < 1$ and $m_3 > 1$, we deduce that for some value of a *between* 2 and 3 the corresponding gradient is *exactly* 1.

This value of a is denoted by the letter e. Thus, for $y = e^x$, the gradient at P is $1 \times e^x = e^x$.

The function $y = e^x$ has the important property that

$$\boxed{\frac{d}{dx}[e^x] = e^x}$$

Estimates for e can be found by drawing graphs of $y = 2{\cdot}5^x, 2.8^x, \dots$ and measuring the corresponding gradients. It turns out that $e = 2{\cdot}7183$ to 4 decimal places.

e is an irrational number and so does not have a terminating or recurring decimal expansion.

Your calculator should have an e^x key enabling quantities such as $e \equiv e^1, e^2, e^3, \dots$ to be evaluated.

Examples

1. $y = e^{3x-5}$

Let $u = 3x-5$ so that $y = e^u$ and $\frac{du}{dx} = 3$.

$$\frac{dy}{dx} = \frac{dy}{du}\frac{du}{dx}$$ change of variable, page 161

$$= e^u \times 3$$ $\frac{d}{du}(e^u) = e^u$, property of e

$$= 3e^{3x-5}$$

2. $y = e^{x^2} - 2e^{-x}$

$$\frac{d}{dx}(e^{x^2}) = 2xe^{x^2}$$ change of variable $u = x^2$

$$\frac{d}{dx}(e^{-x}) = -e^{-x}$$ change to $u = -x$

So

$$\frac{dy}{dx} = 2xe^{x^2} + 2e^{-x}$$

In general

$$\frac{d}{dx}(e^{f(x)}) = f'(x)e^{f(x)}$$

3. $y = \dfrac{1+e^x}{1-e^x}$

Using the quotient rule of page 264 with $u = 1 + e^x$, $v = 1 - e^x$

$$\begin{aligned}\frac{dy}{dx} &= \frac{(1-e^x)e^x - (1+e^x)(-e^x)}{(1-e^x)^2}\\ &= \frac{e^x(1-e^x+1+e^x)}{(1-e^x)^2}\\ &= \frac{2e^x}{(1-e^x)^2}\end{aligned}$$

31.7 Differentiation of Log Functions

$y = \log_e x$ is the inverse function of $y = e^x$. $\log_e x$ is called the **natural log** of x and is usually denoted by the simpler $\ln x$. Your calculator should have an [ln] key. (Exercise: Verify that $\ln 1 = 0$, $\ln 2 = 0{\cdot}6931471$, to 7 decimal places.)

If $y = \ln x$ then $e^y = x$. Differentiate both sides *with respect to x*.

$$\frac{d}{dx}(e^y) = 1$$

$$\Rightarrow \frac{d}{dy}(e^y)\frac{dy}{dx} = 1 \qquad \text{chain rule, page 161}$$

$$\Rightarrow e^y\frac{dy}{dx} = 1$$

$$\Rightarrow x\frac{dy}{dx} = 1$$

$$\Rightarrow \frac{dy}{dx} = \frac{1}{x} \qquad \text{as } e^y = x$$

Thus

$$\boxed{\frac{d}{dx}(\ln x) = \frac{1}{x}}$$

Examples

1. $$\frac{d}{dx}(\log_e(3x)) = \frac{d}{dx}(\log_e 3 + \log_e x)$$
$$= \frac{d}{dx}(\log_e 3) + \frac{d}{dx}(\log_e x)$$
$$= 0 + \frac{1}{x} = \frac{1}{x}$$

(*Note*: $\log_e 3$ is a constant and so has zero derivative. $\frac{d}{dx}(\log_e 3)$ is *not* $\frac{1}{3}$!)

2. $$\frac{d}{dx}(\log_e(x^2 - 2)) = \frac{d}{dx}(\log_e u) \qquad \text{putting } u = x^2 - 2$$
$$= \left(\frac{d}{du}(\log_e u)\right)\left(\frac{du}{dx}\right) \qquad \text{change of variable}$$
$$= \frac{1}{u}2x$$
$$= \frac{2x}{x^2 - 2}$$

In general

$$\boxed{\frac{d}{dx}[\ln(f(x))] = \frac{f'(x)}{f(x)}}$$

3. $$y = \ln\left(\frac{1 + e^x}{2 + 3x}\right)$$
$$\Rightarrow y = \ln(e^x + 1) - \ln(2 + 3x) \qquad \text{simplify first}$$
$$\Rightarrow \frac{dy}{dx} = \frac{e^x}{e^x + 1} - \frac{3}{2 + 3x}$$

4. The general exponential function $y = a^x$ $(a > 0)$ can now be differentiated:

$$y = a^x$$

$\Rightarrow \ln y = x\ln a$ taking $\log_e$ of both sides

$$\Rightarrow \frac{d}{dx}(\ln y) = \frac{d}{dx}(x\ln a)$$

$$\Rightarrow \frac{1}{y}\frac{dy}{dx} = \ln a$$ implicit functions, page 230

$$\Rightarrow \frac{dy}{dx} = (\ln a)y$$

$$\boxed{\Rightarrow \frac{d}{dx}(a^x) = (\ln a)a^x}$$

5. We can also differentiate

$$y = \log_a x \, (a > 0)$$

Change to base e

$$y = \frac{\log_e x}{\log_e a} = \left(\frac{1}{\log_e a}\right)\log_e x$$

$$\Rightarrow \frac{dy}{dx} = \left(\frac{1}{\log_e a}\right)\frac{1}{x}$$ $\frac{1}{\log_e a}$ is *constant*

$$\Rightarrow \frac{dy}{dx} = \frac{1}{(\log_e a)x}$$

31.8 Series Expansions (Maclaurin Series)

We saw earlier that a function of the form $(a + x)^n$ can be expressed as a series of ascending powers of x (page 209). A similar result holds for other functions.

If $f(x)$ is a function such that $f(x), f'(x), f''(x), \ldots$ are all defined and can be evaluated when $x = 0$ then

$$f(x) \equiv f(0) + f'(0)x + \frac{f''(0)x^2}{2\,!} + \frac{f'''(0)x^3}{3\,!} + \ldots + \frac{f^{(n)}(0)x^{(n)}}{n\,!} + \ldots$$

which is an infinite series, convergent for suitable values of x. ($f^{(n)}(0)$ means differentiate n times and then set $x = 0$.)

The series for e^x can be found:

$$f(x) = e^x \Rightarrow f'(x) = f''(x) = \dots = f^{(n)}(x) = e^x$$

so

$$f(0) = f'(0) = \dots = f^{(n)}(0) = \dots = 1$$

Thus

$$e^x = 1 + x + \frac{x^2}{2\,!} + \frac{x^3}{3\,!} + \dots + \frac{x^n}{n\,!} + \dots$$

This series converges for *all* real values of x.

Assuming this series we can now estimate the value of $e = e^1 = 1 + 1 + \frac{1}{2!} + \frac{1}{3!} + \dots$ By taking enough terms a suitable approximation can be found. In fact about 10 terms are required for 7 decimal place accuracy.

n	$\frac{1}{n!}$	sum of first n terms
0	1	1
1	1	2
2	0·5	2·5
3	0·166 666 67	2·666 666 67
4	0·041 666 67	2·708 333 34
5	0·008 333 33	2·716 666 67
6	0·001 388 89	2·718 055 56
7	0·000 198 41	2·718 253 97
8	0·000 024 80	2·718 278 77
9	0·000 002 76	2·718 281 53
10	0·000 000 28	2·718 281 81

$f(x) = \log_e x$ does not have a series like this because $f(0), f'(0), \dots$ are all undefined. However, $f(x) \equiv \log_e(1 + x)$ and all its derivatives *are* defined at $x = 0$.

$$f'(x) = \frac{1}{1+x}, f''(x) = -\frac{1}{(1+x)^2}, f'''(x) = \frac{2}{(1+x)^3}, \dots$$

The series for this function is

$$\log_e(1 + x) = x - \frac{x^2}{2} + \frac{x^3}{3} - \frac{x^4}{4} + \dots$$

which converges when $-1 < x \leqslant 1$. A similar series is found by replacing x by $-x$:

$$\log_e(1-x) = -(x + \frac{x^2}{2} + \frac{x^3}{3} + \frac{x^4}{4} + \ldots)$$

which converges when $-1 \leqslant x < 1$.

These series can usually be quoted without derivation, but you must also specify the ranges of values for which they converge.

Example

Find the first 2 non-zero terms in the expansion of $e^x \log(1+2x)$ in ascending powers of x. State the range of values of x for which the series is valid.

Answer

$$e^x = 1 + x + \frac{x^2}{2} + \frac{x^3}{6} + \ldots$$

$$\log_e(1+2x) = (2x) - \frac{(2x)^2}{2} + \frac{(2x)^3}{3} - \ldots \qquad \text{from above}$$

$$= 2x - 2x^2 + \frac{8x^3}{3} - \ldots$$

$$\therefore e^x \log_e(1+2x) = \left(1 + x + \frac{x^2}{2} + \frac{x^3}{6} + \ldots\right)\left(2x - 2x^2 + \frac{8x^3}{3} + \ldots\right)$$

$$= 2x + (2x^2 - 2x^2) + \left(x^3 - 2x^3 + \frac{8}{3}x^3\right) + \ldots$$

$$= 2x + \frac{5}{3}x^3 + \ldots$$

e^x is convergent for all x, and $\log_e(1+2x)$ is convergent for $-1 < 2x \leqslant 1$.

For the series $e^x \log_e(1+2x)$ to converge, $-\frac{1}{2} < x \leqslant \frac{1}{2}$.

Notice that we had to calculate terms up to x^3 in order to find 2 non-zero terms.

The expansion for e^x can be used to calculate limits such as

$\lim_{x \to \infty} x^2 e^{-x}$

$$x^2 e^{-x} = \frac{x^2}{e^x} = \frac{x^2}{1 + x + \frac{x^2}{2} + \frac{x^3}{3!} + \ldots}$$

$$= \frac{1}{\frac{1}{x^2} + \frac{1}{x} + \frac{1}{2} + \frac{x}{3!} + \ldots}$$ dividing top and bottom by x^2

$$\to 0 \text{ as } x \to \pm\infty$$

$\therefore \lim_{x \to \infty} x^2 e^{-x} = 0$

In general $\lim_{x \to +\infty} x^n e^x = \infty$

$\lim_{x \to -\infty} x^n e^x = 0$ for any constant power n

Thus e^x is 'stronger' than any single power of x.

Related limits are $\lim_{x \to \infty} x^n e^{-x} = 0$ and $\lim_{x \to -\infty} x^n e^{-x} = \infty$.

These results are useful when sketching curves for such functions (see example 5, page 314).

31.9 Integration

Rewriting $\frac{d}{dx}(e^x) = e^x$ as an integral

$$\boxed{\int e^x dx = e^x + K}$$

Similarly, as $\frac{d}{dx}(\ln x) = \frac{1}{x}$, then

$$\int \frac{1}{x} dx = \ln x + K$$

as long as x is positive.

Suppose that we know $x < 0$ and wish to evaluate

$$\int \frac{1}{x} dx$$

Letting $x = -y$, y must be *positive.*

$$\frac{dy}{dx} = -1 \Rightarrow -dy = dx$$

and so

$$\int \frac{1}{x} \mathrm{d}x = \int \frac{1}{-y}(-\mathrm{d}y) = \int \frac{1}{y} \mathrm{d}y = \ln y + K \text{ (since } y \text{ is positive)}$$

$$\Rightarrow \int \frac{1}{x} \mathrm{d}x = \begin{cases} \ln x + K \text{ when } x > 0 \\ \ln(-x) + K \text{ when } x < 0 \end{cases}$$

This can be written in the single form

$$\boxed{\int \frac{1}{x} \mathrm{d}x = \ln|x| + K}$$

(See page 104 for definition of $|x|$.)

Notes: 1. This takes care of the case $n = -1$ for $\int x^n \mathrm{d}x$ (page 173)

2. $\ln x + K = \ln x + \ln A$ for some constant $A (A > 0)$
$= \ln(Ax)$
is an alternative form.

The change of variable rule can be used to apply these results to more general functions.

Examples

1. $\int e^{2x+1} \mathrm{d}x$

let $u = 2x + 1$

$\therefore \frac{\mathrm{d}u}{\mathrm{d}x} = 2$

$\frac{1}{2}\mathrm{d}u = \mathrm{d}x$

$\Rightarrow \frac{1}{2}\int e^u \mathrm{d}u$
$= \frac{1}{2}e^u + K = \frac{1}{2}e^{2x+1} + K$

In general

$$\boxed{\int e^{ax+b} \mathrm{d}x = \frac{e^{ax+b}}{a} + K}$$

2. $\int_0^1 x e^{x^2-2} \mathrm{d}x$

Let $u = x^2 - 2$

$\therefore \frac{\mathrm{d}u}{\mathrm{d}x} = 2x$

$\frac{1}{2}\mathrm{d}u = x\mathrm{d}x$

x	0	1
u	-2	-1

$= \frac{1}{2}\int_{-2}^{-1} e^u \mathrm{d}u$

notice how the x term goes with the dx to form the du term

$= [\frac{1}{2}e^u]_{-2}^{-1} = \frac{1}{2}\{e^{-1} - e^{-2}\}$

$= \frac{1}{2}\left\{\frac{1}{e} - \frac{1}{e^2}\right\} = \frac{1}{2}\left(\frac{e-1}{e^2}\right)$

A useful general rule is

$$\int f'(x)e^{f(x)}\mathrm{d}x = e^{f(x)} + C$$

You should be on the lookout for an $f'(x)$ factor in the integrand to see a suitable change of variable.

3. $\int \frac{1}{2x-3}\mathrm{d}x$

let $u = 2x - 3$

$\Rightarrow \mathrm{d}u = 2\mathrm{d}x$

$\Rightarrow \frac{1}{2}\mathrm{d}u = \mathrm{d}x$

$\Rightarrow \frac{1}{2}\int \frac{1}{u}\mathrm{d}u$

$= \frac{1}{2}\ln|u| + K$

$= \frac{1}{2}\ln|2x-3| + K$

In general

$$\int \frac{1}{ax+b}\mathrm{d}x = \frac{1}{a}\ln|ax+b| + K$$

4. $\int \frac{2x}{x^2+1}\mathrm{d}x$

let $u = x^2 + 1$

$\Rightarrow \frac{\mathrm{d}u}{\mathrm{d}x} = 2x$

$\Rightarrow \mathrm{d}u = 2x\mathrm{d}x$

$\Rightarrow \int \frac{1}{u}\mathrm{d}u$

$= \ln|u| + K$

$= \ln|x^2+1| + K$

$= \ln(x^2+1) + K$

since $(x^2+1) > 0$ *for all* x.

In general

$$\int \frac{f'(x)}{f(x)} dx = \ln[f(x)] + K$$

If the integral is not of standard form it can often be reduced to a simple expression by a suitable change of variable.

5. $$\int \frac{1+e^x}{1-e^x} dx \equiv \int \frac{1-e^x+2e^x}{1-e^x} dx$$
$$= \int 1 + \frac{2e^x}{1-e^x} dx$$
$$= x + \int \frac{2e^x}{1-e^x} dx$$
$$= x + \int \frac{-2}{u} du \text{ (where } u = 1-e^x)$$
$$= x - 2\ln|u| + K$$
$$= x - 2\ln|1-e^x| + K$$

An integral can often be evaluated in different ways. Simplifying the integrand before changing the variable reduces the amount of work.

6. $$\int_1^3 \frac{x^3-3}{x(x+1)} dx \text{ (a rational } \textit{improper} \text{ function)}$$

We must divide out first to get

$$\int_1^3 x^2 + x + \frac{x-3}{x(x+1)} dx$$

see page 78

and using partial fractions

$$\int_1^3 x^2 + x - \frac{3}{x} + \frac{4}{x+1} dx$$

cover up rule

$$= \left[\frac{x^3}{3} + \frac{x^2}{2} - 3\ln x + 4\ln(x+1)\right]_1^3$$

(Note that for $1 \leqslant x \leqslant 3$, x and $x+1$ are positive.)

$$= 9 + \frac{9}{2} - 3\ln 3 + 4\ln 4 - \frac{1}{3} - \frac{1}{2} + 3\ln 1 - 4\ln 2$$

$$= \frac{38}{3} - 3\ln 3 + 4\ln 4 - 4\ln 2 \qquad \ln 1 = 0$$

$$= \frac{38}{3} - \ln 27 + 4\ln\left(\frac{4}{2}\right) \qquad \text{log rules, page 291}$$

$$= \frac{38}{3} - \ln 27 + \ln 16$$

$$= \frac{38}{3} + \ln\left(\frac{16}{27}\right)$$

31.10 Integration by Parts

The integral $\int 2xe^{x^2}\mathrm{d}x$ can be evaluated by changing the variable to $u = x^2$:

$$\frac{\mathrm{d}u}{\mathrm{d}x} = 2x \Rightarrow \mathrm{d}u = 2x\mathrm{d}x$$

$$\Rightarrow \int e^u \mathrm{d}u = e^u + K = e^{x^2} + K$$

However the very similar integral $\int xe^x\mathrm{d}x$ cannot be evaluated by such a change of variable.

Integrals of products of two dissimilar functions can often be evaluated by a method known as **integration by parts**. It is a direct result of the product rule of differentiation.

$$\frac{\mathrm{d}}{\mathrm{d}x}(uv) = \frac{\mathrm{d}u}{\mathrm{d}x}v + u\frac{\mathrm{d}v}{\mathrm{d}x}$$

Integrating

$$\int \frac{\mathrm{d}}{\mathrm{d}x}(uv)\mathrm{d}x = \int\left(\frac{\mathrm{d}u}{\mathrm{d}x}\right)v\mathrm{d}x + \int u\left(\frac{\mathrm{d}v}{\mathrm{d}x}\right)\mathrm{d}x$$

$$\Rightarrow uv = \int\left(\frac{\mathrm{d}u}{\mathrm{d}x}\right)v\mathrm{d}x + \int u\left(\frac{\mathrm{d}v}{\mathrm{d}x}\right)\mathrm{d}x \quad \left(\int \text{and } \frac{\mathrm{d}}{\mathrm{d}x} \text{ are inverses}\right)$$

$$\boxed{\Rightarrow \quad \int\left(\frac{\mathrm{d}u}{\mathrm{d}x}\right)v\mathrm{d}x = uv - \int u\left(\frac{\mathrm{d}v}{\mathrm{d}x}\right)\mathrm{d}x}$$

The rule is applied to integrands which are products. One of the functions in the product is taken as $\frac{du}{dx}$ and the other as v.

In general $\frac{du}{dx}$ and v are functions of different type, where functions are classified as 1. polynomial type, 2. rational type, 3. exponential type, (and other powers) 4. logarithmic type (other types are introduced later).

Example

$$\int xe^x \mathrm{d}x$$

The function chosen to be $\frac{du}{dx}$ must be easy to integrate. Both x and e^x satisfy this condition. However, if we choose $v = x$ so that $\frac{dv}{dx} = 1$ is a *simpler* function then the integral on the right-hand side of the formula should be simpler than the original one.

$$v = x \Rightarrow \frac{\mathrm{d}v}{\mathrm{d}x} = 1$$

$$\frac{\mathrm{d}u}{\mathrm{d}x} = e^x \Rightarrow u = e^x$$

So

$$\begin{aligned}\int xe^x \mathrm{d}x &= xe^x - \int e^x \mathrm{d}x \\ &= xe^x - e^x + K \\ &= e^x(x-1) + K\end{aligned}$$

At this level the essential feature of the method is that a simpler integration is obtained by suitable choices of v and $\frac{du}{dx}$.

Examples

1. $\int x^2 e^{2x+3} \mathrm{d}x$ $\qquad v = x^2 \quad \frac{\mathrm{d}v}{\mathrm{d}x} = 2x$

$$\frac{\mathrm{d}u}{\mathrm{d}x} = e^{2x+3} \quad u = \tfrac{1}{2}e^{2x+3}$$

$= \frac{1}{2}x^2 e^{2x+3} - \int xe^{2x+3} \mathrm{d}x$

The second integral is simpler but cannot be evaluated directly. Applying the method again

$\int xe^{2x+3} \mathrm{d}x = \frac{1}{2}xe^{2x+3} - \frac{1}{2}\int e^{2x+3} \mathrm{d}x$ $\qquad v = x \quad \frac{\mathrm{d}v}{\mathrm{d}x} = 1$

$$\frac{\mathrm{d}u}{\mathrm{d}x} = e^{2x+3} \quad u = \tfrac{1}{2}e^{2x+3}$$

$$= \tfrac{1}{2}xe^{2x+3} - \frac{1}{4}e^{2x+3} + K$$

$$\Rightarrow \int x^2 e^{2x+3}dx = \tfrac{1}{2}x^2e^{2x+3} - \tfrac{1}{2}xe^{2x+3} + \frac{1}{4}e^{2x+3} + K$$

$$= \frac{1}{4}e^{2x+3}(2x^2 - 2x + 1) + K'$$

Notice that only one arbitrary constant, K, is needed.

2. $\int x^3 \ln x dx$.

In this case we cannot set $v = x^3$, $\frac{du}{dx} = \ln x$ as we do not yet have a rule for integrating $\ln x$.

so, set $v = \ln x \Rightarrow \dfrac{dv}{dx} = \dfrac{1}{x}$

$\dfrac{du}{dx} = x^3 \Rightarrow u = \dfrac{1}{4}x^4$

$\left(\dfrac{1}{x}x^4 = x^3\right)$

$$\Rightarrow \frac{1}{4}x^4 \ln x - \int \frac{1}{4}x^3 dx$$

$$= \frac{1}{4}x^4 \ln x - \frac{1}{16}x^4 + K$$

(*Check* this result by differentiating to arrive back with $x^3 \ln x$.)

3. $\displaystyle\int_1^2 \ln x dx$

This is not a product as it stands. However we can write it in product form as

$$\int_1^2 1 \times \ln x dx$$

set $\dfrac{du}{dx} = 1 \Rightarrow u = x$

$v = \ln x \Rightarrow \dfrac{dv}{dx} = \dfrac{1}{x}$

$$= [x \ln x]_1^2 - \int_1^2 x \frac{1}{x} dx$$

$$= [x \ln x]_1^2 - \int_1^2 1 \mathrm{d}x = [x \ln x - x]_1^2$$

$$= (2 \ln 2 - 2) - (1 \ln 1 - 1)$$

$$= 2 \ln 2 - 1$$

which now gives us the rule for integrating $\ln x$.

31.11 Differential Equations

An equation involving x, y and $\frac{\mathrm{d}y}{\mathrm{d}x}$ such as

$$2xy\frac{\mathrm{d}y}{\mathrm{d}x} = 3$$

can often be solved by **separating the variables**.

Rearrange the equation so that the xs appear on the right and the ys on the left.

'$2y\mathrm{d}y = \frac{3}{x}\mathrm{d}x$' but see page 148

Now integrate both sides

$$\int 2y\mathrm{d}y = \int \frac{3}{x}\mathrm{d}x$$

$$\Rightarrow y^2 = 3 \ln|x| + K$$

This is the **general solution** of the equation. Each value of K gives a different function with a corresponding graph. We say that the general solution provides a **family** of **integral curves**.

If we specify a particular point that the curve should contain, the value of the constant can be evaluated. Suppose that when $x = 2$, $y = 5$. Then

$$25 = 3 \ln 2 + K$$

$$\Rightarrow K = 25 - 3 \ln 2$$

$$= 25 - \ln 8$$

$$\therefore y^2 = 3 \ln|x| + 25 - \ln 8$$

Example

Find the solution of the differential equation

$$x(x+1)\frac{dy}{dx} = 3y$$

given that $x > 0$, $y > 0$ and the graph passes through the point (2, 6). Sketch the graph of this solution.

Answer

$$x(x+1)\frac{dy}{dx} = 3y$$

$$\Rightarrow \int \frac{1}{3y}dy = \int \frac{1}{x(x+1)}dx \qquad \text{separating the variables}$$

$$\Rightarrow \frac{1}{3}\ln y = \int \frac{1}{x} - \frac{1}{x+1}dx \qquad \text{partial fractions}$$

$$= \ln x - \ln(x+1) + K \qquad y, x > 0 \text{ so no modulus needed}$$

$$\Rightarrow \ln y = 3\ln\left(\frac{Cx}{x+1}\right) \qquad \text{where } K = \ln C$$

$$\Rightarrow \ln y = \ln\left(\left(\frac{Cx}{x+1}\right)^3\right)$$

$$\Rightarrow y = \frac{Ax^3}{(x+1)^3} \qquad \text{where } A = C^3$$

$$x = 2 \Rightarrow y = 6 \qquad \text{given in the question}$$

$$\Rightarrow 6 = \frac{8A}{27}$$

$$\Rightarrow A = \frac{81}{4}$$

$$\Rightarrow y = \frac{81x^3}{4(x+1)^3}$$

The graph can be sketched using the methods on page 268.

The curve cuts the axes only at the origin. ($x = -1$ is a vertical asymptote; however, we are restricted to $x > 0$.) $y = \frac{81}{4}$ is a horizontal asymptote, on the right.

For turning points $\frac{dy}{dx} = 0$. However we do *not* need to differentiate. The differential equation $x(x+1)\frac{dy}{dx} = 3y$ tells us that when $\frac{dy}{dx} = 0$, $y = 0$.

But $y = 0 \Rightarrow x = 0$ and so there are no turning points.

The graph has the form

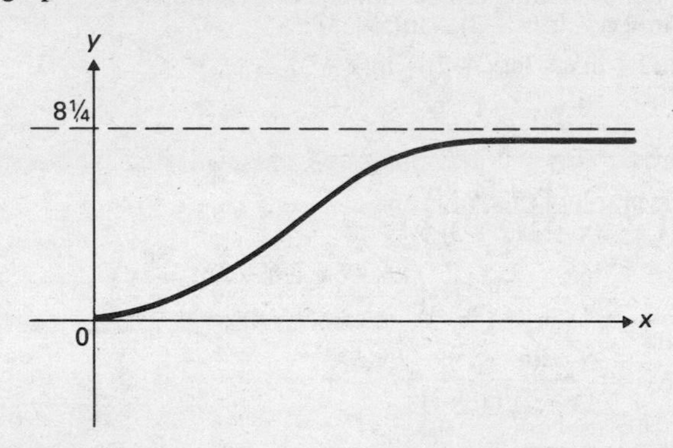

for $x > 0$.

31.12 Logarithmic Differentiation

Some functions can be differentiated most easily by taking $\log_e$ and using implicit function differentiation (page 230).

Examples

1. $y = 4^x$

$\Rightarrow \ln y = x \ln 4$

$\Rightarrow \dfrac{1}{y}\dfrac{dy}{dx} = \ln 4$ differentiating with respect to x

$\Rightarrow \dfrac{dy}{dx} = y \ln 4$

$= 4^x \ln 4$

2. $y = x^x$

$\Rightarrow \ln y = x \ln x$

$\Rightarrow \dfrac{1}{y}\dfrac{dy}{dx} = \ln x + x\dfrac{1}{x}$ product

$\Rightarrow \dfrac{1}{y}\dfrac{dy}{dx} = 1 + \ln x$

$\Rightarrow \dfrac{dy}{dx} = (1 + \ln x)y = (1 + \ln x)x^x$

3. $y = \dfrac{2x}{(x+2)(x+3)}$

$\Rightarrow \ln y = \ln(2x) - \ln(x+2) - \ln(x+3)$

$\Rightarrow \ln y = \ln 2 + \ln x - \ln(x+2) - \ln(x+3)$

$\Rightarrow \dfrac{1}{y}\dfrac{dy}{dx} = \dfrac{1}{x} - \dfrac{1}{x+2} - \dfrac{1}{x+3}$

$\Rightarrow \dfrac{dy}{dx} = y\left(\dfrac{1}{x} - \dfrac{(2x+5)}{(x+2)(x+3)}\right)$

$= \dfrac{2x}{(x+2)(x+3)}\left(\dfrac{x^2+5x+6-2x^2-5x}{x(x+2)(x+3)}\right)$

$= \dfrac{2(6-x^2)}{(x+2)^2(x+3)^2}$

Section 32 Worked Examples

1. $f(x) = 3^{2x+1}$
   (*a*) Evaluate $f(1{\cdot}2)$ to 3 significant figures.
   (*b*) Find the solution of the equation $f(x) = 2{\cdot}3$ to 3 significant figures.

Answer

(*a*) $f(1{\cdot}2) = 3^{3{\cdot}4}$ — calculator x^y,

$= 41{\cdot}9$ — 3 significant figures

(*b*) $3^{2x+1} = 2{\cdot}3$

$\Rightarrow \ln(3^{2x+1}) = \ln(2{\cdot}3)$ — take ln of both sides

$\Rightarrow (2x+1)\ln 3 = \ln(2{\cdot}3)$ — rules for logs, page 291

$\Rightarrow 2x+1 = \dfrac{\ln(2{\cdot}3)}{\ln 3} = 0{\cdot}7581$ — calculator

$\Rightarrow 2x = 0{\cdot}7581 - 1 = -0{\cdot}2419$

$\Rightarrow x = -0{\cdot}121$ — 3 significant figures

2. If $3\log_4 a = 1 - 6b$, express a in terms of b.

Answer

$3\log_4 a = 1 - 6b$

$\Rightarrow \log_4 a^3 = 1 - 6b$ — log rules, page 291

$\Rightarrow a^3 = 4^{1-6b}$

$\Rightarrow a = 4^{\frac{1-6b}{3}}$

3. Solve the equation
$e^{\ln(2x)} + \ln(e^x) = \log_3 27$

Answer

$e^{\ln(2x)} = 2x$

$\ln(e^x) = x$

e^x and $\ln x$ are inverse functions

$\log_3 27 = \log_3 3^3 = 3$

$\Rightarrow 2x + x = 3$

$\Rightarrow 3x = 3$

$\Rightarrow x = 1$

4. Find any turning points on the graph of $y = \frac{x}{\ln x}$ and determine their nature. Sketch the graph for $0 < x < 1$ and $x > 1$.

Answer

$$y = \frac{x}{\ln x}$$

$$\frac{dy}{dx} = \frac{(\ln x)1 - x\left(\frac{1}{x}\right)}{(\ln x)^2}$$

quotient rule

$$\therefore \frac{\ln x - 1}{(\ln x)^2} = 0 \text{ for a turning point}$$

$\Rightarrow \ln x = 1$

$\Rightarrow \quad x = e$

when $x = e$, $y = \frac{e}{\ln e} = e$

$\ln e = 1$

x	$<e$	e	$>e$
$\frac{dy}{dx}$	$-$	0	$+$

(e, e) is a minimum point. $x = 1$ is a vertical symptote, as $\ln 1 = 0$. The graph is

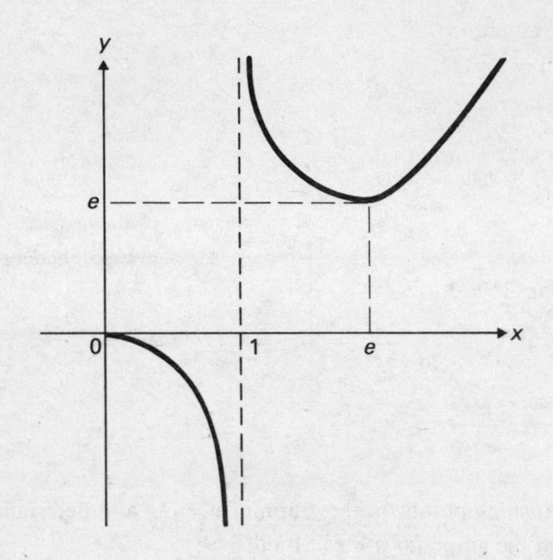

5. Sketch the graph of $y = e^{-x^2}$. Show any turning points and intercepts with the axes. Show also the behaviour as $x \to \pm\infty$.

Answer

$y = e^{-x^2}$

When $x = 0$, $y = 1$ — $e^0 = 1$

Since $e^{-x^2} > 0$, the graph does not cut the x-axis — $e^a > 0$ for all a

As $x \to \pm\infty$

$$e^{-x^2} = \frac{1}{e^{x^2}} \to 0$$ — $e^{x^2} \to \infty$

The x-axis is an asymptote. — $\Rightarrow \frac{1}{e^{x^2}} \to 0$

For turning points

$$\frac{dy}{dx} = -2xe^{-x^2} = 0$$ — change of variable $u = x^2$

$\Rightarrow x = 0$ — $e^{-x^2} \neq 0$ for any x

$\therefore$ (0, 1) is a stationary point.

$$\frac{d^2y}{dx^2} = -2e^{-x^2} + 4x^2e^{-x^2}$$ product rule

$$= e^{-x^2}(4x^2 - 2)$$

When $x = 0$, $\dfrac{d^2y}{dx^2} = -2 < 0$. $e^0 = 1$

$\therefore$ (0, 1) is a maximum point. page 156

The graph is

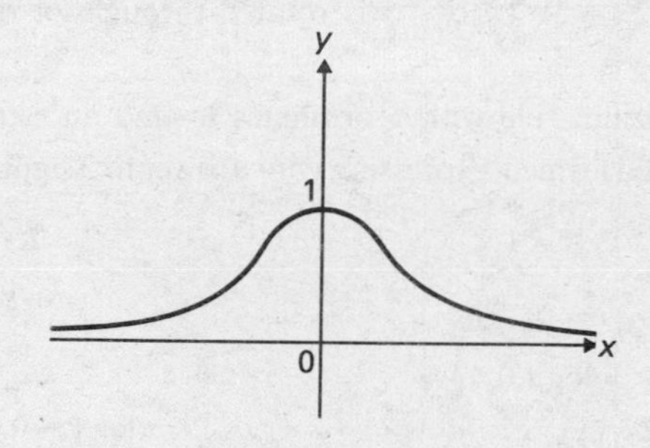

Note the points of inflexion at $x = \pm\dfrac{1}{\sqrt{2}}$

6. Use the substitution $u = \ln x$ to evaluate $\int_e^{e^2} \frac{dx}{x\ln x}$, leaving your answer in terms of natural logarithms.

Answer

Let $u = \ln x$ change variables

$$\Rightarrow \frac{du}{dx} = \frac{1}{x} \Rightarrow du = \frac{1}{x}dx$$

x	e	e^2
u	1	2

$$\Rightarrow \int_e^{e^2} \frac{dx}{x\ln x} = \int_e^{e^2} \frac{1}{\ln x}\frac{1}{x}dx$$

$$= \int_1^2 \frac{1}{u}\,du$$

$$= [\ln u]_1^2$$

$$= \ln 2 - \ln 1$$

$$= \ln 2 \qquad \ln 1 = 0$$

7. Sketch the graph of $y = \log_e(2x + 3)$ for $0 \leqslant x \leqslant 10$. The region defined by $0 \leqslant y \leqslant \log_e(2x + 3)$, $1 \leqslant x \leqslant 5$ is rotated through 2π radians about the x-axis.

Use the trapezium rule with 5 ordinates to find an estimate for the volume of the solid formed, expressing your answer to 3 significant figures.

Answers

$y = \log_e(2x + 3)$

When $x = 0$, $y = \log_e(3)$.

When $y = 0$, $2x + 3 = 1 \qquad \log 1 = 0$

$$2x = -2$$

$$x = -1$$

Vertical asymptote when

$$2x + 3 = 0$$

$$x = -\frac{3}{2}$$

page 289

The graph is

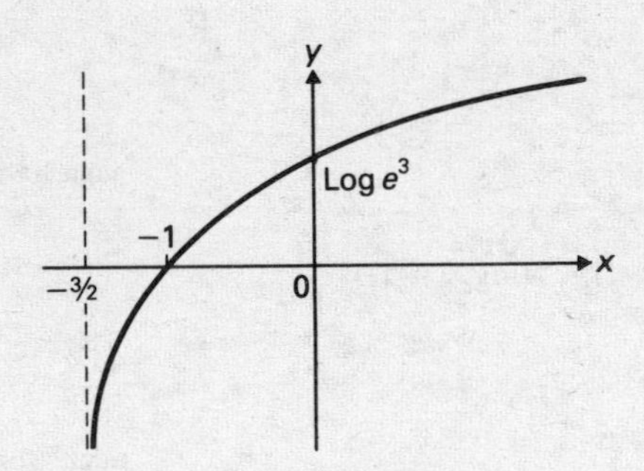

The volume of the solid of revolution is given by

$\pi\int_1^5(\log_e(2x+3))^2dx$ — page 186

Let $f(x) = (\log_e(2x+3))^2$. Evaluating $f(x)$ for

$x = 1, 2, 3, 4, 5$ — 5 ordinates

x	1	2	3	4	5
$f(x)$	2·590	3·787	4·828	5·750	6·579

3 significant figure answer requires 4 significant figure in working

From the trapezium rule — page 248

h = strip width = 1

$$\pi\int_1^5(\log_e(2x+3))^2dx \simeq \frac{1}{3}(2{\cdot}590 + 2(3{\cdot}787 +$$

$$4{\cdot}828 + 5{\cdot}750) + 6{\cdot}579)\pi$$ — $\pi = 3{\cdot}1416$

$$= 39{\cdot}7$$ — 3 significant figures

8. Calculate the mean value of $f(x) = \log_e(5x+2)$ over the interval $0 \leqslant x \leqslant 3$. Express your answer to 3 significant figures.

Answer

$$\text{Mean value} = \frac{1}{3}\int_0^3 \log_e(5x+2)dx$$ — page 189

Let $u = 5x + 2$, $du = 5dx$ — change of variable

x	0	3
u	2	17

$$\Rightarrow \frac{5}{3}\int_2^{17}\log_e u\,du$$

$$= \frac{5}{3}[u(\log_e u - 1)]_2^{17}$$ — page 308

$$= \frac{5}{3}(17(\log_e 17 - 1) - 2(\log_e 2 - 1))$$

$$= \frac{5}{13}(17\log_e 17 - 2\log_e 2 - 15)$$

$$= 12{\cdot}2$$ — calculator

9. The variables x and y are believed to satisfy a relation of the form $y = ax^n$, where a and n are constants.

The table shows approximate values for x and y. By plotting a graph of $\ln y$ against $\ln x$, show that the stated relationship between x and y is reasonable, and find values for a and n correct to 1 decimal place.

x	1	1·5	2	2·5	3	3·5
y	3·95	13·6	32·02	62·5	107·89	171·60

Answer

$y = ax^n$

$\Rightarrow \ln y = \ln a + n \ln x$ taking $\log_e$

If $Y = \ln y$, $X = \ln x$

$Y = \ln a + nX$

which represents a straight line with gradient n and Y-intercept $\ln a$.

$X = \ln x$	0	0·41	0·69	0·92	1·10	1·25
$Y = \ln y$	1·37	2·61	3·47	4·14	4·68	5·15

The graph of Y against X is on a separate sheet of squared paper

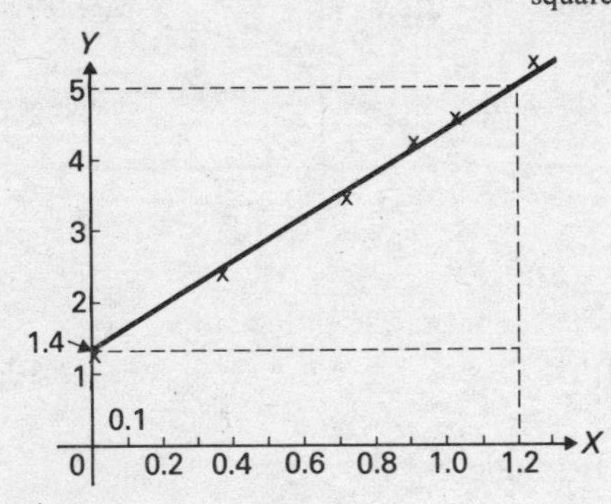

The graph is a straight line and so $y = ax^n$.

$$\text{Gradient } n = \frac{5 - 1{\cdot}4}{1{\cdot}2} = 3{\cdot}0.$$

Y-intercept $\ln a = 1{\cdot}4$

$\therefore a = 4{\cdot}0$ (to 1 decimal place)

10. Show graphically that the equation

$$e^x = \frac{(x+2)^2}{4}$$

has exactly 3 real roots, one of which is $x = 0$. Use your graph to estimate, to 1 decimal place, the negative root. Apply the Newton–Raphson procedure once to $f(x) = e^x - \frac{(x+2)^2}{4}$ to obtain a better estimate, to 3 decimal places.

Answer

$\frac{(x+2)^2}{4}$ touches the x-axis at $(-2, 0)$ and cuts the y-axis at $y = 1$. page 99

The graphs of $y = \frac{(x+2)^2}{4}$ and $y = e^x$ are

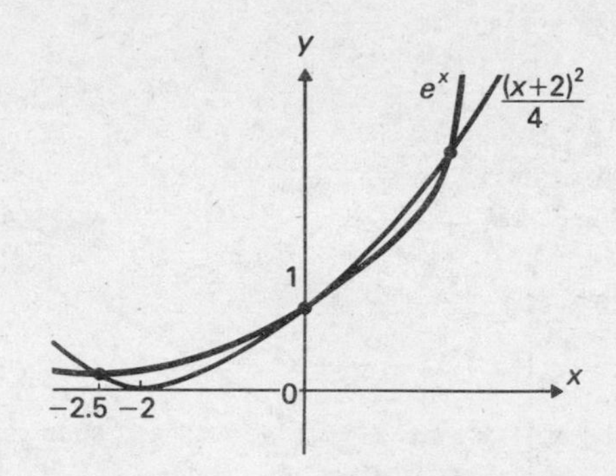

The curves intersect 3 times and so the equation has 3 real roots.

When $x = 0$, $e^0 = 1$

$$\frac{(0+2)^2}{4} = 1$$

$\Rightarrow x = 0$ is one root.

From the graph, the negative root is approximately $x = -2{\cdot}5$. If

$$f(x) = e^x - \frac{(x+2)^2}{4}$$

then

$$f'(x) = e^x - \frac{2(x+2)}{4}$$
$$= e^x - \frac{(x+2)}{2}$$

The Newton–Raphson method gives

$$x_1 = -2{\cdot}5 - \frac{0{\cdot}0196}{0{\cdot}3321}$$ page 169

$$= 2{\cdot}559$$ to 3 decimal places

as a better approximation to the root.

11. Expand $f(x) = \frac{e^{-x^2}}{1+x}$ in ascending powers of x up to the term in x^5, stating the range of values of x for which the expansion is valid. Use the first two terms of your expansion to estimate $f(0{\cdot}1)$.

Obtain an expansion for $f'(x)$ and use the first two terms to estimate $f'(0{\cdot}1)$.

Answer

$$f(x) = e^{-x^2}(1+x)^{-1}$$
$$= (1 - x^2 + \frac{x^4}{2!} - \ldots + \ldots) \times$$ page 299
$$(1 - x + x^2 - x^3 + x^4 - x^5)$$
$$= 1 - x^2 + \frac{x^4}{2} - x + x^3 - \frac{x^5}{2} + x^2 -$$
$$x^4 - x^3 + x^5 + x^4 - x^5$$ up to x^5 term only
$$= 1 - x + \frac{x^4}{2} - \frac{x^5}{2} + \ldots$$

The series converges for $-1 < x < 1$. page 209

$$f(0{\cdot}1) = 1 - 0{\cdot}1 + \frac{(0{\cdot}1)^4}{2} - \frac{(0{\cdot}1)^5}{2}$$
$$\approx 0{\cdot}900045$$

$$f'(x) = -1 + 2x^3 - \frac{5x^4}{2} + \ldots$$ differentiate term by term

$$f'(0{\cdot}1) = -1 + 0{\cdot}002 - 0{\cdot}00025 + \ldots$$
$$\approx -0{\cdot}998\,25$$

Section 33 Examination Questions

1. *Given that $y = 6^x$, find, to 2 decimal places, the value of x when $y = 0{\cdot}5$.* [LON]

2. *Given that $2\log_{10} y = 2x + 1$ then $y =$*

A $\dfrac{10^x}{\sqrt{10}}$ B $10^x\sqrt{10}$ C $10^x - \sqrt{10}$ D $10^x + \sqrt{10}$

E $(\sqrt{10})^x$ [LON]

3. $e^{-3\ln x} =$

A -3^x B 3^{-x} C $-x^3$ D x^{-3} E $(-3)^{-x}$

[LON]

4. $y = x^3 \ln(3x)$

The value of $\frac{dy}{dx}$, when $x = 1$, is

A 1 B 3 C $3\ln 3$ D $\frac{1}{3} + 3\ln 3$ E $1 + 3\ln 3$

[LON]

5. *In which one of the following is the relation between x and y NOT linear.*

A $2x + 3y = 1$ B $e^y = 2e^x$ C $2^y = 3^x$ D $7\ln y = 3\ln x$

E $\ln y = 1 + \ln x$. [LON]

6. *The general solution of $\frac{dy}{dx} = 2xy$, P being an arbitrary constant, is*

A $y = e^{2x} + P$ B $y = Pe^{-x^2}$ C $y = Pe^{x^2}$ D $y = Pe^{2x}$

E $y = e^{x^2} + P$ [LON]

7. *The graph of $y = xe^{-x}$*

1. *is symmetrical about the y-axis,*
2. *lies above Ox for all values of x,*
3. *has zero gradient at $x = 1$.*

A 1, 2 and 3 are true B 1 and 2 only C 2 and 3 only

D 1 only E 3 only [LON]

8. *Differentiate the following with respect to x, simplifying your answers where possible:*

(i) $\dfrac{1}{4-x^3}$, *(ii)* $(x^2+1)\log_e(x^2+1)$ [SUJB – part]

9. *Find the first three non-zero terms of the expansion of* $e^{\frac{1}{2}x}\log_e(1+2x)$ *in ascending powers of x. Use the first two terms to give a value for* $e^{0\cdot01}\log_e 1\cdot04$, *and the third term to estimate the error in your value. Hence correct your first answer to an appropriate number of decimal places.*

[SUJB – part]

10. *(a) Transform the integral* $\int_1^e \frac{dt}{t(2+\log_e t)^2}$ *by the substitution* $u = 2 + \log_e t$ *and hence evaluate it.*

(b) Give a rough sketch of the graph of $y = e^x - 1$. *The area enclosed by the graph, the x-axis and the line* $x = 1$ *is rotated about the x-axis through* 2π *radians. Find the volume of the solid formed. (You may leave your answer in terms of e and* π.*)* [SUJB – part]

11. *Differentiate* $\log_{10}x$ *with respect to x.* [AEB – part]

12. *Prove that* $\int_1^2 \frac{dx}{x^3+x} = \frac{1}{2}\log_e\frac{8}{5}$. [AEB – part]

13. *Sketch the curve* $y = \log_e x$ *for the interval* $1 \leqslant x \leqslant 7$. *The finite region defined by* $0 \leqslant y \leqslant \log_e x$, $1 \leqslant x \leqslant 7$ *is rotated completely about Ox. Tabulating your work, use Simpson's rule with seven ordinates to estimate, to two decimal places, the volume of the solid so formed.* [AEB]

14. *Given that* $p = \log_y x$ *and* $q = \log_z x$, *where* $x \neq 1$, *express, in terms of p and q, (a)* $\log_x(yz)$, *(b)* $\log_z y$.

If $y + z = 1$, *prove that* $\frac{1}{p} = \log_x(1 - x^{1/q})$. [AEB]

15. *The pairs of values of x and y in the table below satisfy approximately the relationships* $e^y = kx^m$, *where k and m are constants.*

x	1	2	3	5	7
y	1·10	2·28	2·97	3·83	4·41

(a) Express y in terms of x, k and m.

(b) Using squared paper draw a suitable linear graph and hence determine values for k and m.

(c) Use your graph to estimate the value of x when y = 4. [AEB]

16. *Given that* $f(x) \equiv \frac{1}{x(x+2)}$ *express* $f(x)$ *in partial fractions. Hence, or otherwise, find (a)* $\frac{d^4f(x)}{dx^4}$, *(b)* $\int_1^2 f(x)\,dx$. [LON]

17. *A water tank has the shape of an open rectangular box of length 1 m, width 0·5 m and height 0·5 m. Water may be drained from the tank through a tap at the bottom of the tank, and it is known that, when the tap is open, water leaves at a rate of 100h litres per minute, where h m is the depth of water in the tank. When the tap is open, water is also fed into the tank at a constant rate of 50 litres per minute and no water is fed into the tank when the tap is closed. Show that, t minutes after the tap has been opened, the variable h satisfies the differential equation* $10\frac{dh}{dt} = 1 - 2h$. *On a particular occasion the tap was opened when* $h = 0{\cdot}25$ *and closed when* $h = 0{\cdot}375$. *Show that the tap was opened for 5 ln 2 minutes.* [LON]

18. *Solve the differential equation* $xy\frac{dy}{dx} = 1 - x^2$, $x > 0$, *given that* $y = 2$ *when* $x = 1$. [LON]

19. *Given that* $(1 + x)y = \ln x$, *show that, when y is stationary,* $\ln x = (1 + x)/x$. *Show graphically, or otherwise, that this latter equation has only one real root, and prove that this root lies between 3·5 and 3·8.*

By taking 3·5 as a first approximation to this root and applying the Newton–Raphson process once to the equation $\ln x - (1 + x)/x = 0$, *find a second approximation to this root, giving your answer to 3 significant figures.*

Hence find an approximation to the corresponding stationary value of y. [LON]

20. *Find (a)* $\int x \ln x\,dx$, *(b)* $\int \frac{x}{\sqrt{(x-2)}}dx$ [LON]

21. *Obtain the expansion in ascending powers of x of the function*

$$f(x) = \ln\left(\frac{(1-3x)^2}{(1+2x)}\right)$$

Give the values of the coefficients of x up to and including x^3, and give an expression for the coefficient of x^n.

For what range of values of x is this expansion valid? [OXF]

22. *Show that $\int_0^1 e^x dx = e - 1$. The integral is approximated by using the trapezium rule, dividing the range into n intervals each of length $h = 1/n$. Show that the result is $\frac{(e-1)(p+1)}{2n(p-1)}$ where $p = e^h$. Hence or otherwise show that $\frac{h(e^h+1)}{2(e^h-1)}$ is very close to 1 when h is small.* [OXF]

8 Trigonometric Functions and Equations

Section 34 Definitions and Properties

34.1 Angles

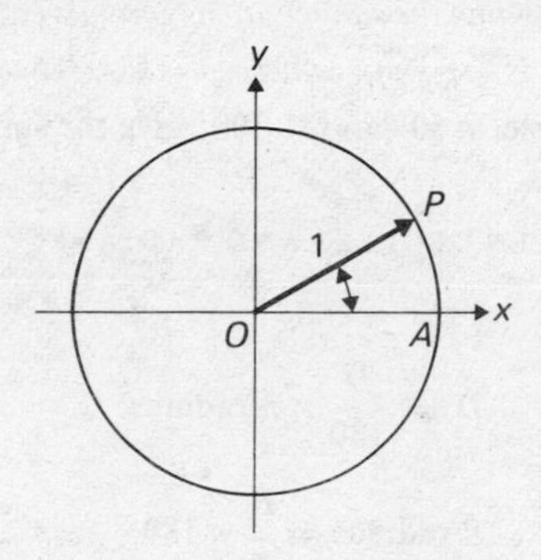

The figure shows a circle, centre O and radius 1 unit. OP is a moving pointer, which rotates anticlockwise about O from **initial line** OA.

Each position of point P on the circumference of the circle defines an angle $\widehat{AOP}$.

A complete revolution returns the pointer to its initial position.

Two systems of angular measurement are in common use:

1. Degrees (°). One revolution $= 360°$, thus a half revolution $= 180°$ and a quarter revolution = a right angle $= 90°$.

One degree is $\frac{1}{360}$th of a revolution.

2. Radians. One revolution $= 2\pi$ radians, where the constant $\pi =$ 3·141 5926 to 7 decimal places. A half revolution $= \pi$ radians and a right angle $= \frac{\pi}{2}$ radians.

You should be familiar with both systems and be able to use them interchangeably.

Angles can be larger than one revolution or negative (measured clockwise).

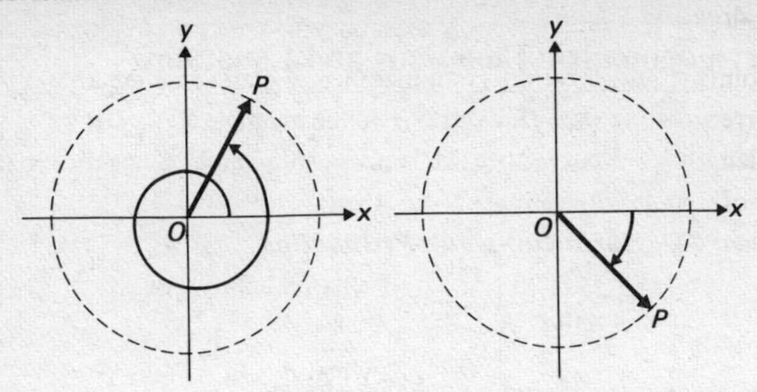

Notice that, for example, $-60°$ and $+300°$ give the same position P.

CONVERSION BETWEEN DEGREES AND RADIANS

Use the formulae

$$D° = \frac{D}{180} \times \pi \text{ radians}$$

$$R \text{ radians} = \frac{R}{\pi} \times 180°$$

The following table is also useful to remember.

radians	0	$\frac{\pi}{6}$	$\frac{\pi}{4}$	$\frac{\pi}{3}$	$\frac{\pi}{2}$	$\frac{2\pi}{3}$	$\frac{3\pi}{4}$	$\frac{5\pi}{6}$	π
degrees	0	30	45	60	90	120	135	150	180

radians	$\frac{7\pi}{6}$	$\frac{5\pi}{4}$	$\frac{4\pi}{3}$	$\frac{3\pi}{2}$	$\frac{5\pi}{3}$	$\frac{7\pi}{4}$	$\frac{11\pi}{6}$	2π
degrees	210	225	240	270	300	315	330	360

The approximations $60° \approx 1$ radian, $90° \approx 1{\cdot}5$ radians are sometimes used. (Angles in radians are often expressed as multiples of π, but this is not always necessary.)

You should *never* mix radians and degrees in the same problem. Use one system only throughout a calculation.

34.2 Arcs and Sectors

Two points A and B on the circumference of a circle define an *arc* AB. The corresponding radii OA and OB define an angle $\theta = \widehat{AOB}$.

The length of the curved arc AB is proportional to θ. Since the circumference of a circle with radius r is $2\pi r$, then

$$\text{arc length} = \begin{cases} \dfrac{\theta\pi r}{180} & \text{when } \theta \text{ is in } \textit{degrees} \\[2ex] \theta r & \text{when } \theta \text{ is in } \textit{radians} \end{cases}$$

The section of the circle cut off by radii OA and OB is called a *sector*. The area of the sector is also proportional to the angle θ.

$$\text{Area of sector} = \begin{cases} \dfrac{\theta\pi r^2}{360} & \text{when } \theta \text{ is in } \textit{degrees} \\[2ex] \tfrac{1}{2}\theta r^2 & \text{when } \theta \text{ is in } \textit{radians} \end{cases}$$

(*Since the area of the complete circle is* πr^2.)

The formulae are simpler for angles measured in radians. In particular, the arc of a circle of radius 1 unit corresponding to an angle of 1 radian is simply 1 unit.

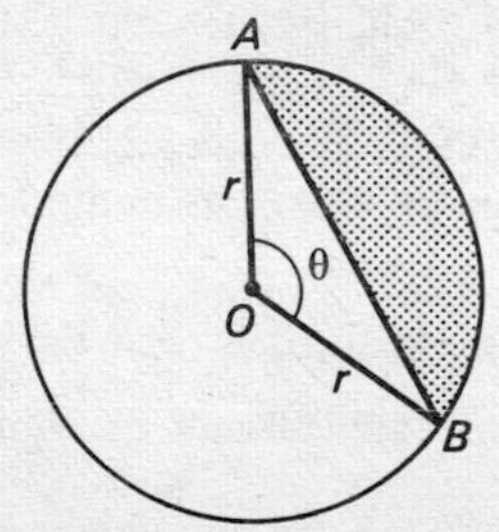

The area of a **segment** cut off by a chord AB is calculated by subtracting the area of the triangle AOB from that of sector AOB.

34.3 Definitions of the Trigonometric Functions Sin, Cos and Tan

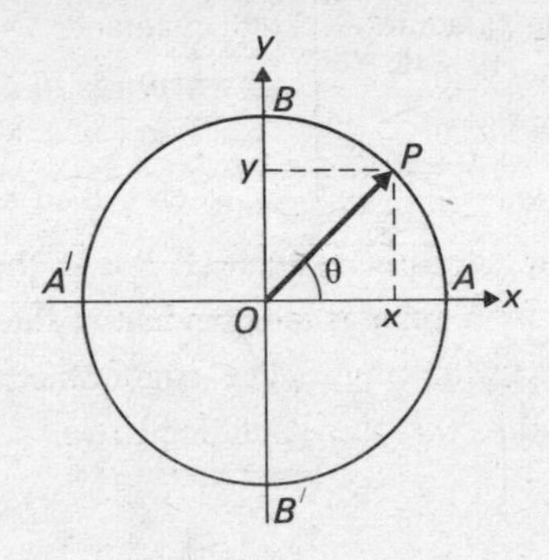

Let $A'OA$ be the x-axis and $B'OB$ be the y-axis, with $OP = OA = OB = 1$ scale unit.

The coordinates of the variable point P depend on the position of P and so are functions of θ. Define

$$\cos\theta = x\text{-coordinate of } P$$

$$\sin\theta = y\text{-coordinate of } P$$

and also

$$\tan\theta = \frac{\sin\theta}{\cos\theta} = \text{gradient of } OP$$

(sin, cos and tan are short forms of sine, cosine and tangent. These are the **trigonometric functions** (or **ratios**).)

The circle is divided into 4 **quadrants**, determined by the signs of the coordinates of P.

y

2nd quadrant	1st quadrant
$x<0$	$x>0$
$y>0$	$y>0$
3rd quadrant	4th quadrant
$x<0$	$x>0$
$y<0$	$y<0$

0 x

For P in the first quadrant, θ is **acute**. If P is in the second quadrant θ is **obtuse**. The size of an angle is independent of the lengths of the line segments which define the angle. The trigonometric ratios are also independent of the radius OP of the defining circle.

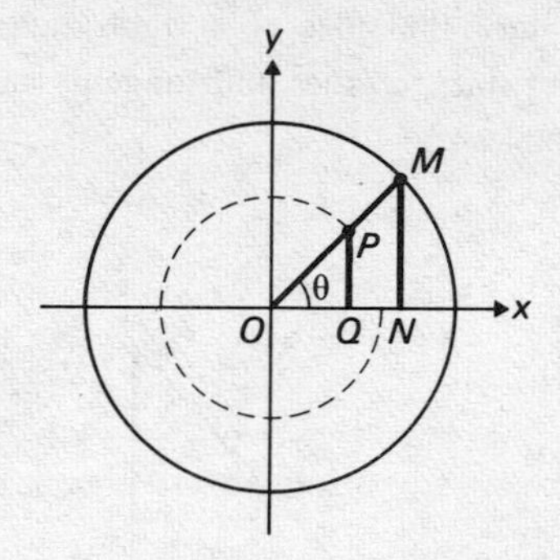

Suppose that $OM = r$ and $M\widehat{O}N = P\widehat{O}Q = \theta$, and $M\widehat{N}O = P\widehat{Q}O =$ a right angle, then $\triangle$s MON and POQ are *similar*.

Since $OM = r$ then $ON = r\cos\theta$ and $MN = r\sin\theta$. Hence $\cos\theta = \frac{ON}{OM}$, $\sin\theta = \frac{MN}{OM}$ and $\tan\theta = \frac{\sin\theta}{\cos\theta} = \frac{MN}{ON}$. Labelling

OM as the **hypotenuse** of $\triangle OMN$
MN as the side **opposite** angle $M\widehat{O}N$ and
ON as the **adjacent** side which connects the angle $M\widehat{O}N$ to the right angle $M\widehat{N}O$

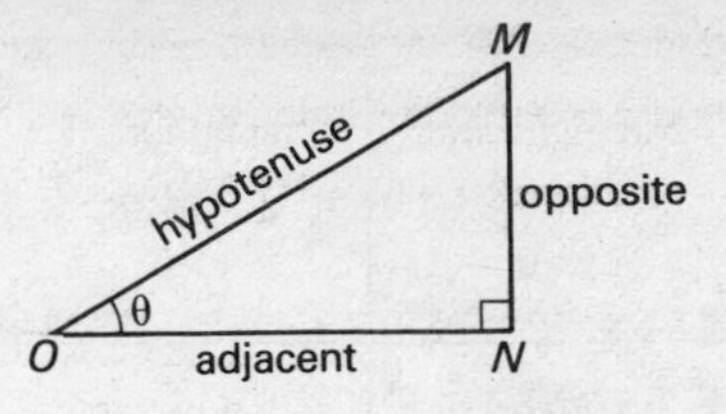

then for *acute angles* θ

$$\sin\theta = \frac{\text{opposite}}{\text{hypotenuse}}, \quad \cos\theta = \frac{\text{adjacent}}{\text{hypotenuse}}, \quad \tan\theta = \frac{\text{opposite}}{\text{adjacent}}$$

(*SOH*, *CAH*, *TOA* for short).

For acute angles, the trigonometric functions can be calculated from the lengths of the sides of a right-angled triangle. Conversely, given values of $\sin\theta$, $\cos\theta$ and $\tan\theta$ the sides of a right-angled triangle may be calculated. (Values of sines, cosines and tangents can be found from a calculator, or from tables.)

Example

To calculate x and y

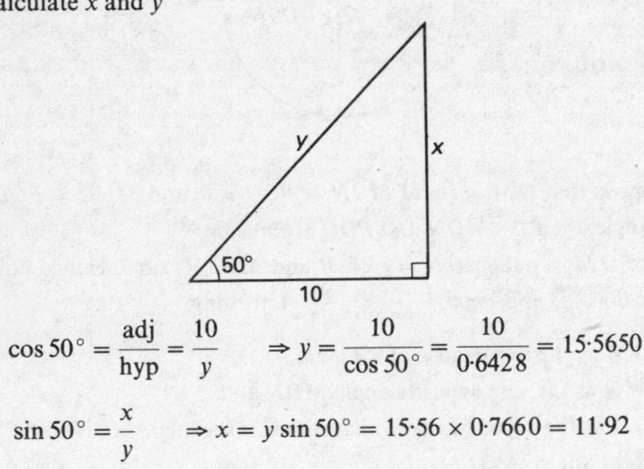

$$\cos 50° = \frac{\text{adj}}{\text{hyp}} = \frac{10}{y} \qquad \Rightarrow y = \frac{10}{\cos 50°} = \frac{10}{0{\cdot}6428} = 15{\cdot}5650$$

$$\sin 50° = \frac{x}{y} \qquad \Rightarrow x = y\sin 50° = 15{\cdot}56 \times 0{\cdot}7660 = 11{\cdot}92$$

34.4 Auxiliary Angles

These triangle formulae can only be used to calculate $\sin\theta$, $\cos\theta$ and $\tan\theta$ when θ is acute. Right-angled triangles cannot be constructed to contain larger angles. However, we can extend these formulae to other angles by making use of **auxiliary acute** angles.

The auxiliary angle α is the acute angle that OP makes with the x-axis.

SECOND QUADRANT

$$\left.\begin{aligned}\cos\theta &= -\cos\alpha\\ \sin\theta &= \sin\alpha\\ \text{and}\tan\theta &= -\tan\alpha\end{aligned}\right\}\text{ from the symmetry of the diagram}$$

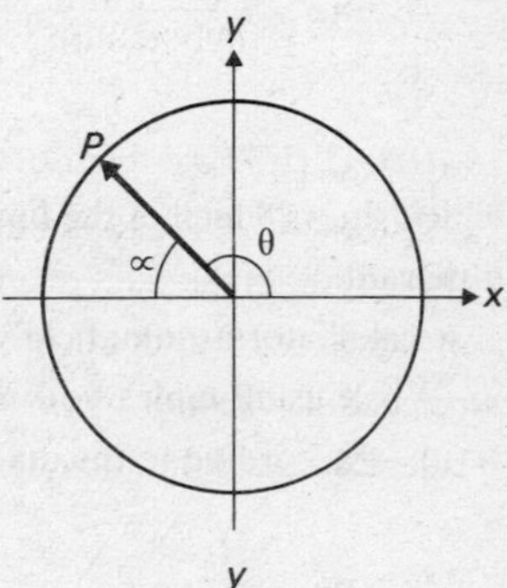

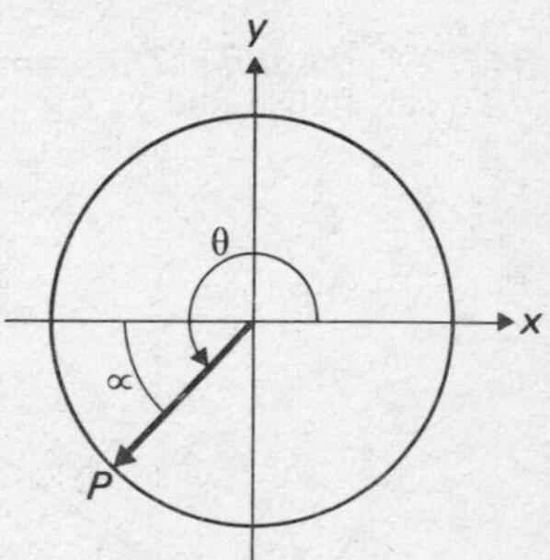

THIRD QUADRANT

$$\cos\theta = -\cos\alpha$$
$$\sin\theta = -\sin\alpha$$
$$\tan\theta = \tan\alpha$$

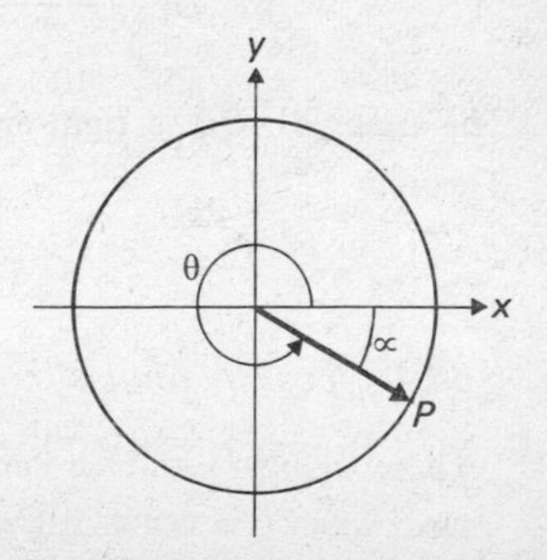

FOURTH QUADRANT

$$\cos\theta = \cos\alpha$$
$$\sin\theta = -\sin\alpha$$
$$\tan\theta = -\tan\alpha$$

The *SOH*, *CAH*, *TOA* formulae can be used with the acute angle α and the correct sign (+ or −) allocated according to the diagram

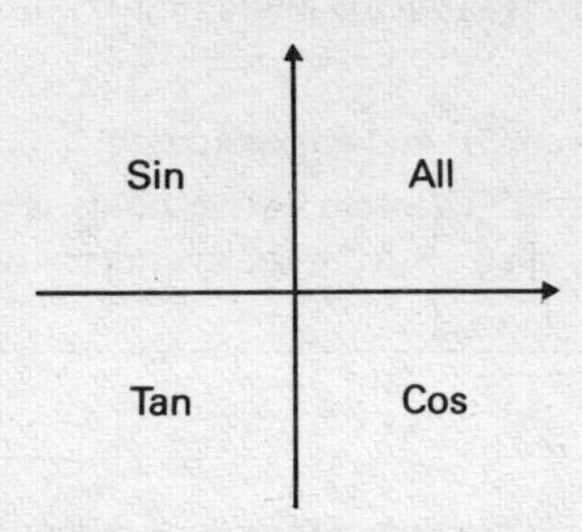

which shows which of the functions ($\sin\theta$, $\cos\theta$, $\tan\theta$) is *positive* for each quadrant.

A calculator automatically puts the correct sign for any angle keyed in. When using tables you must find $\sin\alpha$, $\cos\alpha$ or $\tan\alpha$ and then put + or − according to the diagram above.

34.5 Pythagoras' Theorem, Complementary Angles

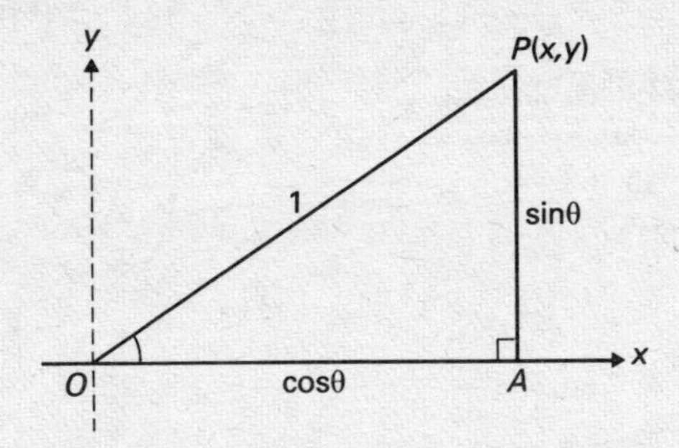

The triangle *AOP* is right-angled and θ is acute. From Pythagoras' Theorem

$$OA^2 + AP^2 = OP^2$$

$$\Rightarrow x^2 + y^2 = 1$$

$$\Rightarrow (\cos\theta)^2 + (\sin\theta)^2 = 1$$

which is more conveniently written as

$$\boxed{\cos^2\theta + \sin^2\theta = 1}$$

Note that $\cos^2\theta$ means $(\cos\theta)^2$ and *not* $\cos(\cos\theta)$!

The form of Pythagoras' Theorem above holds for *any* angle θ. The identity can be rearranged as

$$\boxed{\cos\theta = \pm\sqrt{1-\sin^2\theta} \qquad \text{or} \qquad \sin\theta = \pm\sqrt{1-\cos^2\theta}}$$

These can be used to calculate one of the ratios when the other is given.

Example

Given that $\cos\theta = -\frac{1}{4}$ where θ is an obtuse angle, calculate $\sin\theta$ and $\tan\theta$.

Answer

$$\sin\theta = \pm\sqrt{1-\left(-\frac{1}{4}\right)^2} = \pm\sqrt{1-\frac{1}{16}} = \pm\sqrt{\frac{15}{16}}$$

Since θ is obtuse then $\sin\theta > 0$.

$$\Rightarrow \quad \sin\theta = \frac{\sqrt{15}}{4}$$

$$\tan\theta = \frac{\sin\theta}{\cos\theta} = -\frac{\sqrt{\dfrac{15}{4}}}{\dfrac{1}{4}} = -\sqrt{15}$$

COMPLEMENTARY ANGLES

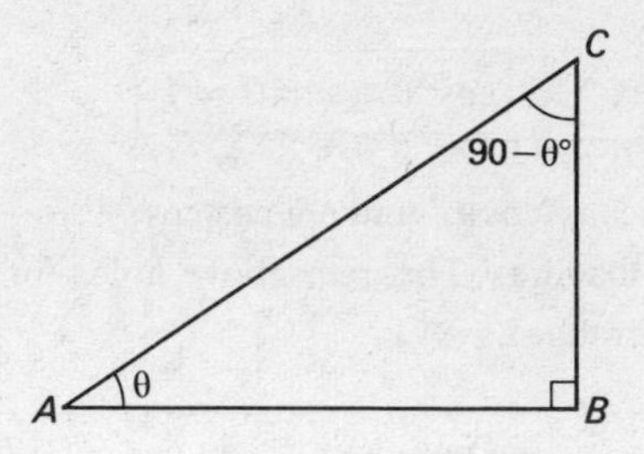

For acute angle θ, the *SOH*, *CAH*, *TOA* formulae give

$$\sin(90° - \theta°) = \frac{AB}{AC} = \cos\theta°$$

and

$$\cos(90° - \theta°) = \frac{CB}{AC} = \sin\theta°$$

These relations also hold when θ is not acute. If $\theta° + \psi° = 90°$, θ and ψ are said to be **complementary**.

34.6 Special Angles

The values of $\sin\theta$, $\cos\theta$ and $\tan\theta$ can be calculated easily for angles $0°, 30°, 45°, 60°$ and $90°$.

$30°$ AND $60°$

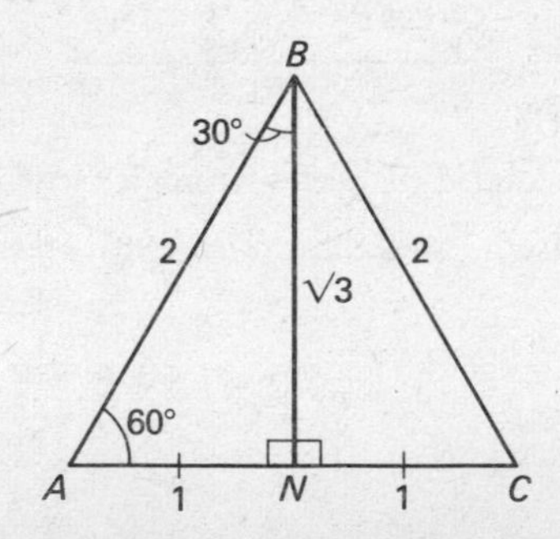

ABC is an equilateral triangle of side 2 units. $\widehat{BAC} = \widehat{CAB} = \widehat{ABC} = 60°$. BN is the perpendicular from B to AC. Hence $\widehat{ABN} = 30°$ and $AN = 1$ unit.

From Pythagoras' Theorem $BN^2 = 2^2 - 1^2 = 3$

$$\Rightarrow \quad BN = \sqrt{3} \text{ units}$$

Thus

$$\sin 60° = \frac{BN}{AB} = \frac{\sqrt{3}}{2}, \quad \cos 60° = \frac{AN}{AB} = \frac{1}{2}, \quad \tan 60° = \frac{\frac{\sqrt{3}}{2}}{\frac{1}{2}} = \sqrt{3}$$

and

$$\sin 30° = \frac{AN}{AB} = \frac{1}{2}, \quad \cos 30° = \frac{BN}{AB} = \frac{\sqrt{3}}{2}, \quad \tan 30° = \frac{\frac{1}{2}}{\frac{\sqrt{3}}{2}} = \frac{1}{\sqrt{3}}$$

0°, 45° AND 90°

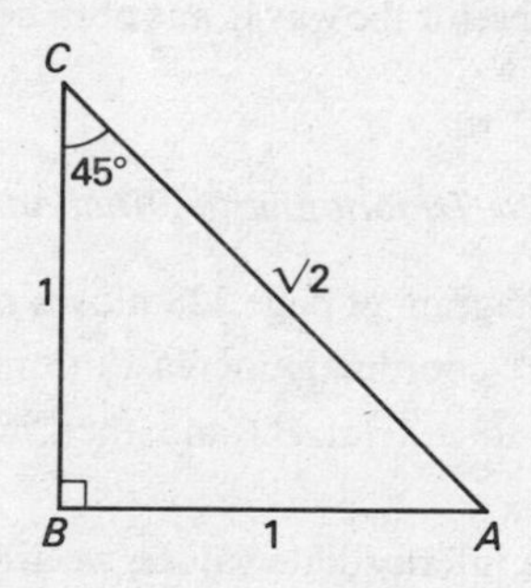

ABC is a right-angled isosceles triangle with $AB = BC = 1$ unit. $AC = \sqrt{2}$ units (from Pythagoras' Theorem). Thus

$$\sin 45° = \frac{AB}{AC} = \frac{1}{\sqrt{2}} \equiv \frac{\sqrt{2}}{2}, \quad \cos 45° = \frac{BC}{AC} = \frac{1}{\sqrt{2}} \equiv \frac{\sqrt{2}}{2}, \quad \tan 45° = 1.$$

and

$\sin 90° = \dfrac{AC}{AC} = 1;$ hence $\cos 90° = \sqrt{1 - \sin^2 90°}$ page 333

$$= \sqrt{1-1} = 0$$

and $\tan 90° = \frac{\sin 90°}{\cos 90°} = \frac{1}{0}$ which is **undefined** (has no finite value).

$0°$ and $90°$ are complementary angles (Section 34.3) thus $\cos 0° = \sin 90° = 1$ and $\sin 0° = \cos 90° = 0$. Hence $\tan 0° = \frac{0}{1} = 0$.

SUMMARY

degrees	0	30	45	60	90
radians	0	$\frac{\pi}{6}$	$\frac{\pi}{4}$	$\frac{\pi}{3}$	$\frac{\pi}{2}$
sin	0	$\frac{1}{2}$	$\frac{\sqrt{2}}{2}$	$\frac{\sqrt{3}}{3}$	1
cos	1	$\frac{\sqrt{3}}{2}$	$\frac{\sqrt{2}}{2}$	$\frac{1}{2}$	0
tan	0	$\frac{1}{\sqrt{3}}$	1	$\sqrt{3}$	undefined

You should *learn* this table (or the way it was obtained using the diagrams above).

34.7 The Graphs of the Trigonometric Functions

As the point P on the diagram of page 328 moves round the circle (anti-clockwise) from A, the y-coordinate increases from 0 (at A) to 1 (at B) then decreases from 1 to -1 (at B') and then increases from -1 to 0 (A again).

Using a calculator for intermediate values, we arrive at the graph.

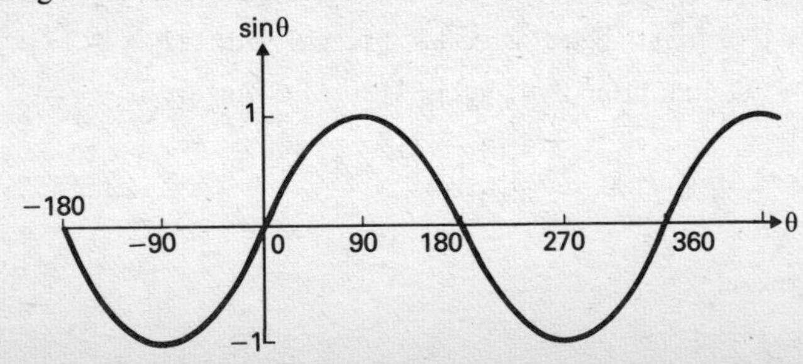

NOTES

1. the function $\sin : \theta \mapsto \sin\theta$ has domain $\mathbb{R}$. The range is $-1 \leqslant \sin\theta \leqslant 1$.
2. $\sin\theta$ is a **periodic** function, that is $\sin(n360° + \theta) \equiv \sin\theta$ for any integer n. The basic *cycle* of the graph is obtained for $0° \leqslant \theta° \leqslant 360°$, and is then repeated indefinitely in each direction. The **period** (length of one cycle) is $360°$ (2π radians). The **amplitude** is 1.
3. $\sin(-\theta) = -\sin\theta$ for all $\theta \in \mathbb{R}$. $\sin\theta$ is an odd function (page 37).

The graph of $\cos\theta$ can be drawn in the same way

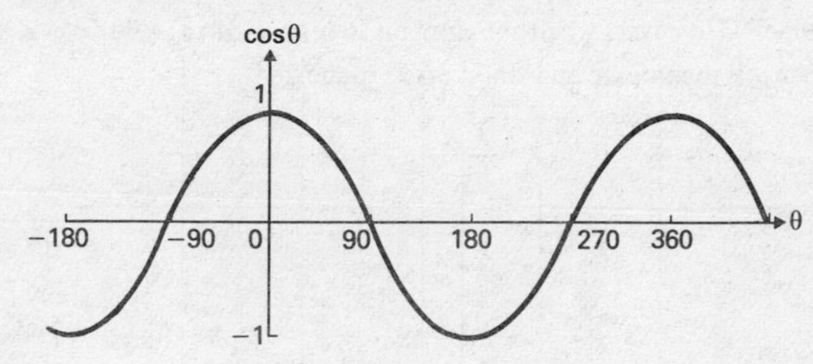

NOTES

1. $\cos : \theta \mapsto \cos\theta$ has domain $\mathbb{R}$ and range $-1 \leqslant \cos\theta \leqslant 1$.
2. $\cos\theta$ is periodic with period $360°$ and amplitude 1.
3. $\cos(-\theta) = \cos\theta$ for all $\theta \in \mathbb{R}$, $\cos\theta$ is an even function.

To draw the graph of $\tan\theta \equiv \frac{\sin\theta}{\cos\theta}$, note that since $\cos\theta = 0$ for $\theta = \pm 90°, \pm 270°, \pm 450°, \ldots$ $\tan\theta$ is undefined for these values. These values of θ correspond to vertical asymptotes in the figure:

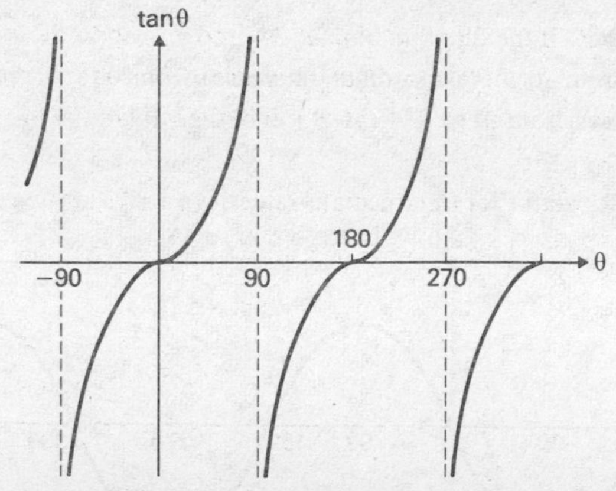

NOTES

1. $\tan\theta$ takes all real values, the range is $\mathbb{R}$.
2. $\tan\theta$ is periodic with period $180°$.
3. $\tan(-\theta) = -\tan\theta$ and so $\tan\theta$ is an odd function.

34.8 The Inverse Trigonometric Functions

The function $\sin\theta$ does not have an inverse function on the whole domain $\mathbb{R}$. However, when the domain is restricted to $-90° \leqslant \theta \leqslant 90°$, then $\sin\theta$ is **monotonic** and $\sin^{-1}$ exists (page 284)

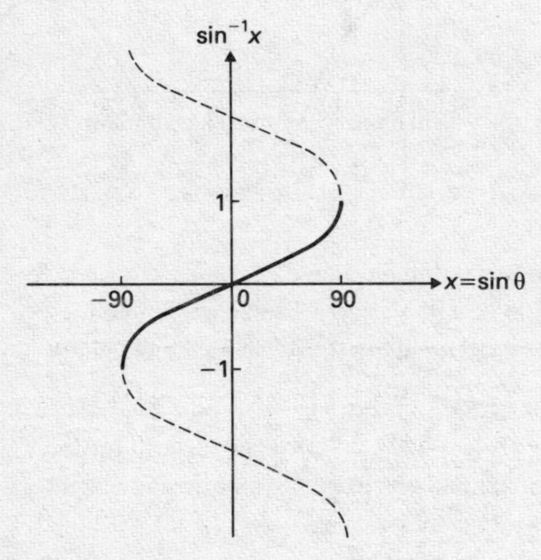

The inverse $\cos^{-1}$ exists when the domain of $\cos\theta$ is restricted to $0 \leqslant \theta \leqslant 180°$.

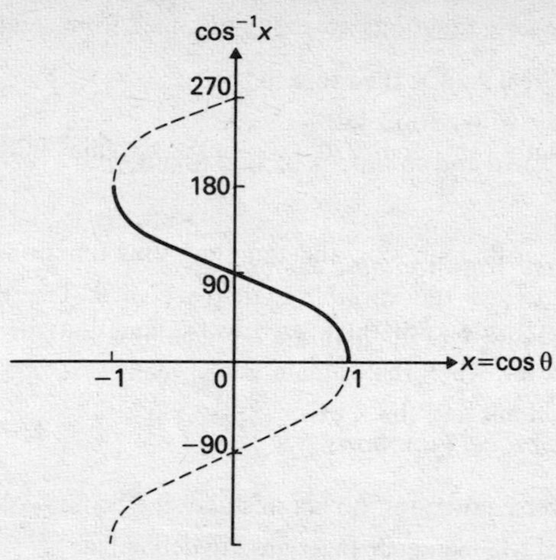

The inverse $\tan^{-1}$ is defined when $\tan\theta$ has domain $-90° < \theta < 90°$.

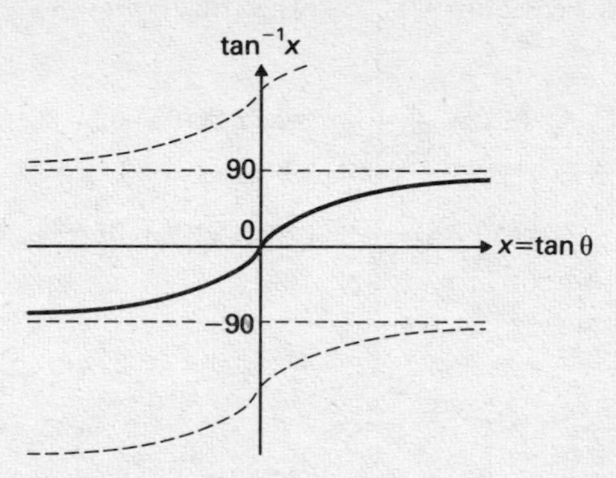

Thus, for $-90° \leqslant x \leqslant 90°$ and $-1 \leqslant y \leqslant 1$

$$\boxed{\sin^{-1}(\sin x) = x \text{ and } \sin(\sin^{-1} y) = y}$$

For

$$0° \leqslant x \leqslant 180° \text{ and } -1 \leqslant y \leqslant 1$$

$$\boxed{\cos^{-1}(\cos x) = x \text{ and } \cos(\cos^{-1} y) = y}$$

For

$$-90° < x < 90° \text{ and } y \in \mathbb{R}$$

$$\boxed{\tan^{-1}(\tan x) = x \text{ and } \tan(\tan^{-1} y) = y}$$

Values for the inverse functions are easily obtained from a calculator.

Exercise

From a calculator $\sin^{-1}(\sin 270°) = -90°$. Explain fully why this happens.

Note: When regarding sin, cos and tan simply as functions on $\mathbb{R}$ it is quite common to use the variable x in place of θ. The x is not the x-coordinate of point P of the diagram on page 328!

34.9 The Reciprocal Functions

When using inverse functions, do *not* mistake $\sin^{-1}\theta$ for $\frac{1}{\sin\theta}$!.

The **reciprocal trigonometric functions** are defined as

$$\operatorname{cosec}\theta \equiv \frac{1}{\sin\theta} \qquad \text{(when } \sin\theta \neq 0\text{)}$$

$$\sec\theta \equiv \frac{1}{\cos\theta} \qquad \text{(when } \cos\theta \neq 0\text{)}$$

$$\cot\theta \equiv \frac{1}{\tan\theta} \qquad \text{(when } \tan\theta \neq 0\text{)}$$

They have graphs

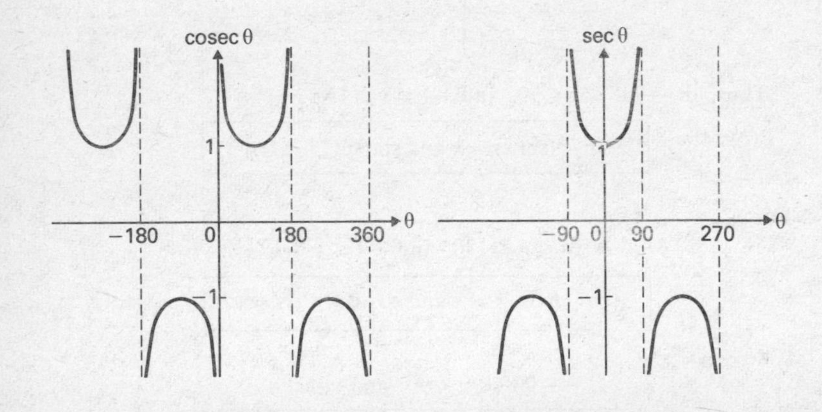

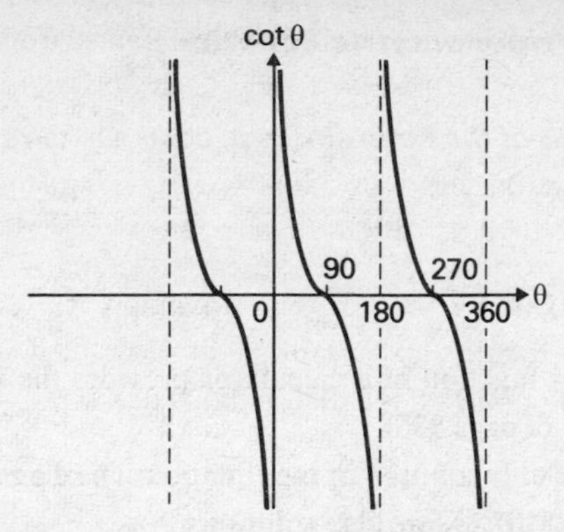

(see page 280).

The Pythagoras identity $\cos^2\theta + \sin^2\theta \equiv 1$ can be written as

$$1 + \tan^2\theta \equiv \sec^2\theta$$ (dividing throughout by $\cos^2\theta$)

or

$$\cot^2\theta + 1 = \operatorname{cosec}^2\theta$$ (dividing by $\sin^2\theta$)

For the complementary angles $\theta°$ and $90° - \theta°$

$$\tan(90° - \theta°) = \cot\theta°$$

and

$$\cot(90° - \theta°) = \tan\theta°$$

Exercise

Prove these two relations.

Section 35 Trigonometric Equations

35.1 Equations of the Form $\sin\theta = a$, $\cos\theta = a$, $\tan\theta = a$

Example

$$\sin\theta = 0{\cdot}5$$

Use of the $\sin^{-1}$ function of a calculator provides the solution $\theta = 30°$ (or use the table of page 336).

This is not the only solution of the equation. The diagram below shows that 150°, 390°, 510°, ... are also solutions.

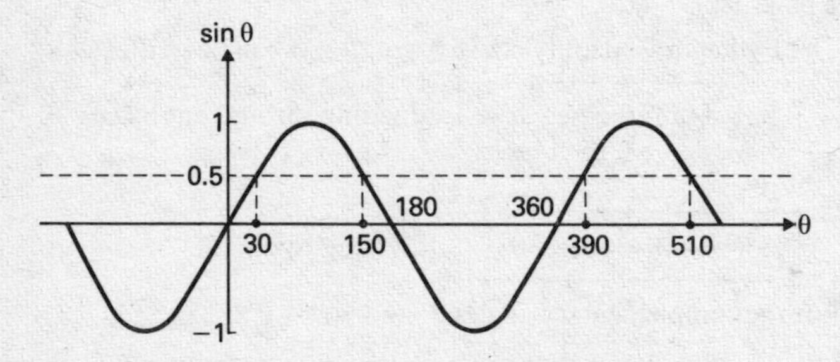

$\theta = 30°$ in the range of the function $\sin^{-1} x$ (page 338).

There are infinitely many solutions of this equation, provided by the formula

$$\theta = n180° + (-1)^n 30°, n = 0, \pm 1, \pm 2 \ldots$$

$\theta = 30°$ is called the **principal value (PV)** of the solution. $\theta = 150° = 180° - 30° = 180° - \text{PV}$ is called the **secondary value (SV).**

The equation $\sin\theta = a$, for $-1 \leqslant a \leqslant 1$, has *general solution*

$$\theta = n\,180° + (-1)^n \alpha° \text{ (degrees)}$$
$$\theta = n\pi + (-1)^n \alpha \text{ (radians)}$$

where $\alpha = \sin^{-1} a = \text{PV}$.

Each value of n provides a particular solution for θ.

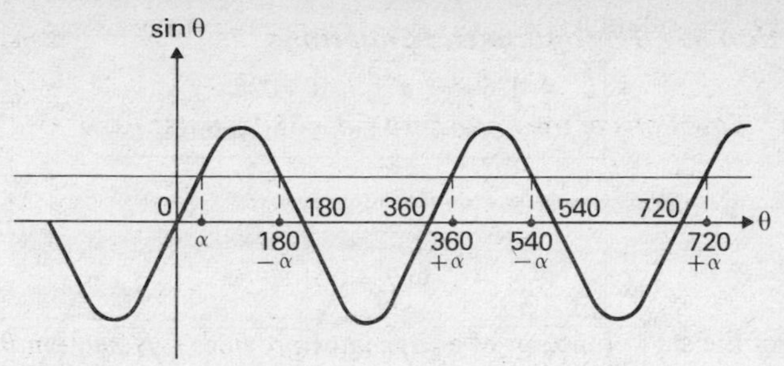

An alternative formula is

$$\theta = \begin{cases} n\,360° + \text{P V} \\ m\,360° + \text{S V} \end{cases} \text{(degrees)}$$

$$\theta = \begin{cases} 2n\pi + \text{P V} \\ 2m\pi + \text{S V} \end{cases} \text{(radians)}$$

for $n, m \in \mathbb{Z}$.

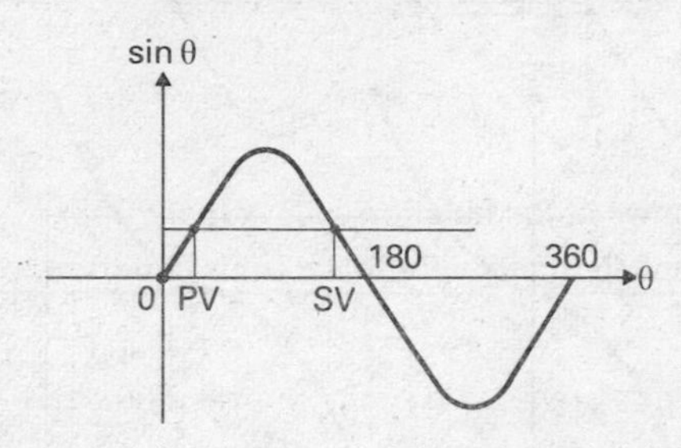

Similarly,

> if $\cos\theta = a$, $-1 \leqslant a \leqslant 1$, the P V is $\alpha \equiv \cos^{-1} a$,
> in the interval $[0, 180°]$ the S V is $-$P V.

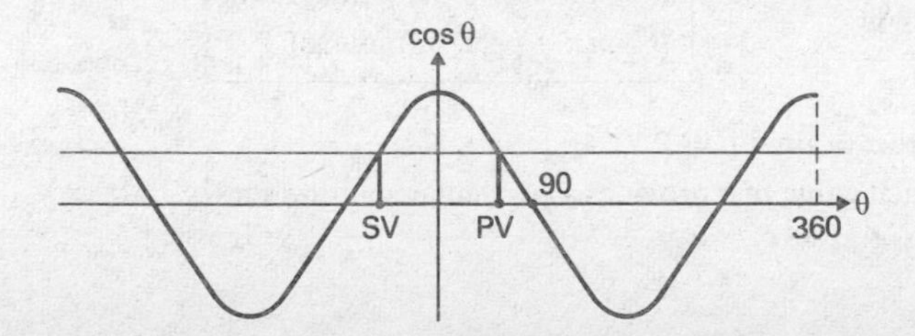

The general solution is

$\theta^\circ = n360^\circ \pm \alpha^\circ$ in degrees	$(\theta = 2n\pi \pm \alpha)$ in radians

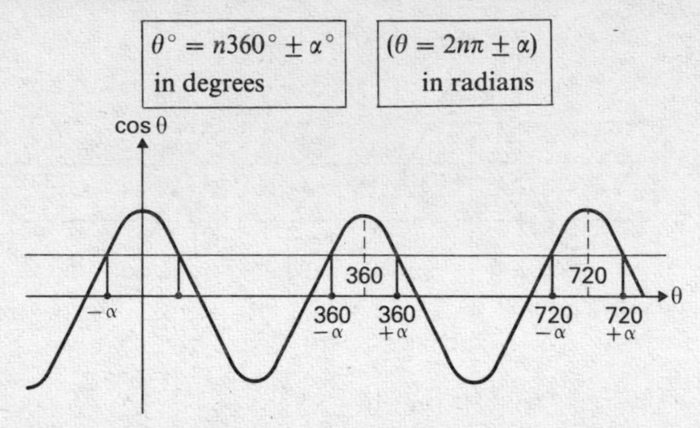

The equation $\tan\theta = a$ $(a \in \mathbb{R})$ has $PV \equiv \tan^{-1} a = \alpha$. The general solution is

$\theta^\circ = n180^\circ + \alpha^\circ$ in degrees	$(\theta = n\pi + \alpha)$ in radians

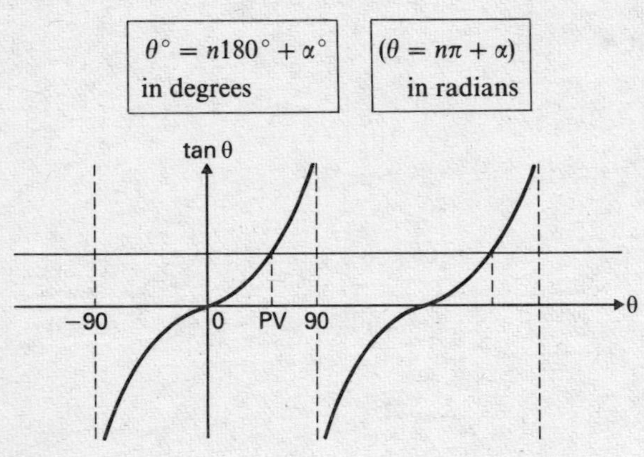

Examples

1. Find the general solution, in degrees, of the equation $\cos\theta = 0{\cdot}5$.

Answer

$\cos\theta = 0{\cdot}5 = \cos 60^\circ$ table on page 336

General solution.

$$\theta = n360° \pm 60°$$

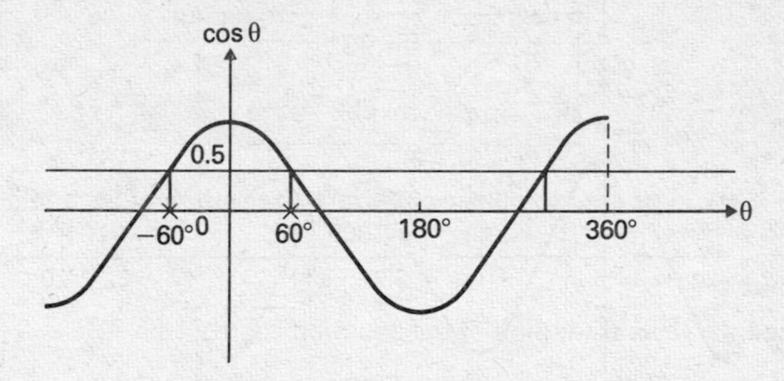

2. Find all the solutions of $\tan 2\theta = 1$ in the range $0 \leqslant \theta \leqslant 2\pi$.

Answer

$$\text{PV} = \frac{\pi}{4} \qquad (\tan^{-1} 1)$$

$$\Rightarrow 2\theta = n\pi + \frac{\pi}{4}$$

$$\Rightarrow \quad \theta = n\frac{\pi}{2} + \frac{\pi}{8}$$

In the range $0 \leqslant \theta \leqslant 2\pi$, the solutions are $\frac{\pi}{8}, \frac{5\pi}{8}, \frac{9\pi}{8}, \frac{13\pi}{8}$ $(n = 0, 1, 3)$.

NOTES

1. The general solution is obtained as an intermediate step. Values of n are substituted for particular solutions.

2. The equations $\sin\theta = 1$, $\cos\theta = 1$, $\sin\theta = -1$, $\cos\theta = -1$ have only *one* solution each in the ranges 0 to 2π or $-\pi$ to π.

3. The equations $\left\{\begin{array}{l}\sin\theta = 0 \\ \tan\theta = 0\end{array}\right.$ have general solution $\theta = n\pi$.

The equation $\cos\theta = 0$ has general solution $\theta = 2n\pi \pm \frac{\pi}{2}$.

35.2 Further Equations

The properties

$$\boxed{\begin{aligned}\cos\alpha^\circ &= \sin(90^\circ - \alpha^\circ)\\ \sin\alpha &= \cos(90^\circ - \alpha^\circ)\end{aligned}}$$

(page 334) can be used to reduce equations to the form of Section 36.1.

Examples

1. Find the general solution of the equation $\cos\theta^\circ = \sin 50^\circ$.

Answer

$$\sin 50^\circ = \cos(90^\circ - 50^\circ) = \cos 40^\circ$$

$$\Rightarrow \quad \cos\theta^\circ = \cos 40^\circ$$

$$\Rightarrow \quad \theta^\circ = n360^\circ \pm 40^\circ$$

2. Solve the equation $\sin\theta = \cos\frac{\pi}{7}$ for $-\pi \leqslant \theta \leqslant \pi$.

Answer

$$\sin\theta = \cos\tfrac{\pi}{7} = \sin(\tfrac{\pi}{2} - \tfrac{\pi}{7}) = \sin(\tfrac{5\pi}{14})$$

$$\therefore \theta = n\pi + (-1)^n\frac{5\pi}{14}, n \in \mathbb{Z}$$

Solutions in $[-\pi, \pi]$ are $\theta = \frac{5\pi}{14}$ and $\theta = \frac{-5\pi}{14}$.

Equations in which the arguments are expressions in the variable can also be solved.

Examples

1. Find the general solution, in radians, of the equation

$$\sin 2x = 0{\cdot}5$$

Answer

$$\left.\begin{aligned}PV &= \sin^{-1}0{\cdot}5 = \tfrac{\pi}{6}\\ SV &= \pi - \tfrac{\pi}{6} = \tfrac{5\pi}{6}\end{aligned}\right\}\quad \text{for } 2x$$

$$\Rightarrow \quad 2x = \begin{cases} 2n\pi + \frac{\pi}{6} \\ 2m\pi + \frac{5\pi}{6} \end{cases} \quad \text{for } m, n \in \mathbb{Z}$$

$$\Rightarrow \quad x = n\pi + \frac{\pi}{12} \quad \text{or} \quad x = m\pi + \frac{5\pi}{12}$$

Note: divide by 2 *as the last step.*

Alternatively,

$$2x = n\pi + (-1)^n \frac{\pi}{6}$$

$$\Rightarrow x = \frac{n\pi}{2} + (-1)^n \frac{\pi}{12}$$

2. Solve the equation

$$\tan(3\theta + 45°) = -1 \text{ for } -90° \leqslant \theta \leqslant 90°$$

Answer

$$\tan^{-1}(-1) = -45°$$

$$\Rightarrow \quad 3\theta + 45° = n180° - 45° \qquad \text{general solution}$$

$$\Rightarrow \quad 3\theta = n180° - 90°$$

$$\Rightarrow \quad \theta = n60° - 30°$$

$$\Rightarrow \quad \theta = -90°, -30°, 30°, 90°$$

on substituting $n = -1, 0, 1, 2$ for solutions in $[-90°, 90°]$.

Note: The expression in θ on the left-hand side is 'unwrapped' *after* the general solution for $\tan^{-1}(-1)$ is put on the right side.

3. Find the general solution of the equation

$$\cos(x + 45°) = \sin(x - 60°)$$

Answer

Rewriting the RHS as a cosine:

$$\cos(x + 45°) = \cos(90° - (x - 60°))$$

$$= \cos(150° - x)$$

$$\Rightarrow \quad x + 45° = n360° \pm (150° - x)$$

$$\Rightarrow \quad x + 45° = n360° + 150° - x \quad or \quad x + 45° = n360° - 150° + x$$

$$\Rightarrow \quad 2x = n360° + 105° \quad or \quad 45° = n360° - 150°$$

thus $\quad x = n180° + 52{\cdot}5° \quad$ which has *no* solutions

35.3 Quadratic Equations in Sin, Cos and Tan

Examples

1. Solve the equation $3\sin^2 x - 2\sin x - 1 = 0$ for $-\pi < x \leqslant \pi$ (giving your answers to 2 decimal places where appropriate).

Answer

Factorizing:

$$(3\sin x + 1)(\sin x - 1) = 0$$

$$\Rightarrow \quad \sin x = -\frac{1}{3} \text{ or } \sin x = 1$$

If $\sin x = -\frac{1}{3} = \sin(-0{\cdot}34)$ calculator

$\Rightarrow x = 2n\pi - 0{\cdot}34$ or $x = 2n\pi + \pi + 0{\cdot}34$

$\Rightarrow x = -0{\cdot}34, -2{\cdot}80$ in the interval $[-\pi, \pi]$

If $\sin x = 1 = \sin\frac{\pi}{2}$ then $x = 2n\pi + \frac{\pi}{2}$ which has only the solution $x = \frac{\pi}{2}$ in the given range.

2. Find the general solution, in degrees, of the equation

$$5 - 5\cos\theta - 4\sin^2\theta = 0$$

Answer

We must write the equation in terms of only one of the ratios sine or cosine.

Using $\sin^2\theta = 1 - \cos^2\theta$ page 333

$$\Rightarrow \quad 5 - 5\cos\theta - 4(1 - \cos^2\theta) = 0$$

$$\Rightarrow \quad 1 - 5\cos\theta + 4\cos^2\theta = 0$$

$$\Rightarrow \quad (1 - \cos\theta)(1 - 4\cos\theta) = 0$$

$$\Rightarrow \quad \cos\theta = 1 \quad \text{or} \quad \cos\theta = 0{\cdot}25$$

$$= \cos 0 \qquad\qquad = \cos 75{\cdot}52°$$

$$\Rightarrow \quad \theta = n360° \qquad \Rightarrow \theta = m360° \pm 75{\cdot}52°$$

3. Solve the equation

$$2\sec^2\theta - 3\tan\theta - 1 = 0$$

for $-360° \leqslant \theta \leqslant 360°$.

Answer

Using the identity $\sec^2\theta \equiv 1 + \tan^2\theta$ page 341

$\Rightarrow \quad 2(1 + \tan^2\theta) - 3\tan\theta - 1 = 0$

$\Rightarrow \quad 2\tan^2\theta - 3\tan\theta + 1 = 0$

$\Rightarrow \quad (2\tan\theta - 1)(\tan\theta - 1) = 0$

$\Rightarrow \quad \tan\theta = \frac{1}{2} \quad \text{or} \quad \tan\theta = 1$

$\qquad = \tan(26{\cdot}6°) \quad = \tan 45°$

$\Rightarrow \quad \theta = n180° + 26{\cdot}6° \quad \text{or} \quad \theta = m180° + 45° \quad m, n \in \mathbb{Z}$

Solutions in the required range are

$$-333{\cdot}4°, -153{\cdot}4°, 26{\cdot}6°, 206{\cdot}6°, -315°, -135°, 45°, 225°$$

35.4 Turning Points (Greatest and Least Values)

The graph of $f: x \mapsto \sin x$ has maximum points when $x = \frac{\pi}{2}, \frac{5\pi}{2}, \ldots$ and minimum points when $x = -\frac{\pi}{2}, \frac{3\pi}{2}, \ldots$

The greatest and least values are $f(x) = 1$ and $f(x) = -1$.

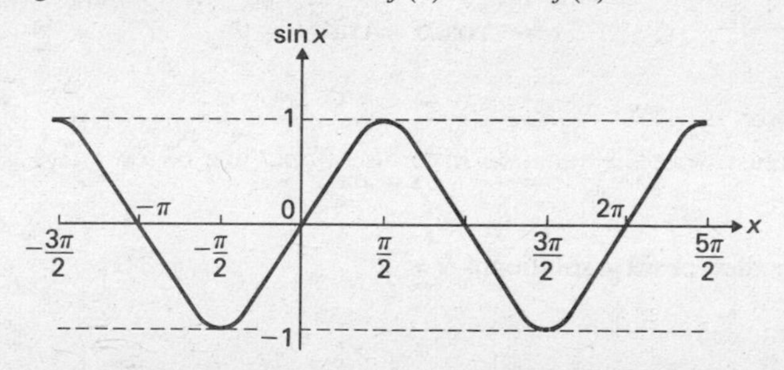

To find the turning points of the more general function $f: x \mapsto a\sin(nx+b)$ we must solve the equations

$$\sin(nx+b) = 1 \quad \text{and} \quad \sin(nx+b) = -1$$

Similarly for $f: x \mapsto a\cos(nx+b)$.

Examples

1. $f(x) \equiv 2\sin(3x + \frac{\pi}{4})$

For a maximum point, $\sin(3x + \frac{\pi}{4}) = 1$

$$\Rightarrow \quad 3x + \frac{\pi}{4} = 2n\pi + \frac{\pi}{2}(n \in \mathbb{Z})$$

$$\Rightarrow \quad 3x = 2n\pi + \frac{\pi}{4}$$

$$\Rightarrow \quad x = \frac{2n\pi}{3} + \frac{\pi}{12}$$

The maxima occur when $x = \frac{\pi}{12}, \frac{3\pi}{4}, \frac{17\pi}{12}, \ldots$ The maximum values are all $f(x) = 2 \times 1 = 2$, and this is the **amplitude** of the function.

2. Find the least value of $f(x) = 3\cos(2x)$ and state the smallest positive value of x for which $f(x)$ takes this least value.

Answer

$\cos 2x$ has least value -1, hence $f(x)$ has least value -3. This occurs when $\cos 2x = -1$

$$\Rightarrow \quad \cos 2x = \cos \pi$$

$$\Rightarrow \quad 2x = 2n\pi \pm \pi$$

$$\Rightarrow \quad x = n\pi \pm \frac{\pi}{2}$$

The smallest positive solution is $x = \frac{\pi}{2}$.

Section 36 Trigonometric Identities

Function brackets are often used in trigonometric expressions: $\sin(2x)$, $\cos(2x-3)$, $\tan(e^x+5)$ for example.

These should *not* be treated as *multiplication* brackets! Sin $(2x)$ and $2\sin x$ are quite different functions.

Exercise

Calculate $\sin(2x)$ and $2\sin x$ for $x=\frac{\pi}{2}$.

Methods for simplifying trigonometric expressions make use of the following identities.

36.1 The Addition Rules

$$\sin(A+B)\equiv\sin A\cos B+\cos A\sin B \quad \text{(i)}$$

$$\sin(A-B)\equiv\sin A\cos B-\cos A\sin B \quad \text{(ii)}$$

$$\cos(A+B)\equiv\cos A\cos B-\sin A\sin B \quad \text{(iii)}$$

$$\cos(A-B)\equiv\cos A\cos B+\sin A\sin B \quad \text{(iv)}$$

You are very unlikely to be required to prove these identities. However, you should *learn* them. (Although they are included in the formula books by most Boards.)

Proofs of these identities can be found in most text books. However, (ii), (iii) and (iv) can easily be derived from (i).

Exercise

Replace B by $-B$ in (i) and using properties of page 336 derive (ii). Replace A by $\frac{\pi}{2}-A$ in (ii) and derive (iii) and then replace B by $-B$ in (iii) to derive (iv).

Example

Calculate (*a*) $\sin 75°$, (*b*) $\cos 135°$ without the use of a book of tables or a calculator. (For example, in a multiple choice paper!)

Answer

(*a*) $\sin 75° = \sin(45° + 30°)$

$$= \sin 45° \cos 30° + \cos 45° \sin 30°$$

$$= \frac{\sqrt{2}}{2}\frac{\sqrt{3}}{2} + \frac{\sqrt{2}}{2}\frac{1}{2}$$

page 336

$$= \frac{\sqrt{2}}{4}(1 + \sqrt{3})$$

(*b*) $\cos 135° = \cos(90° + 45°)$

$$= \cos 90° \cos 45° - \sin 90° \sin 45°$$

$$= (0)\left(\frac{\sqrt{2}}{2}\right) - (1)\left(\frac{\sqrt{2}}{2}\right)$$

$$= -\frac{\sqrt{2}}{2}$$

The corresponding rules for tan can be derived:

$$\tan(A+B) = \frac{\sin(A+B)}{\cos(A+B)} = \frac{\sin A \cos B + \cos A \sin B}{\cos A \cos B - \sin A \sin B}$$

$$= \frac{\dfrac{\sin A \cos B}{\cos A \cos B} + \dfrac{\cos A \sin B}{\cos A \cos B}}{\dfrac{\cos A \cos B}{\cos A \cos B} - \dfrac{\sin A \sin B}{\cos A \cos B}} = \frac{\tan A + \tan B}{1 - \tan A \tan B}$$

dividing all terms by $\cos A \cos B$

Thus

$$\boxed{\tan(A + B) = \frac{\tan A + \tan B}{1 - \tan A \tan B}} \qquad \text{(v)}$$

and

$$\boxed{\tan(A - B) = \frac{\tan A - \tan B}{1 + \tan A \tan B}} \qquad \text{(v')}$$

Example

Calculate the tangent of the acute angle between the lines $y = 2x - 3$ and $y = x + 5$.

Answer

If a line cuts the x-axis at angle θ then it has gradient $\tan\theta$ (see page 133).

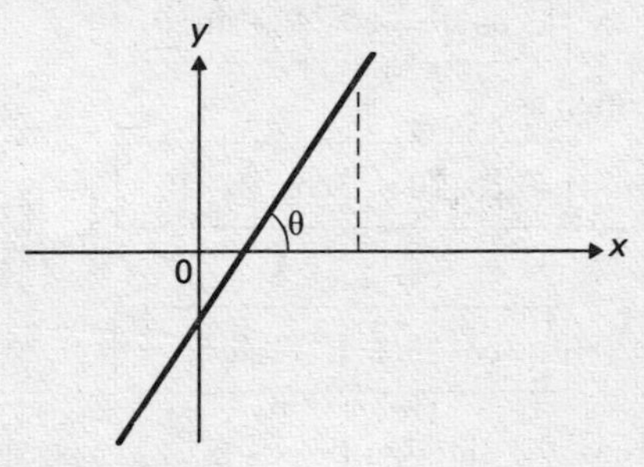

Gradient of $y = 2x - 3$ is 2 so $\tan\ \alpha = 2$
Gradient of $y = x + 5$ is 1 so $\tan\beta = 1$

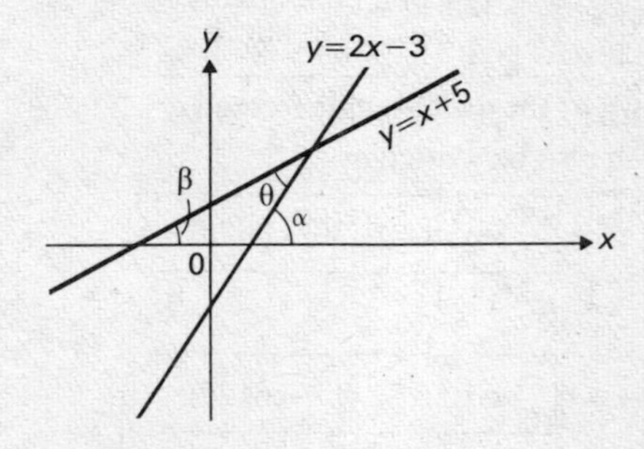

$\theta = \alpha - \beta$ is the required angle.

$$\Rightarrow \quad \tan\theta = \tan(\alpha - \beta) = \frac{\tan\alpha - \tan\beta}{1 + \tan\alpha\tan\beta}$$

$$= \frac{2 - 1}{1 + (2 \times 1)} = \frac{1}{3}$$

36.2 The Double and Multiple Angle Formulae

From identity (i) with $A = B = \theta$ we get

$$\sin 2\theta = 2 \sin \theta \cos \theta \qquad \text{(vi)}$$

and from (iv)

$$\cos 2\theta = \cos^2 \theta - \sin^2 \theta \qquad \text{(vii)}$$

which can be rewritten as

$$\cos 2\theta = 2 \cos^2 \theta - 1 \qquad \text{(viii)}$$

or

$$\cos 2\theta = 1 - 2 \sin^2 \theta \qquad \text{(ix)}$$

using the identity $\cos^2 \theta + \sin^2 \theta = 1$.

Identity (v) leads to

$$\tan 2\theta = \frac{2 \tan \theta}{1 - \tan^2 \theta} \qquad \text{(x)}$$

These are known as the **double angle formulae**.

(viii) and (ix) can also be written as

$$\sin^2 \theta = \tfrac{1}{2}(1 - \cos 2\theta)$$

and

$$\cos^2 \theta = \tfrac{1}{2}(1 + \cos 2\theta)$$

Similar formulae for triple angles and other multiple angles can be derived using the addition rules.

Example

$$\begin{aligned}
\sin 3\theta &\equiv \sin (\theta + 2\theta) \\
&= \sin \theta \cos 2\theta + \cos \theta \sin 2\theta \\
&= \sin \theta (1 - 2 \sin^2 \theta) + \cos \theta (2 \sin \theta \cos \theta) \\
&= \sin \theta - 2 \sin^3 \theta + 2 \sin \theta \cos^2 \theta
\end{aligned}$$

$$= \sin\theta - 2\sin^3\theta + 2\sin\theta(1 - \sin^2\theta)$$

$$= \sin\theta - 2\sin^3\theta + 2\sin\theta - 2\sin^3\theta$$

$$= 3\sin\theta - 4\sin^3\theta$$

Similarly $\cos 3\theta = 4\cos^3\theta - 3\cos\theta$.

The double angle formulae are often used to simplify equations, and in integrations.

Examples

1. Given that $\sin\theta = 0{\cdot}3$ and θ is obtuse, calculate (*a*) $\cos\theta$, (*b*) $\sin 2\theta$, (*c*) $\cos 2\theta$, (*d*) $\sin(\frac{1}{2}\theta)$ expressing your answers to 3 significant figures.

Answer

(*a*) $\cos\theta = -\sqrt{1 - \sin^2\theta}$

$= -\sqrt{1 - 0{\cdot}3^2}$ — negative root since θ is obtuse, page 331

$= -\sqrt{1 - 0{\cdot}09} = -0{\cdot}954$ — 3 significant figures

(*b*) $\sin 2\theta = 2\sin\theta\cos\theta$ — double angle formula

$= 2(0{\cdot}3)(-0{\cdot}954)$

$= -0{\cdot}572$ — 3 significant figures

(*c*) $\cos 2\theta = 2\cos^2\theta - 1$ — double angle formula

$= 2(0{\cdot}91) - 1$

$= 0{\cdot}82$

(Exercise: which quadrant for angle 2θ? Use the answers (*b*) and (*c*).)

(*d*) From $\cos 2\theta = 1 - 2\sin^2\theta$ we obtain

$$\cos\theta = 1 - 2\sin^2(\tfrac{1}{2}\theta)$$

when θ is replaced by $\frac{1}{2}\theta$.

$$\Rightarrow \quad \sin^2(\tfrac{1}{2}\theta) = \frac{1 - \cos\theta}{2}$$

$$\Rightarrow \quad \sin(\tfrac{1}{2}\theta) = \pm\sqrt{\frac{1-\cos\theta}{2}}$$

$$= \pm 0{\cdot}988$$

θ is obtuse and so $\frac{1}{2}\theta$ must be acute.

$\therefore \sin(\frac{1}{2}\theta) = 0{\cdot}988$.

2. Simplify the expression

$$\frac{\sin 2\theta + 1 - \cos 2\theta}{\sin 2\theta + 1 + \cos 2\theta}$$

Answer

From the double angle formulae

$$\Rightarrow \quad \frac{2\sin\theta\cos\theta + 2\sin^2\theta}{2\sin\theta\cos\theta + 2\cos^2\theta}$$

$$= \frac{2\sin\theta(\cos\theta + \sin\theta)}{2\cos\theta(\sin\theta + \cos\theta)}$$

$= \tan\theta$ when the factor $2(\cos\theta + \sin\theta)$ is divided out (provided $\cos\theta + \sin\theta \neq 0$).

3. Solve the equation $\sin 2x = \cos x$ for $-180° \leqslant x \leqslant 180°$.

Answer

The double angle formula for sine gives

$$2\sin x\cos x = \cos x$$

$$\Rightarrow 2\sin x\cos x - \cos x = 0$$

do not 'cancel' the $\cos x$ term. You may miss the solutions of $\cos x = 0$

$$\Rightarrow \cos x\,(2\sin x - 1) = 0$$

$$\Rightarrow \cos x = 0 \text{ or } \sin x = \tfrac{1}{2}$$

$$\Rightarrow x = \pm 90° \text{ or } x = 30°, 150°$$

The solution set is $-90°, 30°, 90°, 150°$

4. Find the cartesian equations of the curves defined parametrically by

(*a*) $x = 3\cos\theta$, $y = 4\sin\theta$, $0 \leqslant \theta < 2\pi$

(*b*) $x = \sec\theta$, $y = \sin\theta$, $0 \leqslant \theta < 2\pi$

(*c*) $x = \cos 2\theta$, $y = 2\sin\theta$, $0 \leqslant \theta < 2\pi$

Answer

(*a*) $\cos\theta = \frac{x}{3}, \quad \sin\theta = \frac{y}{4}$

$$\therefore \left(\frac{x}{3}\right)^2 + \left(\frac{y}{4}\right)^2 = 1$$

page 333

$$\Rightarrow \frac{x^2}{9} + \frac{y^2}{16} = 1$$

(*b*) $\cos\theta = \frac{1}{x}, \quad \sin\theta = y$

$$\therefore \frac{1}{x^2} + y^2 = 1$$

(*c*) $x = \cos 2\theta = 1 - 2\sin^2\theta, \quad \sin\theta = \frac{y}{2}$

$$\Rightarrow \qquad x = 1 - 2\left(\tfrac{y^2}{4}\right)$$

$$\Rightarrow \qquad x = 1 - \tfrac{y^2}{2}$$

$$\Rightarrow \qquad 2x + y^2 - 2 = 0$$

36.3 The Half Angle Formulae

Writing $A = \frac{1}{2}\theta$ in the $\tan 2A$ formula $\Rightarrow \tan\theta = \frac{2\tan(\frac{1}{2}\theta)}{1-\tan^2(\frac{1}{2}\theta)}$. Writing $t = \tan(\frac{1}{2}\theta)$ gives

$$\tan\theta = \frac{2t}{1-t^2}$$

If θ is acute, $\sin\theta$ and $\cos\theta$ can be calculated from the corresponding right-angled triangle. $(1-t^2)^2+(2t)^2 = 1-2t^2+t^4+4t^2 = 1+2t^2+t^4 = (1+t^2)^2$ so that the hypotenuse is $1+t^2$.

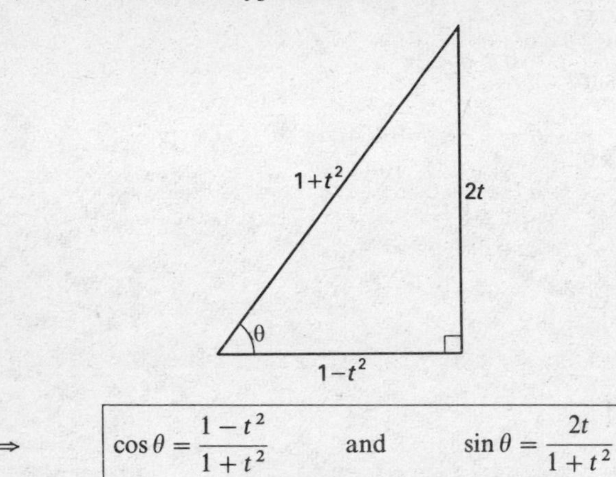

$$\Rightarrow \quad \cos\theta = \frac{1-t^2}{1+t^2} \quad \text{and} \quad \sin\theta = \frac{2t}{1+t^2}$$

In fact these three t-formulae hold for *any* angle θ.

Exercise

Extend the derivation of these formula to cover the case when θ is not acute.

The formulae can also be used in the form

$$\sin 2\theta = \frac{2T}{1+T^2} \qquad \cos 2\theta = \frac{1-T^2}{1+T^2} \qquad \tan 2\theta = \frac{2T}{1-T^2}$$

when $T = \tan\theta$.

Examples

1. Solve the equations $2\tan\theta - \sec\theta = 1$ giving the general solution in radians.

Answer

We can substitute $t = \tan\frac{1}{2}\theta$

$$\Rightarrow \quad 2\left(\frac{2t}{1-t^2}\right) - \left(\frac{1+t^2}{1-t^2}\right) = 1 \qquad \text{as } \sec\theta = \frac{1}{\cos\theta}$$

$$\Rightarrow \quad 4t - 1 - t^2 = 1 - t^2$$

$$\Rightarrow \quad 4t = 2$$

$$\Rightarrow \quad t = \tfrac{1}{2}$$

$$\therefore \quad \tan\tfrac{1}{2}\theta = \tfrac{1}{2} = \tan(0{\cdot}464)$$

$$\Rightarrow \quad \tfrac{1}{2}\theta = n\pi + 0{\cdot}464$$

page 344

$$\Rightarrow \quad \theta = 2n\pi + 0{\cdot}928$$

Exercise

Solve the equation directly by expressing $\tan\theta$ and $\sec\theta$ in terms of $\sin\theta$ and $\cos\theta$.

2. Find the solutions of the equation

$$4\cos\theta + \sin\theta = 1$$

in the degrees in the range $-180° \leqslant \theta \leqslant 180°$. Express your answers to 2 decimal place accuracy.

Answer

Let $t = \tan\frac{1}{2}\theta$. Then $\cos\theta = \frac{1-t^2}{1+t^2}$ and $\sin\theta = \frac{2t}{1+t^2}$

$$\Rightarrow \quad 4\left(\tfrac{1-t^2}{1+t^2}\right) + \left(\tfrac{2t}{1+t^2}\right) = 1$$

$$\Rightarrow \quad 4 - 4t^2 + 2t = 1 + t^2$$

$$\Rightarrow \quad 5t^2 - 2t - 3 = 0$$

$$\Rightarrow \quad (5t+3)(t-1) = 0$$

$$\Rightarrow \quad t = -\tfrac{3}{5} \quad \text{or} \quad t = 1$$

$$\Rightarrow \quad \tan\tfrac{1}{2}\theta = -0{\cdot}6 \quad \text{or} \quad \tan\tfrac{1}{2}\theta = 1$$

$$\Rightarrow \quad \tfrac{1}{2}\theta = n180° - 30{\cdot}96° \quad \text{or} \quad \tfrac{1}{2}\theta = n180° + 45°$$

page 344

$$\Rightarrow \qquad \theta = n360^\circ - 61{\cdot}93^\circ \quad \text{or} \quad \theta = n360^\circ + 90^\circ$$

In the range $-180^\circ \leqslant \theta \leqslant 180^\circ$ the solutions are

$$-61{\cdot}93^\circ,\ 298{\cdot}07^\circ \text{ and } 90^\circ.$$

(The equation can be solved in another way, see page 405.)

36.4 The Product Rules

The addition rules of page 351 can be used to obtain the identities

$$\sin(A+B) + \sin(A-B) \equiv 2\sin A\cos B$$

$$\sin(A+B) - \sin(A-B) \equiv 2\cos A\sin B$$

$$\cos(A+B) + \cos(A-B) \equiv 2\cos A\cos B$$

$$\cos(A+B) - \cos(A-B) \equiv -2\sin A\sin B$$

which enable a product of sine and cosine to be expressed as a sum. Putting $P = A+B$ and $Q = A-B$ so that $A = \frac{P+Q}{2}$ and $B = \frac{P-Q}{2}$

$$\sin P + \sin Q = 2\sin\left(\tfrac{P+Q}{2}\right)\cos\left(\tfrac{P-Q}{2}\right)$$

$$\sin P - \sin Q = 2\cos\left(\tfrac{P+Q}{2}\right)\sin\left(\tfrac{P-Q}{2}\right)$$

$$\cos P + \cos Q = 2\cos\left(\tfrac{P+Q}{2}\right)\cos\left(\tfrac{P-Q}{2}\right)$$

$$\cos P - \cos Q = -2\sin\left(\tfrac{P+Q}{2}\right)\sin\left(\tfrac{P-Q}{2}\right)$$

Examples

1. Solve the equation $\sin\theta + \sin 2\theta + \sin 3\theta = 0$ for $0^\circ \leqslant \theta^\circ \leqslant 360^\circ$.

Answer

Adding the first and last terms and using the formula for $\sin P + \sin Q$

$$(\sin\theta + \sin 3\theta) + \sin 2\theta = 0$$

$$\Rightarrow 2\sin 2\theta\cos(-\theta) + \sin 2\theta = 0$$

$$\Rightarrow \sin 2\theta(2\cos\theta + 1) = 0 \qquad \cos(-\theta) \equiv \cos\theta$$

$$\Rightarrow \sin 2\theta = 0 \quad \text{or} \quad \cos\theta = -\tfrac{1}{2}$$

$$\left.\begin{aligned}\Rightarrow 2\theta &= n180^\circ \\ \Rightarrow \theta &= n90^\circ\end{aligned}\right\} \quad \text{or} \quad \theta = n360^\circ \pm 120^\circ \qquad \cos 120^\circ = -\tfrac{1}{2}$$

The solutions in $[0^\circ, 360^\circ]$ are

$$0^\circ, 90^\circ, 120^\circ, 180^\circ, 240^\circ, 270^\circ, 360^\circ$$

2. Simplify the expression

$$f(\theta) = \frac{\sin 2\theta + \sin 4\theta}{\cos 2\theta - \cos 4\theta}$$

State the largest possible domain for f and find the corresponding range.

Answer

Since

$$\sin 2\theta + \sin 4\theta = 2\sin 3\theta \cos\theta$$

and

$$\cos 2\theta - \cos 4\theta = 2\sin 3\theta \sin\theta$$

then

$$f(\theta) = \frac{2\sin 3\,\theta\cos\theta}{2\sin 3\theta \sin\theta} = \cot\theta$$

$f(\theta)$ is defined whenever $\cos 2\theta - \cos 4\theta \neq 0$, $\Rightarrow$ values of θ for which $\cos 2\theta = \cos 4\theta$ must be excluded from the domain. These values are $\frac{n\pi}{3}$, $n \in Z$ (*exercise*). The domain is $\{\theta \in \mathbb{R},\ \theta \neq \frac{n\pi}{3},\ n \in \mathbb{Z}\}$. The range is $\mathbb{R}$ (page 341).

36.5 *The Expression $a\cos\theta + b\sin\theta$*

Example

Express $2\cos\theta + 3\sin\theta$ in the form $R\cos(\theta - \alpha)$ for some $R > 0$ and $0^\circ < \alpha < 90^\circ$.

Answer

Expanding

$$R\cos(\theta - \alpha) \equiv R(\cos\theta\cos\alpha + \sin\theta\sin\alpha)$$
$$= (R\cos\alpha)\cos\theta + (R\sin\alpha)\sin\theta$$

Comparing with $2\cos\theta + 3\sin\theta$

$$R\cos\alpha = 2 \text{ and } R\sin\alpha = 3$$

$$\Rightarrow \quad R^2\cos^2\alpha + R^2\sin^2\alpha = 4 + 9 = 13$$

$$\Rightarrow \quad R^2(\cos^2\alpha + \sin^2\alpha) = 13$$

$$\Rightarrow \quad R^2 = 13 \qquad \text{as } \cos^2\alpha + \sin^2\alpha = 1$$

$$\Rightarrow \quad R = \sqrt{13}$$

Hence $\sqrt{13}\cos\alpha = 2 \Rightarrow \cos\alpha = \dfrac{2}{\sqrt{13}}$

$$\Rightarrow \alpha = 56{\cdot}3^\circ \text{ (to 1 decimal place)}$$

So

$2\cos\theta + 3\sin\theta \equiv \sqrt{13}\cos(\theta - 56{\cdot}3^\circ)$

In general, such expressions can be transformed as below:

$$\left.\begin{array}{l} a\cos\theta + b\sin\theta \text{ as } R\cos(\theta - \alpha) \\ a\cos\theta - b\sin\theta \text{ as } R\cos(\theta + \alpha) \\ a\sin\theta + b\cos\theta \text{ as } R\sin(\theta + \alpha) \\ a\sin\theta - b\cos\theta \text{ as } R\sin(\theta - \alpha) \end{array}\right\} \begin{array}{l} \text{where } R > 0 \\ \alpha \text{ is } \textit{acute} \\ a, b \text{ positive} \end{array}$$

R is always given by $\sqrt{a^2 + b^2}$. α is best found by expanding the compound angle expression, and comparing with the original.

From the above

$$2\cos\theta + 3\sin\theta = \sqrt{13}\cos(\theta - 56{\cdot}3^\circ)$$

The graph of $y = 2\cos\theta + 3\sin\theta$ is

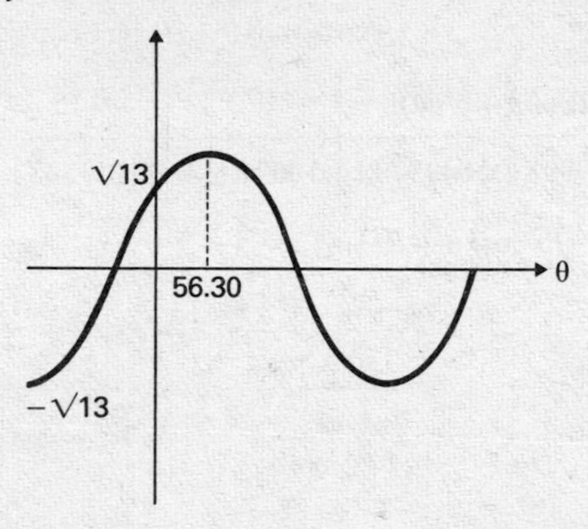

The amplitude is $\sqrt{13}$, and so $2\cos\theta + 3\sin\theta$ has greatest value $\sqrt{13}$ and least value $-\sqrt{13}$.

36.6 Small Angle Formulae

The graph of $y = \sin x$ shows that for small values of x, $\sin x$ is very close to x. The approximation is good for x in *radians* between $-0{\cdot}2$ and $+0{\cdot}2$.

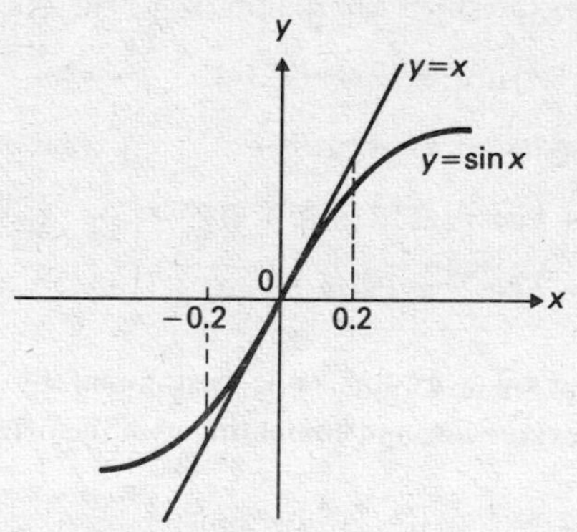

Outside this range the two graphs diverge and the approximation does not hold.

The following table shows that in fact $\sin x$ and x are in good agreement for $-0{\cdot}2 \leqslant x \leqslant 0{\cdot}2$.

x	0	0·01	0·05	0·1	0·15	0·2
$\sin x$	0	0·009 999 8	0·049 979 2	0·099 833 4	0·149 348 1	0·198 669 3

Thus, for small x (in radians)

$$\boxed{\sin x \approx x}$$

which leads to

$$\boxed{\lim_{x \to 0}\left(\frac{\sin x}{x}\right) = 1}$$

Standard text books provide proofs for this statement. However, it is not required for examination questions.

Corresponding results for cos and tan are

$$\boxed{\cos x \approx 1 - \tfrac{1}{2}x^2,\ \lim_{x \to 0}\left(\frac{\cos x - 1}{x}\right) = 0}$$

and

$$\boxed{\tan x \approx x,\ \lim_{x \to 0}\left(\frac{\tan x}{x}\right) = 1}$$

The $\cos x$ approximation follows from that for $\sin x$

$$\cos x = 1 - 2\sin^2(\tfrac{1}{2}x)$$ page 354

$$\simeq 1 - 2(\tfrac{1}{2}x)^2 \quad \text{(if } x \text{ is small)}$$

$$= 1 - \tfrac{1}{2}x^2$$

Also

$$\tan x = \frac{\sin x}{\cos x} \simeq \frac{x}{1 - \frac{1}{2}x^2}$$

$$= x(1 - \tfrac{1}{2}x^2)^{-1}$$

$$= x(1 + \tfrac{1}{2}x^2 + \ldots)$$ page 209

$$= x + \tfrac{1}{2}x^3 + \ldots$$

$$\approx x \text{ for small } x$$

For these approximations to be good, x must be small and measured in *radians.*

Examples

1. Find the limiting value of the expression

$$\frac{2\sin^2(3\theta) - \cos\theta + 1}{\sin^2\theta}$$

as θ approaches 0.

Answer

Notice that when $\theta = 0$ the expression becomes $\frac{0}{0}$ which is *undefined.* Hence it is necessary to consider the limit.

As $\theta \to 0$ we can assume that θ is small, the expression is approximated by

$$\frac{2(3\theta)^2 - (1 - \frac{1}{2}\theta^2) + 1}{\theta^2}$$

$$= \frac{18\theta^2 - 1 + \frac{1}{2}\theta^2 + 1}{\theta^2} = 18{\cdot}5$$

The original expression and this approximation must have the same limiting value. The required limit is 18·5.

2. Find approximations to solutions of the equation

$$20\sin^2\theta + 34\sin 2\theta - 7 = 0$$

in the range $0 \leqslant \theta \leqslant 0{\cdot}2$ in radians.

Answer

The small angle approximations are valid in this range. Solutions are given approximately by

$$20\theta^2 + 34(2\theta) - 7 = 0$$

$$20\theta^2 + 68\theta - 7 = 0$$

$$(10\theta - 1)(2\theta + 7) = 0$$

$$\Rightarrow \qquad \theta = 0{\cdot}1 \quad \text{or} \quad \theta = -3{\cdot}5$$

$\theta = 0{\cdot}1$ is the only solution in the range 0 to 0·2.

Note: The approximations do *not* hold for $\theta = -3{\cdot}5$. In fact $20\sin^2(-3{\cdot}5) + 34\sin(-7) - 7 = -26{\cdot}88$ (2 decimal places).

Section 37 Differentiation and Integration

37.1 Gradient Functions of the Trigonometric Functions

Let $f(x) = \sin x$. To differentiate from first principles we must evaluate

$$\frac{f(x+\delta x) - f(x)}{\delta x}$$ page 145

$$= \frac{\sin(x+\delta x) - \sin x}{\delta x}$$

$$= \frac{\sin x \cos \delta x + \cos x \sin \delta x - \sin x}{\delta x}$$ addition rule

$$= \sin x \frac{(\cos \delta x - 1)}{\delta x} + \cos x \left(\frac{\sin \delta x}{\delta x}\right)$$

Taking the limit as $\delta x \to 0$ and using the small angle approximations of page 364 we obtain

$$f'(x) = \sin x \times 0 + \cos x \times 1$$

$$= \cos x$$

Note that the angle x must be in *radians* so that the approximations may be used.

Note: The product rule may be used instead of the addition rule in this derivation, in which case the calculation is slightly simpler. The addition rule is used here because not all boards include the product rule in their syllabuses.

Hence

$$\frac{d}{dx}(\sin x) = \cos x$$

In a similar way we can show

$$\frac{d}{dx}(\cos x) = -\sin x$$

$\tan x$ can be differentiated using these results and the quotient rule (page 264).

Exercise
Verify that

$$\frac{d}{dx}(\tan x) = \sec^2 x$$

$$\frac{d}{dx}(\operatorname{cosec} x) = -\operatorname{cosec} x \cot x$$

$$\frac{d}{dx}(\sec x) = \sec x \tan x$$

$$\frac{d}{dx}(\cot x) = -\operatorname{cosec}^2 x$$

Recall that

$$\operatorname{cosec} x = \frac{1}{\sin x}$$

$$\sec x = \frac{1}{\cos x}$$

$$\cot x = \frac{1}{\tan x}$$

These rules only apply when x *is in radians.*

Examples

1. Differentiate

(*a*) $f(x) = 3\cos(2x - \frac{\pi}{4})$
(*b*) $g(x) = \sin^2(2x)$

Answer

(*a*) Change to the variable $z = 2x - \frac{\pi}{4}$ so that $f(z) = 3\cos z$ and $\frac{dz}{dx} = 2$

$$\Rightarrow \quad \frac{d}{dz}f(z) = -3\sin z$$

Thus (page 161)

$$f'(x) = 2\left(-3\sin\left(2x - \frac{\pi}{4}\right)\right)$$
$$= -6\sin\left(2x - \frac{\pi}{4}\right)$$

(*b*) Let $y = \sin^2(2x)$ and $z = \sin 2x$

$$\Rightarrow \quad y = z^2 \text{ and } \frac{dz}{dx} = 2\cos 2x$$ change of variable again

$$\Rightarrow \quad \frac{dy}{dx} = \frac{dy}{dz}\frac{dz}{dx} = 2z2\cos 2x = 4\sin 2x\cos 2x$$
$$= 2\sin 4x$$ double angle, page 354

2. A curve is defined by the parametric equations

$$x = 2\cos t \quad \text{for } 0 \leqslant t < 2\pi$$
$$y = 3\sin t$$

(*a*) Find $\frac{dy}{dx}$ at the point where $t = \frac{\pi}{4}$ and hence deduce the equation of the tangent at this point.
(*b*) By eliminating the parameter from the equations, obtain the cartesian equation of the curve. Sketch this curve.

Answer

(*a*)
$$\frac{dy}{dx} = \frac{dy}{dt}\bigg/\frac{dx}{dt}$$
page 240

$$= \frac{3\cos t}{-2\sin t} = -\frac{3}{2}\cot t$$

When $t = \frac{\pi}{4}, \frac{dy}{dx} = -\frac{3}{2}\cot\frac{\pi}{4} = -\frac{3}{2}$ and

$$x = 2\cos\frac{\pi}{4} = \sqrt{2}$$

$$y = 3\sin\frac{\pi}{4} = \frac{3\sqrt{2}}{2}$$

The equation of the tangent is

$$y - \frac{3\sqrt{2}}{2} = -\frac{3}{2}(x - \sqrt{2})$$
page 135

$$\Rightarrow \quad 2y - 3\sqrt{2} = -3x + 3\sqrt{2}$$

$$\Rightarrow \quad 3x + 2y - 6\sqrt{2} = 0$$

(*b*)
$$\cos t = \frac{x}{2}, \quad \sin t = \frac{y}{3}$$

$$\Rightarrow \quad \frac{x^2}{4} + \frac{y^2}{9} = 1$$

since $\cos^2 t + \sin^2 t = 1$.

Now

1. The curve cuts the x-axis when $y = 0$

$$\Rightarrow \quad \frac{x^2}{4} = 1$$

$$\Rightarrow \quad x = \pm 2$$

2. The curve cuts the y-axis when $x = 0$

$$\Rightarrow \qquad \frac{y^2}{9} = 1$$

$$\Rightarrow \qquad y = \pm 3$$

3. When $x = \pm 2$

$\cos t = \pm 1$

$\therefore \sin t = 0$

and $\cot t = \infty$

$\Rightarrow$ gradient $= \infty$

$\Rightarrow$ tangent is vertical

When $x = 0$

$\cos t = 0$

$\Rightarrow \quad \cot t = 0$

$\Rightarrow$ tangent is horizontal

The curve is

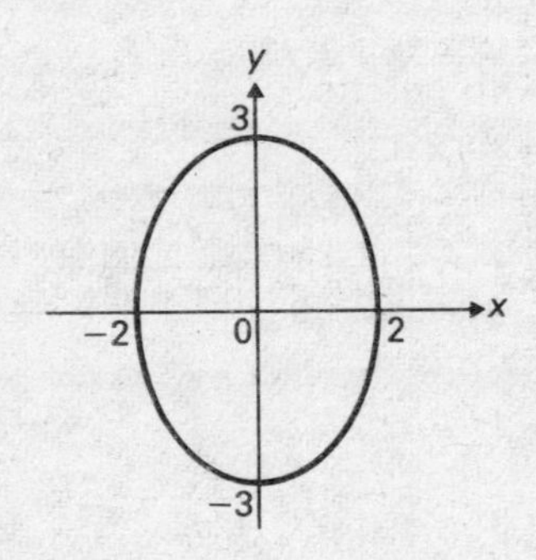

which is an **ellipse**.

3. Differentiate

$$y = \sin^{-1} x \qquad (\arcsin x)$$

Answer
Rewrite as

$$\sin y = x$$

which defines y *implicitly* (page 218). Differentiating with respect to x:

$$\frac{d}{dx}(\sin y) = 1$$

$$\Rightarrow \qquad \cos y \frac{dy}{dx} = 1$$

$$\Rightarrow \qquad \frac{dy}{dx} = \frac{1}{\cos y}$$

as a function of y.

$$= \frac{1}{\sqrt{1 - \sin^2 y}}$$

$$\frac{dy}{dx} = \frac{1}{\sqrt{1 - x^2}} \qquad \left(\text{or } -\frac{1}{\sqrt{1 - x^2}}\right)$$

as a function of x.

SERIES FOR SINE AND COSINE

The series for $f(x) = \sin x$ is

$$\sin x = x - \frac{x^3}{3!} + \frac{x^5}{5!} - \ldots + (-1)^{n+1} \frac{x^{2n+1}}{(2n+1)!} + \ldots$$

and for $f(x) = \cos x$

$$\cos x = 1 - \frac{x^2}{2!} + \frac{x^4}{4!} - \ldots + (-1)^{n+1} \frac{x^{2n}}{(2n)!} + \ldots$$

Both series converge for all $x \in \mathbb{R}$ (see page 299).

Exercise

Derive these series using the definition of page 299.

37.2 Integration of Trigonometric Functions

The differentiation rules of Section 38.1 lead to the integrals (in *radians*)

$\int \sin x\mathrm{d}x = -\cos x + K$	$\int \operatorname{cosec}^2 x\mathrm{d}x = -\cot x + K$
$\int \cos x\mathrm{d}x = \sin x + K$	$\int \sec x \tan x\mathrm{d}x = \sec x + K$
$\int \sec^2 x\mathrm{d}x = \tan x + K$	$\int \operatorname{cosec} x \cot x\mathrm{d}x = -\operatorname{cosec} x + K$

More complicated expressions can be integrated by using the identities of Section 37 and suitable changes of variable.

Examples

1. $$\int_0^{\pi/4} \sin(4x)\,\mathrm{d}x$$

Let $u = 4x$

$\Rightarrow \frac{1}{4}\mathrm{d}u = \mathrm{d}x$

page 175

$$= \frac{1}{4}\int_0^{\pi} \sin u\mathrm{d}u$$

x	0	$\pi/4$
u	0	π

$$= \frac{1}{4}[-\cos u]_0^{\pi} = \frac{1}{4}(-\cos\pi + \cos 0) = \frac{1}{2}$$

2. (i) $$\int \sin(ax+b)\,\mathrm{d}x = -\frac{1}{a}\cos(ax+b) + K$$

(ii) $$\int \cos(ax+b)\,\mathrm{d}x = \frac{1}{a}\sin(ax+b) + K$$

exericse

3. $$\int \sin^2 x\mathrm{d}x$$

Use the identity $\sin^2 x = \frac{1}{2}(1 - \cos 2x)$

double angle, page 354

$$\Rightarrow \frac{1}{2}\int (1 - \cos 2x)\mathrm{d}x = \frac{1}{2}\left\{x - \frac{1}{2}\sin 2x\right\} + K$$

from 2(ii)

$$= \frac{1}{2}x - \frac{1}{4}\sin 2x + K$$

(*Learn* this example.)

4. $$\int \cos^2 x\,dx = \frac{1}{2}x + \frac{1}{4}\sin 2x + K$$

Proof as exercise using double angle formula.

5. $$\int_0^{-\pi/2} \sin 2x \cos x\,dx$$

Let $u = \sin x$

$\Rightarrow du = \cos x\,dx$

x	0	$-\pi/2$
u	0	-1

$$= \int_0^{-1} u^2\,du$$

$$= \left[\frac{1}{3}u^3\right]_0^{-1} = -\frac{1}{3}$$

6. In general

$$\int \sin^n x \cos x\,dx = \frac{1}{n+1}\sin^{n+1} x + K$$

and

$$\int \cos^n x \sin x\,dx = -\frac{1}{n+1}\cos^{n+1} x + K$$

Proof as exercise using the substitutions $u = \sin x$, $u = \cos x$. *Learn these two formulae.*

7. $$\int \sin^3 x\,dx$$

An *odd* power of $\sin x$. Split off a $\sin x$ factor.

$= \int \sin^2 x \sin x\,dx.$

Replace $\sin^2 x$ by $(1 - \cos^2 x)$ page 333

$= \int (1 - \cos^2 x)\sin x\,dx$

$= \int \sin x\,dx - \int \cos^2 x \sin x\,dx$

$= -\cos x + \dfrac{\cos^3 x}{3} + K$ from 6

8. $$\int_0^{\pi/2} \cos^4 x \, dx$$

An *even* power. Write in terms of $\cos^2 x$.

$$= \int_0^{\pi/2} (\cos^2 x)^2 \, dx$$ use double angle formula

$$= \frac{1}{4}\int_0^{\pi/2} (1 + \cos 2x)^2 dx$$ $\cos^2 x = \frac{1}{2}(1 + \cos 2x)$

$$= \frac{1}{4}\int_0^{\pi/2} 1 + 2\cos 2x + \cos^2 2x \, dx$$

$$= \frac{1}{4}\int_0^{\pi/2} 1 + 2\cos 2x + \frac{1}{2}(1 + \cos 4x) \, dx$$ double angle again

$$= \frac{1}{4}\int_0^{\pi/2} \left(\frac{3}{2} + 2\cos 2x + \frac{1}{2}\cos 4x\right) dx$$

$$= \frac{1}{4}\left[\frac{3}{2}x + \sin 2x + \frac{1}{8}\sin 4x\right]_0^{\pi/2}$$ example 2

$$= \frac{1}{4}\left(\frac{3\pi}{4} + \sin \pi + \frac{1}{8}\sin 2\pi - 0 - \sin 0 - \frac{1}{8}\sin 0\right)$$

$$= \frac{3\pi}{16}$$

Other *single* odd or even powers of $\sin x$ or $\cos x$ can be integrated using the methods of 7 and 8. *Learn them.*

9. $$\int \sin^3 x \cos^2 x dx$$

Mixed powers of $\sin x$ and $\cos x$. Split the *odd* power.

$$\Rightarrow \int \sin^2 x \cos^2 x \sin x dx$$

Use $\sin^2 x = 1 - \cos^2 x$

$$\Rightarrow \int (1 - \cos^2 x)\cos^2 x \sin x dx$$

$$= \int \cos^2 x \sin x dx - \int \cos^4 x \sin x dx$$

$$= -\frac{1}{3}\cos^3 x + \frac{1}{5}\cos^5 x + K \qquad \text{example 6}$$

10. $$\int \sin^2 x \cos^2 x dx$$

No odd power to split. Use double angle formulae.

$$= \int \frac{(2\sin x \cos x)^2}{4} dx$$

$$= \frac{1}{4}\int \sin^2 2x \, dx$$

$$= \frac{1}{4}\int \frac{1}{2}(1 - \cos 4x)\, dx \qquad \text{double angle}$$

$$= \frac{1}{8}\left(x - \frac{1}{4}\sin 4x + K\right)$$

$$= \frac{1}{8}x - \frac{1}{32}\sin 4x + K$$

11. $$\int \tan x dx = \int \frac{\sin x}{\cos x} dx$$

$$= -\int \frac{-\sin x}{\cos x} dx$$

$$= -\ln|\cos x| + K \qquad \text{page 305}$$

$$= \ln|\sec x| + K \qquad \text{page 291}$$

12. $$\int \tan^2 x \, dx \qquad \tan^2 x = \sec^2 x - 1 \text{ page 341}$$

$$= \int (\sec^2 x - 1) dx = \tan x - x + K$$

13. $\int \tan^3 x \, dx = \int \tan x \tan^2 x dx$

$= \int (\sec^2 x - 1) \tan x dx = \int \sec^2 x \tan x dx - \int \tan x dx$

Letting $u = \tan x$ in the first integral (so $du = \sec^2 x dx$)

$\Rightarrow \int u du - \int \tan x \, dx$

$= \frac{1}{2}u^2 - \ln|\sec x| + K$

$= \frac{1}{2}\tan^2 x + \ln|\cos x| + K$

14. $$\int \frac{1}{\sqrt{1-x^2}} dx$$

Let $x = \sin\theta$, so that $1 - x^2 = 1 - \sin^2\theta = \cos^2\theta$.

Also $dx = \cos\theta d\theta$

$\Rightarrow \int \frac{1}{\cos\theta} \cos\theta d\theta$

$= \int 1 \, d\theta = \theta + c,$

and, since $\theta = \sin^{-1} x$,

$$\boxed{\Rightarrow \int \frac{1}{\sqrt{1-x^2}} dx = \sin^{-1} x + c}$$

a standard integral.

15. By substituting $x = \tan\theta$ you can show that

$$\boxed{\int \frac{1}{1+x^2} dx = \tan^{-1} x + c}$$

Proof exercise.

More general forms of these integrals are

$$\boxed{\int \frac{1}{\sqrt{a^2 - x^2}} dx = \sin^{-1}\left(\frac{x}{a}\right) + K}$$

and

$$\int \frac{1}{a^2 + x^2}\,dx = \frac{1}{a}\tan^{-1}\left(\frac{x}{a}\right) + K$$

To integrate successfully you must know

1. the standard integrals (table on page 446).
2. the trigonometric identities and logarithm properties.

Section 38 Applications of the Trigonometric Functions

38.1 Polar Coordinates

A point P with cartesian coordinates (x, y) can also be specified by an angle (θ) and a length (r).

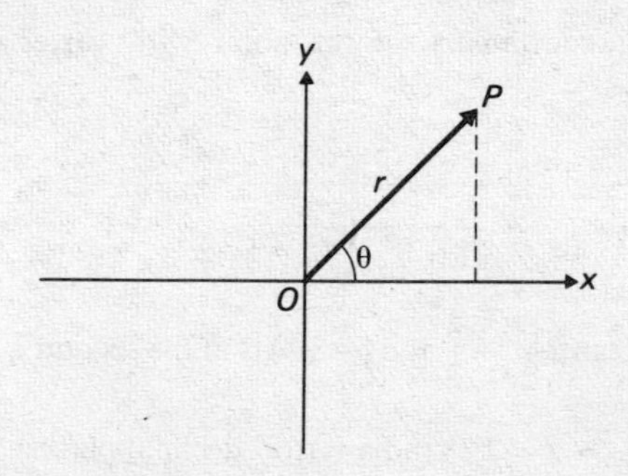

$r = OP =$ distance from O to P, $\theta =$ angle that OP makes with the *positive x-axis* in an *anticlockwise* sense. (r, θ) are the **polar coordinates** of point P.

$$r > 0 \text{ and } 0 \leqslant \theta < 2\pi \text{ (or } -\pi < \theta \leqslant \pi).$$

The origin is called the **pole** and the positive x-axis is the **initial line**.

From page 330 we deduce that cartesian and polar coordinates are related by

$$\left.\begin{aligned} x &= r\cos\theta \\ y &= r\sin\theta \end{aligned}\right\} \text{ and } \left.\begin{aligned} r &= \sqrt{x^2+y^2} \\ \tan\theta &= \frac{y}{x} \end{aligned}\right\}$$

Notice that since there are 2 angles in the range $[0, 2\pi]$ with a given value of $\tan\theta$, θ is *not* uniquely determined by $\frac{y}{x}$. You should consider the signs of x and y to fix the correct quadrant (see page 332).

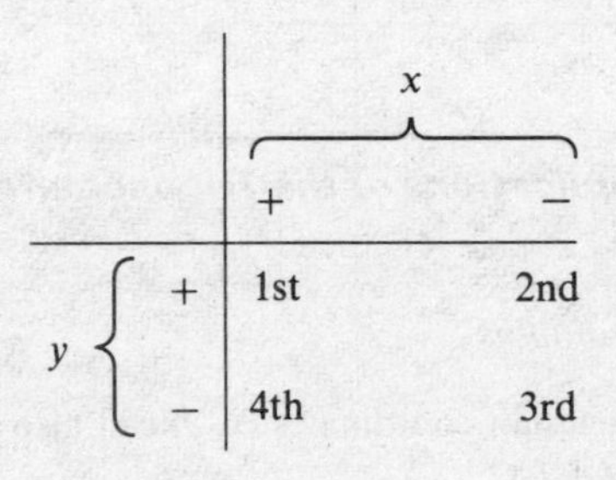

Example

Find the polar coordinates of the point with cartesian coordinates $(-3, 4)$.

Answer

$$r = \sqrt{(-3)^2 + 4^2} = 5$$

$$\tan\theta = -\frac{4}{3} \text{ and } (-3, 4) \text{ is in the second quadrant}$$

$$\Rightarrow \theta = 2{\cdot}21 \text{ radians (to 2 decimal places)}$$

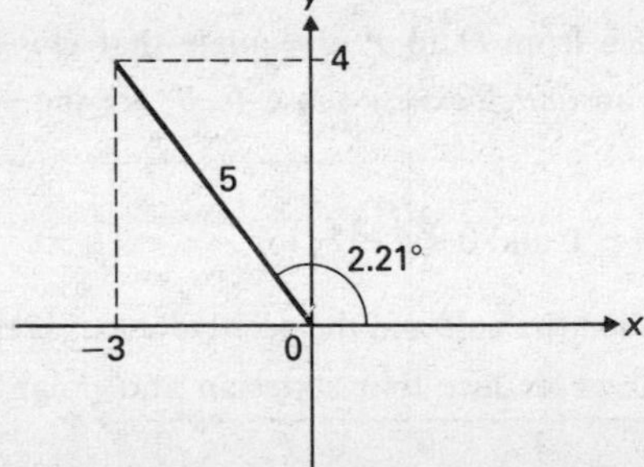

(Degrees may be used for polar coordinates, but radians are more common.)

Note: It is sometimes useful to allow $r < 0$. The convention is to measure distances *backwards* from 0. For instance, the point with the polar coordinates $(-2, \frac{\pi}{6})$ is

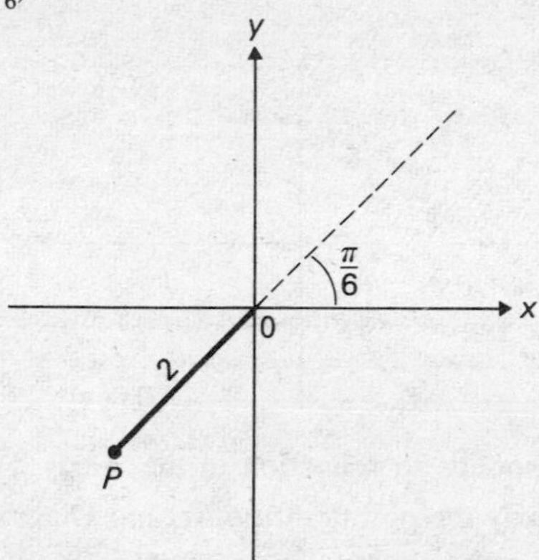

38.2 The Argand Diagram for Complex Numbers

A complex number is determined by two real numbers (real and imaginary parts)

$$z = x + iy,\ x, y \in \mathbb{R} \quad \text{(page 115)}$$

Each $z \in \mathbb{C}$ corresponds to a unique point (x, y) in the plane. A complex number can be represented by a point in the plane (or by a vector; see page 409).

The diagram below shows the points P_1, P_2, P_3 and P_4 corresponding to $z_1 = 1 + 2i$, $z_2 = 2$, $z_3 = 3i$ and $z_4 = -2 + 5i$. This is called an *Argand Diagram.*

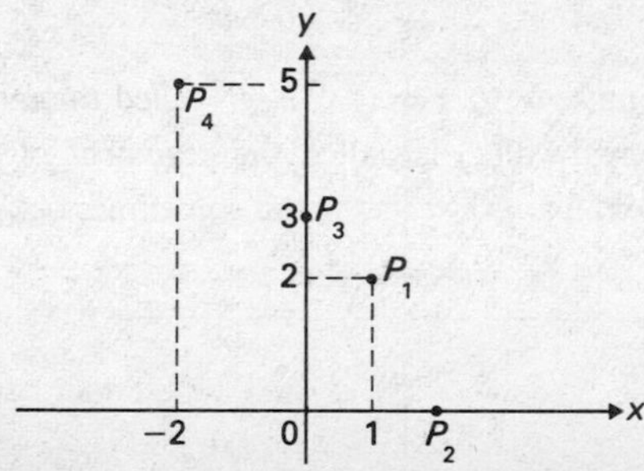

Real numbers correspond to points on the x-axis, which is thus called the **real axis**. Imaginary numbers (i, $2i$, $-3{\cdot}5i$ etc.) correspond to points on the y-axis, or **imaginary axis**.

If $z = x + iy$ is represented by $P(x, y)$ then its conjugate $z^* = x - iy$ is represented by $P'(x, -y)$.

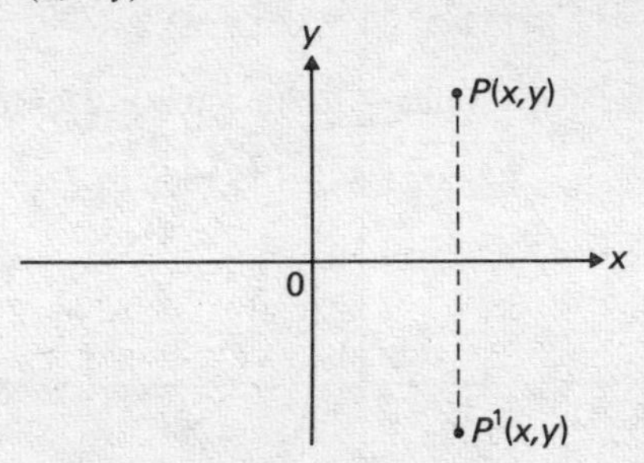

Conjugation corresponds to reflection in the x-axis. Polar coordinates can be used to specify the points in the Argand Diagram. The complex number $z = x + iy$ corresponds to the point $P(x, y)$

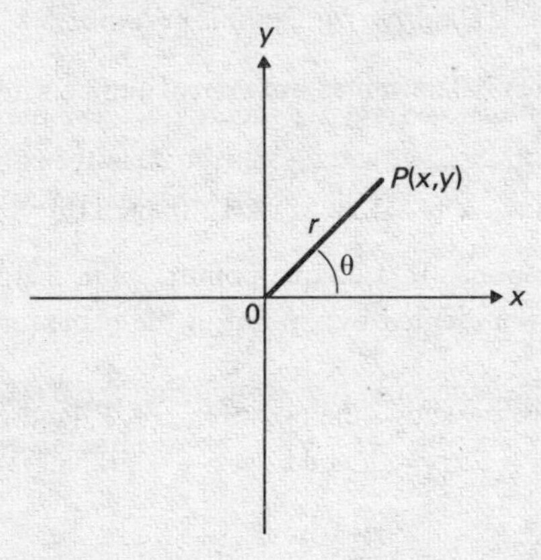

P has polar coordinates (r, θ). $r = \sqrt{x^2 + y^2}$, called the **modulus** of z, $|z|$. $\theta = \tan^{-1}(\frac{y}{x})$ (principal value) is called the **argument** of z, $\arg(z)$. θ is usually taken in the range $-\pi < \theta \leqslant \pi$, but sometimes $0 \leqslant \theta < 2\pi$.

Example

Find the modulus and argument of $z = 2 - 5i$.

Answer

$$|z| = |2 - 5i| = \sqrt{4 + 25} = \sqrt{29}$$

$\tan^{-1}(-\frac{5}{2})$ has principal value $-1{\cdot}19$($x > 0$, $y < 0$ for fourth quadrant).

$$\Rightarrow \arg z = -1{\cdot}19 \text{ radians}$$

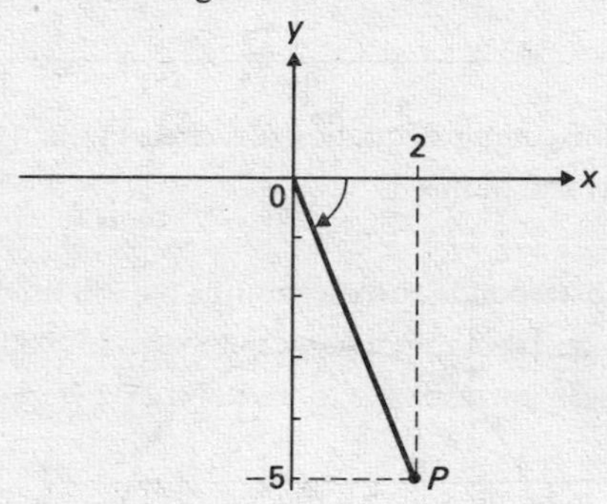

You should always plot the point on the Argand Diagram before calculating $\arg z$, so that you find the angle in the correct quadrant.

LOCI IN THE ARGAND DIAGRAM

If $z_1 = x_1 + iy_1$ and $z_2 = x_2 + iy_2$ are represented by points P and Q, respectively, then

1. $z_1 + z_2$ corresponds to point R such that $OPRQ$ is a parallelogram.

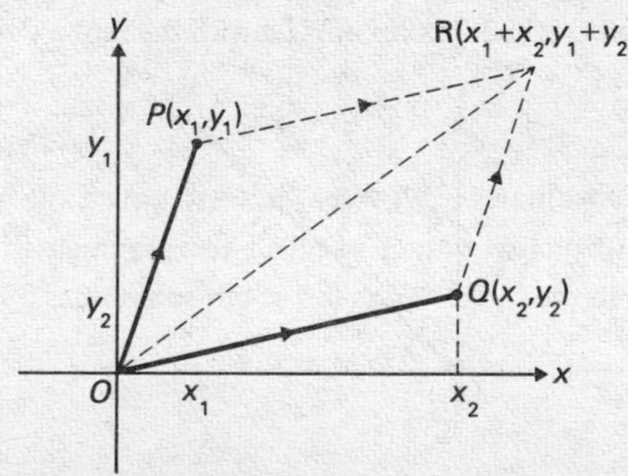

(See also vector addition, page 411.)

2. $|z_1 - z_2| = PQ$

That is $|z_1 - z_2|$ is the distance between the points which represent z_1 and z_2.

Let $z = x + iy$ be a variable complex number, corresponding to the point $P(x, y)$. Let $z_0 = x_0 + iy_0$ be a constant complex number, so that $C(x_0, y_0)$ is a fixed point, and let $r > 0$ be a positive constant.

The equation $|z - z_0| = r$ represents a circle with centre C and radius r, in the Argand Diagram.

Example

$|z - 2 + i| = 3$ is the complex equation of a circle in the Argand Diagram with centre $(2, -1)$ and radius 3.

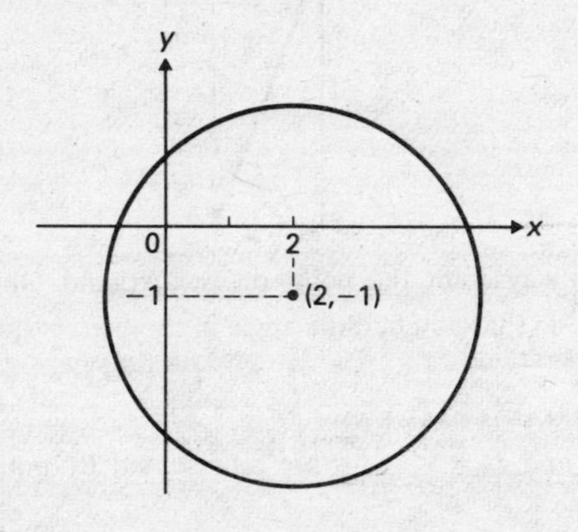

The equation $\arg z = \alpha$, where α is a constant, $-\pi \leqslant \alpha \leqslant \pi$, represents a *half line* through O which makes angle α with the real axis.

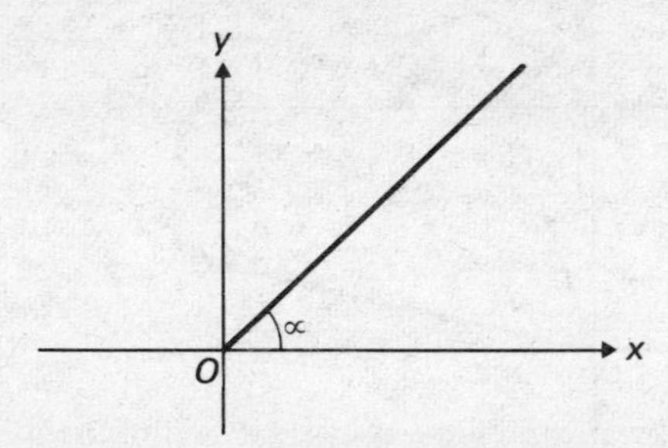

The locus of points corresponding to equation

$$|z - z_1| = |z - z_2|$$

contains points P equidistant from the *fixed points* A and B. It is the **mediator**, or perpendicular bisector, of line segment AB (where A and B represent z_1 and z_2).

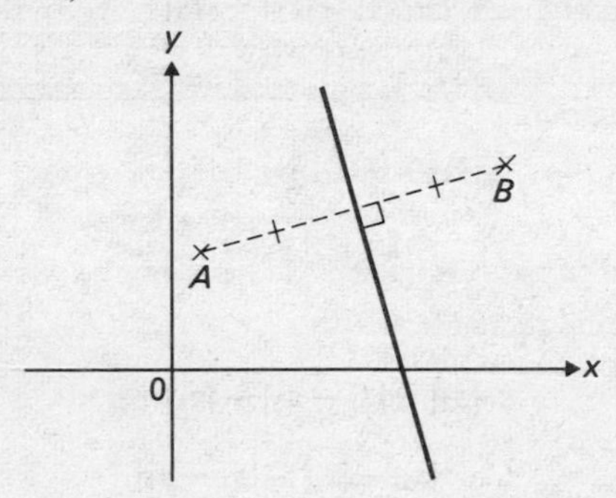

On page 120 we came across the inequality $|z_1 + z_2| \leqslant |z_1| + |z_2|$ for any $z_1, z_2 \in \mathbb{C}$.

We can prove this using the Argand Diagram. If P represents z_1, Q represents z_2 and R represents $z_1 + z_2$ (so that $OPRQ$ is a parallelogram)

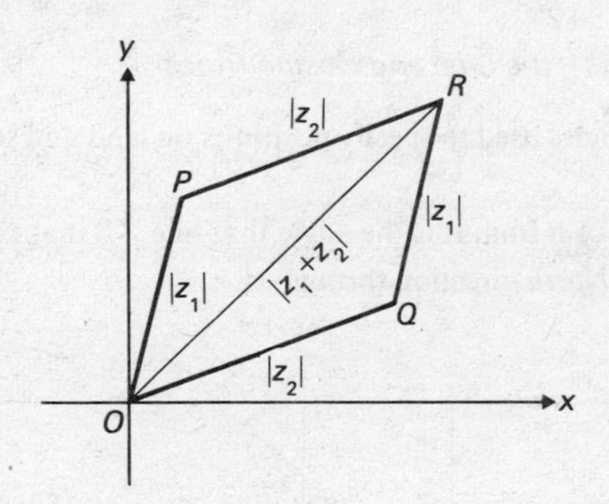

then in $\triangle OPR$

$$OR \leqslant OP + PR$$

since any side of a $\triangle$ is no longer than the sum of the other two sides. But

$$OR = |z_1 + z_2|, OP = |z_1| \text{ and } PR = OQ = |z_2|$$

$$\Rightarrow |z_1 + z_2| \leqslant |z_1| + |z_2|$$

(Equality holds only when *OPQR* is a straight line.)

Another results uses $\triangle OPQ$

$$|z_1 - z_2| \leqslant |z_1| + |z_2|$$

Also

$$|z_1| \leqslant |z_1 - z_2| + |z_2|$$

$$\therefore \quad |z_1| - |z_2| \leqslant |z_1 - z_2|$$

and

$$|z_2| \leqslant |z_1 - z_2| + |z_1|$$

$$\therefore \quad |z_2| - |z_1| \leqslant |z_1 - z_2|$$

so that

$$\Big||z_1| - |z_2|\Big| \leqslant |z_1 - z_2| \leqslant |z_1| + |z_2|$$

38.3 Bearings – the Sine and Cosine Rules

Bearings are angles used to specify positions on land and sea with respect to fixed points.

The bearing of B from A is the angle that line AB makes in a *clockwise* sense with the *North* direction through A.

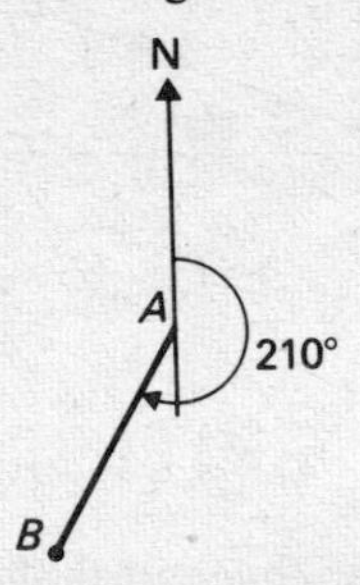

The diagram shows that B has a bearing of 210° from A. Bearings are traditionally written as 3 digit figures (possibly with further decimal digits) 050°, 002°, 010·5°, etc. For points above the horizontal plane, the bearing is taken to be that of the foot of the perpendicular from the point to the plane.

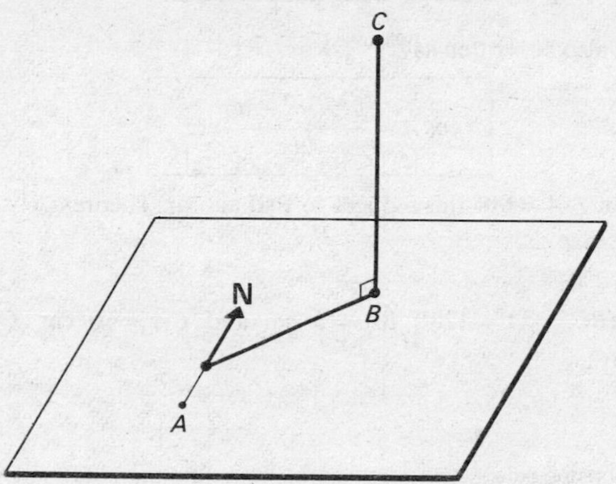

Bearing of C from A = bearing of B from A.

Two useful methods for calculating angles and distances are:

THE SINE AND COSINE RULES

In $\triangle ABC$

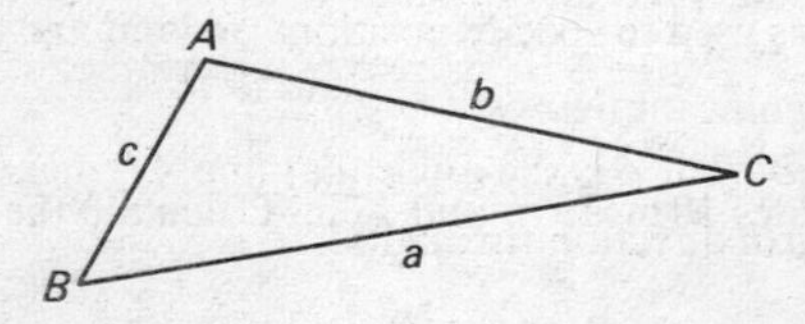

the **sine rule** states that

$$\frac{\sin A}{a} = \frac{\sin B}{b} = \frac{\sin C}{c}$$

The **cosine rule** states

$$a^2 = b^2 + c^2 - 2bc\cos A$$

or

$$b^2 = a^2 + c^2 - 2ac\cos B$$

or

$$c^2 = a^2 + b^2 - 2ab\cos C$$

which can also be written as

$$\cos A = \frac{b^2 + c^2 - a^2}{2bc} \text{ etc.}$$

Note: when $\angle A = 90°$ this reduces to Pythagoras' Theorem.

Examples

1. In $\triangle ABC$, $\angle A = 120°$, $BA = 5$ cm and $CA = 10$ cm. Calculate distance BC.

Answer

From the cosine rule

$$a^2 = 10^2 + 5^2 - 2 \times 5 \times 10\cos 120°$$

$$= 125 - 100 \times \left(-\frac{1}{2}\right)$$

$$= 175$$

$\therefore a = 13{\cdot}2$ cm (3 significant figures)

2. A triangle has sides 10 m, 15 m and 17 m. Calculate the angles of this triangle.

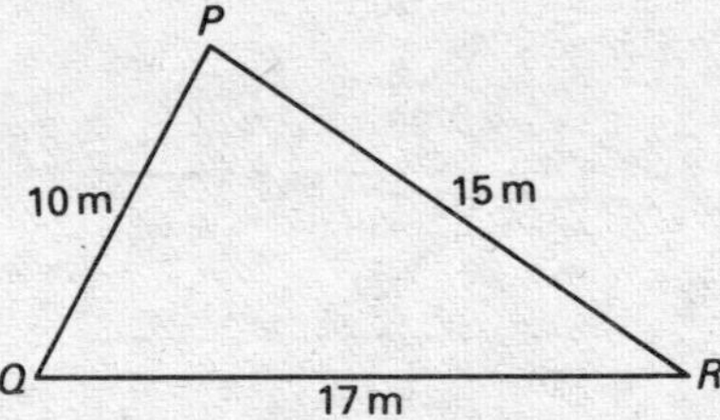

Answer

An angle with a given sine could be either acute *or* obtuse. We first use the cosine rule for the *largest* angle which must be opposite the *longest* side (17 m)

$$\cos P = \frac{10^2 + 15^2 - 17^2}{2 \times 10 \times 15} = 0{\cdot}12$$

$\therefore P = 83{\cdot}1°$ (unambiguously acute as $\cos P$ is positive).

Since the largest angle is acute, so too are the other angles and the sine rule can be safely used:

$$\frac{\sin Q}{q} = \frac{\sin P}{p}$$

$$\Rightarrow \sin Q = \frac{q \sin P}{p} = \frac{15 \sin 83{\cdot}1}{17} = 0{\cdot}8760$$

$$\Rightarrow \angle Q = 61{\cdot}2°$$

Since $\angle P + \angle Q + \angle R = 180°$ (angles in a $\triangle$) then $\angle R = 180° - 83{\cdot}1° - 61{\cdot}2° = 35{\cdot}7°$.

(Show sufficient working in this type of question. Mistakes often slip in when you miss out steps.)

3. Point A is on a bearing 062° from point B and distant 2 km from B. C is on a bearing of 100° from A and $AC = 3$ km. Calculate distance BC and the bearing of B from C. Express your answers correct to 1 decimal place.

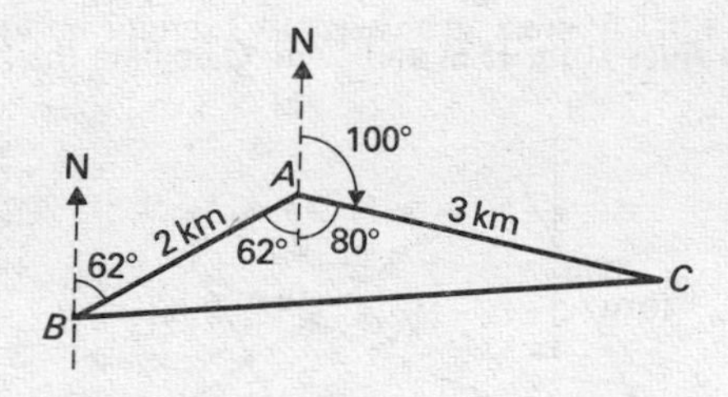

Answer

$\widehat{BAC} = 142°$. Using the cosine rule in ABC

$$BC^2 = 2^2 + 3^2 - 2 \times 2 \times 3 \cos 142°$$

$$BC = 4{\cdot}7388\,\text{km}$$

$$\therefore BC = 4{\cdot}7\,\text{km} \quad \text{(1 decimal place)}$$

Now calculate $\widehat{BCA}$ using the sine rule

$$\frac{\sin C}{2} = \frac{\sin 142^\circ}{4{\cdot}7388}$$

$$\Rightarrow \sin C = \frac{2 \sin 142^\circ}{4{\cdot}7388} = 0{\cdot}260$$

$$\Rightarrow \widehat{BCA} = 15{\cdot}1^\circ \quad \text{(1 decimal place)}$$

B is on a bearing of 264·9° from C.

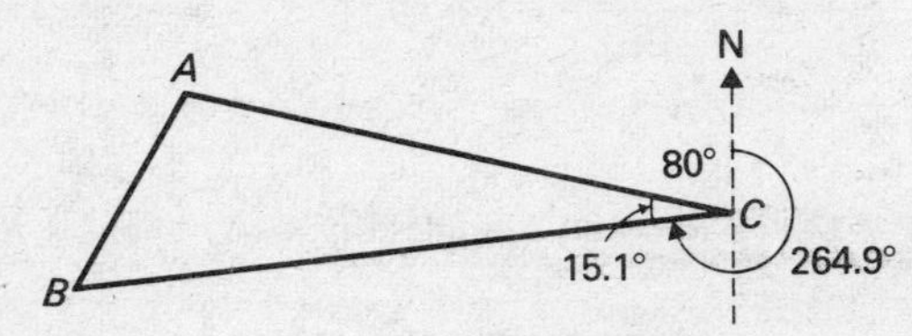

38.4 Two and Three Dimensional Problems

Examples

1. A vertical mast AT, 12 m high, has its foot at the vertex A of triangle ABC. This triangle is horizontal with $AB = 10\,\text{m}$, $AC = 15\,\text{m}$ and $\widehat{BAC} = 70^\circ$. Calculate (*a*) the length BC, (*b*) the angle $\widehat{BTC}$, (*c*) the areas of $\triangle ABC$ and $\triangle TBC$. Express all answers to 3 significant figures.

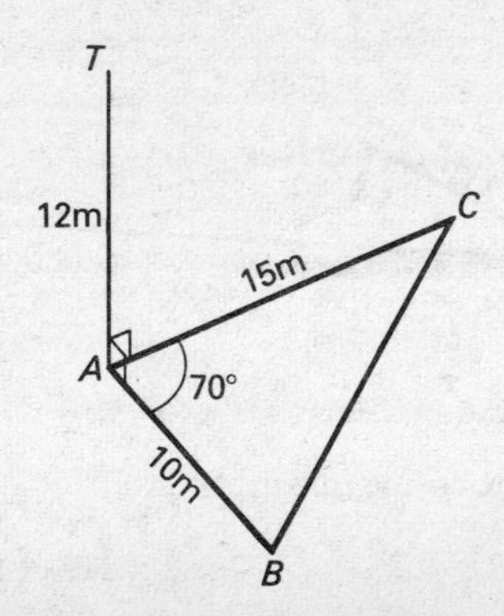

Answer

(*a*) From the cosine rule in $\triangle ABC$

$$BC^2 = 10^2 + 15^2 - 2 \times 10 \times 15 \cos 70°$$
$$= 100 + 225 - 300 \times 0{\cdot}3420$$
$$= 222{\cdot}4$$

Hence $BC = 14{\cdot}9$ m.

(*b*) To calculate $\widehat{BTC}$, BT and CT are needed. $\triangle ACT$ is right-angled and so Pythagoras' Theorem can be used.

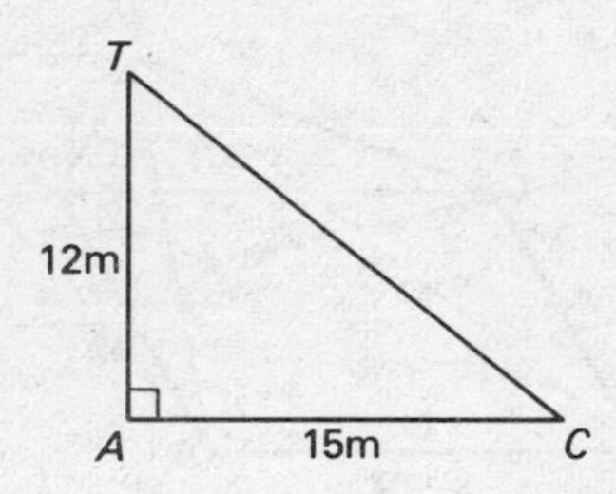

$$CT^2 = 12^2 + 15^2 = 369 \quad \Rightarrow \quad CT = 19{\cdot}209$$

Similarly in the right-angled triangle BAT,

$$BT^2 = 10^2 + 12^2 = 244 \quad \Rightarrow \quad BT = 15{\cdot}620$$

Now using the cosine rule in $\triangle BTC$

$$\cos \widehat{BTC} = \frac{BT^2 + CT^2 - BC^2}{2 \times BT \times CT} = 0{\cdot}65087$$

$$\Rightarrow \qquad \widehat{BTC} = 49{\cdot}4°$$

(*c*) The formula

$$\text{Area} = \tfrac{1}{2}bc \sin A$$ page 441

for triangle ABC can be used

$\Rightarrow$ Area $\quad \triangle ABC = \frac{1}{2} \times 15 \times 10 \times \sin 70° = 70{\cdot}477$

Similarly

Area $\quad \triangle TBC = \frac{1}{2} \times BT \times CT \times \sin \widehat{BTC}$

$$= \tfrac{1}{2} \times 15{\cdot}620 \times 19{\cdot}209 \times 0{\cdot}75919 = 113{\cdot}9$$

2. The pyramid $ABCD$ has horizontal square base $ABCD$ of side a cm. Vertex V is vertically above the mid point M of side BC, and $VM = 2a$ cm. Calculate

(*a*) the length DM, (*b*) the angle of elevation of V from D, (*c*) the angle between planes ADV and $ABCD$, (*d*) the volume of tetrahedron $VMCD$.

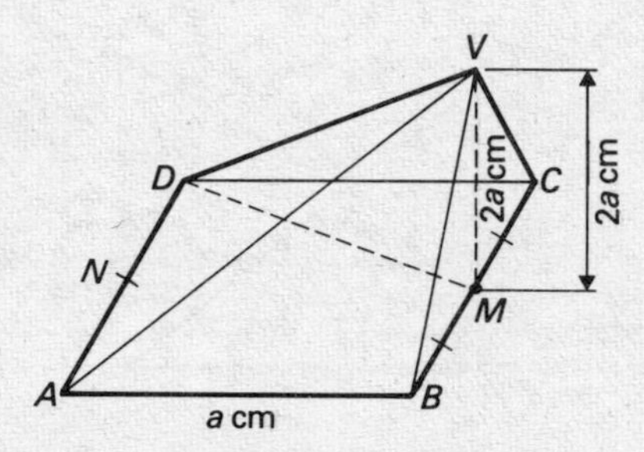

Answer

(*a*) $\triangle\ DMC$ is right-angled.

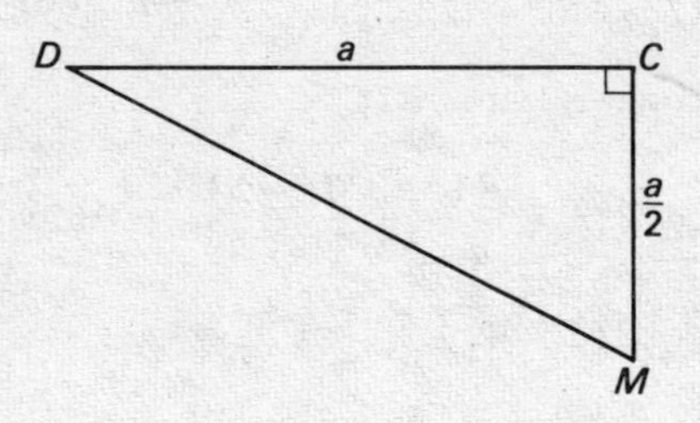

$$DM^2 = DC^2 + CM^2 \qquad \text{Pythagoras}$$

$$= a^2 + \frac{1}{4}a^2 = \frac{5a^2}{4}$$

$$\Rightarrow \qquad DM = a\frac{\sqrt{5}}{2}\,\text{cm}$$

(*b*) The angle of elevation is $\widehat{VDM}$ since VM is vertical.

$$\tan(\widehat{VDM}) = \frac{VM}{DM} = \frac{2a}{\sqrt{5}\frac{a}{2}} = \frac{4}{\sqrt{5}}$$

$$\Rightarrow \qquad \widehat{VDM} = 60{\cdot}8^\circ$$

(*c*) The angle between two planes is defined to be the angle between two lines, one in each plane, which intersect on and at right angles to the line of intersection of the two planes.

If N is the midpoint of AD, the required angle is $\widehat{VNM}$

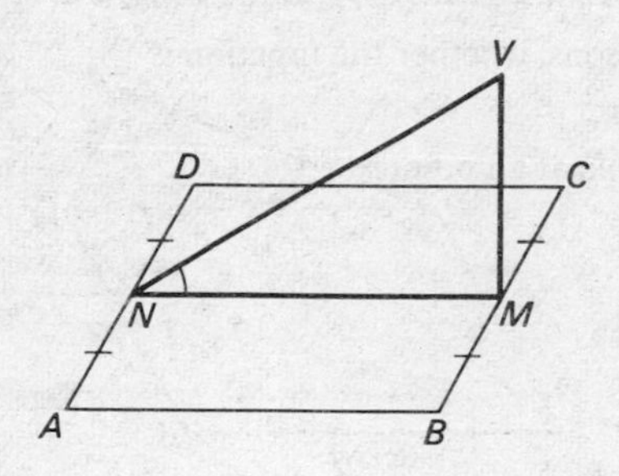

$$\text{Tan}(\widehat{VNM}) = \frac{VM}{NM} = \frac{2a}{a} = 2$$

$$\Rightarrow \widehat{VNM} = 63{\cdot}4^\circ$$

(*d*) Volume of tetrahedron $VMCD$

$= \frac{1}{3} \times$ base area $\times$ height page 442

$= \frac{1}{3} \times \text{area } \triangle CMD \times VM$

$= \frac{1}{3} \times (\frac{1}{2} \times a \times \frac{1}{2}a) \times (2a)\,\text{cm}^3$

$= \frac{1}{6}a^3\,\text{cm}^3$

Section 39 Worked Examples

1. The function $f(x)$ is defined on $\mathbb{R}$ by

$$f(x) = \begin{cases} \sin x, & 0 \leqslant x < \frac{\pi}{2} \\ (x - \frac{\pi}{2})^2, & \frac{\pi}{2} \leqslant x < \pi \end{cases}$$

and $f(x)$ is periodic with $f(x + \pi) = f(x)$ for all $x \in \mathbb{R}$.

(*a*) Sketch the graph of $f(x)$ for $-3\pi \leqslant x \leqslant 3\pi$.

(*b*) Calculate the area bounded by the curve, the x-axis between $x = -3\pi$ and $x = 3\pi$ and the lines $x = \pm\pi$, $x = \pm 2\pi$ and $x = \pm 3\pi$.

(*c*) State, with reasons, whether the function is

(i) continuous,

(ii) differentiable at all points.

Answer

(*a*)

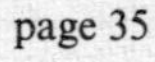
page 35

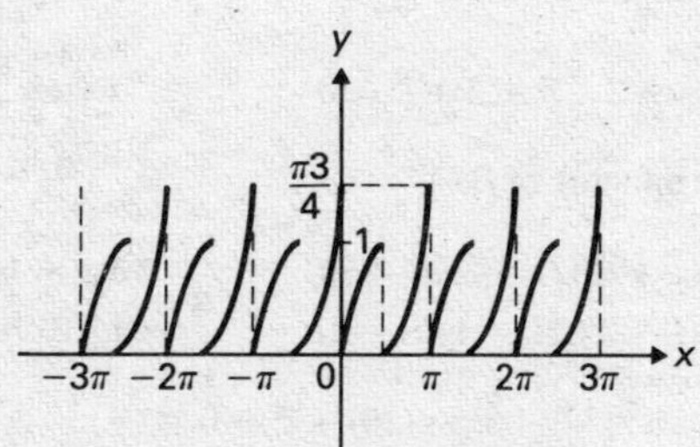

(*b*) One cycle is completed for $0 \leqslant x \leqslant \pi$. The area between this cycle and the x-axis is

$$\int_0^{\pi/2} \sin x \, dx + \int_{\pi/2}^{\pi} (x - \tfrac{\pi}{2})^2 \, dx$$

$$= [-\cos x]_0^{\pi/2} + \left[\frac{(x - \frac{\pi}{2})^3}{3}\right]_{\pi/2}^{\pi}$$

$$= 1 + \frac{\pi^3}{24}$$

The area for $-3\pi \leqslant x \leqslant 3\pi$ contains 6 cycles and so is

$$6\left(1+\frac{\pi^3}{24}\right) = 6 + \frac{\pi^3}{4} \text{ square units}$$

(*c*) (i) The graph is not continuous at values $x = \frac{n\pi}{2}$, $n \in \mathbb{Z}$, since for example $\sin\frac{\pi}{2} = 1$ while $(\frac{\pi}{2} - \frac{\pi}{2})^2 = 0 \neq 1$.

(ii) Since the graph is not continuous at $x = n\frac{\pi}{2}$, it cannot be differentiated at these points. — tangents cannot be drawn at these points

2. By factorizing the expression

$$f(L) = 2L^3 - 3L^2 - 3L + 2$$

find all solutions of the equation

$$2\cos^3(2\theta) - 3\cos^2(2\theta) - 3\cos(2\theta) + 2 = 0$$

in the range $0° \leqslant \theta \leqslant 180°$.

Answer

$$f(-1) = -2 - 3 + 3 + 2 = 0$$ Factor Theorem of page 81

$\therefore$ $L + 1$ is a factor of $f(L)$.

$$f(L) = (L+1)(2L^2 - 5L + 2)$$ e.g. by long division (page 78)

$$= (L+1)(2L-1)(L-2)$$

$$2\cos^3(2\theta) - 3\cos^2(2\theta) - 3\cos(2\theta) + 2 = 0$$

$$\Rightarrow (\cos(2\theta)+1)(2\cos(2\theta)-1)(\cos(2\theta)-2) = 0$$ put $L = \cos(2\theta)$

$\Rightarrow \cos 2\theta = -1$ or $\cos 2\theta = 0{\cdot}5$ or

$$\cos 2\theta = 2 \text{ (no solution)}$$

$$\Rightarrow 2\theta = n360° \pm 180° \text{ or } 2\theta = n360° \pm 60°$$ page 344, general solutions

$$\Rightarrow \theta = n180° \pm 90° \text{ or } \theta = n180° \pm 30°$$

$\Rightarrow$ In the range $0° \leqslant \theta \leqslant 180°$ the solutions are

$$\theta = 90°, \quad \theta = 30°, \quad \theta = 150°$$

3. OA and OB are radii of the circle centre O and radius r cm such that $\widehat{AOB}$ is acute and the area of sector AOB is $\frac{50}{49}$ times the area of triangle AOB.

Show that $49\theta - 50\sin\theta = 0$.

Find an estimate for the solution of this equation by drawing graphs of $y = 49\theta$ and $y = 50\sin\theta$ (for θ in radians).

Use the *first two* non-zero terms of the series for $\sin\theta$ in ascending powers of θ to find a better approximation to the value of θ.

Answer

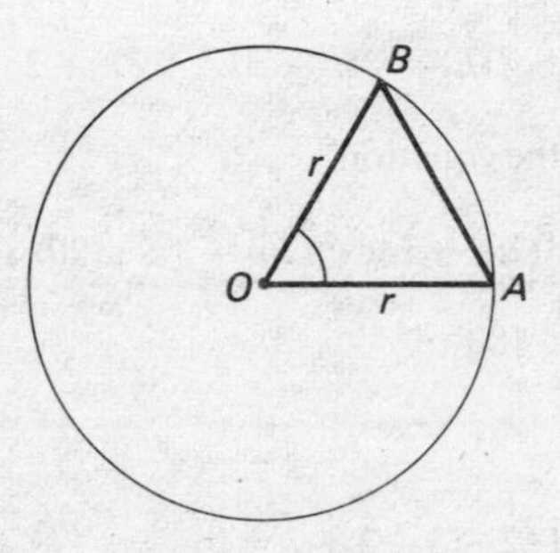

Area of $\triangle AOB = \frac{1}{2}r^2\sin\theta$ page 441

Area of sector $AOB = \frac{1}{2}r^2\theta$

$$\Rightarrow \frac{50}{49}\left(\frac{1}{2}r^2\sin\theta\right) = \frac{1}{2}r^2\theta$$

$$\Rightarrow 50\sin\theta = 49\theta$$

$$\Rightarrow 49\theta - 50\sin\theta = 0$$

The graphs of 49θ and $50\sin\theta$ intersect when $\theta \approx 0{\cdot}4$.

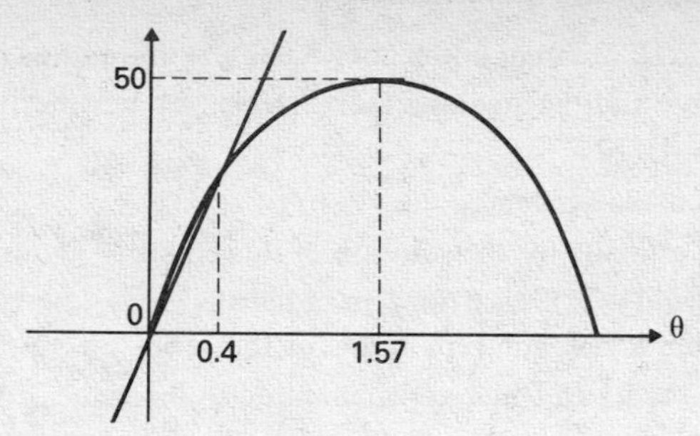

The series for $\sin\theta = \theta - \frac{1}{6}\theta^3 + \ldots$ page 371

$$\Rightarrow 50\left(\theta - \frac{1}{6}\theta^3\right) = 49\theta$$

for approximate solutions for θ

$$\Rightarrow \theta - \frac{25}{3}\theta^3 = 0$$

$$\Rightarrow \theta^2 = \frac{3}{25} = 0{\cdot}12 \qquad \theta \neq 0$$

$$\Rightarrow \theta = 0{\cdot}346 \qquad \text{positive as } \theta \text{ is acute}$$

4. Express $\cos x + \sin x$ in the form $R\cos(x - \alpha)$ where R is positive and $0 < \alpha < \pi/2$. Hence or otherwise find the greatest and least values of the expression

$$\frac{2}{(\cos x + \sin x)^2 + 3}$$

Answer

$$R = \sqrt{1+1} = \sqrt{2}$$ page 362

$$\sqrt{2}\cos(x - \alpha) = \sqrt{2}(\cos x\cos\alpha + \sin x\sin\alpha)$$

$$= (\sqrt{2}\cos\alpha)\cos x + (\sqrt{2}\sin\alpha)\sin x$$

$$\therefore \qquad \sqrt{2}\cos\alpha = 1$$ comparing with $\cos x + \sin x$

$$\Rightarrow \cos\alpha = 1/\sqrt{2}$$

$$\Rightarrow \qquad \alpha = \pi/4$$ page 336

$$\therefore \cos x + \sin x = \sqrt{2}\cos\left(x - \frac{\pi}{4}\right)$$

$$(\cos x + \sin x)^2 + 3 = 2\cos^2\left(x - \frac{\pi}{4}\right) + 3$$

$$0 \leqslant \cos^2(x - \pi/4) \leqslant 1$$

$$\therefore 3 \leqslant 2\cos^2\left(x - \frac{\pi}{4}\right) + 3 \leqslant 5$$

and

$$\frac{2}{3} \geqslant \frac{2}{2\cos^2\left(x - \frac{\pi}{4}\right) + 3} \geqslant \frac{2}{5}$$

Greatest value $\frac{2}{3}$, least value $\frac{2}{5}$.

5. Differentiate (*a*) $\sin x \cos^3 x$, (*b*) $e^{\sec x}$

Answer

(*a*) $y = \sin x \cos^3 x$

$$\frac{dy}{dx} = \cos x(\cos^3 x) + \sin x(3\cos^2 x)(-\sin x)$$ product rule and change of variable (page 161)

$$= \cos^4 x - 3\sin^2 x \cos^2 x$$

$$= \cos^4 x - 3(1 - \cos^2 x)\cos^2 x$$ $\sin^2 x = 1 - \cos^2 x$

$$= \cos^4 x - 3\cos^2 x + 3\cos^4 x$$

$$= 4\cos^4 x - 3\cos^2 x$$

(*b*) $y = e^{\sec x}$

$$\frac{dy}{dx} = \sec x \tan x \, e^{\sec x}$$

$\frac{d}{dx}(\sec x) = \sec x \tan x$

and page 297

6. Find the coordinates of the turning points on the graph of $f(x) = e^{\sin x}$. Sketch this graph for $-\pi \leqslant x \leqslant \pi$.

Answer

For a turning point $f'(x) = 0$ page 151

$\Rightarrow \quad \cos x e^{\sin x} = 0$

$\Rightarrow \quad \cos x = 0$ $\quad e^{\sin x} > 0$ for all x

$\Rightarrow \quad x = 2n\pi \pm \frac{\pi}{2} (n \in \mathbb{Z})$ page 344

$\Rightarrow x = \ldots, -\frac{5\pi}{2}, -\frac{3\pi}{2}, -\frac{\pi}{2}, \frac{\pi}{2}, \frac{3\pi}{2}, \ldots$

$$f\left(-\frac{5\pi}{2}\right) = e^{-1}, \quad f\left(-\frac{3\pi}{2}\right) = e^{1}$$ stationary values

$$f\left(-\frac{\pi}{2}\right) = e^{-1} \quad f(\pi/2) = e^{1} \text{ etc.}$$

$$f''(x) = \cos^2 x e^{\sin x} - \sin x e^{\sin x}$$
$$= e^{\sin x}(\cos^2 x - \sin x)$$
$$= \pm e^{\mp 1} \text{ when } \cos x = 0$$
$$\neq 0$$

These are not points of inflexion. page 158

The turning points are

$$\left(2n\pi + \frac{\pi}{2}, e^{1}\right), \quad \left(2n\pi - \frac{\pi}{2}, e^{-1}\right)$$

for $n \in \mathbb{Z}$.

$f(0) = e^{0} = 1$

and $f(x) = e^{\sin x} > 0$ for all values $x \in \mathbb{R}$. The graph is

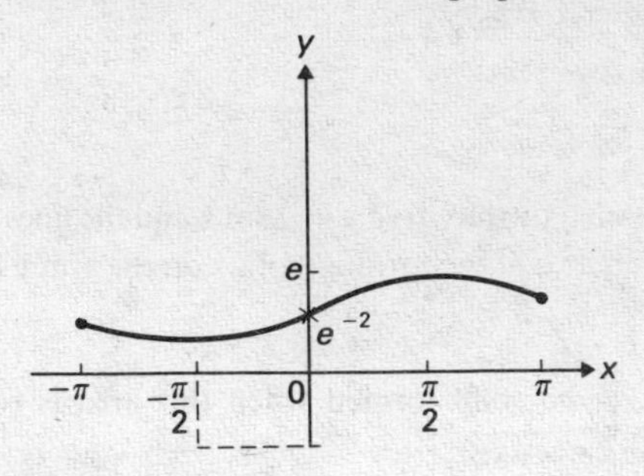

7. Evaluate (i) $\int \frac{\cos x}{1 - \sin x} dx$ (ii) $\int_{\pi/4}^{\pi/2} \frac{\cos x}{\sin^3 x} dx$

Answer

(i) $\displaystyle\int \frac{\cos x}{1 - \sin x} dx = -\int \frac{-\cos x}{1 - \sin x} dx$

$= -\ln|1 - \sin x| + K$ $\qquad \displaystyle\int \frac{f'(x)}{f(x)} dx = \ln|f(x)| + K$

$= \ln\left(\dfrac{1}{|1 - \sin x|}\right) + K$

$= \ln\left(\dfrac{A}{(1 - \sin x)}\right)$ (if $\sin x \neq 1$) $\qquad$ page 303; note that $1 - \sin x \geqslant 0$

(ii) $\displaystyle\int_{\pi/4}^{\pi/2} \frac{\cos x}{\sin^3 x} dx = \int_{\pi/4}^{\pi/2} \sin^{-3} x \cos x dx$ $\qquad u = \sin x$

$= \left[-\dfrac{\sin^{-2} x}{2}\right]_{\pi/4}^{\pi/2} \equiv \left[-\dfrac{1}{2\sin^2 x}\right]_{\pi/4}^{\pi/2}$ $\qquad$ formula of page 373

$= \left(-\dfrac{1}{2}\right) - \left(-\dfrac{1}{2(\frac{1}{2})}\right)$ $\qquad \sin \pi/2 = 1, \sin \pi/4 = \dfrac{\sqrt{2}}{2}$

$$= -\frac{1}{2} + 1 = \frac{1}{2}$$

8. Find

(*a*) the area bounded by the curve $y = 2\sin x$ and the lines $x = 0, x = \pi/2$, $y = \dfrac{4x}{\pi}$,

(*b*) the volume of the solid formed when this area is rotated through 2π radians about the x-axis.

Answer

The line $y = \frac{4x}{\pi}$ and the curve $y = 2\sin x$ intersect at $(0, 0)$ and $(\frac{\pi}{2}, 2)$.

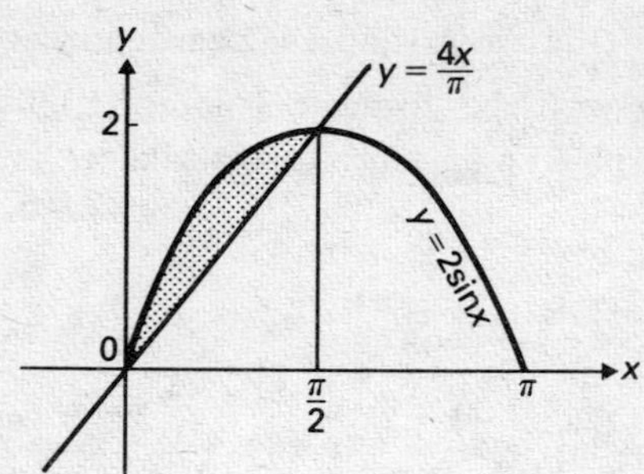

(*a*) The required area is

$$\int_0^{\pi/2} 2\sin x dx - \frac{1}{2} \times \frac{\pi}{2} \times 2 \qquad \text{area } \triangle = \tfrac{1}{2}\text{ base} \times \text{height}$$

$$= [-2\cos x]_0^{\pi/2} - \frac{\pi}{2}$$

$$= 2 - \frac{\pi}{2}$$

(*b*) The required volume is page 186

$$\pi \int_0^{\pi/2} 4 \sin^2 x \, dx - \frac{1}{3} \times \frac{\pi}{2} \times (4\pi)$$

volume of cone = $\frac{1}{3} \times$ height $\times$ base area

$$= 2\pi \int_0^{\pi/2} (1 - \cos 2x) dx - \frac{2\pi^2}{3}$$

$\sin^2 x = \frac{1}{2}(1 - \cos 2x)$

$$= 2\pi \left[x - \frac{1}{2} \sin 2x \right]_0^{\pi/2} - 2\pi^2/3$$

$$= 2\pi \left(\frac{\pi}{2} \right) - 2\pi^2/3 = \pi^2/3$$

9. Points P and Q in the Argand Diagram represent $z_1 = 2 + 2i$ and $z_2 = 1 - \sqrt{3}i$ respectively. Evaluate $|z_1|$, $\arg(z_1)$, $|z_2|$ and $\arg(z_2)$. Calculate $\widehat{POQ}$ without using tables or a calculator.

Answer

$$|z_1| = \sqrt{8}$$

$$\arg z_1 = \tan^{-1}\left(\frac{2}{2}\right) = \pi/4$$

first quadrant

$$|z_2| = 2$$

$$\arg z_2 = \tan^{-1}\left(\frac{-\sqrt{3}}{1}\right) = -\pi/3$$

fourth quadrant

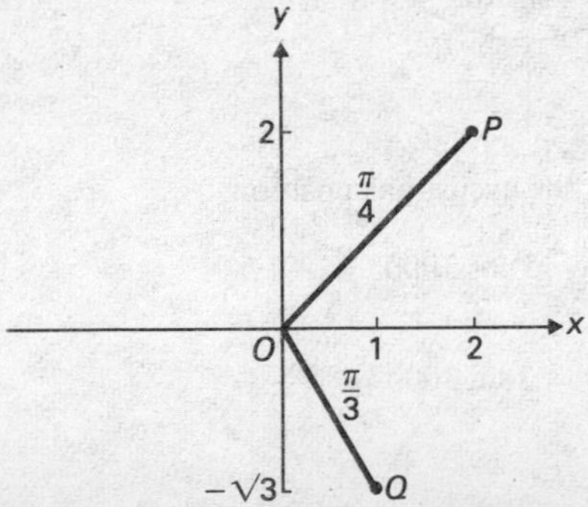

$$\widehat{POQ} = \frac{\pi}{4} + \frac{\pi}{3} = \frac{7\pi}{12}.$$

10. A person cycles in a circle so that their coordinates relative to North–South and East–West axes through the centre of the circle are

$$x = 3\cos 10t^{\circ}$$

$$y = 3\sin 10t^{\circ}$$

at time t minutes after they start cycling. Distances are measured in metres.

A second person is 10 m on a bearing of 030° from the centre (O) of this circle, at point P.

Find the distance (in metres) between this stationary person and the cyclist when $t = 300$ minutes, and also the bearing of the cyclist from point P at this time. (Express your answer to 1 decimal place.)

Answer

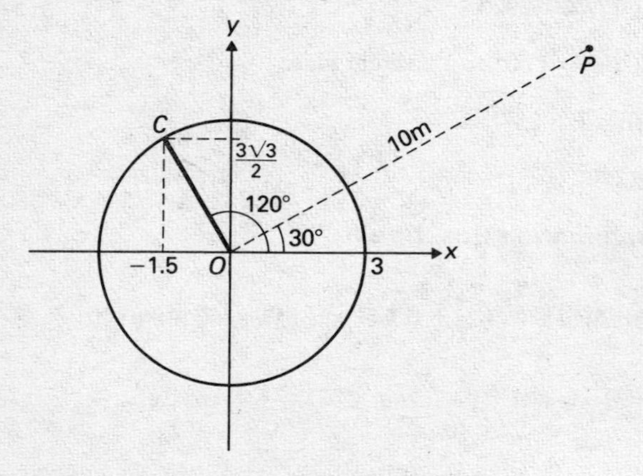

the circle has radius 3 m

When $t = 300$, the cyclist has position

$$x = 3\cos 3000^{\circ} = -1{\cdot}5$$

$$y = 3\sin 3000^{\circ} = 3\frac{\sqrt{3}}{2}$$

and OC makes an angle of 120° with the positive x-axis. — $3000 = 8 \times 360 + 120$

Using the cosine rule in $\triangle OCP$ — page 386

$$CP^2 = 3^2 + 10^2 - 2 \times 3 \times 10 \cos 60^\circ$$

OP makes angle 30° with the North

$$= 9 + 100 - 60 \times \frac{1}{2}$$

$$= 79$$

$\therefore \quad CP = 8{\cdot}9$ metres to 1 decimal place

For the bearing of C from P, $\widehat{CPO}$ is required.
From the sine rule

$$\frac{\sin \widehat{CPO}}{3} = \frac{\sin 60}{CP}$$

page 385

$$\therefore \quad \sin \widehat{CPO} = 0{\cdot}2923$$

$$\Rightarrow \quad \widehat{CPO} = 17{\cdot}0^\circ \text{ to 1 decimal place}$$

$\Rightarrow$ Bearing of C from P is 257°.

Section 40 Examination Questions

1. *Cosec $x = 2$ and $\cot x = -\sqrt{3}$. Which one of the following is true?*

A $\sin x = -\frac{1}{2}$ B $\cos x = \frac{\sqrt{3}}{2}$ C $\tan x = \frac{1}{\sqrt{3}}$ D $\cos 2x = -\frac{1}{2}$

E *None of these* [LON]

2. $y = \cos 2\theta$. *When* $\theta = \frac{\pi}{6}$, $\delta y \approx$

A $\sqrt{3}\,\delta\theta$ B $\frac{1}{2}\sqrt{3}\,\delta\theta$ C $-\frac{1}{2}\sqrt{3}\,\delta\theta$ D $-\delta\theta$ E $-\sqrt{3}\,\delta\theta$ [LON]

3. *The functions f and g are defined by $f: x \mapsto 2 + x - x^2$, $x \in \mathbb{R}$ and $g: \mapsto \frac{1}{1 + \tan x}$, $0 \leqslant x < \pi/2$. Determine the range of each function and state, in each case, whether or not an inverse function exists.* [LON]

4. $f(x) = \sin x$ *for* $0 \leqslant x \leqslant \pi$, $f(x) = 0$ *for* $\pi < x < 2\pi$, $f(x + 2\pi) = f(x)$ *for all* x.

A sketch of the graph of $f(x)$ for $-2\pi \leqslant x \leqslant 2\pi$ could be

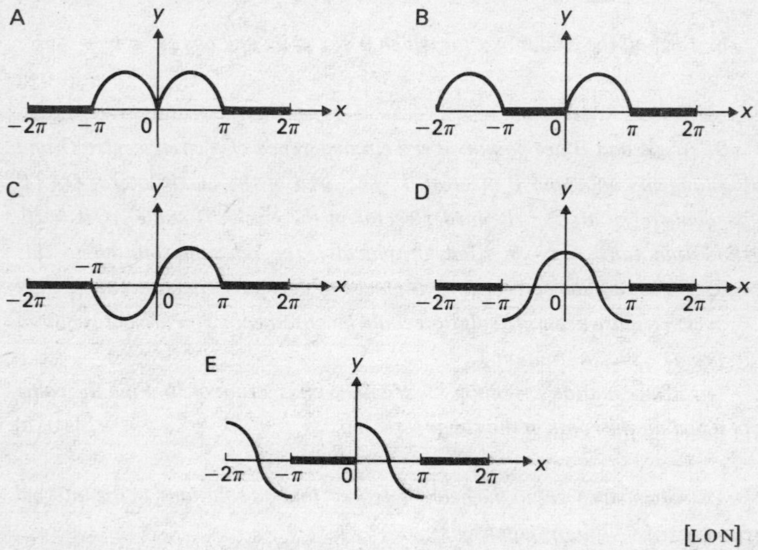

[LON]

5. *The functions f and g each with domain D where $\{x : x \in \mathbb{R}$ and $0 \leqslant x \leqslant \pi\}$, are defined by $f: x \mapsto \cos x$ and $g: x \mapsto x - \frac{1}{2}\pi$. Write down and simplify an expression $f[g(x)]$, giving its domain of definition. Sketch the graph of $y = f[g(x)]$.* [LON]

6. *All solutions of the equation $\cos\theta = \cos\alpha$ are obtained by taking all integer values of n in $\theta =$*

A $2n\pi \pm \alpha$ *B* $n\pi \pm \alpha$ *C* $2n\pi + \alpha$ *D* $2n\pi + (-1)^n\alpha$ *E* $n\pi + (-1)^n\alpha$

[LON]

7. *Using the factor theorem, or otherwise, find the values of x, in terms of p, which satisfy the equation*

$$x^3 - 7p^2x + 6p^3 = 0$$

Hence, or otherwise, find the value of t, in radians to 2 decimal places in the interval $0 \leqslant t < 2\pi$ *which satisfy the equation*

$$4\sec^3 t - 7\sec t + 3 = 0$$ [AEB]

8. *Find all the values of x for which* $0 \leqslant x \leqslant 2\pi$ *and* $\cos 2x = 1 + \sin x$. [LON]

9. *(a) A and B are points on the circumference of a circle centre O and the tangents at A and B meet at T. The area of the quadrilateral OATB is equal to the area of the larger sector of the circle. If angle* $AOB = 2\theta$, *show that* $\tan\theta = \pi - \theta$. *Find, graphically, the relevant solution to this equation in radians correct to two places of decimals. Suggest one method by which a more accurate solution could be obtained. (You are not required to produce such a solution.)*

(b) The equation $1 + \sin^2\phi\,° = a\cos 2\phi\,°$ *has a root of 30. Find the value of a and all the roots in the range 0 to 360.* [SUJB]

10. *Giving answers to the nearest degree, find all solutions, in the interval* $0° \leqslant x \leqslant 180°$, *to the equations*

(a) $\sin + \cos x = \frac{1}{2}$, *(b)* $10\sin(2x + 26°)\cos(2x - 26°) = 1$. [AEB]

11. $p = \cos\theta + \sin\theta$, $q = \cos\theta - \sin\theta$.

1. $p^2 + q^2 = 2$ 2. $pq = \cos 2\theta$ 3. $p^2 - q^2 = \sin 2\theta$

A 1, 2 and 3 are true B 1 and 2 only C 2 and 3 only D 1 only E 3 only [LON]

12. *By using identities for* $\cos(A-B)$ *and* $\cos(A+B)$, *prove that* $1+\cos(A-B)\cos(A+B)=\cos^2 A+\cos^2 B$.

Hence prove that (a) $1+\cos 2\theta = 2\cos^2\theta$ (b) $3+\cos(P-Q)\cos(P+Q)+\cos(Q-R)\cos(Q+R)+\cos(R-P)\cos(R+P) = 2(\cos^2 P+\cos^2 Q+\cos^2 R)$.

[AEB]

13. *Express* $\sin x - \cos x$ *in the form* $R\sin(x-\alpha)$, *where R is positive and* α *is an acute angle. Hence, or otherwise, find, in radians, the general solution of the equation* $\sin x - \cos x = 1$. [LON]

14. *Express* $\sin\theta - \sqrt{3}\cos\theta$ *in the form* $R\sin(\theta-\alpha)$ *where R is positive and* $0<\alpha<\frac{1}{2}\pi$. *Hence find all values of* θ *in the range* $0 \leqslant \theta < 2\pi$ *for which* $\sin\theta - \sqrt{3}\cos\theta = 1$. [OXF]

15. *Given that* $y = A\cos 2x + B\sin 4x$ *where A and B are constants, prove that*

$$\frac{d^4y}{dx^4}+20\frac{d^2y}{dx^2}+64y=0.$$ [AEB – part]

16. *Show that* $\frac{d}{dr}(\sin^{-1}(a/r)) = -\frac{a}{r\sqrt{(r^2-a^2)}}$.

A rectangular field has sides of length 10 m and 20 m. A goat is tethered to a corner of the field by an inelastic rope of length r m, where $10<r<20$. *Show that the goat has access to an area A* m^2 *of the field, where*

$$A = 5\sqrt{(r^2-100)}+\frac{1}{2}r^2\sin^{-1}(10/r)$$

Show that $\frac{dA}{dr} = r\sin^{-1}(10/r)$.

Apply the Newton–Raphson procedure once to the equation $A-100=0$ *with a starting value of* $r=10$, *to show that the goat has access to one half of the area of the field when r is approximately equal to 11·4.*

[LON]

17. *Given that* $f(x) = \frac{\sin x}{2-\cos x}$, *find the greatest and least values of* $f(x)$.

Find the area of the finite region bounded by the curve $y=f(x)$ *and the x-axis between the points where* $x=0$ *and* $x=\pi$. [LON]

18. *Find* $\int \sin 2x\,(\sin x)^{\frac{1}{2}}dx$. [AEB – part]

19. *Find the mean value of* $(x + (1 - x^2)^{\frac{1}{2}})$ *in the interval* $\frac{1}{2} \leqslant x \leqslant 1$, *leaving your answers in terms of* π. [AEB]

20. *After the substitution* $x = \sin\theta$, $\int_0^1 x^2\sqrt{(1 - x^2)}\,dx$ *becomes*

A $\int_0^{\pi/2} \sin^2\theta\cos^3\theta\,d\theta$ B $\int_0^1 \sin^2\theta\cos\theta\,d\theta$ C $\int_0^{\pi/2} \sin^2\theta\cos\theta\,d\theta$

D $\int_0^{\pi/2} \sin^2\theta\cos^2\theta\,d\theta$ E $\int_0^1 \sin^2\theta\cos^2\theta\,d\theta$ [LON]

21. *Evaluate the integrals*

(i) $\int_0^1 \frac{2x - 1}{(x + 1)^3}\,dx$ *(by substitution or otherwise),*

(ii) $\int_0^{\pi/4} \sin^2 3x\,dx$ [OXF]

22. $I_1 = \int_0^{\pi/2} \cos^2\theta\,d\theta$, $I_2 = \int_0^{\pi/2} \sin^2\theta\,d\theta$

1. $I_1 = \frac{1}{2}\int_0^{\pi/2} (1 + \cos 2\theta)\,d\theta$ 2. $I_2 = \frac{1}{2}\int_0^{\pi/2} (1 - \cos 2\theta)\,d\theta$ 3. $I_1 = I_2$.

A 1, 2 and 3 are true B 1 and 2 only C 2 and 3 only D 1 only E 3 only [LON]

23. *Evaluate* $\int_0^{2\pi} x\sin x\,dx$. [LON]

24. *Evaluate* $\int_0^{2\pi} (1 + \sin x)^2\,dx$. [SUJB – part]

25. *Find the modulus and argument of the complex numbers z_1, z_2 and z_3, where $z_1 = (1+i)$, $z_2 = z_1^3$, $z_3 = \dfrac{\sqrt{3}-i}{\sqrt{3}+i}$. Mark on an Argand Diagram the points representing z_1, z_2 and z_3.* [LON]

26. *Mark in an Argand Diagram the points P_1 and P_2 which represent the two complex numbers z_1, and z_2, where $z_1 = 1-i$ and $z_2 = 1+i\sqrt{3}$. On the same diagram, mark the points P_3 and P_4 which represent (z_1+z_2), (z_1-z_2) respectively. Find the modulus and argument of (a) z_1, (b) z_2, (c) z_1z_2, (d) z_1/z_2.* [LON]

27. *(a) $a = 2+5i$, $b = 5+i$ and $c = 10+11i$ are complex numbers represented by the points A, B and C respectively in the Argand Diagram. Express $(c-a)/(b-a)$ in the form $p+iq$ and hence, or otherwise, show that the angle BAC is a right angle. Calculate the angle ABC correct to the nearest degree.*

If the number z (represented by Z) is such that $|z-b| = 12$, sketch the locus of Z in the Argand Diagram and prove that all points of the triangle ABC lie inside the locus.

(b) If $z = x+iy$ and $\bar{z} = x-iy$ solve (for z) the equation $z+5\bar{z} = 6+8i$.

[SUJB]

28. *The complex number z satisfies $\frac{z}{z+2} = 2-i$. Find the real and imaginary parts of z, and the modulus and argument of z.* [OXF]

29. *Three landmarks P, Q and R are on the same horizontal level. Landmark Q is 3 km on a bearing of 328° from P, landmark R is 6 km and on a bearing of 191° from Q. Calculate the distance and the bearing of R from P, giving your answers in km to one decimal place and in degrees to the nearest degree.* [LON]

30. *The triangle ABC is horizontal with $AB = 25a$, $AC = 26a$ and $BC = 17a$.*

The point P lies on BC such that angle APB is 90°. Calculate

(a) *the area of triangle ABC,*

(b) *the length of AP.*

The point Y lies vertically above A, where $YA = 18a$. Calculate, to 0·1°,

(c) *the acute angle between YB and the horizontal,*

(d) *the acute angle between plane YBC and the horizontal.* [OXF]

31. *The square ABCD lies in a horizontal plane. The sides AB, BC, CD and DA each have length a. The points P and Q are at a height h vertically above the points B and D respectively. Show that the triangle APQ has area $\frac{1}{2}(2h^2a^2 + a^4)^{\frac{1}{2}}$ and express the cosine of the angle between AQ and PD in terms of a and h. Prove also that $\cos \widehat{PAQ} = (\cos \widehat{BPC})^2$.* [OXF]

9 Vectors

Section 41 Displacements and Position Vectors

41.1 Displacement Vectors

The movement from one point to another is called a **displacement** or **displacement vector**. This displacement is shown in a diagram as an arrow from the **initial point** to the **final point**.

The displacement shown is denoted by $\overrightarrow{AB}$ or sometimes $\overrightarrow{\mathbf{AB}}$. The arrow above the letter shows the sense of the displacement. Displacements can also be denoted by bold single letters $\mathbf{a} = \overrightarrow{AB}$ for example.

For a given origin and set of coordinate axes the displacement vector is specified by the changes in coordinates from A to B.

In two dimensions, if A is the point (x_1, y_1) and B is the point (x_2, y_2) then $\overrightarrow{AB}$ has **components** $x_2 - x_1$ and $y_2 - y_1$. The displacement is written as a **column vector**

$$\begin{pmatrix} x_2 - x_1 \\ y_2 - y_1 \end{pmatrix}$$

The components completely determine a vector, any two vectors with the same components are equal no matter where the initial points are.

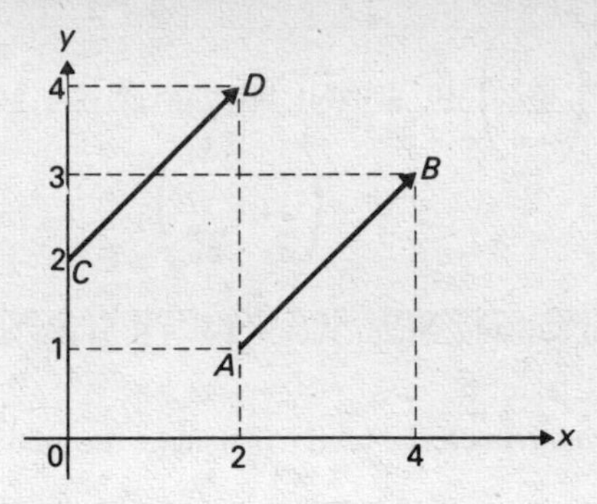

The vectors $\overrightarrow{AB}$ and $\overrightarrow{CD}$ above are equal. They are necessarily parallel and equal in length.

Example

If P has coordinates $(-3, 10)$ and Q has coordinates $(1, 7)$ then $\overrightarrow{PQ}$ is denoted by the column vector $\begin{pmatrix} 4 \\ -3 \end{pmatrix}$

In three dimensions three coordinates axes are required.

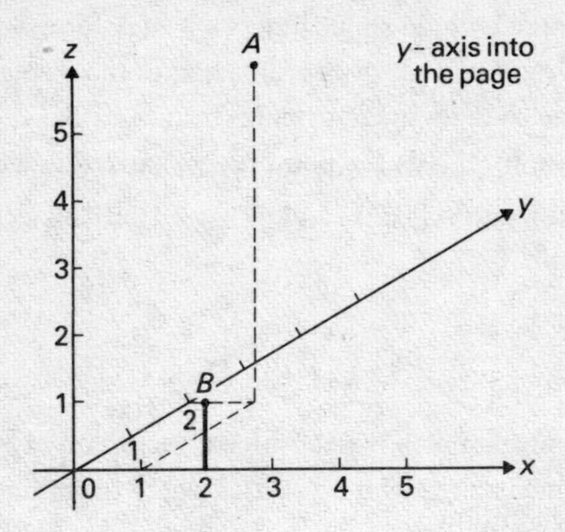

The diagram shows the points $A(1, 2, 5)$ and $B(2, 0, 1)$. The displacement

$\overrightarrow{AB}$ is written $\begin{pmatrix} 1 \\ -2 \\ -4 \end{pmatrix}$. In general for $P(x_1, y_1, z_1)$ and $Q(x_2, y_2, z_2)$

$$\overrightarrow{PQ} = \begin{pmatrix} x_2 - x_1 \\ y_2 - y_1 \\ z_2 - z_1 \end{pmatrix}$$

The *modulus* of a displacement vector $\mathbf{a} \equiv \overrightarrow{AB}$ is the length AB, often denoted by $|\overrightarrow{AB}|$, $|\mathbf{a}|$, or a.

Pythagoras' Theorem can be used to calculate the modulus of a vector.

Example

1. If $\mathbf{a} = \begin{pmatrix} 1 \\ 3 \end{pmatrix}$ then $|\mathbf{a}| = \sqrt{1^2 + 3^2} = \sqrt{10}$.

2. If $\mathbf{b} = \begin{pmatrix} 1 \\ 4 \\ 7 \end{pmatrix}$ then $|\mathbf{b}| = \sqrt{1^2 + 4^2 + 7^2}$
$= \sqrt{66}$

(Note the extension of Pythagoras' Theorem to three dimensions.)

41.2 Addition of Vectors

The displacement $\overrightarrow{AB}$ can be followed by the displacement $\overrightarrow{BC}$ resulting in the displacement $\overrightarrow{AC}$.

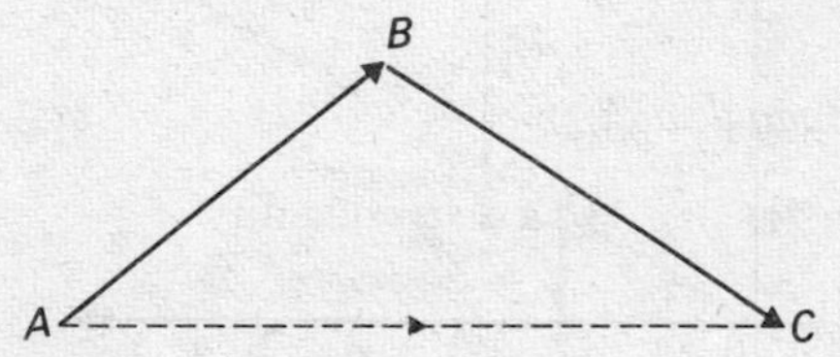

We write this as addition

$$\overrightarrow{AB} + \overrightarrow{BC} = \overrightarrow{AC}$$

This can be generalized to the addition of many vectors. $\overrightarrow{AB} + \overrightarrow{BC} + \overrightarrow{CD} + \overrightarrow{DC} + \ldots + \overrightarrow{YZ} = \overrightarrow{AZ}$.

Two vectors that do not join up can also be added.

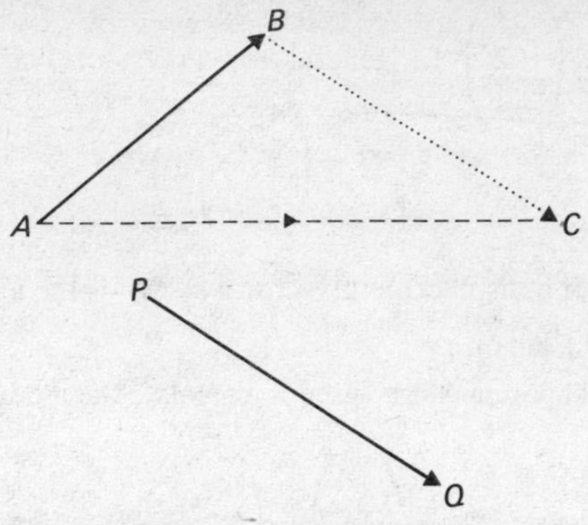

PQ is parallel to vector $\overrightarrow{BC}$ so that $\overrightarrow{PQ} = \overrightarrow{BC}$. Thus

$$\overrightarrow{AB} + \overrightarrow{PQ} \equiv \overrightarrow{AB} + \overrightarrow{BC} = \overrightarrow{AC}$$

$$\text{If } \overrightarrow{AB} = \binom{x_1}{y_1} = \overrightarrow{BC} = \binom{x_2}{y_2} \text{ then}$$

$$\overrightarrow{AC} = \begin{pmatrix} x_1 + x_2 \\ y_2 + y_2 \end{pmatrix}$$

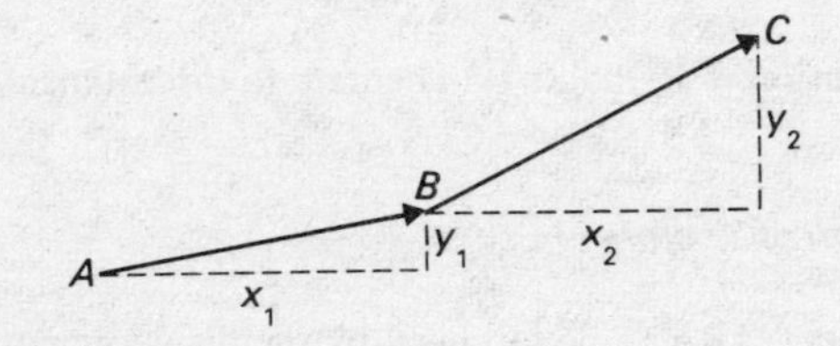

This is why the process of joining displacements is called addition.

41.3 Scalar Multiplication

Any real number $\lambda \in \mathbb{R}$ is called a **scalar** quantity.

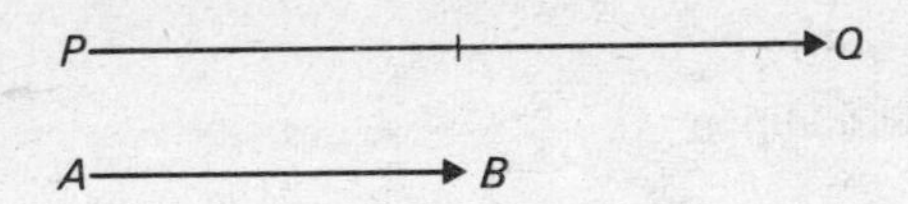

$\overrightarrow{PQ}$ is parallel to and twice the length of $\overrightarrow{AB}$. Thus $\overrightarrow{PQ} = \overrightarrow{AB} + \overrightarrow{AB} \equiv 2\overrightarrow{AB}$.

In general the vector $\lambda\mathbf{a}$ is parallel to $\mathbf{a}$ and has length $|\lambda||\mathbf{a}|$.

If λ is *negative* then $\lambda\mathbf{a}$ and $\mathbf{a}$ are in opposite directions.

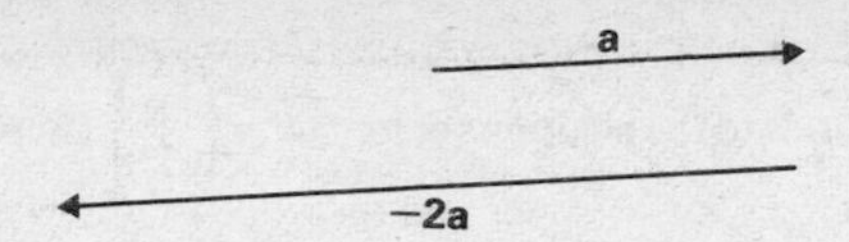

The components of $\lambda\mathbf{a}$ are found by multiplying the components of $\mathbf{a}$ by λ.

Examples

1. $3\begin{pmatrix}2\\1\\5\end{pmatrix}-6\begin{pmatrix}1\\7\\8\end{pmatrix}=\begin{pmatrix}6\\3\\15\end{pmatrix}-\begin{pmatrix}6\\42\\48\end{pmatrix}=\begin{pmatrix}0\\-39\\-33\end{pmatrix}$

2. If $\mathbf{a}=\begin{pmatrix}2\\1\\5\end{pmatrix}$, $\mathbf{b}=\begin{pmatrix}1\\0\\1\end{pmatrix}$ and $\mathbf{p}=\begin{pmatrix}x\\y\\z\end{pmatrix}$ solve the vector equation $2\mathbf{a}-3\mathbf{p}=\mathbf{b}$.

Answer

$$3\mathbf{p}=2\mathbf{a}-\mathbf{b}$$

$$\Rightarrow \quad \mathbf{p}=\tfrac{2}{3}\mathbf{a}-\tfrac{1}{3}\mathbf{b}$$

$$\Rightarrow \quad \begin{pmatrix}x\\y\\z\end{pmatrix}=\frac{2}{3}\begin{pmatrix}2\\1\\5\end{pmatrix}-\frac{1}{3}\begin{pmatrix}1\\0\\1\end{pmatrix}=\begin{pmatrix}\frac{4}{3}-\frac{1}{3}\\\frac{2}{3}-0\\\frac{10}{3}-\frac{1}{3}\end{pmatrix}=\begin{pmatrix}1\\\frac{2}{3}\\3\end{pmatrix}$$

$$\Rightarrow \quad \mathbf{p}=\begin{pmatrix}1\\\frac{2}{3}\\3\end{pmatrix}$$

41.4 Position Vectors

Any point has an associated displacement from the origin. The point

$P(x, y, z)$ corresponds to the **position vector** $\overrightarrow{OP} = \begin{pmatrix} x \\ y \\ z \end{pmatrix}$. (In two dimensions only x and y-coordinates are used.)

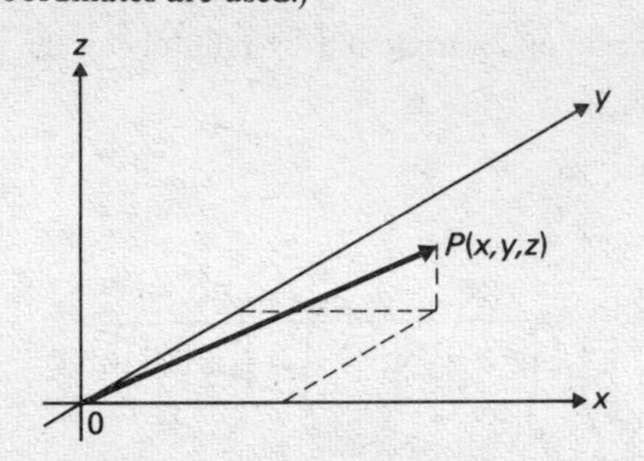

Examples

1. Find the position vector of the midpoint of the line segment joining $A(1, 3, 5)$ and $B(-1, 2, 7)$.

Answer

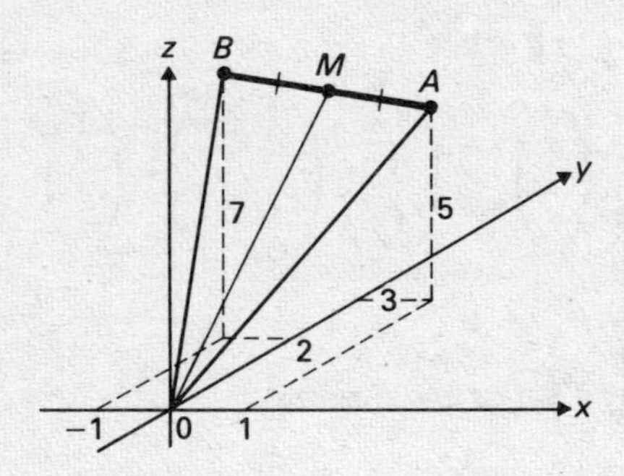

Let the midpoint be M, then M has coordinates

$$\left(\frac{1-1}{2}, \frac{3+2}{2}, \frac{5+7}{2}\right)$$

page 239

$$\equiv (0, 2{\cdot}5, 6)$$

The position vector for M is $\overrightarrow{OM} = \begin{pmatrix} 0 \\ 2{\cdot}5 \\ 6 \end{pmatrix}$. In general, $\overrightarrow{OM} = \frac{1}{2}(\mathbf{a} + \mathbf{b})$.

2. If A has position vector $\mathbf{a}$ and B has position vector $\mathbf{b}$ then $\overrightarrow{AB} = \mathbf{b} - \mathbf{a}$.

Proof

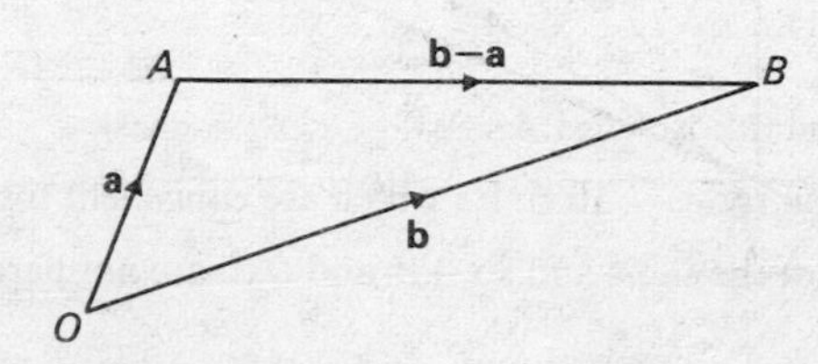

$$\overrightarrow{AB} = \overrightarrow{AO} + \overrightarrow{OB}$$ addition of displacements

$$= -\mathbf{a} + \mathbf{b}$$ $\overrightarrow{BO} = -\overrightarrow{OB}$, reversal of direction

$$= \mathbf{b} - \mathbf{a}$$

$$\therefore \overrightarrow{AB} = \mathbf{b} - \mathbf{a}$$

This is a useful general result which may be quoted.

Section 42 Directions, Lines and Planes

42.1 Direction Ratios and Cosines

The direction of a displacement vector is specified by the ratio of its components.

The **direction ratios** of vector $\begin{pmatrix} x \\ y \\ z \end{pmatrix}$ are $x:y:z$. Two vectors are parallel if they have equivalent direction ratios.

Examples

1. Find the direction ratios of the vector $\overrightarrow{AB}$ where A is the point (2, 5, 7) and B is (−3, 8, 11). The point C has coordinates (−10, 6, 10). Determine whether AB and OC are parallel.

Answer

$$AB = \mathbf{b} - \mathbf{a} = \begin{pmatrix} -3 \\ 8 \\ 11 \end{pmatrix} - \begin{pmatrix} 2 \\ 5 \\ 7 \end{pmatrix} = \begin{pmatrix} -5 \\ 3 \\ 4 \end{pmatrix}$$

$\overrightarrow{AB}$ has direction ratios −5:3:4.

$\overrightarrow{OC}$ has direction ratios −10:6:10, which are equivalent to −5:3:5.

The ratios are not the same and so $\overrightarrow{AB}$ and $\overrightarrow{OC}$ are not parallel.

2. Find the coordinates of the point P such that $\overrightarrow{PQ}$ is parallel to $\begin{pmatrix} 2 \\ 1 \\ 2 \end{pmatrix}$, where

$$\overrightarrow{OQ} = \begin{pmatrix} -1 \\ 5 \\ 7 \end{pmatrix}, \text{ and } |\overrightarrow{PQ}| = 12$$

Answer

Let $\overrightarrow{PQ} = \lambda \begin{pmatrix} 2 \\ 1 \\ 2n \end{pmatrix}$, so that

$|\overrightarrow{PQ}| = 3\lambda$.

But $|PQ| = 12 \Rightarrow \lambda = 4$

$$\text{Hence } \overrightarrow{PQ} = \begin{pmatrix} 8 \\ 4 \\ 8 \end{pmatrix}$$

But $\overrightarrow{PQ} = \mathbf{q} - \mathbf{p}$

$$\therefore \begin{pmatrix} 8 \\ 4 \\ 8 \end{pmatrix} = \begin{pmatrix} -1 \\ 5 \\ 7 \end{pmatrix} - \mathbf{p}$$

$$\therefore \mathbf{p} = \begin{pmatrix} -1 \\ 5 \\ 7 \end{pmatrix} - \begin{pmatrix} 8 \\ 4 \\ 8 \end{pmatrix} = \begin{pmatrix} -9 \\ 1 \\ -1 \end{pmatrix}$$

$\therefore$ P is the point $(-9, 1, -1)$

If vector **a** has direction ratios $x{:}y{:}z$ then the **direction cosines** l, m, n of **a** are defined by $l = \frac{x}{|\mathbf{a}|}$, $m = \frac{y}{|\mathbf{a}|}$, $n = \frac{z}{|\mathbf{a}|}$. The ratios are divided by the modulus of **a**.

Notice that if $\hat{\mathbf{a}} = \begin{pmatrix} l \\ m \\ n \end{pmatrix}$ then $|\hat{\mathbf{a}}| = 1$.

(Proof: *exercise*).

A vector with modulus 1 is called a **unit vector**.

Two vectors are parallel if they have the same direction cosines.

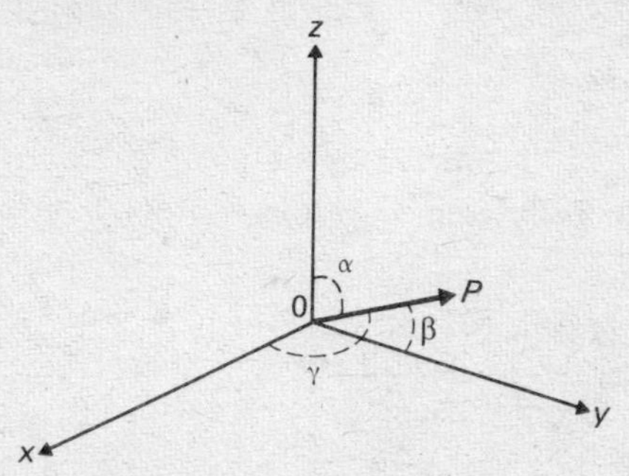

The name direction cosines arises from the fact that $l = \cos\alpha$, $m = \cos\beta$ and $n = \cos\gamma$ where α, β and γ are the angles that **a** makes with the x, y and z-axes respectively.

In two dimensions, the direction ratio of $\overrightarrow{OA} = \binom{x}{y}$ is $x{:}y$, the reciprocal of the gradient of OA. Thus direction ratios and cosines are an extension of the idea of gradient to three dimensions.

Note: If vector $\overrightarrow{AB}$ is perpendicular to one of the coordinate axes, the corresponding direction cosine is 0 (since $\cos 90° = 0$).

Example

The displacement vector $\begin{pmatrix} 1 \\ 0 \\ 1 \end{pmatrix}$ has direction ratios 1:0:1 and direction cosines $\frac{1}{\sqrt{2}}$, 0, $\frac{1}{\sqrt{2}}$. The vector makes angles of 45°, 90°, 45° with the x, y and z-axes respectively

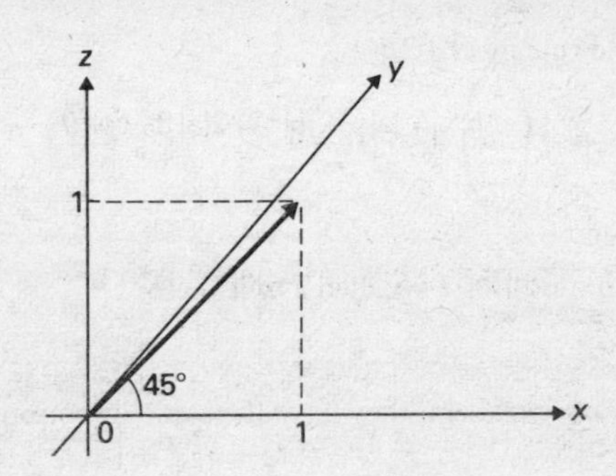

42.2 Scalar Product

The **scalar product** of displacement vectors

$\mathbf{a} = \begin{pmatrix} x_1 \\ y_1 \\ z_1 \end{pmatrix}$ and $\mathbf{b} = \begin{pmatrix} x_2 \\ y_2 \\ z_2 \end{pmatrix}$ is defined as

$$\mathbf{a}.\mathbf{b} = x_1x_2 + y_1y_2 + z_1z_2$$

It turns out that

$$\mathbf{a}.\mathbf{b} = |\mathbf{a}||\mathbf{b}| \cos \theta$$

where θ is the angle between vectors **a** and **b**.

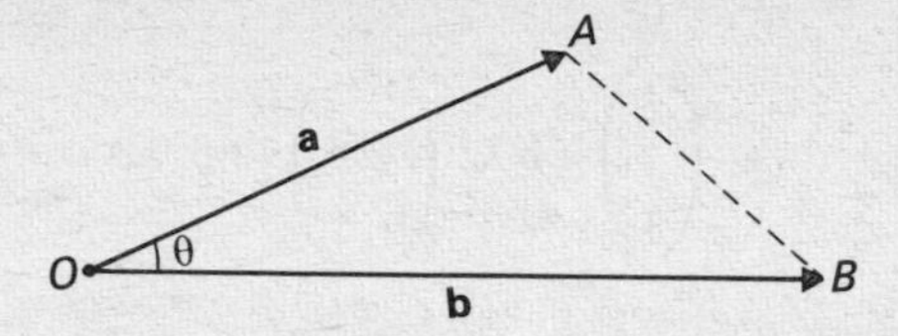

Proof

From the cosine rule in $\triangle AOB$

$$|\mathbf{a}-\mathbf{b}|^2 = |\mathbf{a}|^2 + |\mathbf{b}|^2 - 2|\mathbf{a}|\,|\mathbf{b}|\cos\theta$$

(using $\overrightarrow{AB} = \mathbf{b} - \mathbf{a}$).

$$\Rightarrow \qquad 2|\mathbf{a}|\,|\mathbf{b}|\cos\theta = |\mathbf{a}|^2 + |\mathbf{b}|^2 - |\mathbf{a}-\mathbf{b}|^2$$

$$= x_1{}^2 + y_1{}^2 + z_1{}^2 + x_2{}^2 + y_2{}^2 + z_2{}^2$$

$$-((x_1 - x_2)^2 + (y_1 - y_2)^2 + (z_1 - z_2)^2$$

$$= 2(x_1x_2 + y_1y_2 + z_1z_2)$$

$$\Rightarrow \qquad |\mathbf{a}|\,|\mathbf{b}|\cos\theta = x_1x_2 + y_1y_2 + z_1z_2 = \mathbf{a}.\mathbf{b}$$

From this identity we deduce

1. **a** is perpendicular to $\mathbf{b} \Leftrightarrow \mathbf{a}.\mathbf{b} = \mathbf{0}$ $(\mathbf{a} \neq 0, \mathbf{b} \neq 0)$ (in which case $\theta = 90°$).
2. $\mathbf{a}.\mathbf{a} = |\mathbf{a}|\,|\mathbf{a}|\,|\cos 0° = |\mathbf{a}|^2$.
3. If $|\mathbf{b}| = 1$ then $\mathbf{a}.\mathbf{b} = |\mathbf{a}|\cos\theta \equiv$ *projection* of **a** in the direction of **b**.

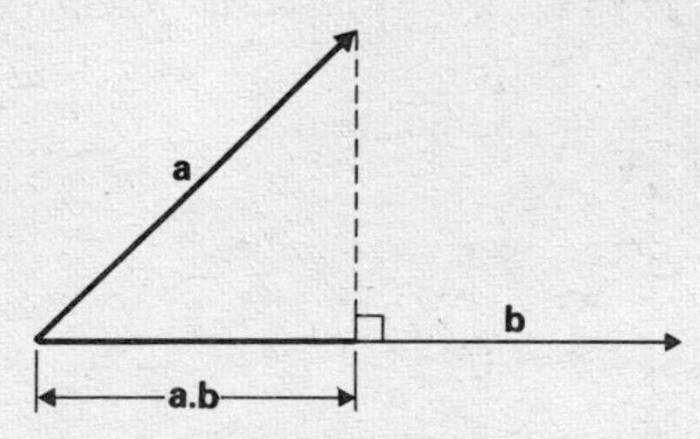

The angle between two vectors **a** and **b** can be calculated from the formula.

$$\boxed{\cos\theta = \frac{\mathbf{a}.\mathbf{b}}{|\mathbf{a}|\,|\mathbf{b}|}}$$

Examples

1.

$$\mathbf{a} = \begin{pmatrix} 1 \\ 1 \\ 1 \end{pmatrix} \quad \mathbf{b} = \begin{pmatrix} 2 \\ -3 \\ 5 \end{pmatrix}$$

$$\Rightarrow \qquad |\mathbf{a}| = \sqrt{3} \qquad |\mathbf{b}| = \sqrt{38}$$

and

$$\mathbf{a}.\mathbf{b} = 1 \times 2 + 1 \times (-3) + 1 \times 5 = 4$$

$$\therefore \qquad \cos\theta = \frac{4}{\sqrt{3}\sqrt{38}} = 0{\cdot}3746$$

$\therefore$ the acute angle, θ, between the vectors is $68°$.

2. $\mathbf{a} = \mathbf{i} + \mathbf{j} + \mathbf{k}$, $\mathbf{b} = \mathbf{i} - 2\mathbf{j} - 2\mathbf{k}$ (see below)

$$\therefore \cos\theta = \frac{-3}{3\sqrt{3}} = \frac{-1}{\sqrt{3}}$$

$$\Rightarrow \theta = 125{\cdot}3°$$

The obtuse angle results from $\mathbf{a}.\mathbf{b} < 0$. If the *acute* angle is required, take $180° - 125{\cdot}3° = 54{\cdot}7°$.

42.3 Basis Vectors

The vectors $\mathbf{i} = \begin{pmatrix} 1 \\ 0 \\ 0 \end{pmatrix}, \mathbf{j} = \begin{pmatrix} 0 \\ 1 \\ 0 \end{pmatrix}, \mathbf{k} = \begin{pmatrix} 0 \\ 0 \\ 1 \end{pmatrix}$ are the position vectors of points 1 unit away from O on the coordinate axes.

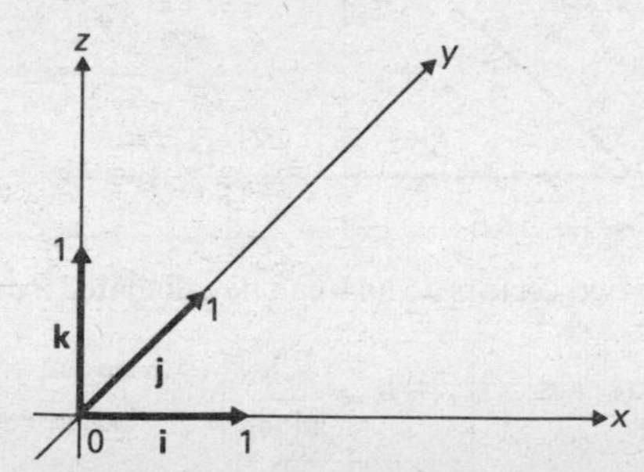

i, **j**, **k** each have unit length and are perpendicular.

Any vector can be written as a linear combination of these basis vectors:

$$\begin{pmatrix} x \\ y \\ z \end{pmatrix} \equiv x\mathbf{i} + y\mathbf{j} + z\mathbf{k}.$$

(In fact any 3 vectors which are not in the same plane form a basis and any vector can be expressed uniquely as a linear combination of these basis vectors.)

Notice that $\mathbf{i}.\mathbf{i} = \mathbf{j}.\mathbf{j} = \mathbf{k}.\mathbf{k} = 1$ and $\mathbf{i}.\mathbf{j} = \mathbf{j}.\mathbf{k} = \mathbf{k}.\mathbf{i} = 0$. An important result is

$$\boxed{\mathbf{a}.(\mathbf{b} + \mathbf{c}) = \mathbf{a}.\mathbf{b} + \mathbf{a}.\mathbf{c}}$$

Proof

Let $\mathbf{a} = \begin{pmatrix} x_1 \\ y_1 \\ z_1 \end{pmatrix}$, $\mathbf{b} = \begin{pmatrix} x_2 \\ y_2 \\ z_2 \end{pmatrix}$, $\mathbf{c} = \begin{pmatrix} x_3 \\ y_3 \\ z_3 \end{pmatrix}$, so that

$$\begin{aligned} \mathbf{a}.\mathbf{b} + \mathbf{a}.\mathbf{c} &= x_1x_2 + y_1y_2 + z_1z_2 + x_1x_3 + y_1y_3 + z_1z_3 \\ &= x_1(x_2 + x_3) + y_1(y_2 + y_3) + z_1(z_2 + z_3) \\ &= \begin{pmatrix} x_1 \\ y_1 \\ z_1 \end{pmatrix} . \begin{pmatrix} x_2 + x_3 \\ y_1 + y_3 \\ z_1 + z_3 \end{pmatrix} \\ &= \mathbf{a}.(\mathbf{b} + \mathbf{c}) \end{aligned}$$

42.4 Vector Equation of a Straight Line

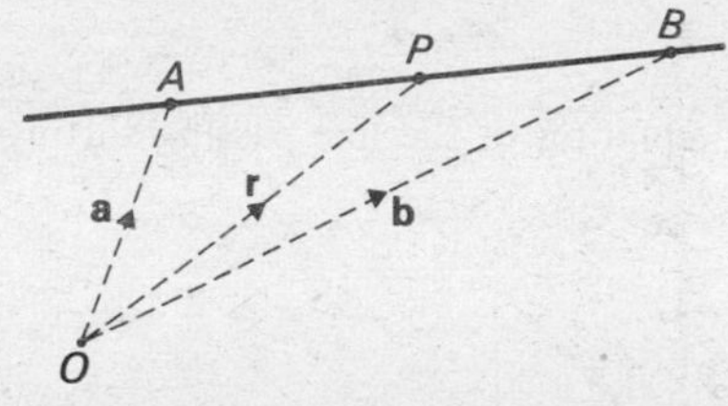

Consider a line passing through points A and B with position vectors **a** and **b**.

The equation of this line should give the position vector of a general point on the line in terms of **a** and **b**.

Let P be any point on the line and $\overrightarrow{OP} = \mathbf{r}$.

Then $\overrightarrow{OP} = \overrightarrow{OA} + \overrightarrow{AP}$

$$= \overrightarrow{OA} + \lambda\overrightarrow{AB}$$

where λ is some real number, the **parameter** (since AP and AB are parallel $\overrightarrow{AP}$ is a scalar multiple of $\overrightarrow{AB}$). Thus

$$\boxed{\mathbf{r} = \mathbf{a} + \lambda(\mathbf{b} - \mathbf{a})}$$

since $\overrightarrow{AB} = \mathbf{b} - \mathbf{a}$, which can also be written as

$$\boxed{\mathbf{r} = (1 - \lambda)\mathbf{a} + \lambda\mathbf{b}}$$

Each value of λ gives a different point on the line. $\lambda = 1$ corresponds to point B, $\lambda = 0$ corresponds to point A.

In general, P divides line segment AB in the ratio $\lambda : 1 - \lambda$.

The line can also be specified by a fixed point and a direction.

The equation of the line through the point with position vector **a** and parallel to vector **m** is

$$\boxed{\mathbf{r} = \mathbf{a} + \lambda\mathbf{m}}$$

where $\lambda \in \mathbb{R}$.

(**m** may be specified by its direction ratios.)

Examples

1. Find the vector equation of the line passing through points $(3, 1, 7)$ and $(-1, 0, 5)$.

Answer

$$\mathbf{a} = 3\mathbf{i} + \mathbf{j} + 7\mathbf{k}$$
$$\mathbf{b} = -\mathbf{i} + 5\mathbf{k}$$

The equation is

$$\mathbf{r} = 3\mathbf{i} + \mathbf{j} + 7\mathbf{k} + \lambda(-4\mathbf{i} - \mathbf{j} - 2\mathbf{k})$$

$$\Rightarrow \quad \mathbf{r} = (3 - 4\lambda)\mathbf{i} + (1 - \lambda)\mathbf{j} + (7 - 2\lambda)\mathbf{k}$$

(It is usual to write the equation in terms of the basis vectors **i**, **j**, **k**.)

2. Find the vector equation of the line passing through the point with position vector $2\mathbf{i} - \mathbf{j} + 3\mathbf{k}$ and parallel to the vector $\mathbf{i} + \mathbf{j} + \mathbf{k}$.

Answer

$$\mathbf{r} = (2\mathbf{i} - \mathbf{j} + 3\mathbf{k}) + \lambda(\mathbf{i} + \mathbf{j} + \mathbf{k})$$

The answer can be left in this form or expressed as

$$\mathbf{r} = (2 + \lambda)\mathbf{i} + (\lambda - 1)\mathbf{j} + (3 + \lambda)\mathbf{k}$$

CARTESIAN FORM OF THE STRAIGHT LINE EQUATION

Since $\mathbf{r} = \overrightarrow{OP} = \begin{pmatrix} x \\ y \\ z \end{pmatrix}$ we can find x, y, z equations to represent a straight line. For example 2 above,

$$\mathbf{r} = x\mathbf{i} + y\mathbf{j} + z\mathbf{k}$$

$\Rightarrow \quad x = 2 + \lambda, \; y = \lambda - 1$ and $z = 3 + \lambda$. matching the
Thus $\lambda = x - 2, \lambda = y + 1$ and $\lambda = z - 3$. components

Hence $x - 2 = y + 1 = z - 3$ are the cartesian equations of the line.

In general, the line through point (x_1, y_1, z_1) with direction ratios $l:m:n$ has cartesian equation

$$\boxed{\frac{x - x_1}{l} = \frac{y - y_1}{m} = \frac{z - z_1}{n}}$$

Conversely given the cartesian form, you can read off the direction ratios and coordinates of the fixed point.

Example

$$\frac{x-1}{2}=\frac{1-y}{3}=\frac{2z+1}{4}$$

$$\Rightarrow \quad \frac{x-1}{2}=\frac{y-1}{-3}=\frac{z+\frac{1}{2}}{2} \qquad \text{(to match general form)}$$

$\Rightarrow$ The line passes through $(1, 1, -\frac{1}{2})$ and is parallel to $2\mathbf{i}-3\mathbf{j}+2\mathbf{k}$.
The vector equation is

$$\mathbf{r}=\mathbf{i}+\mathbf{j}-\tfrac{1}{2}\mathbf{k}+\lambda(2\mathbf{i}-3\mathbf{j}+2\mathbf{k})$$

42.5 Parallel and Intersecting Lines

The direction ratios (cosines) of a line are defined to be the direction ratios (cosines) of a vector parallel to the line.

Thus the direction ratios of line $\mathbf{r}=\mathbf{a}+\lambda\mathbf{m}$ are the same as the ratios of vector $\mathbf{m}$.

Two lines are *parallel* if they have the same direction ratios (or cosines).

Example

$$\mathbf{r}=2\mathbf{i}+\lambda(\mathbf{i}-\mathbf{j})$$

and

$$\mathbf{r}=3\mathbf{i}+\mathbf{j}+\mathbf{k}+\mu(\mathbf{i}-\mathbf{j})$$

are parallel.

Note: different letters must be used for the parameters of different lines.

Two lines are *perpendicular* if their direction vectors are perpendicular.

Example

$$\mathbf{r}=\mathbf{i}+\mathbf{j}+\mathbf{k}+\lambda(\mathbf{i}-\mathbf{j}-\mathbf{k})$$

and

$$\mathbf{r}=2\mathbf{i}+\mathbf{k}+\mu(\mathbf{i}+2\mathbf{j}-\mathbf{k})$$

have direction vectors

$$\mathbf{m}_1 = \mathbf{i} - \mathbf{j} - \mathbf{k}$$

and

$$\mathbf{m}_2 = \mathbf{i} + 2\mathbf{j} - \mathbf{k}$$

respectively. Thus $\mathbf{m}_1 . \mathbf{m}_2 = 1 - 2 + 1 = 0$. The lines are perpendicular.

In two dimensions, any two non-parallel lines must intersect. This is not true in three dimensions, as two lines in different parallel planes cannot intersect.

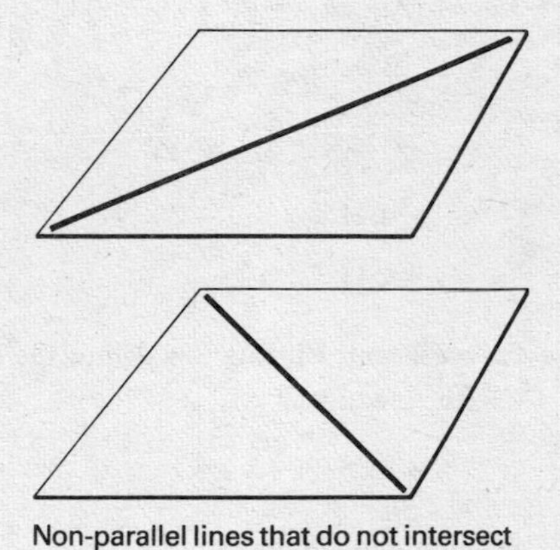

Non-parallel lines that do not intersect

In particular, perpendicular lines need not intersect. To determine whether two lines intersect, we try to solve the corresponding simultaneous equations.

Examples

1. Show that the lines

$$\mathbf{r} = (\mathbf{i} + \mathbf{j} - \mathbf{k}) + \lambda(\mathbf{i} + \mathbf{k})$$

and

$$\mathbf{r} = (2\mathbf{i} - \mathbf{j} + \mathbf{k}) + \mu(\mathbf{i} + 2\mathbf{j} - 2\mathbf{k})$$

intersect, and state the coordinates of the point of intersection.

Answer

For a point of intersection

$$(\mathbf{i}+\mathbf{j}-\mathbf{k})+\lambda(\mathbf{i}+\mathbf{k}) = (2\mathbf{i}-\mathbf{j}+3\mathbf{k})+\mu(\mathbf{i}+2\mathbf{j}-2\mathbf{k})$$

$$\Rightarrow \quad (1+\lambda)\mathbf{i}+(1)\mathbf{j}+(-1+\lambda)\mathbf{k} = (2+\mu)\mathbf{i}+(-1+2\mu)\mathbf{j}+(3-2\mu)\mathbf{k}$$

Matching components:

$$1+\lambda = 2+\mu \qquad (1)$$

$$1 = -1+2\mu \qquad (2)$$

$$-1+\lambda = 3-2\mu \qquad (3)$$

Equation (2) $\Rightarrow$ $\mu = 1$

$$(1) \Rightarrow \lambda = 1+\mu = 2$$

Check in (3) $\quad \text{LHS} = -1+2 = 1$

$$\text{RHS} = 3-2 = 1$$

The equations are **consistent**. Putting $\lambda = 2$ into the equation of the first line (*or* $\mu = 1$ into the second)

$$\mathbf{r} = 3\mathbf{i}+\mathbf{j}+\mathbf{k}$$

The point of intersection is (3, 1, 1).

2. Determine whether the lines

(*a*) through $A(1, 3, 5)$ and $B(-1, 0, 2)$ and
(*b*) $\mathbf{r} = 2\mathbf{i}+s(2\mathbf{i}-\mathbf{j}+\mathbf{k})$ $\qquad (s \in \mathbb{R})$

intersect.

Answer

(*a*) The equation is

$$\begin{aligned}\mathbf{r} &= (1-\lambda)\mathbf{a}+\lambda\mathbf{b}\\ &= (1-\lambda)(\mathbf{i}+3\mathbf{j}+5\mathbf{k})+\lambda(-\mathbf{i}+2\mathbf{k})\\ &= (1-2\lambda)\mathbf{i}+(3-3\lambda)\mathbf{j}+(5-3\lambda)\mathbf{k}\end{aligned}$$

Equating with (*b*)

$$2\mathbf{i} + s(2\mathbf{i} - \mathbf{j} + \mathbf{k}) = (1 - 2\lambda)\mathbf{i} + (3 - 3\lambda)\mathbf{j} + (5 - 3\lambda)\mathbf{k}$$

$$\Rightarrow \qquad 2 + 2s = 1 - 2\lambda \qquad (1)$$

$$-s = 3 - 3\lambda \qquad (2)$$

$$s = 5 - 3\lambda \qquad (3)$$

Adding (2) + (3)

$$\Rightarrow \qquad 0 = 8 - 6\lambda$$

$$\Rightarrow \qquad \lambda = \tfrac{4}{3}$$

$$(3) \Rightarrow s = 5 - 4 = 1$$

Check in (1)

$$\text{LHS} = 2 + 2 = 4 \qquad \text{RHS} = 1 - \tfrac{8}{3} = -\tfrac{2}{3} \neq 4.$$

The equations are not consistent, the lines do not intersect.

42.6 Vector Equation of a Plane

1 PARAMETRIC FORM

Whereas a line is determined by 2 points, 3 points are required to specify a plane.

The vector equation of the plane passing through points A, B, C with position vectors $\mathbf{a}$, $\mathbf{b}$, $\mathbf{c}$ respectively is

$$\boxed{\mathbf{r} = \mathbf{a} + \lambda(\mathbf{b} - \mathbf{a}) + \mu(\mathbf{c} - \mathbf{a})} \qquad (1)$$

where $\lambda, \mu \in \mathbb{R}$ are the two parameters and $\mathbf{r}$ is the position vector of a general point P in the plane

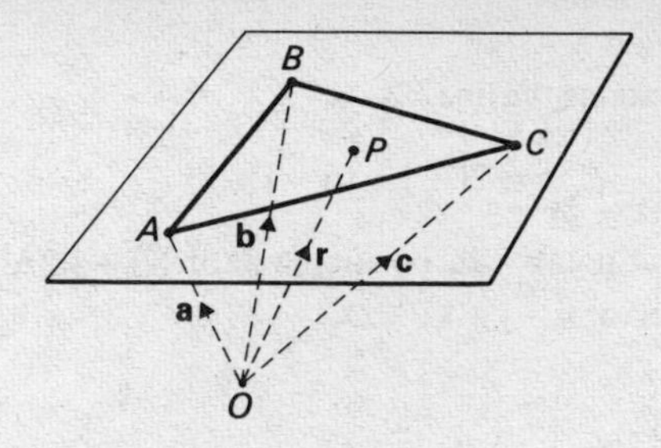

Alternatively the plane can be specified by a point and two direction vectors.

The plane passing through the point with position vector **a** and parallel to vectors **m** and **n** has equation

$$\boxed{\mathbf{r} = \mathbf{a} + \lambda\mathbf{m} + \mu\mathbf{n}} \qquad (2)$$

Each pair of values λ, μ gives the position vector of a point in the plane.

Example

1. Find the vector equation of the plane containing the points $A(1, 0, 1)$, $B(0, 1, 1)$ and $C(1, 1, 0)$.

Answer

The equation is

$$\mathbf{r} = \mathbf{i} + \mathbf{k} + \lambda(-\mathbf{i} + \mathbf{j}) + \mu(\mathbf{j} - \mathbf{k}) \qquad \text{from (1)}$$

or

$$\mathbf{r} = (1 - \lambda)\mathbf{i} + (\lambda + \mu)\mathbf{j} + (1 - \mu)\mathbf{k}$$

2. Find the equation of the plane which contains the line

$$\mathbf{r} = 2\mathbf{i} + \mathbf{j} + t(\mathbf{i} - \mathbf{j} + \mathbf{k})$$

and is parallel to the vector $\mathbf{m} = \mathbf{i} + 2\mathbf{j} + 3\mathbf{k}$.

Answer

Since the plane contains the line

$$\mathbf{r} = 2\mathbf{i} + \mathbf{j} + t(\mathbf{i} - \mathbf{j} + \mathbf{k})$$

it must contain the point with position vector $(2\mathbf{i} + \mathbf{j})$. Also, the plane is parallel to the vector $(\mathbf{i} - \mathbf{j} + \mathbf{k})$.

The equation is

$$\mathbf{r} = 2\mathbf{i} + \mathbf{j} + \lambda(\mathbf{i} - \mathbf{j} + \mathbf{k}) + \mu(\mathbf{i} + 2\mathbf{j} + 3\mathbf{k}).$$

2. SCALAR PRODUCT FORM

A plane can also be specified by a vector $\mathbf{n}$ *perpendicular* to the plane and a point A in the plane.

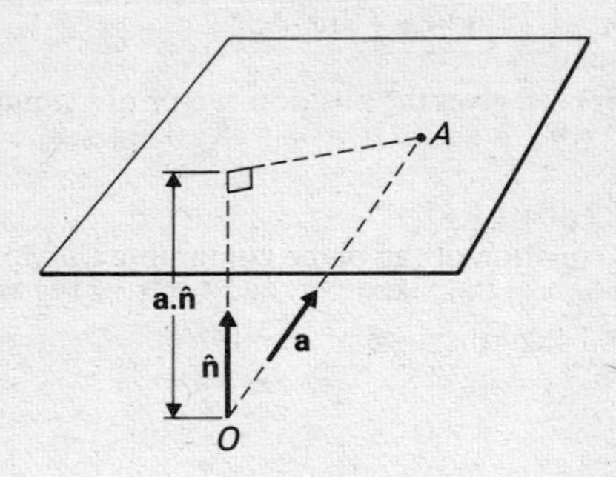

Let $\mathbf{n}$ be perpendicular to the plane and $\overrightarrow{OA} = \mathbf{a}$, where A lies in the plane.

$$\boxed{\hat{\mathbf{n}} = \frac{\mathbf{n}}{|\mathbf{n}|}}$$

is a unit vector and

$\mathbf{a}.\hat{\mathbf{n}}$ = projection of $\mathbf{a}$ in direction of $\hat{\mathbf{n}}$. page 419

This projection is simply the perpendicular distance from O to the plane, and is the same no matter which point, A, is taken in the plane.

In particular $\mathbf{r}.\hat{\mathbf{n}} = \mathbf{a}.\hat{\mathbf{n}} = p$ where $\mathbf{r}$ is the position vector of any point in the plane and p is the perpendicular distance from O to the plane.

Thus we have two equations of this plane

$$\mathbf{r}.\hat{\mathbf{n}} = p$$

$$\mathbf{r}.\mathbf{n} = \mathbf{a}.\mathbf{n}$$

(Multiplying both sides by $|\mathbf{n}|$, so that the perpendicular vector need not be a unit vector in the second equation.)

Examples

1. Find a vector equation of the plane passing through $A(1, 3, 2)$ and perpendicular to the vector $\mathbf{i} + \mathbf{j} + \mathbf{k}$.

Answer

$$\mathbf{n} = \mathbf{i} + \mathbf{j} + \mathbf{k}$$

The plane has equation

$$\mathbf{r}.(\mathbf{i} + \mathbf{j} + \mathbf{k}) = (\mathbf{i} + 3\mathbf{j} + 2\mathbf{k}).(\mathbf{i} + \mathbf{j} + \mathbf{k})$$

$$\Rightarrow \quad \mathbf{r}.(\mathbf{i} + \mathbf{j} + \mathbf{k}) = 1 + 3 + 2 = 6$$

2. Find the equation of the plane perpendicular to the vector $2\mathbf{i} - \mathbf{j}$ and which is a perpendicular distance of 2 units from the origin.

Answer

$$\mathbf{n} = 2\mathbf{i} - \mathbf{j} \quad \Rightarrow \quad |\mathbf{n}| = \sqrt{5}$$

$$\therefore \quad \hat{\mathbf{n}} = \frac{2}{\sqrt{5}}\mathbf{i} - \frac{1}{\sqrt{5}}\mathbf{j}$$

$$\Rightarrow \quad \mathbf{r}.\left(\frac{2}{\sqrt{5}}\mathbf{i} - \frac{1}{\sqrt{5}}\mathbf{j}\right) = 2$$

$$\Rightarrow \quad \mathbf{r}.(2\mathbf{i} - \mathbf{j}) = 2\sqrt{5}$$

is the required equation. ($\mathbf{r}.(2\mathbf{i} - \mathbf{j}) = -2\sqrt{5}$ is also a solution.)

3. A plane has vector equation

$$\mathbf{r}.(2\mathbf{i} - 3\mathbf{j} + 6\mathbf{k}) = 1$$

Find the distance from the origin to this plane.

Answer

Let $\mathbf{n} = 2\mathbf{i} - 3\mathbf{j} + 6\mathbf{k}$

$$\Rightarrow \qquad |\mathbf{n}| = \sqrt{4+9+36} = \sqrt{49} = 7$$

$$\Rightarrow \qquad \mathbf{r}.\frac{1}{7}(2\mathbf{i} - 3\mathbf{j} + 6\mathbf{k}) = \frac{1}{7}$$

Since $\frac{1}{7}(2\mathbf{i} - 3\mathbf{j} + 6\mathbf{k})$ is a unit vector, the required distance is $\frac{1}{7}$.

DISTANCE FROM A POINT TO A PLANE

If a plane containing point A with position vector $\mathbf{a}$ is perpendicular to the unit vector $\hat{\mathbf{n}}$, then the distance of the point X, with position vector $\mathbf{x}$, from the plane is $\mathbf{a}.\hat{\mathbf{n}} - \mathbf{x}.\hat{\mathbf{n}}$

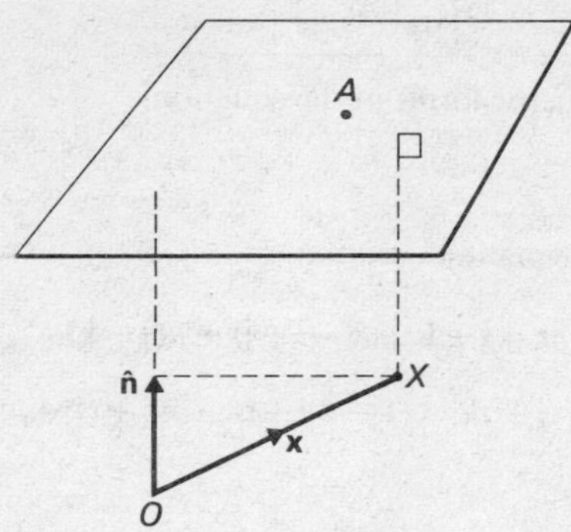

Two points, X and Y, with position vectors $\mathbf{x}$ and $\mathbf{y}$ are on the *same* side of the plane if $(\mathbf{x} - \mathbf{a}).\mathbf{n}$ and $(\mathbf{y} - \mathbf{a}).\mathbf{n}$ have the *same* sign. They are on opposite sides if the signs are different.

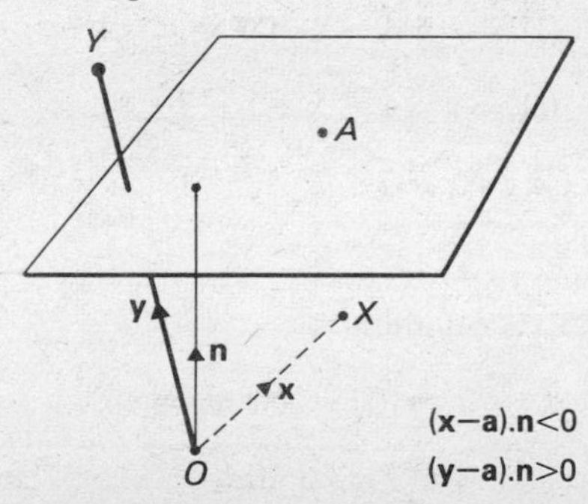

42.7 Cartesian Equation of a Plane

If a plane has vector equation $\mathbf{r}.\hat{\mathbf{n}} = p$, the cartesian equation can be found by setting $\mathbf{r} = x\mathbf{i} + y\mathbf{j} + z\mathbf{k}$.

Example

A plane has vector equation

$$\mathbf{r}.(2\mathbf{i} + 3\mathbf{j} + 5\mathbf{k}) = 7$$

$$\Rightarrow \quad (x\mathbf{i} + y\mathbf{j} + z\mathbf{k}).(2\mathbf{i} + 3\mathbf{j} + 5\mathbf{k}) = 7$$

$$\Rightarrow \quad 2x + 3y + 5z = 7$$

The general cartesian equation of a plane is of the form

$$\boxed{ax + by + cz = d}$$

Similarly, for parametric forms of the equation.

Example

A plane has vector equation

$$\mathbf{r} = \mathbf{i} + \mathbf{k} + \lambda(-\mathbf{i} + \mathbf{j}) + \mu(\mathbf{j} - \mathbf{k})$$

$$\Rightarrow \quad x\mathbf{i} + y\mathbf{j} + z\mathbf{k} = (1 - \lambda)\mathbf{i} + (\lambda + \mu)\mathbf{j} + (1 - \mu)\mathbf{k}$$

$$\Rightarrow \quad x = 1 - \lambda \qquad (1)$$

$$y = \lambda + \mu \qquad (2)$$

$$z = 1 - \mu \qquad (3)$$

$$(1) \Rightarrow \lambda = 1 - x \quad (3) \Rightarrow \mu = 1 - z$$

$$(2) \Rightarrow y = 1 - x + 1 - 7$$

$$\Rightarrow x + y + z = 2$$

42.8 Parallel Planes

If two planes are both perpendicular to the same vector, then these planes must be parallel. Thus

$$\mathbf{r}.\hat{\mathbf{n}} = p$$

$$\mathbf{r}.\hat{\mathbf{n}} = q$$

are parallel.

In cartesian form:

$$ax + by + cz = d$$

and

$$ax + by + cz = e$$

are parallel.

Example

Find an equation of the plane parallel to $\mathbf{r}.(\mathbf{i} - \mathbf{j} + \mathbf{k}) = 2$ which passes through the point (1, 1, 1). Find the distance between these planes.

Answer

The equation must have the form

$$\mathbf{r}.(\mathbf{i} - \mathbf{j} + \mathbf{k}) = c \text{ for some } c \in \mathbb{R}$$

Since (1, 1, 1) lies in the plane

$$(\mathbf{i} + \mathbf{j} + \mathbf{k}).(\mathbf{i} - \mathbf{j} + \mathbf{k}) = c$$

$$\Rightarrow \qquad c = 1$$

The plane has vector equation

$$\mathbf{r}.(\mathbf{i} - \mathbf{j} + \mathbf{k}) = 1$$

The two planes can be expressed as

$$\mathbf{r}.\frac{1}{\sqrt{3}}(\mathbf{i} - \mathbf{j} + \mathbf{k}) = \frac{2}{\sqrt{3}}$$

and

$$\mathbf{r}.\frac{1}{\sqrt{3}}(\mathbf{i}-\mathbf{j}+\mathbf{k})=\frac{1}{\sqrt{3}}$$

in terms of unit vectors.

Thus the distance between the planes is $\frac{2}{\sqrt{3}}-\frac{1}{\sqrt{3}}=\frac{1}{\sqrt{3}}$

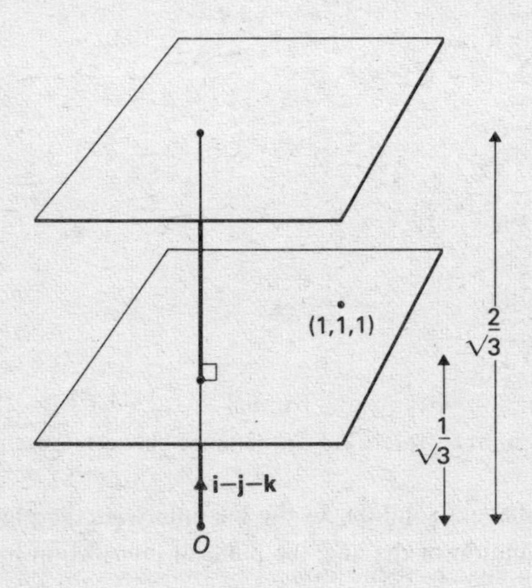

Note: you can only find the distance between *parallel* planes.

42.9 Intersections of Lines and Planes

A line intersects a plane provided it is not parallel to the plane.

Examples

1. Find the point of intersection of the line $\mathbf{r}=(2\mathbf{i}+3\mathbf{j}+\mathbf{k})+\lambda(\mathbf{i}-\mathbf{j}+\mathbf{k})$ and the plane $\mathbf{r}=(\mathbf{i}+\mathbf{j})+s(\mathbf{i}-\mathbf{j}-\mathbf{k})+t(2\mathbf{j}+\mathbf{k})$.

Answer

Equating

$$(2\mathbf{i} + 3\mathbf{j} + \mathbf{k}) + \lambda(\mathbf{i} - \mathbf{j} - 2\mathbf{k}) = (\mathbf{i} + \mathbf{j}) + s(\mathbf{i} - \mathbf{j} - \mathbf{k}) + t(2\mathbf{j} + \mathbf{k})$$

$$\Rightarrow \qquad 2 + \lambda = 1 + s \qquad (1)$$

$$3 - \lambda = 1 - s + 2t \qquad (2)$$

$$1 - 2\lambda = -s + t \qquad (3)$$

$$(1) + (2) \quad \Rightarrow \quad 5 = 2 + 2t \Rightarrow 3 = 2t$$

$$\Rightarrow t = \frac{3}{2}$$

$$(1) \quad \Rightarrow \quad \lambda = s - 1$$

$$(3) \quad \Rightarrow \quad 2\lambda = 1 + s - t = 1 + s - \tfrac{3}{2}$$

$$\therefore \qquad 2(s - 1) = 1 + s - \tfrac{3}{2}$$

$$\therefore \qquad s = \tfrac{3}{2}$$

$$(1) \quad \Rightarrow \quad \lambda = \tfrac{1}{2}$$

The equations have a solution, so the line intersects the plane. Setting $\lambda = \frac{1}{2}$ in the equation of the line, the point of intersection has position vector

$$\mathbf{r} = (2 + \tfrac{1}{2})\mathbf{i} + (3 - \tfrac{1}{2})\mathbf{j} + (1 - 1)\mathbf{k}$$

$$= \frac{5}{2}\mathbf{i} + \frac{5}{2}\mathbf{j}$$

Section 43 Worked Examples

1. Points A and B have position vectors $\mathbf{a} = 2\mathbf{i} + \mathbf{j} - \mathbf{k}$ and $\mathbf{b} = \mathbf{i} + \mathbf{j} + 3\mathbf{k}$ respectively. Find a unit vector parallel to AB.

Answer

$$\overrightarrow{AB} = \mathbf{b} - \mathbf{a} = -\mathbf{i} + 4\mathbf{k}$$ page 415

$$|\overrightarrow{AB}| = \sqrt{1+16} = \sqrt{17}$$

The required unit vector is divide by modulus

$$\frac{1}{\sqrt{17}}(-\mathbf{i} + 4\mathbf{k})$$

2. Find the acute angle between the lines

$$\mathbf{r} = \mathbf{i} + 2\mathbf{j} - 3\mathbf{k} + \lambda(\mathbf{i} - \mathbf{j} + \mathbf{k})$$

and

$$\mathbf{r} = 2\mathbf{i} + 4\mathbf{j} + \mathbf{k} + \mu(2\mathbf{i} + \mathbf{j} + 2\mathbf{k})$$

Answer

The lines are parallel to the vectors

$$\mathbf{a} = \mathbf{i} - \mathbf{j} + \mathbf{k}$$

and

$$\mathbf{b} = 2\mathbf{i} + \mathbf{j} + 2\mathbf{k}$$ page 422

The angle between these vectors is given by

$$\cos\theta = \frac{\mathbf{a}.\mathbf{b}}{|\mathbf{a}||\mathbf{b}|}$$ page 419

$$= \frac{2-1+2}{\sqrt{1+1+1}\sqrt{4+1+4}}$$

$$= \frac{3}{3\sqrt{3}} = \frac{1}{\sqrt{3}}$$

$\therefore \theta = 54{\cdot}7^\circ$ to 3 significant figures.

3.

$$\mathbf{a} = 2\mathbf{i} + \mathbf{j} + \mathbf{k}$$

$$\mathbf{b} = -\mathbf{i} + 3\mathbf{j} + 4\mathbf{k}$$

Find a unit vector **n** which is perpendicular to both **a** and **b**. Hence find in scalar product form the vector equation of the plane passing through the point (1, 5, 7) and parallel to both **a** and **b**.

Answer

Let $\mathbf{n} = x\mathbf{i} + y\mathbf{j} + z\mathbf{k}$

$\mathbf{n}$ is perpendicular to both $\mathbf{a}$ and $\mathbf{b}$

$$\Rightarrow \quad \mathbf{n}.\mathbf{a} = 0 \text{ and } \mathbf{n}.\mathbf{b} = 0$$

page 419

$$\therefore \quad 2x + y + z = 0 \qquad (1)$$

and

$$-x + 3y + 4z = 0 \qquad (2)$$

$$(1) \Rightarrow \quad y = -2x - z$$

$$(2) \Rightarrow \quad -x - 6x - 3z + 4z = 0$$

$$\Rightarrow \quad -7x + z = 0$$

$$\Rightarrow \quad z = 7x$$

$$\therefore \quad y = -2x - 7x = -9x$$

$$\therefore \quad \mathbf{n} = x\mathbf{i} - 9x\mathbf{j} + 7x\mathbf{k}$$

$\therefore$ $\mathbf{m} = \mathbf{i} - 9\mathbf{j} + 7\mathbf{k}$ is perpendicular to both, $\mathbf{a}$ and $\mathbf{b}$.

divide out x for convenience

$$|\mathbf{m}| = \sqrt{1 + 81 + 49} = \sqrt{131}$$

$$\hat{\mathbf{m}} = \frac{\mathbf{m}}{|\mathbf{m}|} = \frac{1}{\sqrt{131}}(\mathbf{i} - 9\mathbf{j} + 7\mathbf{k})$$

is the required vector.

The plane has equation

$$\mathbf{r}.(\mathbf{i} - 9\mathbf{j} + 7\mathbf{k}) = (\mathbf{i} + 5\mathbf{j} + 7\mathbf{k}).(\mathbf{i} - 9\mathbf{j} + 7\mathbf{k})$$

passes through (1, 5, 7)

$$\Rightarrow \mathbf{r}.(\mathbf{i} - 9\mathbf{j} + 7\mathbf{k}) = 5$$

4. The four points A, B, C and D have position vectors $\mathbf{a} = \mathbf{i} + \mathbf{j} + \mathbf{k}$, $\mathbf{b} = -\mathbf{i} + 2\mathbf{j}$, $\mathbf{c} = \mathbf{i} - \mathbf{j} - 3\mathbf{k}$ and $\mathbf{d} = 7\mathbf{i} + 5\mathbf{j} - \mathbf{k}$ respectively.

Find a vector equation of the plane containing A, B and C and determine whether A, B, C, D are coplanar.

Answer

The plane ABC has equation

$$\mathbf{r} = \mathbf{a} + \lambda(\mathbf{b} - \mathbf{a}) + \mu(\mathbf{c} - \mathbf{a})$$ page 428

$$\mathbf{r} = (\mathbf{i} + \mathbf{j} + \mathbf{k}) + \lambda(-2\mathbf{i} + \mathbf{j} - \mathbf{k}) + \mu(-2\mathbf{j} - 4\mathbf{k})$$

If D lies in this plane, then

$$2\mathbf{i} + 5\mathbf{j} - \mathbf{k} = (\mathbf{i} + \mathbf{j} + \mathbf{k}) + \lambda(-2\mathbf{i} + \mathbf{j} - \mathbf{k}) + \mu(-2\mathbf{j} - 4\mathbf{k})$$

for some $\lambda, \mu \in \mathbb{R}$.

$$\Rightarrow \quad 2 = 1 - 2\lambda \quad (1)$$

$$5 = 1 + \lambda - 2\mu \quad (2)$$

$$-1 = 1 - \lambda - 4\mu \quad (3)$$

equating coefficients of **i**, **j** and **k**

$$(1) \Rightarrow \quad \lambda = -\tfrac{1}{2}$$

$$(2) \Rightarrow \quad 2\mu = \lambda - 4 = -4{\cdot}5$$

$$\Rightarrow \quad \mu = -2{\cdot}25$$

Check in (3)

$$\text{RHS} = 1 + 0{\cdot}5 + 9 = 10{\cdot}5$$

$$\text{LHS} = -1$$

The equations do not have a solution and so $ABCD$ are not coplanar.

Section 44 Examination Questions

1. $\overrightarrow{OP} = 3i + 4j$, $\overrightarrow{OQ} = 4i + 3j$, $|\overrightarrow{PQ}| =$

A $\sqrt{2}$ *B* $7\sqrt{2}$ *C* 2 *D* 24 *E* 25 [LON]

2. *An equation of the line which passes through the point* $(1, 0, 2)$ *and has direction ratios* $1:0:2$ *is*

$$A\ \mathbf{r} = \mathbf{i} + 2\mathbf{k} \quad B\ \mathbf{r} = \lambda\mathbf{i} + 2\mu\mathbf{k} \quad C\ \mathbf{r} = \lambda(\mathbf{i} + \mathbf{k})$$
$$D\ \mathbf{r} = \lambda(\mathbf{i} + 2\mathbf{k}) \quad E \text{ none of these}$$

[LON]

3. *Find a unit vector which is in the opposite direction to the sum of the vectors* $(3\mathbf{i} + 2\mathbf{j} + \mathbf{k})$ *and* $(-5\mathbf{i} - 3\mathbf{j} + 6\mathbf{k})$.

Prove that this unit vector is perpendicular to the vector $(9\mathbf{i} - 4\mathbf{j} + 2\mathbf{k})$.

[LON]

4. *Two straight lines are given by the equations*

$$\mathbf{r} = 17\mathbf{i} - 9\mathbf{j} + 9\mathbf{k} + \lambda(3\mathbf{i} + \mathbf{j} + 5\mathbf{k}),$$

$$\mathbf{r} = 15\mathbf{i} - 8\mathbf{j} - \mathbf{k} + \mu(4\mathbf{i} + 3\mathbf{j}),$$

where λ *and* μ *are scalar parameters. Show that these lines intersect and find the position vector of their point of intersection.*

Find also the cosine of the acute angle contained by the lines. [LON]

5. *The position vectors, with respect to a fixed origin, of the points* L, M *and* N *are given by* $\mathbf{l}$, $\mathbf{m}$ *and* $\mathbf{n}$ *respectively, where* $\mathbf{l} = a(\mathbf{i} + \mathbf{j} + \mathbf{k})$, $\mathbf{m} = a(2\mathbf{i} + \mathbf{j})$, $\mathbf{n} = a(\mathbf{j} + 4\mathbf{k})$ *and* a *is a non-zero constant. Show that the unit vector* $\mathbf{j}$ *is perpendicular to the plane of the triangle* LMN.

Find a vector perpendicular to both $\mathbf{j}$ *and* $(\mathbf{m} - \mathbf{n})$, *and hence, or otherwise, obtain a vector equation of that perpendicular bisector of* MN *which lies in the plane* LMN.

Verify that the point K *with position vector* $a(5\mathbf{i} + \mathbf{j} + 4\mathbf{k})$ *lies on this bisector and show that* K *is equidistant from* L, M *and* N. [LON]

6. *The point* A *has position vector* $\mathbf{i} + 4\mathbf{j} - 3\mathbf{k}$ *referred to the origin* O. *The line* L *has vector equation* $\mathbf{r} = t\mathbf{i}$. *The plane* Π *contains the lines* L *and the point* A. *Find*

(*a*) *a vector which is normal to the plane* Π,
(*b*) *a vector equation for the plane* Π,
(*c*) *the cosine of the acute angle between* OA *and the line* L.

[LON]

7. *The lines l_1 and l_2 have the vector equations*

$$l_1 : \mathbf{r} = (1+s)\mathbf{i} + (1-s)\mathbf{j} - 2\mathbf{k}$$

$$l_2 : \mathbf{r} = \mathbf{i} + (1+t)\mathbf{j} - (2+t)\mathbf{k},$$

*where **i**, **j** and **k** are perpendicular unit vectors. Show that l_1 and l_2 meet in the point A with position vector $\mathbf{i}+\mathbf{j}-2\mathbf{k}$. Show also that the lines l_3 and l_4*

$$l_3 : \mathbf{r} = (3-u)\mathbf{i} - (1-u)\mathbf{j} + (-2+u)\mathbf{k},$$

$$l_4 : \mathbf{r} = (1+v)\mathbf{i} - (1+3v)\mathbf{j} - v\mathbf{k},$$

form the other two sides of a quadrilateral ABCD, and find the position vectors of B, C and D which are the intersections of l_1 and l_3, l_3 and l_4, l_2 and l_4, respectively.

Find the angle between the diagonals AC and BD. Determine whether or not the four points A, B, C and D lie in a plane, explaining your method carefully. [OXF]

Formulae for Areas and Volumes

Area of a triangle $= \frac{1}{2} \times \text{base} \times \text{height}$

$$= \tfrac{1}{2}ab \sin C$$

$$= \tfrac{1}{2}bc \sin A$$

$$= \tfrac{1}{2}ac \sin B$$

$$= \sqrt{s(s-a)(s-b)(s-c)}$$

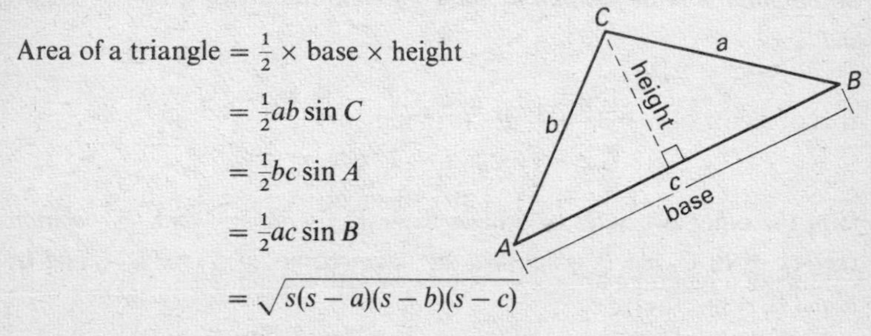

where $s = \frac{1}{2}(a + b + c)$.

Area of a rectangle = base × height

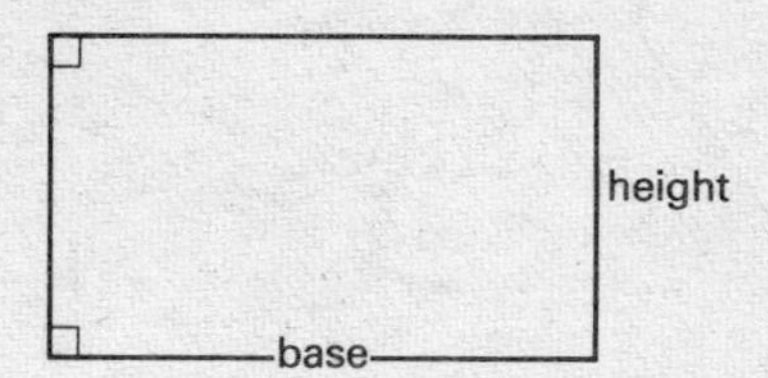

Area of a parallelogram = base × height

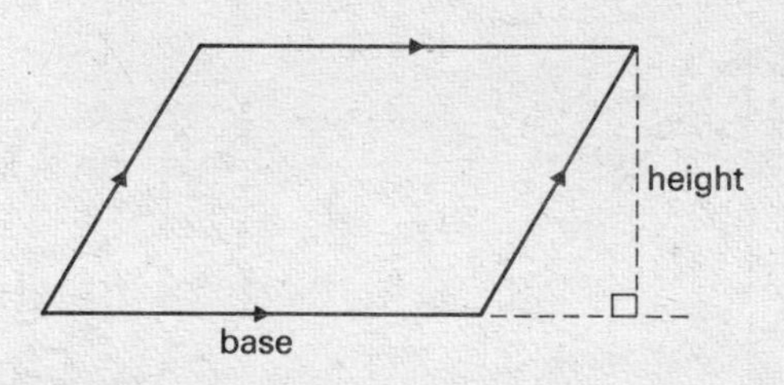

Area of a trapezium $= \frac{1}{2}(a + b) \times h$

= average parallels × height

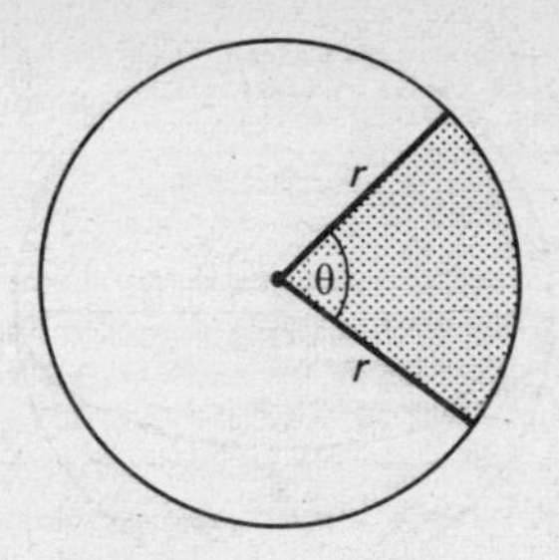

Area of sector of a circle $= \frac{1}{2}r^2\theta$ (θ in radians)

$$= \frac{\theta\pi r^2}{360} \quad (\theta \text{ in degrees})$$

Volume of a rectangular box = length × width × height

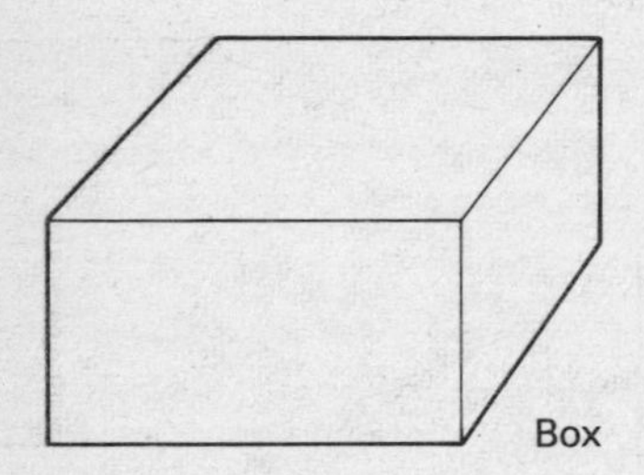

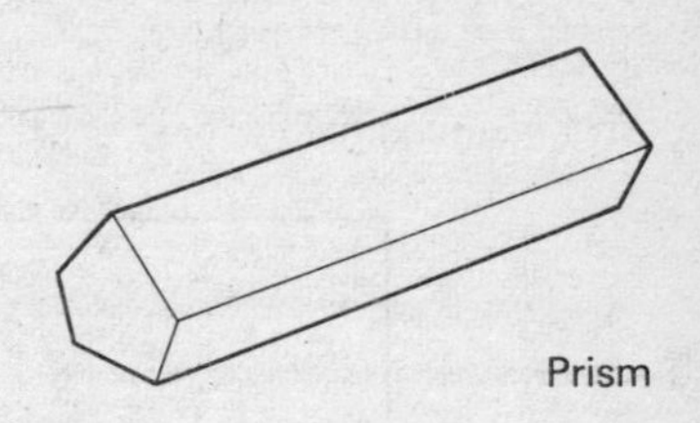

Volume of a prism = base area × height

Volume of a pyramid $= \frac{1}{3} \times$ base area × height

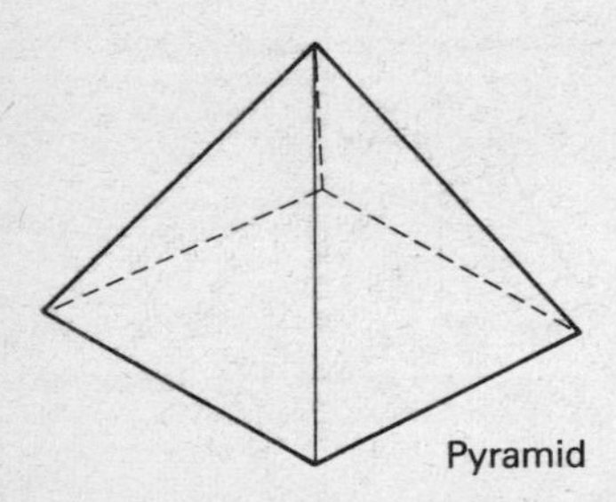

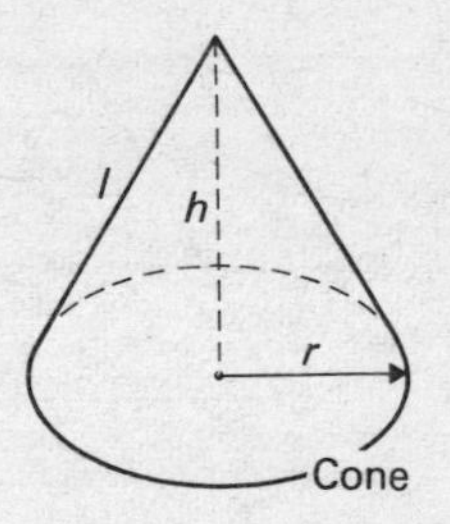

Volume of a cone $= \frac{1}{3}\pi r^2 h$

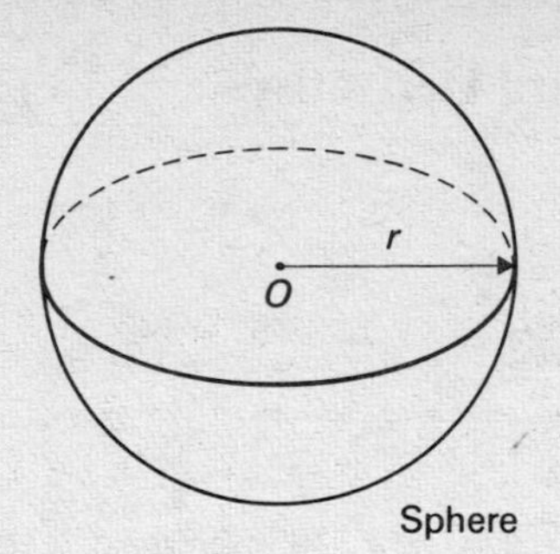

Sphere

Volume of a sphere $= \frac{4}{3}\pi r^3$

Curved surface of a cone $= \pi rl$ (l = slant height)

Surface area of a sphere $= 4\pi r^2$

Table of Standard Derivatives

$f(x)$	$f'(x)$	
x^n	nx^{n-1}	
e^x	e^x	
e^{ax+b}	ae^{ax+b}	
$\ln x$	$\frac{1}{x}$	
$\ln(ax+b)$	$\frac{a}{ax+b}$	
$e^{f(x)}$	$f'(x)e^{f(x)}$	
$\ln(f(x))$	$\frac{f'(x)}{f(x)}$	
$u(x)v(x)$	$\frac{du}{dx}v + u\frac{dv}{dx}$	(product rule)
$\frac{u(x)}{v(x)}$	$\frac{\frac{du}{dx}v - u\frac{dv}{dx}}{v^2}$	(quotient rule)
$\sin x$	$\cos x$	
$\cos x$	$-\sin x$	
$\tan x$	$\sec^2 x$	
$\sec x$	$\sec x \tan x$	
$\operatorname{cosec} x$	$-\operatorname{cosec} x \cot x$	
$\cot x$	$-\operatorname{cosec}^2 x$	
$\sin(ax+b)$	$a\cos(ax+b)$	

$\arcsin x \equiv \sin^{-1}x$	$\dfrac{1}{\sqrt{1-x^2}}$
$\arccos x \equiv \cos^{-1}x$	$-\dfrac{1}{\sqrt{1-x^2}}$
$\arctan x \equiv \tan^{-1}x$	$\dfrac{1}{1+x^2}$

Table of Standard Integrals

$f(x)$	$\int f(x)\,dx$ (constant to be added to each formula)
$x^n \ (n \neq -1)$	$\dfrac{x^{n+1}}{n+1}$
$\dfrac{1}{x}$	$\ln\lvert x\rvert$
e^x	e^x
e^{ax+b}	$\dfrac{1}{a}e^{ax+b}$
$\dfrac{1}{ax+b}$	$\dfrac{1}{a}\ln\lvert ax+b\rvert$
$f'(x)e^{f(x)}$	$e^{f(x)}$
$\dfrac{f'(x)}{f(x)}$	$\ln\lvert f(x)\rvert$
$\sin x$	$-\cos x$
$\cos x$	$\sin x$
$\tan x$	$\ln\lvert\sec x\rvert$
$\cot x$	$\ln\lvert\sin x\rvert$
$\sec^2 x$	$\tan x$
$\operatorname{cosec}^2 x$	$-\cot x$
$\sec x \tan x$	$\sec x$
$\operatorname{cosec} x \cot x$	$-\operatorname{cosec} x$

$\frac{1}{\sqrt{a^2 - x^2}}$	$\sin^{-1}\left(\frac{x}{a}\right)$
$\frac{1}{a^2 + x^2}$	$\frac{1}{a}\tan^{-1}\left(\frac{x}{a}\right)$
$\sin^n x \cos x \, (n \neq -1)$	$\frac{\sin^{n+1}}{n+1}$
$\cos^n x \sin x (n \neq -1)$	$-\frac{\cos^{n+1} x}{n+1}$

Examination Do's and Don't's

Do's

- There is no substitute for thorough revision! You cannot get by on a few hastily learnt topics, or on 'standard' questions that will probably not be set.
- Practise examination type questions beforehand to get the feel for the papers.
- Read the instructions at the head of the paper. If you are required to answer 8 questions you will only waste time by attempting more.
- Read the questions *thoroughly* and make sure you understand what is required.
- Think of how you will attack a question *before* you start answering it.
- Set out your working clearly and with sufficient detail. An examiner cannot mark illegible work and may not give marks if key details are omitted.
- If a certain accuracy is specified for the answers, or the answer should be in a stated form, follow the instructions.
- Make sure you know the format of each paper, and which papers allow the use of formula books and calculators.
- When the examination starts, spend a few minutes reading through the whole paper. Choose the questions that you will start with. It will give you time to relax and recover from 'exam nerves'.
- Try to answer complete questions rather than fragments.
- Check *all* your calculations. It only takes a few minutes but could save you many precious marks.

- In a multiple choice paper it is best to work through the questions in order. Work the answers out thoroughly rather than using half guesses.

Don't's

- Misreading a question will result in low marks and much time wasted.
- Don't launch into a question until you have read it completely through.
- Don't write irrelevant details in your answers.
- Don't try to answer questions on topics that you do not understand!
- Don't guess answers in multiple choice papers, unless you are really stuck. The chances of guessing correctly are very small.
- Don't be complacent. Your judgement in an examination will be subject to time pressure and nervousness. Work through your answer *carefully*.
- Don't make careless mistakes. You could drop at least a grade by throwing marks away.

Answers to Examination Questions and Exercises

Chapter 1 (page 38)

1. $A \cap B = \{1 \leqslant x < 5\}$
2. $\frac{2}{1+x} + 3, \{x \in \mathbb{R}, 0 < x < 5\}$ **3.** (*a*) neither, (*b*) even, (*c*) odd

Chapter 2 (page 63)

1. (i) $7(p+1)$ (ii) $7(p+1)(10p+11)$ **2.** $S_n = 2n(2n+1), u_n = 4^n$
3. £5730 **4.** $a = 51, d = 2$ **5.** D **6.** 20 **7.** C **9.** 2660 **10.** C
11. C **12.** (*a*) (i) $3k(2k+1)$ (ii) $3k^2$ (*b*) 25/333

Chapter 3 (page 111)

1. $2, -2, -\frac{1}{3}, \frac{3}{2}$ **2.** $(3-x)(1-x)^2, x \geqslant 3, x = 0$ **3.** $p = 3, r = -5$
4. C **5.** C **7.** $f(x) = 2(1-x)(x-3)^2$, roots positive, $k > 18$
8. $-2 < x < 0$
9. C **10.** $495/2^8$ **11.** (i) $\lambda = 0, \lambda = -48$ (iii) $\lambda = -1$
12. $x = -\frac{3}{5}, y = -\frac{11}{5}; x = 1, y = 1$ **13.** C **14.** 840
15. (*a*) 224 (*b*) 425

Chapter 4 (page 128)

1. E **2.** (i) $18 - i, \frac{6}{25} + \frac{17}{25}i$ **3.** $x = 1, y = -2$ **4.** B **5.** A
6. $\alpha^2 + \beta^2 = 7p^2, \alpha - \beta = \sqrt{5}p, x^2 - 21\sqrt{5}p^2x - p^4 = 0$
7. (*b*) $((c-1)^2 + b^2)x^2 - (c+1)bx + c = 0$ **8.** $a_1 + a_2 = b_1 + b_2$,
$a_1a_2 = b_1b_2 - c$ **9.** E **10.** (*a*) 6, 7 or $-4, -5$ (*b*) $-1, \pm\sqrt{2}$

Chapter 5 (page 203)

1. C **2.** D **3.** $a = 140, b = 0{\cdot}35$ **5.** $(x+2)(3x-1)^2(15x+16)$
6. A **7.** C **8.** $-1{\cdot}18$ **9.** $1{\cdot}25$ **10.** 1:2 **11.** $\frac{c}{5}$ m s^{-1} **12.** D
13. C **14.** E **16.** $x = 0{\cdot}5, x = -1{\cdot}5$

Chapter 6 (page 258)

1. (*a*) $1 + \frac{1}{2}x - \frac{1}{8}x^2 + \frac{1}{16}x^3 + \ldots$ (*b*) $1 - \frac{x}{4} + \frac{x^2}{16} - \frac{x^3}{64} + \ldots$
2. $m = -\frac{1}{2}, p(-2, \frac{1}{2}), Q(1, -1)$ **3.** $a_0 = 1, a_1 = \frac{1}{2}, a_2 = -\frac{1}{8}$, 0·010,3
4. (26, 9) **5.** centre $(4a, 0)$, radius $2a$. A$(2a, 0)$ B$(6a, 0)$, 60°,
$y = \pm\frac{\sqrt{3}}{3}x, 4a^2\frac{\sqrt{3}}{3}$ **7.** area $= \frac{8}{15}$ square units **8.** $\frac{2}{3}(x+4)\sqrt{x-2}$
11. B **12.** A **13.** E **14.** C **15.** C **16.** C **17.** $\frac{24}{5}, \frac{64\pi}{7}$
18. $tx + y = 2at + at^3, R(\frac{81a}{4}, -9a)$

Chapter 7 (page 285)

1. (*a*) $y \in \mathbb{R}, y \neq 1$ (*b*) x (*c*) $\frac{x+3}{x-1}$ **3.** $1 - \frac{1}{x-1} + \frac{4}{x-2}, f(x) = \frac{1}{2}x^2 + \frac{3}{4}x^3 + \ldots, -1 < x < 1$ **4.** $y = \frac{x^4 - 20x + 48}{3x}$, (2, 4) minimum, $(-2, 17\frac{1}{3})$
maximum, no point of inflexion **5.** D **6.** D **7.** $\frac{1}{2r} - \frac{1}{2(r+2)}, \frac{3}{4} - \frac{2n+3}{2(n+1)(n+2)}$ **8.** $\frac{6x}{(2x^2+1)^2}, x > 0$, 0 and -1 **9.** $g^{-1}(x) = \frac{3x+5}{x-2}$,
$x \in \mathbb{R}, x \neq 2$ **10.** $\{-3 < x < -1\} \cup \{1 < x < 3\}$ **11.** $-\frac{1}{72}$

(page 321)

1. $-0{\cdot}39$ **2.** B **3.** D **4.** E **5.** D **6.** C **7.** E
8. (i) $-\frac{3x^2}{(4-x^3)^2}$ (ii) $2x(1 + \log_e(x^2+1))$ **9.** $2x - x^2 + \frac{23}{12}x^3$, 0·03961
10. (*a*) 1/6 (*b*) $\pi(\frac{1}{2}e^2 - 2e + \frac{5}{2})$ **11.** $\frac{1}{x \ln 10}$ **13.** 35·43 **14.** (*a*) $\frac{p+q}{pq}$
(*b*) $\frac{q}{p}$ **15.** (*a*) $y = \ln k + m \ln x$ (*b*) $k = 3, m = 1{\cdot}7$ (*c*) 5·47
16. (*a*) $-12(\frac{1}{x^5} + \frac{1}{(x+2)^5})$ (*b*) $\frac{1}{2}\ln(\frac{3}{2})$ **18.** $\frac{1}{2}y^2 = \ln x - \frac{1}{2}x^2 + \frac{5}{2}$
19. 3·59, 0·278 **20.** (*a*) $\frac{1}{4}x^2(2\ln x - 1)$ (*b*) $\frac{2}{3}(x+4)\sqrt{x-2}$
21. $-8x - 7x^2 - \frac{62x^3}{3} - \ldots, \frac{1}{n}((-1)^n 2^n - 2(3^n)), -\frac{1}{3} \leqslant x < \frac{1}{3}$

Chapter 8 (page 402)

1. E **2.** E **3.** $f(x) \leqslant \frac{9}{4}, 1 \geqslant g(x) > 0, g^{-1}$ exists **4.** B
5. $fg(x) = \sin x, \frac{\pi}{2} \leqslant x \leqslant \pi$ **6.** A **7.** $p, 2p, -3p, 0, 2{\cdot}30, 3{\cdot}98$
8. $0, \pi, \frac{7\pi}{6}, \frac{11\pi}{6}, 2\pi$ **9.** (*a*) 1·11 (*b*) $a = \frac{3}{2}$, 30°, 150°, 210°, 330°
10. (*a*) 114° (*b*) 144° **11.** B **13.** $R = \sqrt{2}, \alpha = \frac{\pi}{4} x = 2n\pi + \frac{\pi}{2},$
$(2n+1)\pi$ **14.** $R = 2, \alpha = \frac{\pi}{3}$ **17.** $\pm\sqrt{3}/3, \ln 3$ **18.** $\frac{4}{5}\sin^{5/2}x$
19. $2(\frac{3-\sqrt{3}}{8} + \frac{\pi}{3})$ **20.** D **21.** (i) 17/8 (ii) $\frac{\pi}{8} - \frac{1}{12}$ **22.** A **23.** -2π
24. 3π **25.** $\sqrt{2}, \frac{\pi}{4}; 2\sqrt{2}, \frac{3\pi}{4}; 1, -\frac{2\pi}{3}$ **26.** (*a*) $\sqrt{2}, -\frac{\pi}{4}$ (*b*) $2, \frac{\pi}{3}$ (*c*) $2\sqrt{2}, \frac{\pi}{12}$
(*d*) $\sqrt{2}, -\frac{7\pi}{12}$ **27.** (*a*) 63° (*b*) $1 - 2i$ **28.** $-3, -1, \sqrt{10}, 3{\cdot}5^c$
29. 4·3 km, 256° **30.** (*a*) $204a^2$ (*b*) $24a$ (*c*) 35·8°

Chapter 9 (page 438)

1. A **2.** D **3.** $\frac{1}{3\sqrt{6}}(2\mathbf{i} + \mathbf{j} - 7\mathbf{k})$ **4.** $11\mathbf{i} - 11\mathbf{j} - \mathbf{k}, \frac{3}{\sqrt{35}}$
5. $\lambda(2\mathbf{i} + \mathbf{k}), \mathbf{r} = a(\mathbf{i} + \mathbf{j} + 2\mathbf{k}) + \lambda(2\mathbf{i} + \mathbf{k})$ **6.** (*a*) $\lambda(3\mathbf{j} + 4\mathbf{k})$
(*b*) $\mathbf{r}.(3\mathbf{j} + 4\mathbf{k}) = 0$ or $\mathbf{r} = \lambda\mathbf{i} + \mu(\mathbf{i} + 4\mathbf{j} - 3\mathbf{k})$ (*c*) $\frac{1}{\sqrt{26}}$ **7.** $B(3\mathbf{i} - \mathbf{j} - 2\mathbf{k}),$
$C(2\mathbf{j} + \mathbf{k}), D(\mathbf{i} - \mathbf{j}), \arccos\sqrt{\frac{8}{11}}$

Index of Definitions and Terms

Base (of logarithms)	$\log_a b = c$ means $b = a^c$, a is the base	*289*
Basis vectors	Any vector can be expressed as a linear combination of basis vectors Usually denoted by **i**, **j**, **(k)**	*420*
Bearings	Angles used to specify position	*384*
Best fit line	Straight line which lies closest to a set of plotted points	*137*
Binomial coefficient	$\binom{n}{r} = {}^nC_r = \frac{n!}{r!(n-r)!}$. Coefficient in	
Binomial expansion	$(1+x)^n = 1 + \binom{n}{1}x + \binom{n}{2}x^2 + \ldots + \binom{n}{r}x^r + \ldots$	*71*
Bisector	(1) Of an angle, a line dividing the angle into equal halves (2) Of a line segment, divides the segment into equal halves	
Cardinality	Number of elements in a set	*25*
Cartesian coordinates	(x, y) relative to chosen perpendicular axes	*33*
Cartesian equation	Equation in terms of x and y coordinates	
Chord	Line joining two points on a curve	
Coefficient	Of a term, the constant factor	*67*
Collinear	On the same straight line	
Column vector	$\begin{pmatrix} x \\ y \\ z \end{pmatrix}$ or $\begin{pmatrix} x \\ y \end{pmatrix}$	*409*
Complement	Of set A, A', contains all elements outside A	*26*
Complementary angles	Add up to 90° ($\frac{\pi}{2}$ radians)	*334*
Complex number	Has the form $a + ib$, where a and b are real numbers, and $i = \sqrt{-1}$	*115*
Component	Vector $x\mathbf{i} + y\mathbf{j} + z\mathbf{k}$ has components x, y and z	*409*

Displacement vector	$\overrightarrow{AB}$ describes the translation from A to B	*409*
Divergent	Not convergent	*45*
Domain	Of a function, consists of all possible values of the argument	*29*
Double root	Corresponds to a squared factor	*99*
Empty set	$\varnothing$, contains no elements	*26*
Equation	Relation satisfied by a number of values of the variable(s)	*78*
Even function	Satisfies $f(-x)=f(x)$ for all x	*37*
Exclusive sets	Sets which do not overlap	*26*
Exhaustive sets	Sets which contain all elements in the universal set	*26*
Exponent	Power or index	*19*
Exponential function	Has a variable as exponent	*287*
Factorial	$n! = n(n-1)(n-2)\ldots 2 \times 1$	*71*
Finite	Not infinite	
Focus	Reference point of a parabola, ellipse or hyperbola	*234*
Function	Many–one or one–one mapping	*29*
General solution	Formula for generating solutions of a problem	*342*
Geometric mean	Of a and b, $\sqrt{ab}$	*42*
Geometric progression	Progression in which pairs of successive terms have the same ratio	*41*
Gradient	$\frac{y_2-y_1}{x_2-x_1}$, rate of change of a function, $\frac{dy}{dx}$	*133*
Graph	Points in a plane representing a function	*33*
Hypotenuse	Longest side of a right-angled triangle	
Identity	Relation satisfied by all values of the variables	*78*
Identity function	$I: x \mapsto x$	*32*

Term	Definition	Page
Logarithmic differentiation		*311*
Logarithmic function		*289*
Maclaurin series	Expansion of a function as a series in ascending powers of the variable	*299*
Many–many Many–one	Mapping types	*29*
Mapping	$m: A \mapsto B$	*29*
Maximum point		*151*
Minimum point		*151*
Modulus	(1) $\|x\|$ = positive part of x	*104*
	(2) $\|x + iy\| = \sqrt{x^2 + y^2}$	*118*
	(3) $\|\mathbf{a}\|$ = length of $\mathbf{a}$	411
Monotonic	Increasing or decreasing	*284*
Natural logarithm	(Napierian), $\log_e$, ln	*289*
Natural numbers	$\mathbb{N} = \{0, 1, 2, 3, \ldots\}$	*26*
Normal	(1) At a point on a curve, a line perpendicular to the tangent at that point	*148*
	(2) To a plane, perpendicular to the plane	
Numerator	Top part of a fraction	*20*
Obtuse	Angle between 90° and 180°	*329*
Odd function	Satisfies $f(-x) = -f(x)$ for all x	*37*
One–many One–one	Mapping types	*29*
Order	Of a polynomial = degree	*67*
Ordered pair	(a, b)	*35*
Ordered sequence	$a_0, a_1, a_2, a_3, \ldots$	*39*
Ordered triple	(a, b, c)	
Orthogonal	Cut at right angles	*229*

Term	Definition	Page
Radius	Line joining the centre of a circle to its circumference	*219*
Range	Set of all possible values a function takes	*29*
Rational function	Of the form $\frac{f(x)}{g(x)}$, f and g polynomials	*262*
Rational number	A fraction	*26*
Real numbers	$\mathbb{R}$, numbers represented by the whole number line	*26*
Real part	Of $z = x + iy$, $\text{Re}(z) = x$	*116*
Reciprocal	Of A, $\frac{1}{A}$	*22*
Remainder theorem		*79*
Scalar	Quantity without direction	*412*
Scalar product	$\mathbf{a}.\mathbf{b} = x_1x_2 + y_1y_2 + z_1z_2$	*418*
Secant	Line which cuts across a circle or curve	
Secondary value		*342*
Sector	Part of interior of a circle cut off by two radii	*327*
Segment	Part of interior of a circle cut off by a chord	*327*
Sequence	$a_0, a_1, a_2, \ldots$	*39*
Series	Sum of a sequence	*46*
Set	Collection of items	*25*
Simpson's rule		*250*
Sine	$\sin\theta = \frac{\text{opposite}}{\text{hypotenuse}}$ for acute θ. y-coordinate of P on the unit circle where OP defines angle θ, $OP = 1$	*328*
Stationary point	Where a curve has zero gradient	*151*
Subset	A is a subset of B if the elements of A are also in B ($A \subset B$)	*25*
Tangent	(1) Line touching a curve	*148*
	(2) $\tan\theta = \frac{\text{opposite}}{\text{adjacent}}$ for acute θ	*328*
	Gradient of OP where OP defines θ	
Trapezium rule	Method for approximating a definite integral	*248*

Penguin Masterstudies

This comprehensive list, designed to help advanced level and undergraduate studies, includes:

Subjects

Applied Mathematics
Biology
Drama: Text into Performance
Geography
Pure Mathematics

Literature

Dr Faustus
Eugenie Grandet
The Great Gatsby
The Mill on the Floss
A Passage to India
Persuasion
Portrait of a Lady
Tender Is the Night
Vanity Fair
The Waste Land

Chaucer

The Knight's Tale
The Miller's Tale
The Nun's Priest's Tale
The Pardoner's Tale
The Prologue to The Canterbury Tales
A Chaucer Handbook

Shakespeare

Hamlet
King Lear
Measure for Measure
Othello
The Tempest
A Shakespeare Handbook

'Standing somewhere between the literal, word-by-word explication of more usual notes and the abstractions of an academic monograph, the Masterstudies series is an admirable introduction to mainstream literary criticism for A Level students, in particular for those contemplating reading English at university. More than that, it is also a model of what student notes can achieve' – *The Times Literary Supplement*